DANCING QUEEN: MARIE DE MÉDICIS' BALLETS AT THE COURT OF HENRI IV

Under glittering lights in the Louvre palace, the French court ballets danced by Queen Marie de Médicis prior to Henri IV's assassination in 1610 attracted thousands of spectators ranging from pickpockets to ambassadors from across Europe. Drawing on newly discovered primary sources as well as theories and methodologies derived from literary studies, political history, musicology, dance studies, and women's and gender studies, *Dancing Queen* traces how Marie's ballets underscored her incipient political authority through innovative verbal and visual imagery, avant-garde musical developments, and ceremonial arrangements of objects and bodies in space. Making use of women's semi-official status as political agents, Marie's ballets also manipulated the subtle social and cultural codes of international courtly society in order to more deftly navigate rivalries and alliances both at home and abroad.

At times the queen's productions could challenge Henri IV's immediate interests, contesting the influence enjoyed by his mistresses or giving space to implied critiques of official foreign policy, for example. Such defenses of Marie's own position, though, took shape as part of a larger governmental program designed to promote the French consort queen's political authority not in its own right but as a means of maintaining power for the new Bourbon monarchy in the event of Henri IV's untimely death.

MELINDA J. GOUGH is a professor in the Department of English and Cultural Studies at McMaster University.

Dancing Queen: Marie de Médicis' Ballets at the Court of Henri IV

MELINDA J. GOUGH

UNIVERSITY OF TORONTO PRESS
Toronto Buffalo London

© University of Toronto Press 2019
Toronto Buffalo London
utorontopress.com

Reprinted in paperback 2020

ISBN 978-1-4875-0366-6 (case)   ISBN 978-1-4875-2679-5 (paper)

Library and Archives Canada Cataloguing in Publication

Title: Dancing queen : Marie de Médicis' ballets at the court of Henri IV / Melinda J. Gough.

Names: Gough, Melinda J., 1967– author.

Identifiers: Canadiana 20200274252 | ISBN 9781487526795 (softcover)

Subjects: LCSH: Marie de Médicis, Queen, consort of Henry IV, King of France, 1573–1642. | LCSH: Marie de Médicis, Queen, consort of Henry IV, King of France, 1573–1642 – Knowledge – Ballet. | LCSH: Queens – France – Biography. | LCSH: Ballet – France – History – 17th century. | LCSH: France – Court and courtiers – History – 17th century. | LCSH: France – History – Henry IV, 1589–1610. | LCGFT: Biographies.

Classification: LCC DC122.9.M3 G68 2020 | DDC 944/.031092–dc23

This book has been published with the help of a grant from the Federation for the Humanities and Social Sciences, through the Awards to Scholarly Publications Program, using funds provided by the Social Sciences and Humanities Research Council of Canada.

University of Toronto Press acknowledges the financial assistance to its publishing program of the Canada Council for the Arts and the Ontario Arts Council, an agency of the Government of Ontario.

 Canada Council for the Arts   Conseil des Arts du Canada

 ONTARIO ARTS COUNCIL
CONSEIL DES ARTS DE L'ONTARIO
an Ontario government agency
un organisme du gouvernement de l'Ontario

Funded by the Government of Canada   Financé par le gouvernement du Canada

Contents

List of Illustrations vii
Acknowledgments ix
Abbreviations xiii
Principles of Transcription and Translation xv

Introduction 3
1 Magnificence, Mistresses, and Marie's Dance of Maternity 17
2 Royal Women's Ballet and/as Royal Ceremonial 54
3 Alliances and Others 92
4 Eros and "Absolutism" 125
5 Dances of Diplomacy: London, Valladolid, Paris 171
Conclusion 207

Appendices 211
Appendix 1: Verse Texts for the Ballet of the Sixteen Virtues *(1602)* 212
Appendix 2: Verse Texts for the Ballet of Diana and her Nymphs *(1609)* 218
Appendix 3: Verse Texts for the Ballet de Madame *(1609)* 230
Notes 237
Bibliography 313
Index 349

Illustrations

1.1 Henri IV and Marie de Médicis kneeling before the Virgin Mary and Christ child. Title page for Père Louis Richeome's 1601 *Tableaux Sacrez des figures mystiques* ... (1601), dedicated to Marie 43
2.1 First manuscript page of the anonymous eye-witness spectator's account describing "Le Balet de la Reine dansé à Paris le 23 janvier 1605," archived among Nicolas-Claude Fabri de Peiresc's collected papers at the Bibliothèque-Musée Inguimbertine in Carpentras, France 61
2.2 Costume drawing for Janus in the *Ballet de la nuit*, 1653. Image by an unknown artist of the French school, possibly Henri de Gissey 69
2.3 Portrait of Marie de Médicis next to a decorated chair, ca. 1606–7, by Frans Pourbus the Younger (1569–1622) 82
4.1 A noblewoman wearing a mirror hanging from her waist, framed by the explanation that "this Beauty is from God, and her ornaments are ornaments of virtue." Title page from André Du Chesne's *Figures mystiques du riche et précieux cabinet des dames* (1605) 136
4.2 Wisdom as a beautiful woman, regarding herself in a mirror. Engraved title page from Pierre Charron's *De la sagesse* (second edition, 1604) 137
5.1 Portrait of James I of England and VI of Scotland wearing the Grand Sancy diamond in his hat badge. After John De Critz the Younger's portrait likely painted in connection with James's coronation as English king 201
5.2 Portrait of Marie de Médicis by Frans Pourbus the Younger, presumed to have been painted ca. 1609–10 in connection with her impending coronation 202

Acknowledgments

This study is based on documents held at a number of libraries, archives, and records offices in North America and especially Europe. For their generous aid, I am grateful to staff members at these institutions, especially Laurence le Bras and Anne Mary at the Bibliothèque Nationale de France, Département des Manuscrits, and Jean-François Delmas at the Bibliothèque Inguimbertine, Carpentras. Luc Duerloo helped with initial information about microfilm copies of correspondence authored by the archducal ambassadors in France, held at the Johns Hopkins University Library, and put me in touch with Dr Michael Göbl at the Haus-, Hof- und Staatsarchiv in Vienna, who kindly provided additional assistance with original documents.

Éliane Roux's correspondence on my behalf with staff at a number of archives in Italy and France, together with her expert advice regarding paleography and translation, have been central to this project's success. Others to whom I am indebted for research assistance include Lourdes Amigo, Sheila Barker, Sarah Hipworth, Sarah Johnson, Stephanie Millikin, and Erik di Trani. For additional advice regarding passages in French and Italian, I am grateful to Richard Andrews, Luca Boschetto, James K. Farge, Perry Gethner, Veronica Ghizzi, George Hoffmann, Margaret McGowan, Gabriel Moyal, and Maria Galli Stampino. For assistance with analysis of early music and dance, I thank Jeanice Brooks, David J. Buch, Tim Carter, Rebecca Harris-Warwick, Anne MacNeil, Jeffrey Pollock, and Alexander Silbiger.

Research for this project at its early stages received financial support from the Folger Shakespeare Library, the Mellon Foundation, the National Endowment for the Humanities, the National Humanities

Center, the Oklahoma Humanities Research Council, the Oklahoma State University Faculty of Arts and Sciences, the Renaissance Society of America, and the Social Sciences and Humanities Research Council of Canada. For grants toward costs of publishing the manuscript, I am grateful to the McMaster University Arts and Research Board and Canada's Federation for the Humanities and Social Sciences. I thank the University of Michigan's Department of English and Department of Romance Languages and Literature for providing material and intellectual support during my year in Ann Arbor as a visiting scholar. I am grateful to McMaster's Faculty of Humanities for two sabbatical leaves during which I was able to undertake sustained reading, thinking, planning, writing, and revising.

At Oklahoma State University, my former departmental colleagues Edward Jones, Carol Moder, and Jeffrey Walker provided incisive mentoring at the time that I was beginning research related to this project. A fellowship year at the National Humanities Center provided the necessary material and intellectual conditions enabling me to further hone the book's focus and scope. At McMaster University, the Department of English and Cultural Studies and Graduate Program in Gender Studies and Feminist Research have fostered my continued growth as a teacher and scholar. I am particularly grateful to Donald Goellnicht, Mary O'Connor, and Peter Walmsley for their encouragement and support as department chairs, and to my colleagues and graduate students Chandrima Chakraborty, Nicole Lamont, Susie O'Brien, Mary O'Connor, Jessica Swain, and Gena Zuroski for reading and commenting on chapter drafts.

For additional stimulating conversations regarding ideas in this book, I thank Lawrence Bryant, Katherine Crawford, Nicola Courtright, Sheila ffolliott, Caroline Hibbard, Michele Janette, Rebecca Laroche, Éliane Roux, Malcolm Smuts, the late Virginia Scott, Sara Sturm-Maddox, and Abby Zanger. For invitations to speak or write about ideas developed at more length here I thank Christian Billing, Pamela Allen Brown, Rob Henke, Susan O'Malley, Peter Parolin, Mihoko Suzuki, and Ellen Welch, along with Amherst College, the American Comparative Literature Association, the Massachusetts Center for Renaissance Studies, the Modern Language Association, the Newberry Library, the North Carolina Research Group on Medieval and Early Modern Women, the Renaissance Society of America, the Rudé Seminar in French History and Civilisation, the Society for Court Studies, the Society for the Study of Women in the Renaissance, the University of Miami, the University of Michigan's Early Modern Colloquium and Premodern Colloquium, the University of North Carolina at Chapel Hill, and the University of Warwick. I am particularly honored to have been able to vet early portions of this project at meetings of the Theater Without Borders research collaborative, a group whose work on transnational early modern theatre continues to inspire and sustain me intellectually, professionally, and personally.

I gratefully acknowledge permission to reproduce parts of this book that appear, in germinal form, in "Marie de Medici's 1605 *ballet de la reine*: New Evidence and Analysis," *Early Theatre* 15.1 (June 2012): 109–44, and "Marie de Medici's 1605 ballet and the Virtuosic Female Voice," *Early Modern Women: An Interdisciplinary Journal* 7 (2012): 127–56.

Michele Janette read a number of early chapter drafts and provided much needed commentary and encouragement. Malcolm Smuts gave especially generously of his time and expertise, providing incisive feedback on a draft of the complete manuscript; his insights about its larger argumentative contributions were crucial in guiding the project's final shape. Bunny Siegel's support was instrumental in helping me to prioritize completion of the manuscript. Jennifer Askey at Energized Academic offered valuable professional advice and helped keep me on task with deadlines.

I thank Suzanne Rancourt and Barb Porter, at the University of Toronto Press, for their support and expert guidance in seeing this book into print. I am indebted to the book's two anonymous readers, whose suggestions have greatly strengthened the project's argument and presentation.

I am grateful to my parents, and my brothers, for their continued love and support. For allowing me to devote myself to research and writing, even when it meant absenting myself from them for long periods of time, I owe a monumental debt to Jeffrey, Henry, and Cecilia. Each of them has encouraged me to persevere. Each has also called me back to a rich sense of belonging. I cannot express adequately my gratitude for their patience and their belief in me. I dedicate this book to them.

Abbreviations

500 Colbert	Cinq cents de Colbert collection, BNF
ASF	Archivio di Stato di Firenze
ASMa	Archivio di Stato di Mantova
ASR	Archivio di Stato di Roma
ASV	Archivio Segreto Vaticano
ASVe	Archivio di Stato di Venezia
BAV	Vatican Apostolic Library (Biblioteca Apostolica Vaticana)
Barb. lat.	Barberiniani latini collection, BAV
BI	Bibliothèque-Musée Inguimbertine, Carpentras
BNF	Bibliothèque Nationale de France
CSP	Calendar of State Papers, TNA
HHS	Haus-, Hof- und Staatsarchiv, Vienna
Mss, Fr.	Manuscrits Français, BNF
N.S.	New Style dating
OED	*Oxford English Dictionary Online*
O.S.	Old Style dating
Segr. Stato	Segreteria di Stato, BAV
Vat. lat.	Vaticani latini collection, BAV
TNA	The National Archives (UK), formerly the Public Record Office

Principles of Transcription and Translation

When seventeenth-century texts and documents have been available in modern editions, I have relied on those editions, cited in notes. When transcribing passages directly from seventeenth-century French manuscripts and printed texts, I have followed the principles outlined by Bernard Barbiche and Monique Chatenet in their *L'Édition des textes anciens, XVI*ᵉ*–XVIII*ᵉ *siècle* (second ed.) as well as Barbiche's revised guidelines, on the l'École nationale des chartes website, for editing seventeenth-century documents.[1] Specifically, I have retained source orthography with the following exceptions. In cases where "i" and "u" have the value of consonants, I have substituted "j" where the source uses "i," and "v" where the source uses "u." Additionally, in cases where source othography uses "v" as a vowel, I have substituted "u." I have inserted accents to indicate the relevant sounds for the letter(s) "e" and "ee" in final syllables only, and have not accented letters when they are given interior placement within words. And I have employed the *accent grave* for the letters "a," "e," and "u" in propositions and monosyllabic adverbs in order to distinguish homographic words (e.g., *à, où*). In Italian transcriptions, I have been more liberal with the addition of accents ("piu" becomes "più," for example, to conform with modern spelling). For both French and Italian, however, I have retained separation between words that in modern usage would form a single word (eg., "su la" rather than the modern "sulla"), since these forms are typically found in older documents. When transcribing seventeenth-century English manuscripts and printed texts, I have substituted "u" for "v" where relevant.

---

1 Barbiche and Chatenet, *L'Édition des textes anciens, XVI*ᵉ*–XVIII*ᵉ *siècle*; Barbiche, "Conseils pour l'édition des textes."

Throughout the book, English translations are my own unless otherwise noted. When translating non-literary documents, such as diplomatic correspondence, my primary aim has been to clearly render the text, but where possible I have also attempted to convey tone, for example by replicating figures of speech that have English equivalents. When translating seventeenth-century verse texts, including in the book's three appendices, I have prioritized the poems' communicative functions. I have retained line breaks, for example, but have not attempted to wrest word choice or syntax in order to reproduce rhyme schemes, and when I have attempted to convey the literary nature of a particular word choice, I have provided additional, more literal possibilities in notes.

DANCING QUEEN

Introduction

Under glittering lights in the great hall of the Louvre palace and other Paris residences, the ballets danced by Marie de Médicis (1573–1642), queen consort to the French king Henri IV (1553–1610), attracted thousands of spectators ranging from pickpockets to ambassadors from across Europe. Court ballets and masques performed by members of the royal family were by definition events of state. Yet women's contributions to this politically consequential genre of court entertainment remain understudied, especially during the period that witnessed the beginnings of Bourbon "absolutism."

To begin filling this gap, this book offers the first sustained treatment of Queen Marie de Médicis' social, cultural, and political interventions prior to Henri IV's assassination in 1610. Using court ballet as a window into Marie's use of the performing arts as a vehicle for politically engaged queenship, the book provides readings of productions in this genre that Marie de Médicis organized and danced in 1602, 1605, and 1609, together with several spin-off entertainments performed by figures close to the queen.[1] To correct the historical record regarding these performances, the project draws on a wealth of primary sources largely unknown to French scholars, including manuscripts held in lesser-known municipal libraries within France as well as foreign state archives. Analysing these documents through theories and methodologies derived from literary studies, social and political history, theatre and art history, sociology, anthropology, musicology, dance studies, festival studies, and women's and gender studies, the book's interdisciplinary approach reveals how the ballets that Marie orchestrated and danced prior to her husband's death promoted the queen's incipient political authority on a number of intersecting levels.

One such level involved innovative verbal and visual imagery as well as avant-garde musical developments. Another centred on adaptations of protocols, gestures, and interactions of royal bodies with material objects typically found in official royal ceremonial. Thanks to the queen's direct role in inviting international ambassadors to her ballets and in choosing the French nobles who danced alongside her, moreover, these productions choreographed not only members of the kingdom's highest-ranking princely families but also representatives of foreign rulers seated in the audience. In all of these ways combined, Marie's ballets advertised and enacted the queen consort's role in rebuilding a strong French monarchy capable of uniting the kingdom while simultaneously authorizing her social and political agency within a larger international geopolitical nexus. At times Marie's productions challenged the king's immediate interests: contesting the influence of her husband's mistresses or giving space to implied critiques of official foreign policy, for example. But because Marie's authority as queen was ultimately inseparable from that of the Bourbon dynasty as a whole, even these aspects of her ballets took shape as part of a larger defence of Bourbon legitimacy.

One of the main challenges the new Bourbon monarchy faced was the shadow Henri IV's history of apostacy threw over his authority as claimant to the throne of France on the basis of lineage. In 1584, the future Henri IV (then Henri de Navarre) had become next in line for the crown upon the death of François, duc d'Anjou et d'Alençon, the childless Henri III's brother and heir. Because Navarre was a Huguenot, however, the Catholic League soon used against him arguments for elective (as opposed to hereditary) monarchy that had been initially developed by Protestants in support of Navarre himself.[2] Navarre was called to the throne in 1589, after Henri III was assassinated. Because he was a Huguenot, his accession was hotly contested, not only discursively but also militarily. Only with his abjuration of Protestantism in 1594 and subsequent absolution by Pope Clement VIII did Henri IV's kingship gain a firmer footing. Yet numerous tensions remained. Aided by Habsburg Spain, the Catholic League had argued that as a lapsed heretic Henri should not be welcomed back into the Church. Ultimately, the pope declared otherwise, but suspicions regarding the king's religious sincerity and hence political authority persisted. Henri IV ruled as a Catholic (and "Most Christian") king, but with the 1598 promulgation of the Edict of Nantes, the Bourbon regime's controversial grant of toleration to the Huguenots, he announced his refusal to impose religious unity on French subjects. Because Henri needed to maintain alliances with Protestant and Islamic rulers abroad in order to counter Habsburg aggression against France, moreover, opponents of his authority continued to cast doubt on his commitments to Catholicism both at home and internationally.

Henri IV's marriage to Marie de Médicis, together with his subjects' strong appetite for civic peace after decades of violence and economic devastation, helped to balance out such concerns. Marie's devout Catholicism was a crucial factor in this effort; so was her fertility. Henri IV's immediate predecessor, the last Valois ruler Henri III, had not been able to provide the legitimate male heir needed for a smooth succession; nor had his brothers, François II and Charles IX. Determined to break with this pattern, the first Bourbon king of France finally secured an annulment of his childless union with Marguerite de Valois, in 1599, in order to marry Marie de Médicis. The wedding took place in October 1600, and in September 1601, thanks to the king's new wife, France experienced its first birth of a dauphin in eighty years. With this dauphin's arrival, Henri IV finally gained a legitimate male heir whose Catholicism, unlike the king's own, would not be questioned.

And yet Marie's own status was never fully beyond dispute thanks to the rival claim to the title of queen forwarded by Henri's mistress Henriette d'Entragues, marquise de Verneuil. Indeed, Henri's continued philandering, together with ongoing questions about the morality and legality of his divorce from Marguerite de Valois, provided powerful ammunition for ambitious French nobles from Henriette's family who, backed by Spain, conspired against the new royal house of Bourbon. In light of such plots, as well as the king's declining health and advancing age, many contemporaries believed that France remained vulnerable to yet another war of succession.

To address such concerns and to help ensure a smooth succession should the future Louis XIII accede to the throne as a minor, both Henri and Marie took concrete steps to promote her incipient political authority as legitimate consort and mother to the true dauphin. In France, the consort queen's public authority was officially limited thanks to the designation of the Salic law, and its alleged proscription of female rule, as fundamental to the political nation. An important catalyst for this new understanding of the Salic law had been Henri III's official designation of the Huguenot Henri de Navarre as his heir, in 1584. Members of the Catholic League, opposing this decision on religious grounds, threw their support behind the resolutely Catholic Infanta Isabel Clara

Eugenia, Philip II of Spain's eldest daughter and the future archduchess of the Spanish Netherlands.[3] Isabel Clara Eugenia's proximity to the throne on the basis of lineage was in fact many times closer than Navarre's, yet ultimately French anti-Habsburg sentiment combined with a more general fear of foreign rule prevailed, as did beliefs regarding female weakness. By nature and hence in accordance with God's plan, arguments in favour of Navarre's rights ran, women were the weaker sex. By embracing the same principles of patriarchal dynastic succession that favoured Navarre, his supporters claimed, French public law mirrored the gendered hierarchy of natural law. This argument was bolstered by a misreading of the Salic law; in this misreading, the customary exclusion of women from rule became conflated with actual legal precedent for devolution of property on the basis of inheritance.[4] Acceptance of Henri IV's claims to kingship, then, went hand in glove with France's new standing as Europe's only monarchical state to officially bar women from the throne.

The perceptions of women's weakness that this proscription both relied on and reinforced had important implications for royal efforts to promote Marie de Médicis as a capable political agent. Support for her incipient authority was necessary during Henri IV's lifetime because patriarchal dynastic succession contained a significant structural weakness. Should the king be forced to leave the kingdom in times of war, or should he die before his eldest son reached the age of fourteen, royal authority would be partially eclipsed – due in the former case to physical absence, in the latter case to the weakness that childhood implied. Such a situation might facilitate seizure of monarchical functions by other corporate groups (parliamentarians, princes of the blood).[5] A female regent, however, could help to stave off such dangers. A queen consort or queen mother, because her gender precluded her from rule, could not usurp the throne (unlike a prince of the blood). Her actions in relation to official power, therefore, were de facto less threatening to the rightful king. Should her son accede while still a child, moreover, a queen mother would possess the authority as an adult royal that he still lacked, while her selfless love for her son would lead her to guide him appropriately until he reached the age of majority.[6]

Such understandings, together with the related fact that for quite some time, regents in France had typically been women, helped Marie de Médicis to gain acceptance during her husband's lifetime as worthy of the more weighty political roles of guardian and regent, should the need arise. Nonetheless, significant opposition to the idea of female regency remained. This resistance stemmed in part from the pressure on French kings to marry princesses from other ruling families outside the kingdom as a means of promoting royal authority based on social and familial distinctiveness over and above the subjects they ruled. These dynastic marriages meant that French consort queens, who already faced general prejudice against female participation in the public realm and in governance, were often attacked on the basis that their access to power, even as placeholders for minor kings, was not only unnatural but also anti-Gallican.[7] Catherine de Médicis' ability to safeguard France, for example, had been sharply condemned on the basis of her foreign and allegedly base parentage, which her detractors claimed made her an adherent to Machiavellian methods and an enemy to the French nobility and French traditions more broadly.[8]

The queen of France, then, needed to appear capable of rule even during her husband's lifetime so as to preserve royal authority should the king be called away to war or should her eldest son accede as a minor, and this exigency required representations of the queen consort's incipient political capacity. For such representational efforts to be effective, however, they needed to take into account the political deficits implied both by femaleness and by foreignness, especially when the foreign princely family into which that queen had been born was a relatively less prestigious one, as was the case with both Catherine and Marie de Médicis.

It was within the context of such challenging political circumstances that Marie drew on her considerable training in cultural production at the grand ducal court in Tuscany in order to arrange and dance in a series of court ballets and related entertainments that promoted her new authority as Henri IV's domestic and political partner. *Ballet de cour*, as usefully defined by Marina Nordera, was "a type of composite theatre performance, made up of instrumental and vocal music, texts declaimed in verse and prose, stage design, scenic accessories, costumes, masks and, not least dance."[9] The Medici court, even if it did not produce *ballet de cour* per se, was famous across Europe for converting wealth into status by means of conspicuous consumption within representational court performance. When she arrived in France, Marie came equipped with direct knowledge of such practices. She had been an honoured spectator, for example, at the famous celebrations in honour of Christine of Lorraine's 1589 marriage to Marie's uncle and guardian, Ferdinando I de' Medici, including a series of elaborately staged and sung *intermedii* for the play *La Pellegrina*.[10] A year later, in

1590, Marie organized and acted in a production of Tasso's *Aminta*, for which she personally commissioned new vocal music.[11] In 1596, she danced at the Palazzo Pitti before Christine of Lorraine in a *ballo* with verses by Ottavio Rinuccini, entitled *La mascherata di stelle*. Marie even took a direct and active role along with her aunt in planning the opera *Euridice* that would be performed as part of the official celebrations in honour of her wedding to Henri IV in October 1600: as Tim Carter has noted, the two women seem to have conferred on a number of artistic choices featured in a trial run of this production, performed in May 1600 at apartments in the Pitti Palace.[12] Marie's experiences with court spectacle in Florence thus included a number of genres – *balli, mascherate, intermedii*, and early opera – that were similar to, although not identical with, French *ballet de cour*. When in France Marie faced a pressing need to assert her own legitimacy along with that of the new Bourbon dynasty more generally, then, she not surprisingly lost little time in taking up her new prerogatives as queen within the magnificent tradition of royal women's ballet that had begun with Catherine de Médicis in the late 1570s and early 1580s but which had been forced into abeyance by protracted violence and penury during the French wars of religion.

Catherine de Médicis did not herself dance in ballets at the French court. Initially, as queen regnant, she had been sidelined both politically and culturally by Henri II's powerful mistress, Diane de Poitiers. Then, after her husband's death, Catherine's self-depiction as devoted royal widow – a representational strategy that scholars note helped to authorize her as regent for the young Charles IX – made dancing on her part unthinkable.[13] As dowager queen, however, Catherine served as impresario for at least two ballets performed by her daughter-in-law Queen Louise de Lorraine, wife of Henri III, including the famous 1581 *Ballet comique de la royne*. Lengthy interruptions to court life caused by the wars of religion and then by Henri IV's military engagements against the Catholic League prior to his 1595 coronation meant that for a significant period of time, the French crown was unable to mount elaborate *divertissements*, including royal women's ballets. Henri's sister Catherine de Bourbon danced in at least one ballet at Henri IV's court in the early 1590s; she also presided over others at the ducal court of Lorraine prior to her death in 1604.[14] But it was not until after Marie de Médicis arrived in the French capital that Paris would again see magnificent ballets danced by the royal consort.

One important level at which Marie's ballets promoted her incipient political authority involved textual and visual iconographies that, by merging Christian with classical imagery, emphasized the new queen's divinely ordained status as Henri's legal consort. Marie's February 1602 *Ballet of the Sixteen Virtues* discussed in chapter 1, for example, overlaid textual allusions to Astraea, the pagan goddess of justice, with Marian imagery from Franco-Florentine Neoplatonic discourse. Read in light of this ballet's casting choices, divinizing imagery in this instance not only promoted the Bourbon regime by resacralizing the French monarchy but also defended Marie's contributions to that regime by insistently placing her, rather than the king's mistress Henriette d'Entragues, marquise de Verneuil, in the role of mother to the true dauphin through whom peace, plenty, and political stability would be secured. Marie's January 1609 *Ballet of Diana and her Nymphs*, discussed in chapters 4 and 5, also worked to displace and debunk the marquise's rival claims to queenly authority – this time via Marie's eroticized yet resolutely virtuous self-representation as Diana, the ancient Roman goddess of nature. Dancing this version of Diana, Marie reconciled her own feminine (and hence "weak") participation in the natural world with her share in the charismatic aura of divinity enjoyed by the sovereign, her husband Henri IV.

To analyse the political messages conveyed by such uses of classical and Christian imagery combined, this book draws on several generations of revisionist work treating Marie's patronage of the visual arts, in particular the heroic cycle of portraits depicting Marie's life by the painter Peter Paul Rubens.[15] Thanks to this body of scholarship, critical consensus now views Marie as an informed and discerning artistic patron, but it is only recently that scholars have begun to study the revival of the arts at Henri IV's court more generally and Marie's role in this revival more specifically.[16] Particularly useful among this work, for my purposes, is a set of articles by Nicola Courtright that takes up a number of projects, from royal *jetons* to garden sculpture and architecture at royal palaces, designed to promote Henri's second marriage as not only a domestic but also a political partnership.[17] Marie's own contributions to this representational program during her husband's lifetime have not yet been mapped in any sustained way, but by studying in detail the ballets that she organized and danced during this period, my own project offers a new, more precise lens through which to view Marie's cultural activities prior to her regency.

Marie's ballets during Henri IV's lifetime have received almost no previous attention, though, in part because scholars of *ballet de cour* going back more than a century have had little if anything to say about entertainments at Henri IV's court.[18] On one level, this neglect is unsurprising since, as Michele Fogel has shown, the Bourbon monarchy was just beginning to take up "ceremonies of information" – descriptions of royal occasions which circulated in print as a means of authorizing monarchical authority for a wider readership.[19] For this reason, we lack printed *livrets* (brochures with collected verses) for almost all court entertainments during Henri IV's reign, including Marie's.[20] By attending to a wider range of contemporary sources, however, including occasional early printed newsletters, verse texts scattered in other print and manuscript sources, texts by royal historiographers, and last but not least ambassadorial correspondence from the period, the present project begins to correct the historical record regarding royal women's performance in France during Henri IV's reign. The picture that emerges challenges what little has been said by previous scholars regarding the sole ballet danced by Marie for which we have a set of collected texts: her production for winter 1609. Critics have credited Henri's set-aside first wife Marguerite de Valois, rather than Marie herself, for this production's artistic and intellectual innovations – despite what art historians have taught us about Marie's incisive patronage of painting, sculpture, and architecture.[21] Evidence provided by the wider range of sources treated in the present study, however, reveals the importance of Marie's shaping influence, even prior to her regency, in a series of sustained cultural interventions on the French court ballet stage designed to affirm not only her own contested political authority but also that of the new Bourbon dynasty as a whole.

From one of these sources in particular – an eye-witness account of the queen's January 1605 ballet danced at the Louvre palace – we gain particular insight into the ways Marie's productions used elements from royal ceremonial to position her as an "actor" on the French political stage. Close readings of this and other documents indicate that each of the queen's ballets, as was typical of this genre, included a *grand ballet* or set of choreographed dances performed by high-ranking members of the court. In Marie's ballets for 1605 and 1609 in particular, archival documents show, the women she selected to dance in her troupes included members of the kingdom's most powerful noble families. The on-stage presence of these women, dancing under Marie's direction, helped infuse the new queen with the same aura of moral and physical superiority that attended their own longstanding noble bloodlines in accordance with early seventeenth-century "ideas of race."[22] The social priority Marie claimed by entering the playing space before these women, however, helped to establish her unique standing over and above them, as the royal consort: the only French subject who in juridical discourse also shared in the king's sovereign majesty, through marriage. These and other spatial and kinetic protocols, together with the ballets' use of rare objects and costly materials typically seen in official royal ceremonial, mustered Marie's literal, symbolic, and political capital as a princess from a wealthy foreign princely family to viscerally reinforce more abstract theoretical and juridical understandings of Henri's kingship as an instantiation of sovereign, as opposed to suzerain, rule.

In pursuing this argument, I take an important cue from the attentiveness to symbolic dimensions of royal power that characterizes scholarship associated with the so-called American "neo-ceremonialist school" of French political history, as well as related work on the French queen's participation in coronations, royal entries, *lits de justice*, and royal funerals.[23] Political historians, even of this "ceremonialist" stripe, tend to hive off court spectacle, including court ballet, from constitutive political ritual. And yet as Fanny Cosandey notes, early modern antiquarians and other collectors of texts describing royal ceremonial from this and earlier periods gathered accounts that covered a much wider range of royal occasions: for these authors, whatever concerned the *mise en scène* of the king or queen, no matter the precise nature of the event, seems to have counted as royal ceremony.[24] Extending this insight, the current study seeks to further elucidate the queen's political role in early modern France by considering how it was shaped by, and in turn shaped, a form of ceremonial political expression – court ballets – all too often dismissed, even now, as frivolous entertainment. To this end, the book draws on Janette Dillon's study of ceremonial in early modern English court performance to trace in contemporary eye-witness accounts of the ballets organized and danced by Marie de Médicis a heightened attentiveness to temporal, spatial, and kinetic protocols, ostentatious displays of wealth, and the number and status of royal attendants.[25] By means of these production values, this analysis shows, Marie's productions emphasized the foreign queen consort's role in securing and advertising the French monarchy's membership in a supra-national European sovereign caste, the exclusivity and distinction of which anchored its members' claims to the prerogatives of rule.

Marie's court ballets also registered a number of politically significant avant-garde aesthetic innovations involving lesser status performers, including the Italian female singer discussed in chapters 2 and 5 and the "living breathing luxury items" associated with the Islamicate world discussed in chapter 3. These innovations, particularly when combined with imagined crossings of gendered and animal-human divides, helped to set in relief the queen's participation in sovereign grace, and in this way the queen's productions made an especially ingenious contribution to French monarchical self-representation. Kings in early modern France were understood to possess both mortal (natural) bodies and immortal (divine) ones. The queen's gender compromised her divinely sanctioned authority more than the king's did, since in contemporary thinking women's bodies were baser and women as a whole were weaker with respect to sins of the flesh.[26] Working against such assumptions in ways that championed Marie's moral and political role, the ballets' allegorical efforts to divinize the queen through iconography and verbal imagery were important. Equally significant, though, was the *form* through which such iconographies of rule made themselves felt and understood. When in her ballets Marie appeared alongside professional women singers, whose open throats connoted sexual availability according to early modern understandings, or when her *grand ballet* was framed on either side by burlesque entries performed by animals and human "monsters" whose awkward choreographies revealed their closeness to unimproved, bestial nature, the grace her decorous comportments enacted, by contrast with these lesser-status "others," came to signal her perfected, rather than corrupted, natural body, and thus made visible on a kinetic and gestural, not just a visual or verbal, plane the queen's participation through Christian marriage in her husband's (divinely given) sovereign status.

Abstract, textual allegory worked together with the immediacy of embodied, live performance, then, to render the queen's natural body in positive, divinizing terms. And yet Marie's productions did not function solely as apologies for an "absolutist" Bourbon regime; nor were these productions straightforwardly decorous in tone and content. Rather, queens' ballets at the court of Henri IV involved both collaboration and contestation. Studies of French burlesque ballet c. 1620–36, the sub-genre most noted for its "playful resistance" to royal ideology, show that in this variant, no women danced.[27] At the court of Henri IV, however, queens' ballets could and did incorporate not only the dignified comportments typically associated with royal women's ballet under Catherine de Médicis but also a number of surprisingly edgy moments – the king's eldest illegitimate son costumed *en travesti* as a girl, a group of "savage" figures representing "beast-like" denizens from the Ottoman empire, or the scantily clad daughter of France's most notorious financier, for example. The surprise coda to Marie's 1605 ballet, with its burlesque gestures and choreographies performed by a troupe of "Turks," "Tartars," and "Moors," chapter 3 argues, engaged proto-Orientalist fantasies of encounter with the Mediterranean world and Near East that challenged, if only implicitly, the Franco-Ottoman alliance officially renewed by Henri IV in 1604. The casting choices for the January 1609 *ballet de la reine* discussed in chapter 4, meanwhile, not only underscored Marie de Médicis' participation in sovereign majesty but also trafficked in negative attitudes towards the crown's new tax on venal office, the *paulette*, through which hereditary office helped to fill the crown's coffers, albeit at the expense of the older nobility's claims to exclusiveness.

Taking these complexities into account, the book illuminates, from a new angle, the "dynamism and struggle at the heart of [Bourbon] 'absolutism'" emphasized in revisionist understandings of state formation in early modern Europe.[28] By attending to the work of gender within the production and reproduction of civility by means of courtly entertainments, my particular project surfaces new insights regarding women's contributions to both the promulgation of divine right rhetoric and the ways that this rhetoric managed, or failed to manage, the negotiated give and take that characterized actual relations between "absolute" monarchs and the subjects that they governed. Following sociologist Norbert Elias, numerous scholars have analysed sixteenth- and seventeenth-century civility discourse in relation to the centralization of power at royal courts, yet as a recent state-of-the-field article on affect theory in connection with the history of the emotions points out, cultural historians have failed to attend to the importance of gender within courtesy literature and related genres.[29] In highlighting intersections of social rank with norms of gendered embodiment in the formation and contestation of noble status, this book extends the claim put forward by feminist musicologists and literary scholars that early modern civility *required* women.[30] The court ballets sponsored and danced by Marie de Médicis, it shows, both exemplified and self-reflexively thematized such gendered contributions to the making of civility and, by extension, to the (contested) centralization of power under Bourbon rule. Taken together, the micro-histories of the queen's particular productions offered in this book's individual chapters provide a fuller, more concrete picture of the ways that female performance per se could both promulgate a (patriarchal) rhetoric of divine right *and* simultaneously manipulate the push and pull between rival forces that characterized the actual on-the-ground dynamics of "absolutist" Bourbon rule in order stake out more politically significant roles for Marie de Médicis specifically.

Because these productions took shape within scenes of political contest specific to French governance within the kingdom but also within a larger set of geopolitical, dynastic rivalries, attention to the ways Marie's ballets engaged foreign audiences forms a thread that runs throughout the book, while chapter 5 turns in particularly concerted fashion to diplomatic ceremonial as an important feature of Marie's productions. Published work on royal women's French court ballets as diplomatic events tends to focus on Catherine de Médicis and on the ballets that Marie presided over as regent, while leaving aside, almost entirely, the ballets Marie sponsored and danced while her husband was alive.[31] And yet diplomacy was especially crucial to French governance during this earlier period, since the crown's need to rebuild the royal treasury and assure civic peace after the wars of religion required it to stave off direct military action whenever possible while still advancing French interests abroad. Given such political exigencies, combined with what other chapters of this book show to have been the multiple levels on which Marie's ballets engaged political objectives, we should not be surprised to find, from diplomatic correspondence, that the ballets Henri IV's consort sponsored and performed in navigated not only domestic political relations within the French kingdom but also France's relations with foreign states.

In pursuing this argument, the book's fifth chapter brings into view another level at which court ballets allowed women like Marie to "act" and "speak" on a political stage – in this case, an international one. Most obviously, ballets could send messages internationally through dramatic allegories that drew on "the literature of classical antiquity" – a shared "repertoire of stories and visual symbols that might be variously 'applied' to comment on contemporary politics" in diplomatic settings.[32] Yet production values in these ballets were also designed to "exhibit the wealth and artistic talent amassed by the monarch for international appreciation."[33] These spectacles marked the relative status of their royal patrons through displays of wealth – including the use of rich fabrics decorated with rare gems and metals.[34] Simultaneously, when royal courts mounted entertainments noteworthy for their technical ingenuity – innovations in stage machinery that could produce masterful visual or sonic effects, for example, or avant-garde virtuosity in music and dance – this was partly so that these displays of artistic talent, appreciated as such within a larger pan-European frame, together with the showing off of rare and costly objects, could augment their royal patrons' prestige relative to that of foreign rivals and affines (members of foreign dynasties related by marriage to the host court's rulers).[35] Invitations to attend such performances were also meaningful, diplomatically speaking, as were the spatial and temporal arrangements such invitations might encompass.[36] Because court spectacle conveyed meanings at these various levels, it could be deployed to achieve nuanced political objectives within the field of foreign policy negotiations.

Here, though, forms of communication proved useful in part through their capacity to encompass ambiguity, even disingenuousness. Theorizing the place of the visual arts in the world of early modern diplomacy, Anthony Colantuono has outlined how the Barberini deployed paintings and other forms of figurative art "to encode and transmit thoughtfully contrived, ideologically laden political arguments" by carefully controlling not only the iconographic content of art works that they commissioned and sent via diplomats to foreign courts, but also the rhetorical contexts in which these objects were exchanged and discussed.[37] Colantuono's related notion of paintings as "mute diplomats" – objects that spoke eloquently without saying a word – may usefully be extended to considerations of court ballets as occasions of diplomatic ceremonial. The productions organized and danced by Marie de Médicis, my own project argues, succeeded in conveying favour to certain foreign governments while slighting others in ways that could not easily be pinned down in part through the "mute diplomacy" they put in motion through subtle, non-verbal social codes involving the relative spatial positioning of ambassadors at these events. Because nothing had been said explicitly, messages sent by means of the particular location at which a given ballet was performed or by means of the relative rank or status of its host, for example, allowed for denial that anything important had been intentionally signified at all. In this sense, court ballet proves to have been a particularly useful locus for what Nathalie Rivère de Carles, drawing on Lawrence Lessig, calls "diplomatic *ambiguation*" in early modern fictional and non-fictional texts: a strategy that involves "cultivating ambiguity … not always as a means of deception but rather in Lessig's sense of the word which is to give 'a particular act (…) a second meaning as well, one that acts to undermine the negative effects of the first.'"[38]

The larger topic of women's interventions in court theatre has gained in scholarly popularity over the past two decades in part because of the ways it can illuminate, from new angles, the influence of female consorts on government by means of a larger politicization of the arts.[39] Much important work in this vein continues to focus on the English context, yet as the current study centred on just one performance genre at a single court indicates, the resolutely transnational nature of royal women's entertainments offers rich possibilities for further comparative work.[40] The marked success of Albert Rabil, Jr and Margaret King's "The Other Voice in Early Modern Europe" series, moreover, indicates a readership eager for scholarly English translations of texts by and about early modern women. The present study therefore concludes by offering, as appendices, lightly annotated dual-language editions of printed verses for the 1602 *Ballet of the Sixteen Virtues*, 1609 *Ballet of Diana and her Nymphs*, and 1609 *Ballet de Madame*. By making translations of texts for these three royal women's ballets at the court of Henri IV available for the first time, I hope that this project will help to facilitate future research on early modern women's theatrical and political agency across linguistic and geographic borders.

Chapter One

Magnificence, Mistresses, and Marie's Dance of Maternity

The first full winter following Marie de Médicis' initial arrival in Paris, the French court celebrated carnival with numerous balls and ballets, including one queen's ballet for which she was the principal masked dancer.[1] Biographers, historians, and *ballet de cour* scholars alike have remained virtually silent regarding this production, largely because we lack an extant *livret* containing its collected verses. This chapter identifies two printed verse texts for this ballet and uses the information they offer about the production's structure and iconographies, together with theories of early modern magnificence, gift giving, and the accumulation of cultural capital, to articulate what was at stake for the French crown and for Marie de Médicis in the performance.

At this time of this production, France was undergoing a number of complex, intersecting transitions. Thanks in part to the political and biological failures of François II, Charles IX, and Henri III, the last three Valois kings, the sacral aspects of the French monarchy had lost much of their authority for both Huguenots and Catholics alike. After thirty-five years of civil and religious war, however, desire for stability and peace among French subjects, together with the advent of a new monarchical regime – the Bourbons – opened an important space for royal efforts to reclaim notions of divine right in connection with dynastic monarchy. So did the shift from a protracted period during which France's traditions of courtly activity had been disrupted by violence and penury, to one in which magnificent courtly pastimes were beginning to be restored.

Henri IV's accession and pacification of the realm promised greater peace and prosperity. His politico-military victories had vindicated the hereditary principle; registration of the Edict of Nantes by the Parlement of Paris had also upheld the king's right to act as the ultimate arbiter of religious discord within his kingdom. Religious peace had been achieved through Henri's somewhat problematic conversion, however, while the grant of toleration to Huguenots remained controversial. In order to protect French interests internationally, moreover, Henri needed to keep Habsburg ambitions in check, and this required him to foster networks of mutual support with Protestant states abroad as well as the Ottoman empire, alliances which risked bringing his own religious sincerity into further question. Even more crucially, if he failed to provide an heir – or even if he failed to secure recognition of that heir by the political nation – everything he had achieved would be in danger of collapsing at his death.

It was within this challenging set of circumstances that the king's new wife, Marie de Médicis, needed to establish herself – in part through sponsorship of, and performance in, court entertainments. Indeed, the first of Marie's ballets, danced on the last day of the 1602 carnival season, took up imagery directly relevant to the Bourbon regime's pressing need to reassert the divinely sanctioned nature of dynastic monarchy and ensure unquestioned recognition for the king's legitimate male heir. The queen's allegorical role on stage as the first of the sacred virtues crowned the joyous return of another golden age made possible thanks to Henri's own virtue: his greatness as a military commander but also his political acumen in having used clemency in order to pacify a kingdom that had been devastated, under late Valois rule, by warfare and penury. Likening the brightness that reflected from Marie's opulent dancing habit to a powerful celestial light normally blinding to mortal eyes, Neoplatonic imagery in this ballet's verse texts and in contemporary accounts of the production, like that found in descriptions of Marie's dancing authored by Medici court poets, tied the luminous effects of Marie's bejeweled appearance on stage to a brightness and beauty frequently associated in contemporary writings with pagan goddesses but also with the Virgin Mary, celestial queen of the sacred virtues. Presenting Marie's on-stage arrival as coinciding with the return of Astraea, pagan goddess of justice – and with it the arrival of a child born to save the world, as prophesied in Virgil's Fourth Eclogue – the ballet associated Marie's infant son with the Christ child, whose birth at the time of the Pax Romana under Augustus coincided with the restoration of peace following civil war. In these ways, the new queen's 1602 ballet combined classical with Christian imagery in order to celebrate in sacralizing terms the French monarchy's success in having secured, through her, the first birth of a dauphin in eighty years.[2]

This production's combination of conspicuous consumption with symbolic expression would lay the groundwork for magnificence as a tool for political legitimization in subsquent ballets organized and danced by Marie prior to Henri IV's death in 1610. At this particular moment in time, however, magnificence on the French court stage proved especially useful given the serious threat to Marie's legitimacy posed by Henriette d'Entragues, marquise de Verneuil. In late September 1601, Marie had given birth to the future Louis XIII. But this child's status as Henri IV's legitimate heir was challenged by d'Entragues, who not only possessed a written promise of marriage from the king but had also given Henri IV another son just weeks after Marie had birthed hers. The queen could not force Henri IV to end his affair with the marquise, despite the fact that Henriette's ambiguous claims could well end up feeding into yet another civil war for the succession. And yet, the prerogatives that Marie enjoyed as royal consort, including her privileges as an impresario of magnificent spectacles, helped to contain such threats. It was Marie, not Henriette, whose institutional position as queen allowed her to sponsor this ballet, and with it to position herself as the more powerful giver of gifts – including the gift of a dauphin – to the king and his subjects. As events leading up to this performance reveal, moreover, this production was also part of a more subtle gift exchange between queen and mistress, one in which Marie's standing as chief performer and organizer afforded her significant advantages.

Peace, Plenty, and the Pleasures of Courtly Pastimes Restored

The most detailed contemporary account of Marie's *Ballet of the Sixteen Virtues* appears in royal historiographer Pierre Matthieu's history of France, first published in 1605. Describing carnival festivities at the French capital three years earlier, Matthieu writes:

> à la cour ... le Caresme-prenant fut celebré avec toutes sortes de rejouyssances. La Royne fist un Ballet à Paris aussi memorable que celuy de Lycurgus au Pirée. Elle choisit à cest effect quinze des plus belles Princesses & Dames de la Cour: Berthaud fait un poesme sur ce subject, & dit qu'elles representoient seize vertus, dont la royne estoit la premiere. L'entrée fut d'un Apollon la lyre en main avec les neuf Muses, qui chantoient, dansoient & jouoient des instrumens de Musicque, finissant tousjours la cada[n]ce en ceste reprinse. *Il faut que tout vous fasse homage, Grand Roy miracle de nostre aage.* Huit filles de la Royne danserent la seconde partie du

Balet. A la troisiesme parut la Royne & sa suitte en quatre trouppes, dont les testes estoient couvertes & parées de tant de brillans & de pierreries, que qua[n]d les flambeaux eussent refusé leur lumiere à la Salle, on y eust veu assez clair, tant elles esclattoient & esclairoient.[3]

[at court... carnival was celebrated with all kinds of festivities. The queen made her ballet in Paris, as memorable as that of Lycurgus in Piraeus. To that end, she chose fifteen of the most beautiful princesses and ladies of the court: Bertaut made a poem on this subject, and says that they represented sixteen virtues, of which the queen was the first. The entry was of an Apollo lyre-in-hand with the nine muses, who sang, danced, and played some musical instruments, always finishing the cadence with this refrain: *Everyone must pay tribute to you, Great King, miracle of our age*. Eight of the queen's *filles* danced the second part of the ballet. For the third, the queen and her followers appeared in four troupes, heads covered and adorned with so many jewels and gems that even if the torches had refused to give their light to the hall, one would have seen quite clearly, so much did they sparkle and shine.]

Using Matthieu's description, it is possible to identify two poetic texts for this ballet: the anonymously authored verses for the air "Maintenant les Vertus Sacrées" [Now the Sacred Virtues] and Jean Bertaut's *récit* with the incipit "Voyant la douce Paix et la divine Astrée" [Seeing gentle Peace and divine Astraea]. (For full transcriptions of both sets of verses, with English translations, see Appendix 1.) These texts together have not previously been attributed to this 1602 ballet. Correcting the record on this point is important, however, because when read side by side, "Maintenant les Vertus Sacrées" and "Voyant la douce Paix et la divine Astrée" make legible a number of allegories evoked by the queen's appearance on stage and, with them, this ballet's larger dramatic and political interventions.

"Maintenant les Vertus Sacrées" was performed as a sung air by Apollo and the muses during the ballet's first entry. Matthieu's printed history, as we have seen, specifies that this production featured Apollo, in song, accompanied by the nine muses. "Maintenant les Vertus Sacrées" does not directly mention Apollo. However, the fourth stanza's declaration that "Ces Muses viennent pour offrande / Vous donner le plus beau des lieux" [These Muses have come to give you, as an offering, the most beautiful of places] indicates the arrival of a group of muses on the court stage. This connection alone would not be sufficient to assign this air to the new queen's 1602 ballet. The striking overlap between its refrain and the reprise that Matthieu says finished each cadence of Apollo's song during the performance establishes this match with certainty, however. The refrain for "Maintenant les Vertus Sacrées" reads: "Il faut que tout vous rende homage, / Grand Roy, merveille de nostre age" [Everyone must pay tribute to you, Great King, marvel of our age]. According to Matthieu, the air sung by Apollo and the muses featured the refrain "Il faut que tout vous face hommage, Grand Roy miracle de nostre aage." Matthieu replaces "rende" with "face" and "merveille" with "miracle," but otherwise his version of the refrain's text is identical to that of the printed air. As set to music, "Maintenant les Vertus Sacrées" appeared in print in 1608 in two different versions: Pierre Guédron's polyphonic rendition for four voices and Gabriel Bataille's adaptation for solo voice with lute.[4] Both publications indicate that this air was composed for a court ballet without specifying which one. Clearly, though, when Apollo and the muses sang for the first entry of Marie's 1602 ballet, their text was that of "Maintenant les Vertus Sacrées."[5]

A closer look at this air's poetic text indicates its rousing announcement of the ballet's central theme: legitimate power, founded on virtue, brings another golden age of peace and prosperity and a flourishing of the courtly arts.[6] "Maintenant les Vertus Sacrées" consists of five stanzas. The first informs Henri IV and other members of the ballet's audience that they will soon witness on the court ballet stage the Sacred Virtues, deities who will descend from the heavens in order to offer "Leurs clartés comme un nouveau jour" [their pure illumination like the dawning of a new day]. The air's second stanza identifies the king's own divine ornaments of equity, faith, and clemency as the reason why France is now able to taste a thousand diverse happinesses ["L'équité, la foi, la clemence, / Qui sont vos divins ornemens, / Ores font gouter à la France / Mille divers contentemens"], including the felicities these Sacred Virtues bring with them from the heavens above. These lines, with their reference to divine qualities, to faith, and to clemency, allude to Henri IV's conversion to Catholicism as well as his subsequent policy of pardoning former Catholic Leaguers, both of which had helped bring peace to a kingdom decimated by years of religious warfare and political upheaval.[7] Ruling equitably, with piety and clemency, the king's divinely sanctioned governance of the realm ensures a propitious setting for the Sacred Virtues here below.

When these celestial virtues arrive and present themselves on stage during the ballet, the text continues, they will appear in mortal guise as dancing women and cause to march before themselves "Les jeux, les ris, les gaietés" [light pastimes, laughter, and delights], including "Nymphes d'une autre bande" [a group of nymphs] who offer "leurs plaisirs plus délicieux" [their even more delicious pleasures]. According to Matthieu, as we have seen, eight of Marie's *filles* danced the ballet's second entry; it is they, therefore, who most likely performed as these nymphs preceding the queen's own entrance. This troupe of nymphs, the air tells us, was itself preceded by the muses who offered "les plus beaux des lieux" [the most beautiful of places]. Having thus explained the allegories that underpinned the ballet as a whole, the air concludes by calling on the king to accept an exchange: "Recevez, Monarque invincible, / Ces délices et ses ebats, / Au lieu de ce glaive terrible / Qui vous faisoit craindre aux combats" [Receive, invincible monarch, these delights and these frolics in place of this terrifying two-edged sword which caused you to be feared in battle]. Henri IV, the great military commander, now rules virtuously in accordance with divine justice; in consequence, he is graced with the delightful yet virtuous recreations this ballet offers him. In fact, such pleasing pastimes only reinforce Henri IV's glory, for when witnessing them, the refrain insists, "Il faut que tout vous rende hommage, / Grand Roi, merveille de nostre age" [Everyone must pay tribute to you, Great King, marvel of our age]. If France is now home to Apollo and the muses as well as the Sacred Virtues with their joyful pleasures, as the ballet's on-stage action confirms, this happy development occurs both thanks to the king's own greatness and in honour of it.

"Maintenant les Vertus Sacrées" conveys this encomiastic program textually but also aurally. Assuming that the musical setting for this air as it appears in print lines up with that used in the actual ballet performance, careful matching of syllables with note values during the air's verses would have rendered more clearly the air's textual assertion that these performers' appearance on stage was possible only because Henri IV himself had restored peace to the realm.[8] Ornamentation and harmonic modulation in the refrain further underscore this encomiastic message. As Don Lee Royster argues, the air's use of ornament at the phrase "rende homage" enacts aurally what its poetry forwards conceptually: courtly diversion as an offering to the monarch. Royster notes further that although "Maintenant les Vertus Sacrées" displays harmonic consistency throughout, one marked alteration occurs during the refrain's sudden shift from minor to major (G- to G+) at the word "merveille" [marvel].⁹ Enhancing musically the textual phrase describing Henri IV as the "merveille de nostre age" [marvel of our age], this modulation lends further emphasis to the air's most striking instance of verbal praise.

Adding to such honouring of Henri IV was the encomium implicit in this entry's bucolic fictional setting. Apollo tells the king in stanza four that the muses have come to France in order to present him with "le plus beau des lieux" [the most beautiful of places]. Festivities at the court of Charles IX (1550–74) had often featured pastoral versions of the god Apollo in his guise as poet, accompanied by the muses, as part of an attempt to evoke civic peace and harmony. Due to religious violence and continued dynastic infertility, however, the appropriateness of such themes came under increasing strain. Kate Van Orden notes that throughout the wars of religion and immediately afterward during the first years of Henri IV's rule, pastoral versions of Apollo as the god of poetry disappeared from French royal encomium; royal panegyric instead made use of myths in which Apollo engaged in violent struggle, defeating the Python and other monsters, for example. By the time of Henri IV's 1595–6 entries at Lyon and Rouen, though, the pastoral Apollo of music and poetry began to be partly restored,¹⁰ and following the king's October 1600 Florentine wedding by proxy to Marie de Médicis, allusions to this version of the god resurfaced with greater frequency and insistence in connection with the Bourbon dynasty. At the Medici court, the opera *Il rapimento di Cefalo* (The Abduction of Cephalus) performed in honour of this royal wedding included Apollo and the muses at the Heliconian spring together with Poetry personified descending from the heavens to delight the court with song.¹¹ Marie's royal entry at Avignon on 19 November 1600 featured similar tropes. André Valladier's printed account of this entry, emphasizing the Bourbon dynasty's sacred legitimacy and its enactment of virtues associated with royalty, features verse texts for an "Odelette" of praise performed by Phoebus playing his lute accompanied by seven muses on various other instruments; it also includes an engraving representing the arch dedicated to Henri IV as Apollo Economo, "the god who governs the universe with his rays," along with the inscription "Redeunt Saturnia regna," a motto that evokes Virgil's famous prophecy of the ruler destined to restore Saturn's age of gold.¹² Published that same year, Siméon-Guillaume de La Roque's *Hymne sur l'embarquement de la royne, et de son arrivée en France* also calls on the muses to descend from Mount Helicon and other lofty regions to the temple of France in order to proclaim in song the glory and power of Henri and to sing of Marie, "ceste Princesse où l'on voit que les Cieux / Ont mis leur plus beaux dons & les plus precieux" [this princess adorned with the heavens' most beautiful and precious gifts].[13] Proclaiming this new queen's arrival as heralding an end to the discord and envy that had troubled France and as the beginning of "l'heureux siècle d'or" [the happy golden age] now shining again ["à ce regne nouveau puisse reluire encore"], La Roque invokes the muses, infused with the spirit and golden hair of Apollo ["Apollon ce Dieu tant reveré, / D'où vous tenez l'esprit & le beau poil doré] to "Sonnez dessus vos Luts" [sound here below your lutes] in order to "Renflammez les esprits de Bertaut & Desportes" [inflame the hearts of Bertaut and Desportes], along with other famous poets, so that they will "encore chanter, / La gloire Bourbons" [again sing the glory of the Bourbon line] and thereby "augmenter le bal, / Des nopces que l'on fait dans ce Palais Royal" [heighten the nuptial ball that is made at this royal palace].[14]

As if answering La Roque's call, the *Ballet of the Sixteen Virtues* not only restores Apollo and the muses to the French court stage but also offers a *récit* by Jean Bertaut, one of the two poets La Roque invokes by name. We have seen how Matthieu's printed account mentions in connection with this ballet a poem by "Berthaut."[15] Printed editions of Bertaut's collected verses published in 1602, 1606, and 1620 indicate that his *récit* "Voyant la douce Paix et la divine Astrée" [Seeing sweet Peace and the divine Astraea] was written "Pour le Ballet de seize Dames representant les Vertus, dont la Royne estoit l'une" [For the ballet of the sixteen women representing the virtues, of which the queen was the first].[16] Using Matthieu's history and the text for Guédron's air "Maintenant les Vertus Sacrées" noted above, I have identified as the central action for Marie's first major court ballet in France her appearance leading a troupe of fifteen other princesses and ladies representing the sacred virtues. Putting these pieces of the puzzle together thus clarifies that Bertaut's "Voyant la douce Paix et la divine Astrée" describes this same queen's ballet rather than any other.[17]

Like other court ballet *récits*, "Voyant la douce Paix et la divine Astrée" introduces a danced entry and lauds its own dedicatee; it also elucidates further the allegories found in "Maintenant les Vertus Sacrées."[18] "Voyant la douce Paix et la divine Astrée" begins by proclaiming that all the virtues have arrived in the performance hall and in France more generally because gentle peace and justice, heralded by the arrival of

Astraea, now inhabit this beautiful country and seem to promise for it another golden age:

> Voyant la douce Paix et la divine Astrée
> Habiter maintenant ceste belle contrée,
> Et sembler y promettre un second âge d'or,
> La Foy, la Pieté, la Bonté, la Clemence,
> L'Equité, la Raison, la Douceur, l'Innocence,
> Bref, toutes les Vertuz y retournent encore.[19]

> [Seeing gentle Peace and divine Astraea
> Now inhabiting this beautiful country
> And seeming to promise here a second Golden Age,
> Faith, Piety, Generosity, Clemency,
> Equity, Reason, Gentleness, Innocence,
> In Brief – all of the Virtues return here again.]

This list of virtues recalls the qualities of rule emphasized in Seneca's "On Clemency," translated into French during the 1590s by Simon Goulart.[20] The second book of Seneca's treatise defines clemency – the liberty and power to judge equitably, and not only with rigor – as essential for those who would rule wisely. Writing at the end of the first century CE, Seneca also proclaims the time nigh for world-wide agreement to follow justice and equity; for piety, integrity, faith, and modesty to reveal themselves; and for the vices, long responsible for fostering abuse and disorder, to give way to a more sacred and happy age. Bertaut's poem incorporates this imagery associated with the Pax Romana in its first stanza, as we have seen; its third stanza then revisits these same tropes while directly addressing Henri IV himself:

> Grand Monarque François, l'heure de nos destinées,
> C'est par vous qu'elles sont en France retournées:
> Vous en avez chassé leurs mortels ennemis:
> Aussi, c'est pres de vous qu'elles se viennent rendre,
> Saçhant que de vous seul elles doivent attendre
> Le permanent sejour qu'elles s'y sont promis.

> [Great French Monarch, good fortune of our destinies,
> It is through you that they [the Virtues] have returned to France.
> You chased away their deadly enemies:

Therefore, it is to be near you that they have come,
Knowing that from you alone can they expect
The everlasting sojourn that they have been promised here.]

Such lines imply that only now, at the dawn of another new century, has Seneca's promise of peace and plenty finally been fulfilled in France. As Denis Crouzet has shown, writings by royalist intellectuals in the late 1580s and early 1590s, propagandist pamphlets from the 1590s in support of Henri IV's reign, and royal entries from the early 1600s borrowed from Stoic thought to depict the king, in contrast to his Leaguer enemies, as possessing the virtuous control over his own passions that allowed him to serve as heroic renewer of the world.[21] In early 1602, Bertaut's verses for the queen's *Ballet of the Sixteen Virtues* similarly frame Henri IV's military victories and religious pacification of the realm along Stoic lines, as the precursor to his virtuous restoration of another golden age of peace and prosperity in keeping with the workings of divine providence.

According to Bertaut's *récit*, the arrival of the queen and her troupe on stage as if from the heavens, accompanied by pleasure and abundance, crowned this providential scheme's fulfilment:

> Les voicy qui s'ornant de figures mortelles
> Font, à pas mesurez, cheminer devant elles
> La Richesse, et la Joye, et les chastes Esbats:
> A fin qu'il se remarque en ces ombres parlantes,
> Que les seules Vertus par la paix fleurissantes
> Font fleurir la richesse et la joye icy bas.

[Behold them, who adorning themselves with mortal appearance
Make Plenitude, Joy, and chaste Pastimes
Walk in measured steps before them:
So that, through these talking shadows, it may be known
That only Virtues, when flourishing through Peace,
Make Abundance and Joy flourish here below.]

Led by Marie, this troupe of virtues ensures that "La Richesse, et la Joye, et les chastes Esbats" [Plenitude, Joy, and chaste Pastimes] "Font, à pas mesurz, cheminer devant elles" [walk in measured steps before them]. Thus ascribing to the queen's own dancing the virtuous capacity to chasten and control the pleasures made possible through Henri IV's peace, Bertaut recalls the famous dancing master

Fabrizio Caroso's claim that recreation in dance is itself a virtue when joined with poetry and music.[22] According to Bertaut's *récit*, Marie de Médicis appeared on stage following an entry danced by young girls (the same *filles* who according to "Maintenant les Vertus Sacrées," this ballet's other verse text, represented peacetime's "plaisirs … délicieux" [delicious pleasures]). These young women in turn were preceded on stage by court musicians in the guise of Apollo and the muses (allegories for poetry and music). Thus enacting the harmonious joining of dance and poetry with music, the ballet as a whole thematized its own enactment of pleasing yet virtuous pastimes of the kind defended by Caroso and tied, in French royal panegyric from this period more widely, to the glorification of the new Bourbon regime.

Franco-Florentine Neoplatonism and the (Medicean) Magnificence of Bourbon Rule

Proclaiming in direct address to Henri IV that it is "de vous seul" [through you alone] that peace and the permanent restoration of virtue are now made possible in France, Bertaut's "Voyant la douce Paix et la divine Astrée" emphasizes the king's uniqueness. As the analysis above suggests, however, this *récit* also brings into encomiastic focus the king's new wife. Like other texts associated with her ballet production, moreover, Bertaut's poem draws on notions of beauty and light found in Florentine Neoplatonism to harness in connection with the visual effects created on stage by Marie's bejewelled dancing costume a larger discursive pattern, useful to the sacralization of the Bourbon dynasty, in which female beauty carried resonances of pagan as well as Christian divinity.

Particularly important to Florentine Neoplatonic discourse is Marsilio Ficino's theory that beauty in humans reveals, through the veil of corporeality, the light that derives from God himself. Ficino's *Commentary on Plato's Symposium* (1484–5) outlines this concept in its definition of true Beauty as the splendour of the Good that shines through Matter and which resembles "the supreme light of the sun," or God.[23] This divine ray attracts admirers, Ficino notes, yet the lover of such luminous beauty is virtuous, "[f]or he does not desire this or that body, but he admires, desires, and is amazed by the splendour of the celestial majesty shining through bodies." Such amazement in turn leads to deference: "Hence it also always happens that lovers fear and worship in some way the sight of the beloved … that splendour of divinity, shining in the beautiful, like a statue of God, compels lovers to marvel, to be afraid, and to worship."[24]

The 1602 queen's ballet evokes such notions from its first entry, performed by musicians performing as Apollo and the muses. Ficino's treatise *De sole* (1494) identifies the nine muses as lights around the Sun, whom the ancients called Apollo: "Indeed in the same way that this sensible light is experienced by the senses, illuminating, invigorating and forming all sensible things and faculties of sense and converting them to higher planes, so a certain intelligible light in the soul of the Sun illuminates, kindles and recalls the inner spiritual eye. I think for this reason the Sun was called Apollo by the ancient Theologians, and creator of all harmony, and leader of the Muses, since he releases minds from a certain confused turmoil, not so much by visible but by hidden influxes of rays, and he tempers them proportionately, and finally leads them to understanding."[25] In the *Ballet of the Sixteen Virtues*, we have seen, Apollo and the muses praise in song the "clartés comme un nouveau jour" [pure illumination like a new dawning] that Marie with her troupe emits when entering the performance space. This purity, these singers assert, inheres even as "ces déitées" [these deities] leave their celestial dwelling place to "se présente dessous des figures mortelles" [present themselves here below, in the guise of mortals]. Voiced on stage by Apollo and the muses, figures for the art of poetry but also for the sun and its divine powers, such imagery both underscored the ballet's larger thematic emphasis on the luminous beauty and virtuous pleasures of just, divinely sanctioned Bourbon rule and prepared its audience for this theme's fullest instantiation in the entry danced by the troupe of women led on stage by the queen.

The celestial nature of Marie's luminous beauty and that of her troupe receives similar emphasis in Matthieu's print account of the papal nuncio's response to their arrival on stage. Describing this ballet, as we have seen, Matthieu explains that the queen and her followers appeared wearing headdresses decorated with gems which sparkled so brightly that "qua[n]d les flambeaux eussent refusé leur lumiere à la Salle, on y eust veu assez clair, tant elles esclattoient & esclairoient" [even if the torches had refused to give their light to the hall, one would have seen quite clearly so much did they sparkle and shine]. He then recounts the following conversation in the ballet's audience at the moment this troupe appeared in view:

> De loing que le Roy les veit il se tourna devers le Nunce du Pape qui estoit un peu à quartier, avec les autres Ambassadeurs, & luy demanda ce qu'il luy en sembloit, & si un tel esquadron n'estoit pas beau? Bellissime, respond le Nunce, & bien perilleux. Tant de beautez estoient assez

puissantes pour acquerir un autre Empire à l'Amour. Tant de vertus estoient assez puissantes pour destruire & desesperer tous les desseins d'Amour. Ce sont beautez qu'il faut regarder comme les rayons du Soleil en ligne oblique avec de l'admiration, car tout autre regard est perilleux.[26]

[Seeing them coming from a distance the king turned toward the papal nuncio who was close by, with the other ambassadors, and asked him how it seemed to him, and whether such a squadron was not beautiful? "Bellissimo," responded the nuncio, "and quite dangerous. So many beauties were powerful enough to acquire another Empire for Love. So many virtues were strong enough to destroy and frustrate all of Love's designs. They are beauties that must be looked at as one looks at rays of sunlight, indirectly and with great esteem, for looking any other way is perilous."]

Matthieu's account draws attention to the amplified brightness made possible through the rich gems and precious metals on the women's headdresses reflecting light from the torches that decorated the hall. He also records how this powerful light, seen from a distance across the playing space, evoked in the king and the pope's representative a shared appreciation for the dancers' exceptional beauty. The nuncio's reference to love's empire alludes to Ovidian myth in ways that link the queen's allegorical role, as queen of the virtues, to Venus, goddess of love and sun of beauties. In the fifth book of Ovid's *Metamorphoses*, Venus incites her son Cupid (also known as Love) to wound Pluto with one of his arrows.[27] By thus subjecting the king of the underworld to the power of love, Ovid explains, Cupid will extend his mother's empire, for by controlling Pluto's heart she will herself control not only the skies and seas but even hell, the third and only remaining part of the world still free from Venus' power. Matthieu's description informs us that Marie entered this ballet's performance space preceded by the young César de Vendôme costumed as Cupid or Love: "Le Duc de Vendosme estoit vestu en Cupidon, & marchoit devant la Roine."[28] This appearance of Love followed immediately by the queen explains the nuncio's frank warning about the risks of responding erotically to a beauty embodied in fleshly female form. Putting concerns of any such response to rest, however, the nuncio as recorded in Matthieu's description references the familiar Neoplatonic dictum that beauty, when embodied in virtuous femininity, has the capacity to thwart all lustful designs by commanding the indirect gaze of a respectfully deferential admiration.

In its emphasis on virtue as revealed through light, brightness, and beauty, Matthieu's account of the nuncio's comments echoes a pattern of figurative imagery found in this ballet's verse texts as well as depictions of Marie's dancing authored by Medici court poets. Of the latter, perhaps the earliest example is the dedicatory epistle by Ottavio Rinnucini for the 1596 *Mascherata di stelle*, described by one contemporary as "un ballo della signora Principessa Maria fatto in concorso con altre sette dame" [Princess Maria's *ballo* made together with seven other ladies].[29] Rinuccini's prose dedication to Marie's aunt, the grand duchess Christine of Lorraine, begins with a rhetorical question: "E quando vide mai, o questa o altra etade, le stelle del cielo discese sopra la terra, esporsi alla vista de' mortali?" [When, in this age or any other, have we ever witnessed the stars of the heavens descending to earth and exposing themselves to the sight of mortals?].[30] Rinuccini next explains that the eight stars who perform this *ballo* are the comet Berenice, the lovely Callisto, and the Pleiades. According to Rinuccini, these stars – formerly the daughters of Atlas – have been transformed into astral beings by Jove as a reward for their purity and chastity.[31] As his verses for the *mascherata* further emphasize, "queste danzatrici snelle / Donne non son, ma de'l ciel lumi e stele" [these nimble dancers are not women, but stars and lights of the sky].[32] Brighter than any earthly treasure, they now graciously make themselves visible to humans. Under normal circumstances, mere mortals would be blinded by the bright light these stars emit, "Ma ne l'antica lor tenera veste / Velano i raggi luminosi et d'oro" [But in this instance they have veiled their rays in antique dress].[33] Appearing before the grand duchess, disguised as mortal women, their dancing is made visible to humans: "E com'in cielo a l'armonia celeste / Guidano eternamente i balli loro, / Si, transformate ne'l primiero aspetto, / Muovon danzando il piè per tuo diletto" [Just as in the heavens these astral beings tune their dances eternally to cosmic harmonies, so now these celestial bodies appear changed back into their first guise as women and moving their feet in harmonious dance formations for your delight].[34] Ilaria Ciseri and Maria Adelaide Bartoli Bacherini have suggested thematic continuity between this *mascherata*'s central trope of dancing stars and elements of the famous 1589 *intermedii* for the wedding of Grand Duke Ferdinando I de' Medici to Christine of Lorraine.[35] But Rinuccini's imagery also offers intertextual connections with Marie's 1602 ballet as queen of France, for both the *Mascherata di Stelle* and the *Ballet of the Sixteen Virtues* compare Marie as dancer to a virtuous and beautiful celestial light that, descending to earth, appears veiled in mortal female form.

Verses written by Medici court poets in praise of the new queen's dancing at the time of her marriage also find intextual echoes in the 1602 ballet's emphasis on virtuous divinity made luminously manifest through opulent feminine self-display. Gabriello Chiabrera's "Canzone in lode della Reina" [Song in praise of the queen] performed on 8 October 1600 as one of the *rime* sung in the Riccardi gardens to celebrate Marie's wedding, for example, extols the new queen's beautiful hair, lips, and hands but also her dancing feet, so regally majestic and graceful that one would believe her to be Venus or Diana ["Con maestà reale / E laggiadria move lo snello piede, / Che Ciprigna esser crede / O Latona"].[36] Marie's glorious attire also receives tribute: "Nè dèi tacer de' manti suoi, canzone, / De' vari portamenti, / De' superbi ornamenti / Chà al variar di tempo e di stagione / Cangia con Flora e Rea veste e corone" [And you, o song, should never stop speaking of her dress, of her varied attire, of her superb ornaments, and she, with the change in weather and season, changes dresses and crowns with Flora and Rhea]. These lines imply that Marie, with her ornamented and varied dress, rivals the goddesses of ancient Rome. Moreover, such divine authority, crowned by the new queen's virtue, makes her a source of light and brightness so compelling that it occasions this very poem in praise of her:

Questa cortese e saggia,
Magnanima, gentil, benigna e pia,
È l'illustre Maria:
Maria che d'ogn'intorno il mondo irragia
Di chiara leggiadria,
E splende e luce con sue alte e sole
E maniere e virtude
Che dentro a sè richiude:
Che, chi lodar, chi palesar le vuole
Porge acqua al mar, reca splendore al sole.

[This, courteous and wise,
Magnanimous, gentle, kind and pious,
Is the renowned Maria:
Maria who in every place bestows her light on the world
With bright gracefulness, and shines
With manners and virtues
That she alone holds within herself:
Such that one wishes to compliment her,

And to reveal to her that
She brings water to the sea, and grants brightness to the sun.]

Three days earlier, at the famous banquet entertainment for the wedding festivities, six golden statues set in niches represented visually the virtues this new bride was said to embody: Glory, Justice, Peace, Abundance, Charity, and Prudence.[37] Chiabrera's poem expands on this theme by declaring the new queen to be a source of virtue so bright that even the sun, that most powerful of stars, owes his illumination to her. Recalling Rinuccini's flattering comparison of the dancing princess to a heavenly star in the 1596 *Mascherata di stelle*, Chiabrera's "Canzone in lode della reina" ups the encomiastic ante in keeping with Marie's now greater social status, four years later, as wife to the king of France.

An undated poem by Rinuccini in the style of Ovid's *Heroides* also praises the new queen's dancing as a source of divine brightness made visible here below.[38] This poem's unnamed speaker, a victim of love's wounds, declares herself unmoved by springtime courtly festivities and pastimes. She nonetheless recalls a happier time: one beautiful evening when, "Inebriato di diletto immenso" [drunk with delight], her heart had been free from pain ["Respirò il cor dagli amorosi affanni"].[39] At the royal palace where she used to live, the speaker explains, knights and ladies danced all night and into the morning. On one such occasion, "Quand'ecco risonar d'alto concento / S'odon de' regii alberghi i tetti aurati / E mille lumi e mille faci ardenti / Tanti intorno vibrar raggi e splendori / Ch'io non vidi giammai sul mezzo giorno/ Splender di sì gran luce armato il sole" [the high golden ceilings of the palace resonated with noble music and the room, filled with light from a thousand lamps and a thousand burning torches, was brightened with more splendour than even the sun is armed with at mid-day]. Amidst this brightness appeared "l'inclita Donna, / Sovra il cui biondo crin ripose il cielo / Qual più degna corona il mondo ammiri, / Sovra ogni uso mortal sì bella apparve / Che l'alta maestà, gl'alti sembianti / Sostener non potea guardo terreno" [the woman whose beauty exceeded that of any mortal, whose majesty and features, like the light of the sun, caused all human eyes to look away, and on whose blonde hair the heavens had placed a crown, the most precious in the world]. This famous woman wore a skirt woven with gold, the borders of which were so artfully decorated with jewels that it demanded admiration. Beneath the skirt could also be seen a foot so decorated with jewels and gold that it was well worthy of tracing the stars ["Succinta gonna le scendea dal fianco / D'oro contesta, e per mirabil arte / Di varie gemme ricamata il limbo, / Sotto a cui si scorgea gemmato e d'oro / Il piè ben degno di calcar le stelle"]. "Ricco splendor di lucidi diamante / Arder parea tra le dorate chiome" [lustrous diamonds appeared to burn in her golden hair], and "del bel collo l'animate nevi / Cingea puro candor di perle elette" [the living snow of her beautiful neck was surrounded by the white purity of rare pearls]. Followed by a group of beautiful and proud ladies, this dancer resembled in her legendary and immortal beauty the tall queen Penthisilea appearing on the river Xanthus amidst her armed phalanxes ["Tal già, come risuona immortal fama, / Su la riva del Xanto apparve adorna / Fra l'armate falangi alta regina. Schiera di donne, d'ogni pregio altere, / In guisa pur d'Amazzoni superbe / L'orme seguin dell'onorate piante"]. "Ed ella al suon delle soavi lire / Cotal movea qual per le selve antiche / Vide il mondo danzar Delia e Ciprigna" [To the sound of the lyre, this famous woman moved with all the grace of Delia and Cypria dancing in the ancient forests].

In Rinuccini's *heroide*, as in Chiabrera's *canzone*, a goddess-like woman dances bedecked with gems and jewels; glittering with light, this dancer resembles a blinding sun from which mortals must avert their gaze. In keeping with such tropes, the air sung by Apollo and the muses during the 1602 ballet praises the new queen's "clarté" [luminousness], while the nuncio's response to the production as recounted by Matthieu likens her virtuous beauty to a light from the celestial spheres, deserving of worshipful deference. As I will now explore, Bertaut's *récit* for this *Ballet of the Sixteen Virtues* concludes by glorifying Marie de Médicis in similar terms. In particular, Bertaut's poem emphasizes the celestial charms embodied by her richly dressed troupe and praises as divine and admirable the love that such celestial beauties and especially their leader, "La reine des Vertus" [the queen of the Virtues], evokes in this ballet's spectators. Unlike Rinuccini or Chiabrera, though, Bertaut's language hints at a particular difficulty the new Bourbon monarchy faced when reinstating at the court of France a magnificence still associated, in the minds of many French subjects, with the last Valois king Henri III and his mother Catherine de Médicis.

Bertaut's final stanzas describing the women dancers gloss the impact of the queen and her female troupe entering the ballet's performance space as follows:

Vous les verrez venir superbement parées,
Et non comme Platon les auroit desirées

Pour charmer tout d'amour à les voir seulement:
Mais, ny leur riche habit n'empesche point leurs charmes
Ny ce n'est point de honte à vos heureuses armes,
Qu'en France la Vertu s'habille richement.

Ce ne sont que beautez, qu'attraits, que mignardises
Dignes d'assujettir les plus libres franchises,
Et dont mesme les Dieux se sentent combatus.
Amour les accompagne, et dans ses vives flames
Fait pour elles bruler les plus celestes ames:
Mais est-il rien si beau que l'amour des Vertus?

L'amour en est divin, la flamme en est loüable,
Et digne de bruler d'une ardeur perdurable
Dans les plus beaux esprits jusqu'au point du trépas:
Car tant s'en-faut qu'aimer (mesme avec violence)
Leurs celestes beautez ce puisse estre une offence,
Que ce seroit peché de ne les aimer pas.[40]

[You will see them coming superbly arrayed,
And not as Plato would have desired them
To charm everyone with love at mere sight of them.
But their luxurious dress does not hinder their charms,
Nor is there any shame to your fortunate arms
That in France Virtue dresses herself richly.

They are nothing but beauty, charms, daintiness
Worthy of subduing the freest resistant hearts
And by whom even the Gods feel assailed.
Love accompanies them and, in his ardent flames,
Makes even the most celestial souls burn for them:
But is anything so beautiful as the love of the Virtues?

To love them is divine, to desire them admirable
And worthy of burning with an eternal flame
In the most beautiful of minds until the point of demise:
Because, rather than it being an offence to love
(Even with violence) their celestial beauties,
It would be a sin not to love them.]

In Matthieu's description of this occasion, I have suggested, the nuncio's conversation with the king registers a certain ambivalence regarding divine beauty's material embodiment in the form of sumptuously attired women. Bertaut's final stanzas, too, acknowledge the potentially seductive power wielded by these female dancers. "[S]uperbement parées" [superbly dressed] with "leur riche habit [qui] n'empesche point leur charmes" [their luxurious garb which prevents none of their charms], the queen and her troupe will incite amorous desire "à les voir seulement" [merely on sight]. As embodiments of sacred virtue, however, these women can only enhance the honourable reputation that Henri IV's court has come to enjoy as a result of his military leadership ["vos heureuses armes"].

Insisting that admiration for these opulently dressed dancers constitutes a virtue rather than a vice and that under Henri IV's virtuous rule France's military greatness cannot be shamed by the enticements of elite (women's) spectacle, Bertaut's *récit* registers concerns pertinent to the kingdom's transition from a realm torn apart by protracted wars of religion and of succession to one in which court life was being restored. The last Valois kings Charles IX and Henri III along with their mother Catherine de Médicis had sought (and ultimately failed) to navigate political difficulties in part through magnificent royal entertainments. These *divertissements* aimed to bolster the French monarchy's reputation abroad while simultaneously inducing civic harmony.[41] Expensive costumes worn by members of the royal family and courtiers who danced alongside them under their direction were one vehicle through which courtly productions such as these promoted images of a powerful French crown. The famous *Ballet comique de la royne* organized in 1581, for example, had sought to mobilize such messages in its plot centred on Henri's III's defeat of Circe, a figure who, according to this ballet's allegory, represented the dangers of rebellion and civil war. The king's gaze from the audience, this ballet's *livret* claims, had the power to free from this enchantress's immobilizing powers the troupe of high-ranking women dancers, headed by Queen Louise de Lorraine, who appeared on stage covered head to toe with precious gems that resembled, in their qualities of brightness, the starry lights of the heavens.[42]

In the face of crippling factionalism, protracted violence, and economic as well as political impoverishment, however, the crown's expenditure of "over a million écus" for this and other elaborate *divertissements* celebrating the 1581 marriage of Henri III's male favourite to the queen's sister, including the *Ballet comique*, "appeared to many as an act of royal irresponsibility," perhaps even "a project of criminal folly."[43] The new Bourbon dynasty, as Nicolas le Roux has argued, drew much of its symbolic legitimacy from a "demonization" of the last Valois kings and their entourages.[44] During the earliest years of Henri IV's reign, therefore, the practices of economic restraint with respect to courtly entertainments necessitated by the royal treasury's depletion had a silver lining, in that they helped to signal an important distance between this first Bourbon king's style of rule and that of his immediate predecesors.

And yet, royal magnificence of the type Marie de Médicis knew firsthand from her upbringing in Florence also offered its own political advantages. In late sixteenth- and seventeenth-century Italy and particularly in Florence, Iain Fenlon notes, *magnificenza* "acted as a mechanism for converting wealth into status and power."[45] Fenlon traces praise for magnificence back to humanist defenses of Cosimo il Vecchio's building projects, particularly their invocations of Saint Thomas, who described magnificence as a virtue and recalled Aristotle's statement in the *Nichomachean Ethics* that "great expenditure is becoming to those who have suitable means to start with, acquired by their own efforts or from ancestors or connections, and to people of high birth and reputation, and so on; for all these things bring with them greatness and prestige." During Marie's years in Florence, the ducal court of Tuscany continued to draw on the wealth it had acquired through banking in order to fund patronage of the visual arts and architecture as well as courtly festivities including *balli*, plays, *intermedii*, and early opera.[46] For the still relatively new Medici dynasty, this patronage of the arts had usefully converted financial advantage into social preeminence and political power.

In winter 1602, when Marie danced her *Ballet of the Sixteen Virtues* in Paris, the Bourbon dynasty had only recently established itself within the larger set of territories that made up early modern France. Given Henri's rather distant claims on the French crown by means of inheritance, as well as persistent scepticism regarding his religious sincerity, his government needed to make use of all available means for establishing its own legitimacy. Claims to authority on the basis of Henri's rights of acquisition, as conquerer in arms and pacifier of the realm, were one important means of authorizing his kingship,[47] as were Henri's conspicuous performances of piety at royal entries and in Paris ceremonies strongly associated with the medieval *religion royale*.[48] But so, too, was the magnificence endemic to courtly festivity. The 1581 *Ballet comique* had been performed at a time of military and political weakness as well as penury. By contrast, the 1602 *Ballet of the Sixteen Virtues* took place after Henri IV had captured League strongholds and pacified others through policies of clemency, after the king had promulgated the Edict of Nantes and had succeeded in having it registered by the Parlement of Paris, and after he had married a Catholic princess from a wealthy foreign dynasty. In winter 1602, when this new consort danced on the court ballet stage wearing the French crown jewels, augmented no doubt by gems she brought with her from Florence, the meanings and reception of her opulent attire thus occurred in a topical political context quite different from that of late Valois festivities. As Thierry Crépin-Leblond has noted, official documents which describe in detail Marie's collection of precious stones and her fine clothing, including the rich attire she brought with her to France from Tuscany, provide evidence for the renewed prosperity her marriage brought to the French royal treasury; in this sense, the gems and precious metals that she wore on ceremonial occasions and in visual portraiture dovetailed with contemporary understandings of magnificence as not merely a prerogative but also a duty of virtuous rule.[49] Extending this insight to consider the queen's ballet appearances, we can see that the visual effects of light and brightness made possible through Marie's opulent dancing habit for her *Ballet of the Sixteen Virtues* worked similarly: framed textually as a complement to Henri IV's politico-military successes and resacralization of the French monarchy, these aspects of the production's magnificence underscored on both visual and material registers a larger set of claims legitimating the Bourbon crown: in particular, its claim to have finally restored to France, after protracted civil unrest and economic hardship, the orderly pleasures of divinely sanctioned, hereditary rule.

Virtually everyone in Paris, it seems, ran to see this "ballet magnifique" [magnificent ballet] in its various locations – first at the Louvre, and then at the residence of Madame de Retz, the Évêché (the bishop of Paris' palace), and elsewhere, with crowds being so great that several curious spectators found themselves sorely inconvenienced.[50] Even the future duc de Sully, Maximilien de Béthune, who carefully guarded Henri IV's finances, found himself suitably impressed, recalling in his memoirs for winter 1602 how the court on this occasion prepared a truly magnificent ballet: "[o]n travailla par ordre, & pour le divertissement de la reine, à la composition *d'un ballet d'une grande magnificence*" [we worked by command, and for the diversion of the queen, at the composition *of a very magnificent ballet*].⁵¹ Visiting ambassadors seem to have been especially taken with this performance's magnificence. The Florentine representative, for example, wrote that "Qui s'è fatto il Carnevale allegramente con un bellissimo ballo inventato dalla Regina" [here carnival is made very gaily with a very beautiful ball invented by the queen].⁵² More detailed and directly pertinent to the previous discussion of gems on display are the nuncio Innocenzo del Bufalo's comments, not only as we have seen them via Matthieu's printed history but also directly, in his own letters. To Cardinal Pietro Aldobrandini, secretary of state for the Holy See, the nuncio wrote of "una festa che faceva la Regina con quindici Principesse, le quali insieme mascherate e *vestite di sontuosissimi habiti a livrea* dovevano far certi balli ... Et invero la festa riuscì bella et honesta" [a festivity organized by the queen with fifteen princesses, the which together, masked and *dressed in very sumptuous habits* of the same design and colours, were obliged to make some ballets ... *and in truth the festivity was beautiful and honest*].⁵³ To his brother Muzio, as well, del Bufalo describes this ballet as "vaghissimo" [very beautiful].⁵⁴ Not only panegyric – Bertaut's *récit* and Matthieu's official royal history – but also contemporary accounts by visiting dignitaries, then, record this ballet's conversion of royal wealth, in the form of rich costumes and precious jewels, into signs of moral and social pre-eminence. Thus the queen's actions as impresario for and lead dancer in this opulent production seem to have paid off handsomely; as Matthieu reports: "Ceste nuict valut à la Roine une journée: car en tous les lieux où le Balet fut veu & admiré, tous les coeurs & toutes les voix s'accordoient à ses louanges" [The night's efforts were well worth it to the queen, because in all places where the ballet was seen and admired ... all hearts and all voices sung her praises].⁵⁵

Marie as (Virgin) Mother

The conspicuous consumption that this ballet put in motion through the richly decorated costumes worn by its high-ranking women dancers, I have indicated, helped to establish production values of reflected light and brightness, while texts for and about this ballet drew on Franco-Florentine Neoplatonic language to situate these luminous material effects in a supra-human register. These material and textual specificities worked together to convert wealth into status for both the queen and the new Bourbon dynasty. Building on this argument, I now turn to an additional set of textual allegories deployed for similar purposes in this production: namely, this ballet's implicit comparison of Marie de Médicis, queen of the sacred virtues and mother of the king's first son born in wedlock, to the Virgin Mary, celestial queen of the virtues and mother of the Christ child.

For many contemporaries, luminous beauty of the type that this ballet's verse texts ascribe to Marie de Médicis would have found its highest human instantiation in the Virgin Mary, queen of the virtues. When arguing for the superior virtue of women, Henricus Agrippa's influential *Declamation on the nobility and preeminence of the female sex* (1529, and translated from Latin into French as early as 1530) had turned readers' attention to "the stories of the holy virgins" who in Catholic teachings are accorded "astonishing beauty," especially "the first among all ... whose praise should surpass all others ... the Virgin Mary, mother of God, immaculate virgin, whose beauty the sun and moon admire and from whose face so much chastity and holiness of beauty shines forth that even though she dazzles all eyes and all hearts, never did a single mortal man entice her with his inducements or with even the least thought."[56] More temporally proximate to Marie's *Ballet of the Sixteen Virtues* was André Du Chesne's 1605 *Figures mystiques du riche et précieux cabinet des dames*. This text's discussion of female beauty builds on Agrippa's when lauding "La glorieuse vierge Marie ... [qui] portoit en son corps les rayons de ses divines vertus" [the glorious Virgin Mary ... who wore in her body the rays of her divine virtues] and in whose face one reads "les caracteres de la charité, de la modestie, de l'humilité, de la gravité, de la pudicité, de la prudence, de la temperance, & des autres rares & divines qualités qui furent couchées en cette du tout divine" [the characters of chastity, modesty, humility, gravity, pudeur, prudence, temperance, and other rare and divine qualities].[57] Although Helen of Troy's rare beauty is often deemed so perfect that it is impossible to represent, Du Chesne claims, the qualities of this woman from antiquity pale by comparison with the beauty that makes itself admired in the holy mother of God who truly and divinely, in her body, gathers in herself the beauties of the women of all past centuries and all the perfections and excellences of the corporeal world ["On dit qu'Helene fille de Leda & de Jupiter fut si parfaitement belle que ... jamais tous les Peintres de l'antiquité ne peurent [sic] par leur art, ny par la perfection des plus belles femmes toutes nuës la representer au naïf ... Mais qu'estoit cette Beauté au parangon [sic] de celle, qui se faisoit admirer en [l]a Saincte Mere de Dieu? Elle estoit comme un recueil des beautés de toutes les femmes des siecles passés, toutes les perfections & excellences du monde corporel estoient vrayment & divinement ramassées en son corps"]. Indeed, within the Virgin Mary are found such virtues that in her, according to Saint Jerome, shines the mysterious ray of divinity, through which she attracts the eyes and hearts of all to admire and love her ["Aussi estoit elle au dedans ac-[c]omplie de mille vertus ... Ce qui occasionna S. Hierôme d'écrire qu'en elle resplandissoit je ne sçay quell rayon de la divinité, par lequel elle attiroit l'oeil & l'ame d'un chacun à l'admirer & aymer"].[58]

Texts by and about the *Ballet of the Sixteen Virtues*, discussed above, assign to Marie de Médicis, queen of France, the same virtuous powers of light, brightness, and beauty linked in texts such as these with the Virgin Mary, queen of heaven. In Agrippa's account, Mary stands as the "first among all" virtuous women, while in Du Chesne's, she gathers in herself the beauty and virtue of all other women. Similarly, Marie as lauded in the final stanza of Bertaut's *récit* draws to herself even the most cruel hearts, so worthy of love she seems ["Mais quand quelque inhumain les voudroit prendre en haine, / Encor ne sçauroit-il qu'il n'en aime la Reine, / Tant elle semble aimable aux coeurs moins amoureux"], since as Queen of the Virtues she contains all of them in herself: "La reine des Vertus les a toutes en elle."

Adding another important layer of meaning to these parallels between the queen and the virgin mother, Bertaut's poem asserts that Marie's arrival on the court ballet stage follows the return to France of Astraea, goddess of justice and equity. As we have seen, Bertaut's *récit* begins by specifying that the ballet's troupe of dancing virtues led by the queen owes its appearance to Astraea's arrival:

Voyant la douce Paix et la divine Astrée
Habiter maintenant ceste belle contrée,
Et sembler y promettre un second âge d'or,
La Foy, la Pieté, la Bonté, la Clemence,
L'Equité, la Raison, la Douceur, l'Innocence,
Bref, toutes les Vertuz y retournent encore.

[Seeing gentle Peace and divine Astraea
Now inhabiting this beautiful country
And seeming to promise here a second Golden Age,
Faith, Piety, Generosity, Clemency,
Equity, Reason, Gentleness, Innocence,
In Brief – all of the Virtues return here again.]

In pagan mythology, Astraea's rule in the heavens symbolized cosmic order and with it a golden age of peace and prosperity for humankind, such that in Virgil's fourth eclogue Astraea's return presaged the birth of a child destined to rule with justice and equity. In Christian thought Astraea's departure from earth came to symbolize the Fall and the loss of perfection in Eden, while the saviour child foretold by this goddess's return in Virgil's poem became a type for Christ, both the agent of divine reconciliation with humans and the sovereign adjudicator of God's justice.[59] As Frances Yates has shown, references to Astraea were ubiquitous in late sixteenth-century dynastic culture, particularly in England and France.[60] In the final decade of that century and the first years of the next, both visual and literary imagery celebrated Henri IV's military and political victories, under the guise of the Gallic Hercules, in connection with hopes for a restoration of peace thanks to the return of Astraea. Honoré d'Urfé's widely read *L'Astrée*, for example, the first books of which were published during Henri IV's reign, suggested that the king's wise and virtuous rule had brought about the return of Astraea, goddess of justice, to a kingdom devastated by succession crises and religious wars.[61] Bertaut's *récit* for Marie's 1602 ballet, too, praises Henri I's pacification of the realm in part by drawing on Christianized versions of the myth in which Astraea's reappearance went hand in hand with prophecies of a saviour's birth following the Pax Romana. This aspect of Bertaut's poem likens Henri IV to the Roman emperor Augustus, who had brought an end to civil war, ushered in a golden age of peace and cultural renewal, and paved the way for Christianity's arrival. In doing so, however, the poem also insists on the contributions of Henri's new wife to the Bourbon monarchy's heroic renewal of the world, through its subtle assimilation of the new French queen to the virgin mother of God.

This production's inclusion of Marian imagery constituted an important innovation within French court ballet. Identifications of French queens with the Virgin can be traced back to Anne de Bretagne, Claude de France, and Louise de Savoie.[62] Visual and literary imagery, for example, likened Louise de Savoie to the virgin mother as the fountain of virtues, such that Louise's son François Ier became by extension another Christ, God's lieutenant on earth and agent of divine order.[63] François Ier's reign had been celebrated "as an imperial *renovatio*" complete with "the rebirth of letters, arts, and sciences," and such panegyric continued at the courts of his son Henri II and grandsons Charles IX and Henri III.[64] None of the three ruling sons born to

Henri II and Catherine de Médicis – François II, Charles IX, and Henri III – produced a legitimate male heir, however, nor had any of these three kings been declared dauphin at his own birth, since the eldest of them, François II, was born before his father acceded to the throne. Biological failure in the later Valois royal line thus meant that Marian imagery in connection with the French queen as mother to the dauphin could no longer combine with references to imperial renewal in visual and literary imagery that promoted dynastic monarchy, including in *ballet de cour*, a magnificent new genre of court entertainment that developed in France under the aegis of the dowager queen Catherine de Médicis. With the arrival of Marie de Médicis, however, thematic parallels between the queen of France and the Virgin Mary again found inspiration, not only because this new consort shared her first name with the woman whom god had chosen to mother the Christ child, as Fanny Cosandey notes, but also because the birth of a legitimate male heir to Henri and Marie in late September 1601 provided the perfect occasion for reviving Marian imagery in connection with the hereditary principle.[65]

Cosandey notes such tropes in connection with Marie de Médicis in ecclesiastical writing beginning in 1611, the first full year of her regency; she also points to Marian imagery in Rubens' heroic cycle of portraits depicting Marie's life presented in 1625, and in printed texts that championed Marie following her exile from France in 1631. Yann Rodier, too, finds in royal imagery from the period 1605–17 a "culte marial" [Marian cult] designed to legitimize Marie's authority as regent through her standing as mother to Henri IV's heir, Louis XIII.[66] My analysis locates such imagery even earlier, however, not only in Léonard Gaultier's engraved title page for Louis Richeome's *Tableaux sacrez des figures mystiques du très-auguste sacrifice et sacrement de l'Eucharistie*, dedicated to Marie de Médicis and published in 1601 [Figure 1.1], but also, the winter following, in an instance of live performance by the queen herself. This same production thus occasioned not only the restoration of magnificent royal ballet at the French court but also an innovation within this genre: its merging of imperial imagery in praise of the French king with Marian imagery lauding his consort.

Scholars of court ballet have missed this important vector of political meaning in Marie's first major production as queen of France in part because of its subtley of expression: this entertainment's printed verses, I believe, anticipate the care with which Rubens himself, to avoid charges of sacrilege, would partly camouflage his comparisons

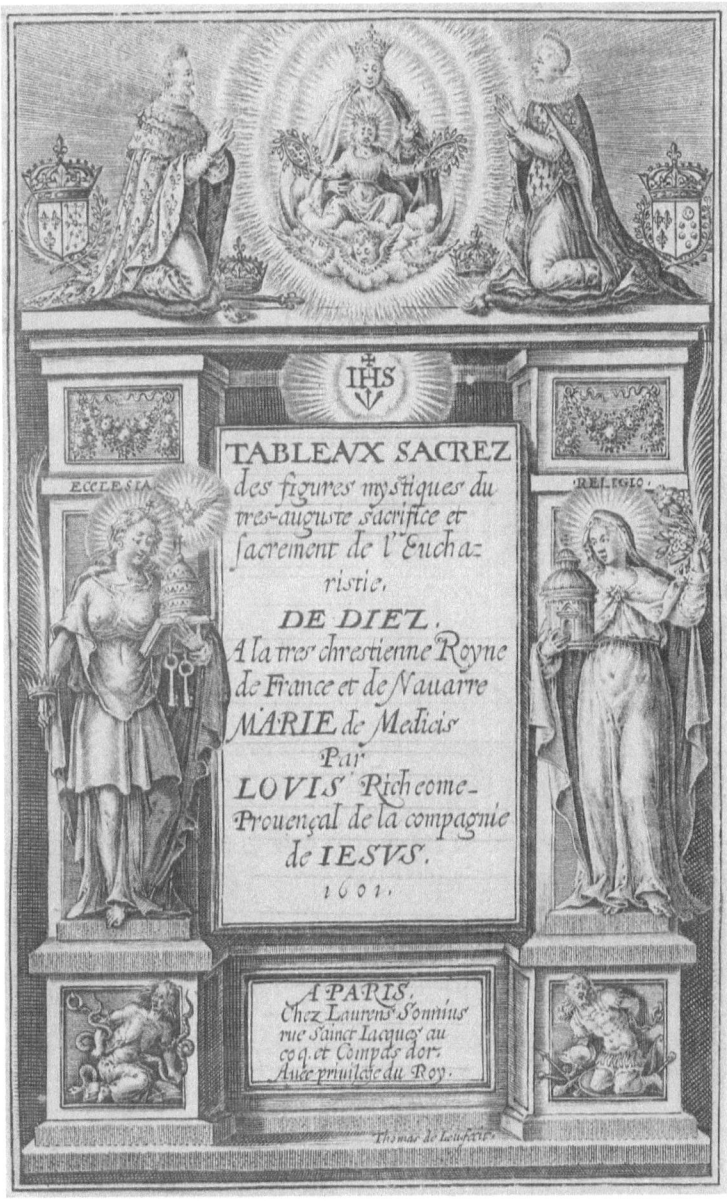

Figure 1.1. Title page, *Tableaux sacrez des figures mystiques du très-auguste sacrifice et sacrement de l'Eucharistie, dediez a la tres chrestienne Royne de France et de Navarre Marie de Médicis*. Paris: Laurens Sonnius, 1601. Gordon 1601. R54. Special Collections, University of Virginia, Charlottesville, VA.

of Marie to the Virgin Mary by merging Christian with pagan imagery.[67] Analysis of this court ballet has also been stymied by confusion regarding its performance date. Relying on Michel Henry's manuscript table of ballet music at the court of Henri IV, *ballet de cour* scholars have assumed that Marie danced her first ballet before, rather than after, the dauphin's birth.[68] Henry's manuscript references a queen's ballet performed in the great hall at the residence of the bishop of Paris on Fat Sunday (the Sunday before Lent), 1601.[69] And yet, for this ballet Henry outlines the same structure that Matthieu ascribes to the queen's winter 1602 ballet: a sung entry by Apollo and the muses, a second entry involving singers with lutes, and a series of dances first by Marie's *filles* (unmarried girls who lived at court under the queen's protection and patronage, as members of her household) and then by Marie de Médicis herself, accompanied by other women.[70] In the year 1601, the last Sunday before Lent fell on 4 March.[71] Marie had entered Paris for the first time on 8 February of that year.[72] It is unlikely that she would have been able to organize, rehearse, and execute a ballet of this magnitude less than four weeks after her arrival in the French capital. Instead, as numerous additional contemporary sources confirm, this ballet was danced the year following. Pierre de L'Estoile's diary for February 1602 mentions a ballet performed by the queen on "Le jour de Carême-prenant" [Mardi Gras] at the bishop's palace and other Paris locations, including the Louvre and the residence of the maréchale de Retz (Claude-Catherine de Clermont).[73] The French statesman Jacques-Auguste de Thou notes (as does Matthieu) that this production was danced in the presence of numerous foreign ambassadors, including the papal legate ["en présence des ambassadeurs des Princes étrangers, & du Légat même"].[74] Extant correspondence by visiting dignitaries makes no mention of a queen's ballet in 1601 but does report one for Fat Tuesday 1602: for example, as we have seen, two letters by the papal nuncio describe a production he attended that was danced by the queen and fifteen princesses in the French royal palace on the final evening of carnival that year, i.e., 19 February 1602.[75] On this basis, and barring any future discovery of evidence to the contrary, it seems safe to conclude that this *Ballet of the Sixteen Virtues*, performed before large audiences and featuring Apollo and the muses together with Marie's *filles*, other ladies, and the new queen, took place just months after Marie had given birth to the future Louis XIII, and that it was in part this dauphin's arrival, and its implications for the Bourbon regime, that her first French court ballet celebrated.

With this birth Marie successfully achieved her most important task as queen: the production of a legitimate royal heir. As the king's wife, Marie had attained the rank of queen at the moment of her marriage. And yet, as Cosandey notes, for a royal consort to possess fully the honours and prerogatives that attended sovereign dignity, her spouse had to be willing to concede them, and for this, her fecundity was paramount – a point that had recently been driven home by Henri IV's broken first marriage to the childless Marguerite de Valois.[76] The English ambassador at the court of France, Ralph Winwood, reports that in the weeks leading up to the birth of Marie's first child she had indicated that if the fetus she was carrying turned out to be a boy, "she would *begin* to be queen" (emphasis mine).[77] After the dauphin's birth, according to the *Histoire des amours du Grand Alcandre* – a historical *roman à clef* believed to have been authored by one of Marie's favoured companions, Louise Marguerite de Lorraine, princesse de Conti – "il fut question de se rejoüir l'hyver. La Reyne fit un ballet qu'elle estudia 2 ou 3 mois" [it was time for the winter celebrations; the queen made a ballet that she had studied for two or three months].[78] Drawing on this account, the queen's nineteenth-century biographer Julia Pardoe recounts that Marie "had been heard to declare that in the event of her becoming the mother of a Dauphin, she would, at the earliest possible period, dance a ballet in honour of the King, which should exceed in magnificence every exhibition of the kind that had hitherto been attempted."[79] Georgie Durosoir – relying on Michel Henry's dating, no doubt – has expressed puzzlement over the apparent lack of a court ballet marking the future Louis XIII's birth in late September 1601.[80] Lying-in time followed by a period of rehearsal, though, together with the dating of carnival festivities that year, easily accounts for the four-month gap between the dauphin's birth in late September 1601 and the *Ballet of the Sixteen Virtues* danced in mid-February 1602.

This production's subtle figuration of Marie de Médicis as the Virgin Mary marked the queen's ascension in social and political status, as mother to the dauphin.[81] It also made Marie as divinely chosen mother a central figure in the reconsolidation of dynastic monarchy and the principle of hereditary succession. When the French queen consort wears the traits of the Virgin Mary, Cosandey notes, the birth of a dauphin becomes the expression of divine will: "Dans un contexte d'affirmation de la loi salique, l'arrivée d'un dauphin est un événement capital qui devient l'expression de la volonté et de l'intervention divines dès lors que la reine revêt les traits de la Vierge ... Saluer la maternité royale – effective ou espérée – en l'identifiant à la maternité divine revenait à inscrire d'emblée les principes dynastiques de la couronne dans le domaine des intentions célestes" [To greet the royal maternity – effective or expected – by identifying it with divine maternity is to inscribe the dynastic principles of the crown in the domain of celestial intention. In this way the political consequences of associating the queen with the Virgin by virtue of her birth of a son contributed to the shoring up of the mythic vision of the statutory devolution of the realm].[82] Dynastic monarchy by definition needs to make crown succession on the basis of bloodline appear inevitable and god-given. In the decades immediately following the protracted crises of the French monarchy in the late sixteenth century, such framings were especially crucial to the restoration of political and economic stability, since during the French civil wars and after, arguments for elective monarchy authored initially by Huguenots had been cleverly turned by the Catholic League against Henri de Navarre, whose claim to kingship rested, instead, on the hereditary principle.[83] At Fontainebleau, the Bourbon princes of the blood had been present in the room for Marie's birthing of Henri's heir – an arrangement that Pierre Matthieu says accorded with "l'ancienne loy des Ceremonies de la Coronne" [the ancient law of crown ceremonies].[84] This alleged restoration of ancient tradition in connection with rituals of royal birth set the new Bourbon regime apart from its more "secretive" predecessors, the late Valois dynasty; it may also have been designed to strengthen Bourbon authority by emphasizing both dynastic monarchy's hereditary principle and the corollary mystique of royal bloodline: the notion that members of the royal family, like others belonging to the "race" of nobles, enjoyed exceptional qualities, granted by god and nature, which in turn entitled them to positions of power and authority.[85] Shortly thereafter, the ringing of bells at the Louvre and all Paris churches, and the singing of a Te Deum at Notre Dame cathedral, celebrated the dauphin's arrival as a gift from God.[86] Then, on 29 October, the child himself was shown to Parisians while travelling from Fontainebleau to Saint-Germain-en-Laye: to ensure that people could see the dauphin as he passed through the city, his wetnurse held the infant to her breast, a sight that Matthieu declares only augmented the thanks rendered to God for the increase of favours he had showered on the French kingdom.[87] This public procession effectively eclipsed Marie de Médicis' own contributions as the dauphin's mother, but three months later, her own court ballet performed in multiple Paris locations ensured that her standing as the vessel chosen by God for his gift of a dauphin to Henri IV and to France would be properly acknowledged and celebrated.

Marie's Primitive Accumulation of (Marian) Cultural Capital

Marian imagery on this occasion also represented the royal marriage as an indissoluble Catholic union. In this sense, the queen's ballet worked to offset challenges to Bourbon legitimacy raised by Henri's history of apostasy as well as his broken first marriage to Marguerite de Valois. It also helped to navigate the immediate threat to Henri's political achievements – and to Marie's own position – posed by his ambiguous relationship with Henriette d'Entragues.

Prior to his liaison with d'Entragues, the king's most beloved mistress had been Gabrielle d'Estrées, duchesse de Beaufort. After Gabrielle had helped him to secure the throne, and gave birth to two of his sons, Henri publicly declared his wish to marry her.[88] This wedding did not take place because the duchesse died unexpectedly in 1599 due to pregnancy complications,[89] but shortly thereafter, the king took up with Henriette d'Entragues. Emboldened perhaps by measures Henri had taken towards making Gabrielle his legitimate wife and hence queen, Henriette acceded to the king's sexual advances only after he promised in writing that he would marry her should she succeed in giving him a son. Even after his wedding to Marie de Médicis in October 1600, this letter, combined with the marquise's remarkable emotional hold on the king, gave her considerable power. Henri IV had married Marie with the pope's blessing, yet Henriette still actively hoped to become queen. In 1601 she openly attacked Marie's dignity by calling her a concubine. In the fall of that year, moreover, Henriette gave birth to a son merely six weeks after Marie had presented France with the future Louis XIII. Henri IV did not help matters. Having installed his mistress in apartments at the Louvre little inferior in quality (and in close proximity) to those of Marie herself, he showed marked preference for his illegitimate progeny by Henriette: according to L'Estoile, the king upon seeing this infant kissed him, called him his son, and declared that he was more comely than the infant of the queen his wife, whom he said resembled the Medici, being dark and fat like them, a statement that, when reported to Marie, made her cry greatly.[90]

Thereafter, Henriette insisted on calling her own son the dauphin and Marie's son the king's natural, i.e., bastard, child.[91] Less than one month prior to the queen's *Ballet of the Sixteen Virtues*, in fact, an anonymous printed book questioned the validity of Henri IV's second marriage. Reporting this incident, del Bufalo informed the papal secretary of state, Pietro Aldobrandini, that "gl'heritici" [the heretics], thinking that the king had betrayed them by turning Catholic, were promising to make the marquise's son their leader and to eventually secure his rule by military means, "[d]icendo questo essere il vero delfino, poché lei è la vera regina di Francia per la promessa, et consenso mutuo, che tra lei et il re è stato con scrittura, la quale è appresso detta marchesa" [saying that he is the real dauphin, because she is the true queen of France, through promise and mutual approval gained between her and the king through a contract that is currently in her possession].[92] This particular rumour of alliance between Henriette d'Entragues and Huguenot factions was likely calumnious.[93] In reporting it, though, the nuncio voiced more general concerns about the very real danger that Henriette's claims posed to Marie's legitimacy as the king's legal consort and mother to his heir.[94]

Given this acute competition between women at France's highest social echelons, it is useful to revisit this 1602 ballet's iconographies and its use of conspicuous consumption by way of Fenlon's assertion that in late sixteenth- and seventeenth-century Italy, "for families who had already arrived at the summit, conspicuous consumption was regarded as a duty ... necessary to avoid loss of face and to sustain the honour of the dynasty; the function of such consumption was to distinguish between two families who, as well as being dynastically linked, were also both rivals and equals at the same time. In this process, awareness of the power of symbolic forms of expression of precisely the kind with which contemporary courtly theatre is crowded is fundamental in this struggle."[95] Marie de Médicis, given her own direct experience with courtly spectacle in Florence, would have been fully cognizant of the ways in which symbolic expression combined with conspicuous consumption could be deployed to sustain dynastic honour and assert preeminence over other elites. She had gained this experience as a spectator at productions organized by others and also in more immediate fashion, as we have seen, as a performer in her own right in productions such as the 1596 *Mascherata di stelle*.

As a vehicle by which to convert wealth into symbolic capital, court spectacle must have seemed particularly compelling to Marie given the threats to her own status posed by Henriette's claims.[96] In this topical context, it is useful to recall Peter Burke's observation that conspicuous consumption and gift giving at times function as linked cultural activities.[97] In his verses for the *Mascherata di stelle* danced by Marie in 1596, Rinuccini had emphasized women's participation in courtly dance as a magnificent benefice. Just as in the heavens the daughters of Atlas were transformed into astral beings by Jove as a reward for their purity and chastity tune their dances eternally to cosmic harmonies, so these celestial bodies appeared before the Medici court audience, changed back into their first guise as women and moving their feet in harmonious dance formations for the delight of Rinuccini's patron, Christine of Lorraine ["E com'in cielo a l'armonia celeste / Guidano eternamente i balli loro, / Si, transformate ne'l primiero aspetto, / Muovon danzando il piè per tuo diletto"].[98] These dancers not only sought to please the grand duchess, though; they also aimed to lighten the soul of Christine's husband and Marie's uncle, the grand duke, who willingly took upon himself the burdens and cares of rule.[99] In a barely disguised bid for ducal patronage, Rinuccini's dedicatory epistle concludes: "Voi poi, serenissima Donna, le scorgerete alla presenza del gran Ferdinando, al quale fra i suoi nobili pensieri non sarà forse discaro per mezzo vostro e come vostro dono rimirare le celesti danze" [You, then, most serene Lady, will observe them in the presence of the great Ferdinando who, through you and as a gift from you, might not be unwilling to admire the heavenly dances, including this observation of them among his noble thoughts]. Praising its female dancers as stellified women, Rinuccini's dedicatory epistle to Christine of Lorraine figures this troupe's return to earth as both a gift *to* his female patron and a gift *from* her, to the grand duke. During the first years of her marriage, Marie de Médicis under threat from Henriette d'Entragues needed a similar means through which to assert her own position. A court ballet sponsored and performed by her for the king's delight and asserting her own pre-eminence as munificent gift giver must have seemed just such a vehicle. I have argued that the new Bourbon monarchy figured its own power in part through this ballet's assertion of the French royal court's restoration of excellence in the courtly arts. But the crown's need for this initiative in turn gave Marie de Médicis a uniquely privileged opportunity when undertaking this task: as official royal consort, her access to material and symbolic capital of the type needed to organize and mount this *Ballet of the Sixteen Virtues* enabled her to give gifts to the king – including this ballet itself – that no mere mistress could give.

Elements of this ballet also positioned Marie herself as a divinely willed gift to Henri IV, worthy of his respect but also his passionate attachment. We have seen how poems for this production contend that Marie and her troupe of dancing women companions merited deferential admiration. Bertaut's text insists that this virtuous effect on spectators retains a specifically erotic appeal: "Amour les accompagne, et dans ses vives flames / Fait pour elles bruler les plus celestes ames" [Love accompanies them and, in his ardent flames, makes even the most celestial souls burn with desire for these women]. In its final stanza, however, the poem carefully clarifies that it is the queen, more than any other woman she leads in the dance, who most merits such passionate regard:

> Mais quand quelque inhumain les voudroit prendre en haine,
> Encor ne sçauroit-il qu'il n'en aime la Reine,
> Tant elle semble amiable aux coeurs moins amoureux.
> La reine des Vertus les a toutes en elle:
> Aussi, vous la donnant pour compagne eternelle,
> Les cieux vous ont rendu contant & bienheureux.[100]

> [But should some cruel person decide to hate them
> Still he would know that he loves their queen
> So worthy of love she seems, even to the least amorous heart.
> The queen of the Virtues contains them all within herself:
> Therefore, in giving her to you as eternal companion,
> The heavens have made you happy and blessed.]

Emphasizing Marie's superior qualities in relation to her women companions on stage, Bertaut's final stanza positions the queen as "the one," or "first," referred to in this composition entitled "Pour le Ballet de seize Dames representant les Vertus, dont la Royne estoit *l'une*" (emphasis mine). Literally, this phrase indicates that Marie was the ballet's lead dancer, entering the playing space first in an ordering that marked her superiority in social rank. But according to Bertaut's final stanza, the queen was also the first in the sense of moral ordering. Marie, like the Virgin Mary, brings together in herself the virtues of all women. "Containing" all of the other virtues embodied by her female dancing companions "within herself," the queen as praised in Bertaut's *récit* harnesses their appeal to hers: if even "les plus libres franchises" and "les plus celestes ames" [the freest resistant hearts and the most celestial souls] cannot resist the powerful beauty of these women, and if Marie as queen of virtues contains this entire troupe's qualities within herself, then no one – none of the king's subjects and not even the king himself – has the capacity to resist her charms.

Such emphasis on Marie's relative priority in rank and in affective intimacy with the king was especially important on this occasion because of a fact tellingly absent from official printed history: among the group of women who danced alongside her as one of the sixteen virtues was none other than Henriette d'Entragues. Legend has it that in relation to this ballet, the marquise and the queen had struck a deal.

Henriette would use her influence with the king in order to obtain his permission for the marriage Marie desired between her childhood companion Leonora Galigaï and the Florentine nobleman Concino Concini. In return, Marie would favour the marquise socially, even going so far as to honour Henriette with an invitation to dance in her first *ballet de la reine*.[101] The opportunity to perform in this production would have had special resonance for the marquise, since it was in part her dancing that had initially attracted Henri IV's attentions to her.[102] Even outside of these particular circumstances, however, this gesture would have been remarkable. As Sharon Kettering has noted, to dance in a royal ballet was a "rare opportunity to be seen by the whole court in a glamorous setting," such that to be chosen to dance alongside the monarch and/or his consort was a form of social and political patronage greatly coveted by even the most high ranking princes and princesses of the realm.[103]

The power to confer such favour, in the case of Marie's ballets, seems to have rested solely with the queen herself.[104] On this basis Julia Pardoe has denounced as a "most unbecoming concession" Marie's willingness to grant Henriette an appearance in her first court ballet.[105] To the extent that this particular instance of gift exchange between the queen and the marquise enacted a cycle of reciprocity, it would have asserted equality among the two parties and in this sense would have worked against Marie's long-term interests. We can read the exchange between the marquise and the queen another way, however, for gift giving, as anthropologists and sociologists note, often solidifies bonds of vertical hierarchy and domination rather than horizontal equality and reciprocity; in this sense, gift exchange also acts as a form of symbolic or ritualized violence.[106] Following this line of thought, we can trace in this legendary agreement between the marquise and the queen two laws of gift exchange as outlined in the work of Marcel Mauss: the obligation to receive or accept, and the obligation to repay.[107] When the marquise used her influence to gain for Marie the king's assent to her childhood friend's marriage, she in effect obliged the queen to receive this gift and to repay it. Marie then paid her metaphorical debt to Henriette by favouring her socially, even choosing her as one of the privileged women who danced in her ballet. With this act, the queen in turn obliged the marquise to both receive this gift and to pay it back. Yet Henriette enjoyed neither the wealth nor the status that would allow her to patronize a social occasion of equal magnificence and socio-political importance to that of a royal ballet. In other words, there was no gift with which the marquise could adequately reciprocate the one she received when

Marie chose her to dance in her queen's ballet. As Mauss and others have noted, gifts that cannot be returned function as vehicles for humiliating one's opponent under the guise of generosity. Describing systems of gift exchange, for example, Pierre Bourdieu asserts that "Friendly transactions between kinsmen and affines are to market transactions as ritual war is to total war."[108] Bourdieu's analogy seems wonderfully appropriate here. Sixteenth- and seventeenth-century French commentary, as Kate Van Orden has shown, likened ballet to war,[109] and indeed, this very metaphor informs Henri IV's words to the nuncio comparing the women's disciplined dance steps in this 1602 *ballet de la reine* to the movements of a beautiful "squadron." But it was not only the women's collective movements that functioned as a form of orchestrated competition in this instance. The ballet itself, as a vehicle for magnificence and for gift exchange, enacted a specific instance of symbolic violence or ritual war: that between the queen and her chief political rival, the marquise.

In this struggle, Marie's institutional position gave her additional access to forms of writing that were sponsored, approved, and printed "avec Privilège du Roy." No verse texts for this ballet seem to have been printed in a collected volume. This lack of a *recueil* was in fact largely typical of verses for royal ballets prior to 1610 (the exception being the 1581 *Ballet comique de la royne*). In 1605, though, Pierre Matthieu, in his official capacity as royal historiographer, published the account of Marie's *Ballet of the Sixteen Virtues* discussed earlier in this chapter.[110] Then, three years later, in 1608, the poetic verses for the air "Maintenant les Vertues Sacrées" set to lute tablature by members of the royal musical establishment also began to circulate in print, again with royal privilege. According to Bourdieu, technologies of literacy, particularly writing, enable social actors with symbolic capital or social status to "accumulate" in textual form instances of cultural capital "previously conserved" in an "incorporated state."[111] Applying Bourdieu's insights here, we can see that Bourbon social capital enabled the new dynasty to gather to itself, in official court panegyric and historiography, a form of culture – this particular court ballet occasion – initially presented in an "incorporated state." In 1602, Marie de Médicis as wife to the king and mother to the dauphin already possessed the wealth, opportunity, and socially prescribed duty to conspicuously display her own and hence her husband's magnificence before the French court as well as representatives of foreign courts. Yet her legitimacy required vigorous assertion. As time went on, the crown's pressing need to solidify her incipient political authority as a bulwark against plots and factions – discussed at greater length in chapter 2 – compelled its recourse to printed panegyric capable of "primitively accumulating" in written form the cultural capital Marie herself had gained access to in 1602 via live, ephemeral performance.

Indeed, the printed record concerning this ballet registers the exigencies faced by the crown not only through what it says regarding this performance – its emphasis on Marie's preeminent virtue revealed through the magnificence of opulent self-display – but also what it leaves unsaid. Traces of Henriette d'Entragues' danced participation in this ballet remain limited to biographical legend only. In their telling silence regarding the marquise's dancing, official sources register the extent to which Marie's role with respect to dynastic imperatives ultimately trumped Henriette's. In this way, not only Marie de Médicis but also the new Bourbon dynasty of which she was now a crucial part arguably achieved a mode of domination over the king's mistress rooted in what Bourdieu calls "the primitive accumulation of cultural capital, the total or partial monopolization of the society's symbolic resources in religion, philosophy, art and science, through the monopolization of these resources ... henceforth preserved *not in memories but in texts*."[112] Marie's arch-rival may have gained unprecedented access to the space of royal ballet on the level of live performance, but the Bourbon monarchy's burgeoning textual apparatus preserves quite another story.

Chapter Two

Royal Women's Ballet and/as Royal Ceremonial

The first court ballet Marie de Médicis danced in Paris, as chapter 1 has outlined, used classical as well as Franco-Florentine Neoplatonic imagery overlaid with imperial and religious allusion to proclaim her recently elevated status as the dauphin's mother. For the queen's next major production three years later, in winter 1605, no extant verses have as yet been identified, while contemporary references previously known to scholars offer only the most skeletal clues regarding its staging.[1] Ambassadorial correspondence held in repositories outside of France provides additional information, however, as does a detailed eye-witness account of this production's performance at the Louvre palace. Reading these documents together with a letter by Marie de Médicis requesting a particular noblewoman to dance in her ballet, this chapter elucidates basic aspects of performance history such as when, and for what socio-political occasion, this production was danced. It also analyses the ballet's appropriation of non-verbal forms of expression typically found in royal ceremonial from the period to explore how by means of these and other production values embodied by particular performers at this particular moment during Henri IV's reign the queen's ballet for carnival 1605 undertook the work of regime-building as part of a larger governmental program designed to bolster Bourbon dynastic continuity in the face of considerable threat.

Elements of royal ceremonial seem to have framed this occasion even prior to the ballet proper, when Henri IV's actions among the assembly at the Grande Salle du Louvre offered a remarkable symbolic performance of his own authority placed in service to that of his wife. Thereafter, the particular female attendants who accompanied Marie on stage, together with the ballet's temporal and spatial placement of the queen in relation to these dancers, fashioned a *mise en scène* of royal authority whereby Marie's literal leadership on the dance floor signalled her incipient capacity to lead in harmonious unity the kingdom's most powerful noble families. The choreographies danced by this troupe, under Marie's leadership, framed the queen as a humble servant to her husband. And yet, through its deployment of rich and rare objects and materials, including magnificent costumes, emblematic furnishings, and even "living breathing luxury items" such as a dwarf and an Italian female singer, this production also drew on the queen's symbolic and political capital as a princess from a powerful foreign ruling family to showcase Marie's participation in the royal dignity through her unity with the king in Christian marriage.[2] In these ways, the second *ballet de la reine* performed at Henri IV's court presented Marie both as the king's loyal subject and as his partner in sovereignty – all with an eye to securing an uncontested succession for the still vulnerable Bourbon regime.

Threats to Dynastic Continuity and Images of Joint Rule, 1603–5

Although Marie had given birth to a dauphin in September 1601, Henri IV's subjects still worried that if the king died while his heir was still a minor, "much harm would befall the kingdom."[3] In such circumstances, royal authority would be partially eclipsed by the weakness that childhood implied.[4] Such a scenario could well invite political instability in the form of attempted usurpation by princes of the blood. This and other forms of internal political and/or military disorder under a minority government would in turn heighten the kingdom's susceptibility to foreign powers. A queen mother acting as guardian and regent for her son could help to mitigate such risks. As an adult member of the French royal house she possessed royal authority, but because she was precluded from rule on the basis of her gender, a queen mother (unlike a prince of the blood) could not usurp the throne. Her maternal prerogatives, obligations, and affections, moreover, were thought to tie her interests closely to those of her son, making her the best person to protect and guide him until he came of majority.[5] The queen of France thus needed to appear capable of rule even during her husband's lifetime, so that if her eldest son were to accede as a minor, contemporaries would already be inclined to accept her as guardian and regent.

During her first years as queen consort, Marie's incipient political capacities remained underdeveloped, in part because Henri IV seems to have purposefully kept his new wife at a distance from the business of statecraft.[6] The shortcomings of this approach became immediately apparent, however, when in summer 1603, after decades of hard living as a warrior, hunter, gambler, and womanizer, the king succumbed to a near-fatal illness. Sir Thomas Parry, the English ambassador in France at this time, reported that if Henri were to die, France would be plunged into chaos.[7] Anticipating just this outcome, the king, from what he believed to be his deathbed, commanded his secretary of state Nicolas IV de Neufville, seigneur de Villeroy, to get ready letters "to all the governors of the provinces and fortresses and to all the princes, that they should come to swear fealty, all of them, to the Queen whom he wished to declare and create guardian of the Dauphin."[8] To help prepare her for this position, the king immediately began "instructing his wife in affairs of state."[9] By the end of the summer, Henri seemed to rally, only to continue to suffer intermittent spells of physical incapacitation throughout the fall.[10] Initiatives to secure an uncontested succession for the dauphin, by representing Marie's legitimacy as a political actor capable of stepping in temporarily, as placeholder for an adult king, thus became a priority for the Bourbon regime.

As a first step, Henri brought Marie onto the royal council so that his consort could begin acquiring first-hand knowledge regarding governmental affairs. For the queen's incipient political capacity to be accepted by contemporaries, however, the crown needed to frame that capacity in ways that did not overtly contradict prevalent beliefs regarding women's inherent weakness. The new Bourbon dynasty in a sense owed its very existence to such beliefs, for discourses of sexual difference had been crucial to securing Henri's accession against the claim of his chief rival to the throne, the Habsburg princess Isabel Clara Eugenia: it was in connection with Henri's succession that jurists in late sixteenth-century France designated the Salic law and its alleged proscription of female rule as fundamental to the French political nation. Images of Marie de Médicis designed to support the new regime could not therefore champion the queen's authority in her own right, but only as an extension of her husband's.

To meet this need, Henri IV began to involve himself publicly in representing the royal marriage as a domestic but also a political partnership, one in which the queen's participation in governance supported, rather than undermined, patriarchal dynastic rule. Art historians have alerted us to one of the first such undertakings: Henri's commission of a *jeton*, designed by Guillaume Dupré in 1603, announcing and commemorating the queen's admission to the royal council that year. As Nicola Courtright outlines, this medal featured on one side Henri IV's profile overlapping Marie's and on the other the royal couple as Mars and Pallas with the dauphin between them. Analysing their intersecting portraits on the medal's front along with the "balanced, equally weighted stances" of their allegorical figurations on the medal's obverse, Courtright shows how this *jeton* proclaimed visually the royal couple's shared embodiment of sovereign power. Moreover, the king took steps to advertise his role in authorizing and disseminating the medal: having involved himself personally in its creation, Henri IV also wrote and signed a letter patent explaining his approbation of the medal's imagery and its inscription. This letter notes with satisfaction the *jeton*'s representation of Marie, "our very dear and very beloved companion," and repeats the medal's inscription "PROPAGO IMPERII," meaning propagation or perpetuation of power.[11] In this way, mythological allusion linked Marie's divine authority as the allegorical personage Minerva, goddess of wisdom and war, to the power vested in her position as the king's wife and mother of his heir.

Already pressing in the wake of Henri IV's summer 1603 near-fatal illness, the need for representations such as these became even more acute following the discovery, in summer and fall 1604, of a well-developed conspiracy against the king, queen, and dauphin. This scheme involved machinations by Spain together with Charles Valois, comte d'Auvergne, d'Auvergne's half-sister, Henri IV's powerful mistress Henriette Balzac d'Entragues, marquise de Verneuil, and the marquise's father, Charles Balzac d'Entragues. According to this plot, d'Auvergne would unseat Henri IV by force of arms, Philip III would declare the king's marriage to Marie illegitimate, and Gaston Henri (Henri IV's illegitimate son born to Henriette) would be proclaimed heir to the French throne.[12] Revelations of this scheme to establish a new royal house did nothing to calm longstanding French suspicions of Habsburg perfidy. They also intensified fears of domestic political instability in the event of the king's untimely death.

To stave off future challenges to the dauphin and his mother, the marquise's father was forced to relinquish Henri's written promise of marriage to Henriette (this document was one of the weapons that the conspirators had wielded in their efforts to discredit Marie and the dauphin). In spring 1605, Henri also recalled to court his first wife, Marguerite de Valois, in part so that her public acceptance of Marie and the dauphin would help put the lie to rumours, fostered by the conspirators, that the king's earlier marriage had not been properly annulled.[13] Additionally, the crown redoubled its efforts to emphasize by means of symbolic expression the legitimate royal authority in which Henri IV's second wife Marie participated. In 1605, for example, the government recycled the representational program outlined in Dupré's 1603 *jeton* by issuing a second variant of the medal in which the facial features of the dauphin, positioned between his parents, were featured with greater visual clarity.[14] Scholars have not linked this *jeton*'s reissue to the d'Entragues conspiracy, but the plot's discovery may well have prompted this second version of the token, with visual features designed to put to rest any confusion of the illegitimate Henri de Verneuil for Henri IV's legitimate son by Marie.

After the conspirators had been arrested but while they were still awaiting sentencing by the Parlement of Paris, moreover, the king and queen worked together to advertise Bourbon dynastic resiliency through Marie's January 1605 *ballet de la reine*. It is to this production, and the qualities of ceremonial political expression it harnessed in connection with the queen consort's inicipient political authority, that I now turn.

The Occasion, the On-stage Action, and the Ballet's Framing as Royal Ceremonial

Letters written by Henri IV's captain of the guards Jacques Nompar, duc de La Force, indicate that this ballet was performed at the Louvre at around midnight on 23 January, with rehearsals having begun no later than 10 January 1605.[15] Michel Henry's table of ballet music assigns Marie's second French ballet a performance date of 13 January 1605, but if we add ten days to Henry's date of 13 January, to adjust Old Style to New Style dating, his account and La Force's add up.[16] Other sources, too, confirm a 23 January performance date: the Florentine ambassador to France, Baccio Giovannini, writes on 23 January that the queen's ballet was expected to be danced that evening, for example, while a lengthy manuscript letter archived among the papers collected by Nicolas-Claude Fabri de Peiresc specifies that the ballet began in the Grande Salle of the Louvre palace at around one o'clock in the morning on 24 January.[17]

These sources also indicate that the ballet was repeated at multiple Paris locations over the course of several hours. Immediately after its presentation at the Louvre, according to the letter found among Peiresc's papers, the production was danced at "autres assemblé[e]s" [other assemblies] between four and eight o'clock in the morning, the first being the Arsenal – the home of Maximilien de Béthune, the future duc de Sully.[18] La Force, too, states that after the ballet was danced to a packed crowd at the Louvre it was again mounted before large gatherings at the Arsenal and the palace of the bishop of Paris.[19] These sources together therefore verify that a sizeable audience gathered at the Louvre on the evening of 23 January and that after this performance, which began at around midnight, the ballet continued into the morning at two additional Paris residences.

We learn a great deal more about what these audiences witnessed from a letter written by one spectator at the Louvre. According to this detailed account, the entertainment proper began after the king had brought order to the assembly and taken his place. First came thirty violins, who marched softly up to the king.[20] Next entered thirteen lutes; then came the king's Music or chorus composed of thirty voices, at the centre of which appeared "une Italienne" [an Italian woman] whom our letter writer tells us was "si bien atifée quil me seroit impossible de vous la depeindre" [so well decked out that it would be impossible for me to describe her].[21] These musicians all wore costumes made from carnation and white taffeta covered in cloth of silver. Once each group had come before the king and had been directed to its appropriate position in the hall by the master of ceremonies, "soudain entre un petit nain de la reyne avec une soutane de taphetas noier couverte de clinquans aiant deux visages comme on depeint Janus faisant milles grimaces cabriolles et entrechats" [suddenly there entered a little dwarf belonging to the queen wearing a black taffeta cassock covered in *clinquant* – tinsel, in the sense of thread of gold, silver, or other rich metal – having two faces as one depicts Janus, making a thousand grimaces, leaps, and capers].[22] Completing two or three tours of the room accompanied by the violins, this dwarf returned to the door from which he had entered, from which next appeared twelve pages, each holding in his hands two white torches. Dressed like the musicians in carnation and white with little white boots covered in *clinquant*, these pages danced "mille passages et figures" [a thousand passages and figures]. After the pages took their places, the Music then played for the entry of the king's natural son César de Vendôme, dressed "en fille" [as a girl]. After coming up to his father, Vendôme performed a reverence or choreographed bow; he then returned to the door from which Marie de Médicis herself finally entered the room accompanied by eleven princesses.[23]

These women appeared costumed in white and carnation, as were the musicians, but in this instance their dance habits were so richly decorated that "on ne voioit que diamans que perles qu'enseignes que joyaux que pierraries" [one saw only costumes diamonds, pearls, gem ornaments, precious stones, and jewels]. "[M]archant d'une façon grave faisant des petis pasages" [marching in a grave fashion, making little passages], the queen and her companions arrived at the centre of the room, at which point "les musiciens chantarent le louanges du Roy" [the musicians sang the king's praises]. The queen approached her husband, the instruments ceased, and she with her companions saluted him. Marie's troupe then continued their ballet accompanied sometimes by the violins, sometimes the lutes, sometimes the Music. The dancing seems to have been extensive, for the queen, eventually tiring, seated herself on a specially constructed chair of carnation-coloured satin all covered with *clinquant*. At this point, the musicians suddenly exited their places to come before the king, where the Italian woman previously mentioned "commença de charmer les oreilles de la companie par sa voix plustot divine que humayne" [began to charm the ears of the company by her voice more divine than human]. Following this song, the queen resumed her dancing until she had completed her ballet.[24]

This detailed description by a spectator at the Louvre performance is crucial for situating this ballet as an occasion worth studying for what it can teach us about the French queen's political role. So is the provenance of the document that preserves this eye-witness account. The manuscript itself comes down to us as part of two bound sets of papers dedicated to the topic of royal ceremonial gathered and organized by the famous seventeenth-century antiquarian Nicolas-Claude Fabri de Peiresc.[25] Peiresc has been described as "one of the most erudite ... collectors of *curiosa* of the seventeenth century."[26] His library included printed books, ancient and medieval manuscripts, and voluminous collections of personal papers (*registres*). These *registres* include his own notes on various topics, letters he himself had received, copies of letters he had sent to others, and "other original or copied letters which had come into his possession."[27] Among the one hundred and twenty volumes of Peiresc's personal papers now housed at the municipal library in Carpentras, two are dedicated to descriptions of royal and other court ceremonies such as Te Deums, processions, baptisms, and royal entries.[28] In one of these volumes is found the seventeenth-century manuscript account of the 1605 *ballet de la reine* performed at the Louvre, indicated by the title "Le Balet de la Reine dansé à Paris le 23 janvier 1605."

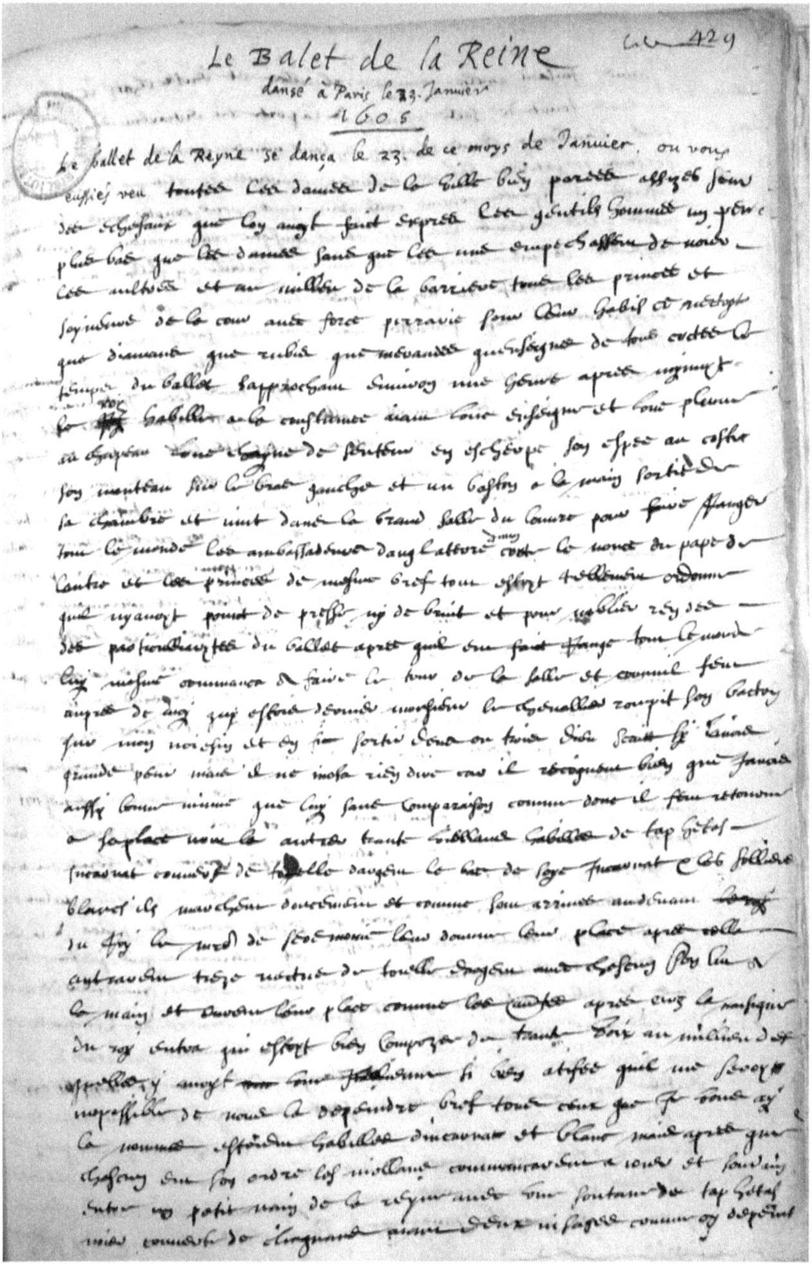
429

Le Balet de la Reine
dansé à Paris le 23. Janvier
1605

Le ballet de la Reyne se dança le 23. de ce moys de Janvier, ou vous eussiés veu

Figure 2.1. "Le Balet de la Reine dansé à Paris le 23 janvier 1605." Carpentras, Bibliothèque-Musée Inguimbertine, ms 1794, f. 429r. Photo by Éliane Roux.

This manuscript found its way into Peiresc's possession, I believe, as a copy from a letter, most likely made at the request of Peiresc himself, for inclusion among a series of documents pertaining to royal ceremonial (for which supposition I rely heavily on insights by Éliane Roux communicated via personal correspondence). Peiresc's interest in ceremonial at around the time of this 1605 ballet becomes clear from Roux's analysis of the manuscript placed immediately following our document within the same gathering. This document describes a royal "carouzère" (or carousel) performed in Paris in February 1606.[29] A carousel was a tournament in which nobles, arranged in companies or quadrilles, undertook various martial exercises before a royal or courtly audience.[30] Peiresc had travelled to Paris, for the first time, in August 1605.[31] The manuscript hand responsible for the document describing the carousel is definitely his, Roux notes, and though at least one printed catalogue indicates that Peiresc was this document's copyist, she contends that Peiresc must have been the description's original author: not only did he correct content as he was writing – interrupting some words, cancelling others, and adding lengthy descriptions of particular performance elements – but François de Malherbe, who consulted Peiresc when composing verses for this carousel, expressed in a letter to Peiresc his satisfaction that his friend had been able to attend the event.[32] If the 1606 "carouzère" description is an original report authored by Peiresc himself, he must have been personally interested in court entertainments and in their eye-witness descriptions. Indeed, Peiresc's correspondence includes several letters requesting descriptions of ceremonials: the volume that includes accounts of the 1605 ballet and 1606 carousel, for example, also includes an undated letter from him asking an unknown addressee to provide him with a description of a Te Deum.[33] This same *recueil* also contains correspondence between Peiresc and his younger brother, Palamède de Valavez, concerning ceremonial occasions. To one letter from Valavez dated 18 September 1610, for example, Peiresc added the title "Cérémonies du renouvellement de l'Alliance d'Angleterre" [ceremonies of the renewal of the English alliance],[34] while in a letter dated 29 November 1622, Valavez ends a lengthy description of a royal entry at Aix by asking Peiresc not to give away a copy of what he has written because "il ne ma pas fallu peu de paine pour ramasser ces pièces" [it has taken me no little effort to gather these documents] and "pourceque l'on doigt imprimer toutes ces entrées avec les tailles douces et les inscriptions &, Et cet abregé osteroit le courage aux autheurs de les imprimer" [because we must print all these entries with musical settings and inscriptions etcetera, and this synopsis if circulated will remove the incentive of printers to publish the project].[35] Peiresc and his brother, it appears, had in mind a project that would publish descriptions of ceremonial occasions. Like Théodore Godefroy's *Cérémonial françois*, which appeared in two volumes in 1619 and 1649, this book would have disseminated to a wider public the descriptions of French royal ceremonial that Valavez and Peiresc had so assiduously gathered. Ultimately the brothers' vision did not result in any extant printed book with their names on it, but along with Roux I believe it likely that Peiresc acquired and filed the 1605 ballet description with an eye to its inclusion in an initiative of this type.

Among the two bundles of papers Peiresc put together concerning royal ceremonial, however, the only ballet described is this one. Godefroy's printed volumes, too, contain no accounts of royal ballets, and while François-Antoine Jolly transcribed the description of this 1605 ballet that he found in Peiresc's *registres* in the eighteenth-century manuscript for a book he hoped to publish on royal ceremonies,[36] Jolly's printed table advertising this project did not end up listing it among the content for his projected work.[37] What accounts, then, for the inclusion of this lone ballet description among Peiresc's two manuscript bundles dedicated to royal ceremonies?

Work on the symbolic dimensions of royal power by political historians such as Ralph Giesey, Richard Jackson, Sarah Hanley, and Lawrence Bryant offers a useful entry point for thinking about royal ballet's relationship to French ceremonial.[38] When discussing royal ceremonies in medieval and early modern France, however, these scholars focus primarily on kingship. Moreover, they concentrate primarily on what Giesey has termed four key, defining rituals: the *sacre* (or coronation), the *lit de justice* (the king's appearance before parliament for its registration of royal edicts), the royal entry (or set of festivities accompanying a city's reception of the ruler), and the royal funeral.[39] Fanny Cosandey's important study of French queenship also focuses its analysis of royal ceremonial on coronations, funerals, and entries. And yet Cosandey herself notes that while early modern ceremonialists were nearly unanimous in the importance their writings accorded to the *sacre* – this particular ceremony almost always takes pride of place in writings on royal ceremonial from the sixteenth, seventeenth, and eighteenth centuries – they otherwise considered with equal interest a wide range of royal occasions, including marriages, births and baptisms,

Te Deums, processions, receptions, openings of Estates General, etc. "Pour ces auteurs," Cosandey concludes, "est finalement cérémonie royale tout ce qui touche à la mise en scène du roi ou de la reine" [For these authors whatever concerns the *mise en scène* of the king or of the queen, no matter the precise nature of the event, counts as royal ceremony].[40] Given this more expansive definition of royal ceremonial as implied by the broad range of events that garnered the attention of early modern ceremonialists and antiquarians themselves, Peiresc's choice to include a description of the 1605 *ballet de la reine* in a *fagot* (packet of papers) dedicated to the topic of ceremonial is less surprising than it first seems. For what registered as "ceremony" for Peiresc in Marie's ballet as described in this account must have been qualities of its *mise en scène* of royalty that seemed familiar to him from other instances of royal ceremonial typically named as such by present-day "neo-ceremonialist" scholars.

Because over time printed taxonomies of French royal ceremonials and fêtes came to privilege types of royal performance that, by means of reiterated forms and rules, became prescribed rituals of kingship, the "more precarious, haphazard performance traditions of kings" have been erased from view, Bryant notes.[41] To this insight, we might add that such earlier performance traditions included occasions involving queens, such as *ballets de cour*. Women's court performance has gained popularity as a topic of research among early modern scholars in part because attending to the politicization of the arts at early modern courts helps to surface new evidence regarding the (sometimes unofficial) influence of female consorts on governance and rule. And yet, present day "neo-ceremonialists" along with scholars working in festival studies tend to insist on ceremonial's distinction from spectacle – the former understood as royal performances that brought power structures into being, the latter being defined as royal performances that functioned primarily as entertainment and amusement or as allegorical representations that, although commenting heuristically on power structures, did not themselves intervene in such structures.[42] In an essay promoting the benefits of a heuristic of space for studies of the *ancien régime* and its courts, however, Marcello Fantoni argues that attention to court spaces, in conjunction with analysis of rituals, clienteles, and iconologies, reveals political activities and meanings that would otherwise remain "in the shadows." More specifically, he calls for work that productively brings together scholarship on ceremonial and ritual with work on festivals, spectacle, and theatre.[43] The fact that a detailed contemporary report on the 1605 *ballet de la reine* appears in one of Peiresc's *fagots* on royal ceremonial, I believe, can help us towards the kind of work that Fantoni calls for.

Specifically, attentiveness to this manuscript's provenance provides an initial clue that this occasion, rather than hiving itself off from the constituitive political work "neo-ceremonialists" have claimed for royal ritual, incorporated ceremonial elements within an ephemeral instance of royal performance. In this sense, questions of manuscript provenance can help restore to view how at Henri IV's court in winter 1605, in keeping with both abstract theories of monarchy and more local circumstances relating to the persons who occupied the institutionally defined roles outlined by those theories, Marie's prerogatives as court ballet patron-performer promoted her unique institutional role as both sovereign and subject as part of a larger emphasis on partnership within the royal marriage as a means for ensuring political stability.

"Pour faire ranger tout le monde"

This ballet's codified staging of the king and queen's joint participation in dynastic rule began with actions by Henri IV to prepare the performance hall for Marie's entrance. From the captain of the royal guards, the duc de La Force, we know that the king attended all of this ballet's performances.[44] The eye-witness spectator's account archived by Peiresc also tells us that at the Louvre, at least, Henri took on the role of *uber*-master of ceremonies by personally arranging the audience in preparation for the entertainment proper.[45] When the king appeared in this royal palace's great hall, this document reports, he carried a sword and a baton and wore a sash, a cape, and a cap on which appeared an *enseigne*[46] – an elaborately fashioned jeweled hat badge of the kind long favoured by French kings as a sign of both piety and military leadership.[47] Signalling the ruler's authority as a feudal warrior but also his membership in the priesthood by way of his *sacre* and by extension his divinely sanctioned sovereign power, this attire proved appropriate for the task Henri IV now undertook: ordering the spectators ["pour faire ranger tout le monde"] so that the ballet itself could begin.[48]

On one level, such actions responded to practical necessity: contemporary references, testifying to the large numbers of people who saw this ballet at its three performance locations, note that the Grande Salle du Louvre that evening was particularly crowded.[49] During the queen's 1602 ballet in this same room, discussed in chapter 1, vast numbers of spectators had made the occasion uncomfortable for many in the audience. For her ballet three years later, an even larger number of spectators seems to have gathered: La Force states outright that he had never seen such a great assembly at the Louvre, the court being so large.[50] The Florentine ambassador Baccio Giovannini, too, complained that the packed crowd interfered with his enjoyment of the event: "Il Balletto fù assai bello, havendolo io visto provare con li habiti, che su la mez[z]a notte et in tanta frequenza et confusion[e] di popolo simil disagi non son più da me" [Having seen the ballet rehearsed with costumes, I know it was very beautiful, but the ballet being around midnight and with so great a crowd of spectators and confusion of people, I have to admit that I can't stand such discomfort any more].[51] Giovannini's experience was not unique: Henri IV's secretary of state Nicolas de Neufville, seigneur de Villeroy, reported to Christophe de Harlay, comte de Beaumont (the French ambassador in England), that he had heard "the press was so great that one had little pleasure there."[52] A further sense of crowded confusion comes through in the first-hand account of this ballet found among the papers archived by Peiresc, which jestingly references the dozens of cutpurses and cunning thieves of hats and cloaks who had infiltrated the audience, the great quantity of lackeys and pages, and the huge numbers of horses, litters, and carriages required by those attending.[53]

When Henri IV as this ballet's host took steps to determine the casting of the ballet's audience, as it were, his actions also enacted symbolically his capacity to govern his court and kingdom. According to Jeroen Duindam, early modern European dynastic monarchies used court spaces to "project ... images of power and order, secure ... protection against infringements, and manage ... measured contacts between the ruler and the outer world."[54] In keeping with this wider practice, Henri IV's efforts that evening to organize the space of his own court began with his arrangement of the ambassadors, such that those of England were placed on one side and the papal nuncio and representatives of other Catholic powers on the other.[55] (For a more detailed discussion of this action by the king and its stakes for French foreign policy, see chapter 5.) Once this organization of the ambassadors had been achieved such that "tout estoyt tellement ordonné quil ny avoyt poinct de presse ny de bruit" [all was so ordered that there was no more scuffle nor noise], those present in the hall saw several spectators expelled from their midst on the basis of inferior dress and status. As our letter writer recounts, "Après qu'il [Henri IV] eut faict rangé tout le monde luy mesme commança à faire le tour de la salle et comm'il feut auprès de moy qui estois dernier monsieur le chevallier rompit son baston sur mon voiesin et en fit sortir deus ou trois Dieu sçait sy javois grande peur mais il ne mosa rien dire car il recogneut bien que javois aussi bonne minne que luy sans comparaison" [After the king had everyone arranged in their place, he himself began to tour the hall and when he was near me, who was last, monsieur le chevallier broke his baton on my neighbour and made two or three leave. God knows I was greatly afraid, but he didn't dare say anything to me because he recognized that I carried myself as well as he without any comparison].[56] Enacting his royal prerogative to judge who among those present were of sufficient status to remain among the assembly, Henri IV's actions at the start of his wife's performance represented, in miniature, his authority as sovereign.

The king's rousting of civic disorder was a major theme in early Bourbon panegyric: for example, sung verses for the first entry of Marie's 1602 *Ballet of the Sixteen Virtues*, as we saw in chapter 1, asserted that Apollo and the Muses could only return to France and to the French court stage because of Henri IV's equity, faith, and clemency, royal virtues which in turn had established in France the necessary conditions for another golden age of peace, prosperity, and cultural revival. Three years later, a printed account of a stylized combat performed in February 1605, published under the title *Le romant des chevaliers de Thrace*, credits the king along similar lines. According to this text, "La paix estoit universelle parmy tous les peoples de la France, sous l'Empire du tres-grand & tres-victorieux Henry quatriesme, toutes sortes de rebellions & d'animositez estoient estouffées de l'ombre des lauriers de cet auguste Monarque, comme les serpens de l'odeur du Cedre: quand l'ordre & le repos ayans chassé les tumultes des guerres, convierent chacun à rechercher de nouveaux plaisirs, pour effacer le souvenir des infortunes passées" [Peace was universal among all of people of France, under the empire of the very great and very victorious Henri the fourth, all sorts of rebellions and animosities were stifled by the shade of this august monarch's laurels, as serpents are suffocated by the scene of cedar: when order and repose have chased away the tumults of war, the time calls for each to seek new pleasures, in order to erase the memory of past misfortunes].[57] It was Henri's success in snuffing out rebellions and animosities within the kingdom, in other words, that had made possible that year's carnival festivities at court – not only the February 1605 combat but also the January 1605 *ballet de la reine* that preceded it. When in the Grande Salle du Louvre on the evening of 23 January Henri IV carefully arranged this ballet's assembly, his actions in ordering the audience thus enacted, on a smaller scale, the rousting of domestic political disorder on which his fame as a ruler rested.[58]

Only after having ordered the hall did the king take his place. And only after Henri IV was seated did the ballet proper begin, starting with the musicians and pages followed by the sudden entrance of "un petit nain de la reyne" [a little dwarf belonging to the queen]. As the king had done previously, this dwarf made a tour of the hall – this time leaping and grimacing, however, and wearing "une soutane de taphetas noier couverte de clinquans aiant deux visages comme on depeint Janus" [a robe made of black taffeta covered in tinsel having two faces as one depicts Janus]. A familiar figure from Renaissance statuary, medals, and emblem books, Janus also made frequent appearances in court festivals across Europe.[59] In Figure 2.2's costume design for a royal ballet at the court of Henri IV and Marie de Médicis' grandson Louis XIV, for example, we see him wearing a mask with two faces.

Janus traditionally marked the new year, with the month of January being named after him; in this sense he would have been an appropriate figure to inaugurate Marie's ballet, performed in January 1605 at the start of the new year's winter festivities. Janus was also the god who guarded the gates of Rome and marked that ancient city's achievement of civic peace under the emperor Augustus, and in this sense, Janus imagery held particular resonance at Henri IV's court, given the challenges his new dynasty faced in its efforts to unite the political nation after thirty-five years of religious war.

Prior to Marie's February 1601 arrival in the French capital, her royal entry at Avignon had referenced Janus in its praise for Henri IV as the Gallic Hercules. Organized by the city's Jesuit college, the Avignon entry commemorated the king's reconciliation with Rome, capped by the pope's willingness to annul Henri's union with Marguerite de Valois so that he might marry Marie de Médicis. Describing the Temple of Janus that appeared along Marie's route into the city, André Valladier's print account explains that the Roman god Janus is given two heads not only because he, like the month of January, looks in two directions, back to the previous year and forward to the year to come, but also because Janus presides over transformations from a bloody and brutal life to a peaceful, better one; it is for this reason, Valladier recalls, that Rome in times of war left open the gates of Janus' temple so that all could visit this god to request peace and a more secure

Figure 2.2. Seventeenth-century French School, "Janus costume for the *Ballet de la Nuit* by Jean-Baptiste Lully (1632–87) danced by Louis XIV, 23rd February 1653" (watercolour on paper). Bibliothèque de l'Institut de France, Paris, France, Archives Charmet. Bridgeman Images.

life. Valladier then compares Janus to Henri IV: like the Roman god, this French king had not only put an end to foreign wars (the Peace of Vervins, which Henri had signed with Philip II of Spain in 1598) but had also achieved internal pacification: it was he who, closing the gates on the wars and adversities that for thirty or forty years had disfigured France and the greater part of Christianity, had seen out the last century of iron only to inaugurate a new (seventeenth) century of gold.[60] Here, the entry's printed account draws on emblematic imagery found on a 1596 *jeton* or token that had featured Henri IV's name and arms on the front and on its reverse the image of Janus' closed temple accompanied by the phrase "Je veille sur la paix et sur les combats" [I oversee peace and battles]. This *jeton*'s image of the closed temple of Janus commemorated Henri's 1595 absolution by Clement VIII as well as his successful pacification of rebellious Catholic subjects, while its legend "ET PACEM ET PRÆLIA CURO" [I preside over both peace and battles] spoke to the kingdom's unity following his 1595 declaration of war against a foreign enemy: Spain. The king's marriage to Marie de Médicis had been arranged by her uncle Ferdinando I de' Medici partly in hopes that financial and political support for France would help to curtail Habsburg efforts to dominate the Italian peninsula. In Avignon, Marie received a copy of Valladier's description, complete with engravings, to take to her new husband, and Valladier's text also circulated more widely in print. At the time of Marie's January 1605 ballet, the allegorical associations between Henri IV and Janus remained pertinent: for example, a bellicose French pamphlet published in 1604 and again in 1605 praised Henri's IV's greatness by comparing his kingdom – a site of domestic tranquility threatened interminably, it seemed, by Habsburg ambition – to Janus' temple.[61]

In Marie's ballet for carnival 1605, the queen's dwarf, wearing a mask, reminded our unknown letter writer of Janus, and in this sense the performer's costume may have called up this Roman god's various topical associations, particularly given the threats to France caused by Spain's recent peace treaty with England, signed by James I at Hampton Court in summer 1604 (for a more detailed discussion of this treaty along with other aspects of French foreign policy during Henri IV's reign, see chapter 5). Neither the dwarf's entry nor Henri IV's ordering of the ballet hall by means of inclusions and exclusions that it mirrored were stand-alone performances, however. Rather, these moments worked in tandem to prepare spectators for the evening's main event: the *grand ballet* of which Marie de Médicis was the principal organizer and first dancer. Making two or three danced tours of the hall, the queen's dwarf imitated, in his navigation of the performance space, the king's earlier "tour de la salle" [tour of the hall] to arrange the ballet's spectators. Like Janus, this performer looked back in time – in this case, to the king's actions moments previously. Also like Janus, however, he simultaneously looked forward by anticipating the queen's entrance. In continental treatises on the *basse danse*, Skiles Howard notes, "dance was fixed and framed by the interior walls of the *palazzo* as an aesthetic emblem of containment; simultaneously, the clearing of space for the performance of dance was a metonym of 'spatial entitlement.'"[62] Applying these elements of contemporary dance theory to events in the Grande Salle du Louvre, we can see that by means of Henri IV's actions, followed by the entry danced by a dwarf from Marie's own household, this ballet claimed a ceremonial, spatial entitlement belonging jointly to the king and to the queen, in part as an emblem of political containment. For, as I explore in the next section, when Marie herself entered the playing space, the social make-up of her troupe of women dancers, together with their costuming and choreography, complemented the emphasis on civic peace under a strong French monarchy emblematized moments earlier in the king's ordering of the hall, as well as in the Janus imagery deployed in her dwarf's danced entry imitating that ordering.

Casting Choices: "Those Who Could Make her Queen"

When Marie de Médicis finally appeared on stage to dance her *grand ballet*, spectators witnessed the fruits of her efforts behind the scenes to involve the court's highest ranking noblewomen, across confessional divides, in scripted gestures of loyalty to their king. Casting choices significantly impacted the political import of all courtly *divertissements*, since part of each performance's contemporary meaning inhered in the audience's knowledge of high-ranking dancers' social identities as these intersected with the ballet's allegories and iconographies. In the case of this particular ballet, Marie's choice of women who performed in her troupe helped to advertise the royal marriage as a partnership in which Henri IV and Marie de Médicis worked together to ensure order within the kingdom.

The specific occasion shaping the casting of female dancers for this performance was the marriage Henri IV had recently arranged between Henri II, duc de Rohan, and Marguerite de Béthune, daughter of Maximilien de Béthune, future duc de Sully.[63] We learn of the connection between the queen's ballet and this marriage from La Force's letters to his wife. In a missive dated 10 January, La Force explains that an engagement had just been accorded between Henri II de Rohan and Marguerite de Béthune and that "Toutes les dames sont empressées avec la Reine tous les soirs à apprendre un grand ballet, il leur faut plus de quinze jours à l'apprendre. Madame la Duchesse de Deux-Ponts en est, quoiqu'elle soit grosse. Je crois que l'on commencera à crier les annonces du mariage dans sept à huit jours" [Every evening, all the ladies gather attentively around the queen to learn a great ballet. It will take more than fifteen days to learn. Madame the duchess of Deux-Ponts is in it, even though she is pregnant. In seven to eight days, I think we will announce the marriage].[64] In 1596, Henri IV's sister Catherine de Bourbon had suggested such a match between Marguerite de Béthune and Henri de Rohan, but the king initially vetoed this idea – partly because his sister had proposed the alliance without first consulting him, partly because he was still angry with Henri II de Rohan's mother, Catherine de Parthénay, duchesse de Rohan, who in 1595 had allegedly published a pamphlet attacking the king for favouring former (League) enemies over longstanding allies.[65] More recently, however, the king had gone out of his way to favour the Rohan family. In 1602 Henri IV had helped to broker the marriage between the eldest Rohan daughter, Catherine, and Jean II de Bavière, the future duc de Deux-Ponts, and in 1603 he had raised Henri de Rohan to the rank of duke and peer.[66] Then in December 1604, a month before his wife's ballet for carnival 1605, Henri IV caused Sully to break off his daughter Marguerite's engagement to François de Coligny, Guy XX de Laval, so as to personally put in place a new match for her with Henri de Rohan.[67]

The house of Rohan (like many others in France) was greatly in debt; revenues from its holdings in Brittany had been decimated during the civil wars. Auguste Laugel suggests that by facilitating Henri II de Rohan's marriage to Marguerite de Béthune, who brought a dowry of 50,000 *livres*, the king sought to lighten Rohan's financial burdens in order thereby to secure his loyalty; at the same time, the king flattered Sully's pride by allying his daughter, and hence Sully himself, with this great family.[68] In order to underscore his personal involvement in this new alliance, Henri gave the bride and groom 10,000 écus each to cover the cost of their wedding clothes and related festivities, and told Sully that his future son-in-law would be given great advantages (in fact, Rohan was very soon after made Colonel General of the Swiss guards).

Moreover, the king himself signed the engagement papers; in this way, the marriage contract linked the two families not only to each other but also to him.[69]

The king's arrangement of this marriage placed the Rohans, a great military family with its own claims to sovereignty in Navarre, in the crown's debt. In this sense, it formed part of a larger effort to neutralize potential for future civil unrest by establishing closer ties between the French crown and the kingdom's most powerful nobles. Other unions arranged for similar ends included the engagement of Henri's sister Catherine de Bourbon to Henri de Lorraine, duc de Bar and heir to Charles III, duc de Lorraine, set in place as part of the 1598 treaty of Saint-Germain-en-Laye outlining terms for the duchy's recognition of Henri IV's kingship; the 1605 marriage of Armand de Bourbon, prince de Conti, to Louise Marguerite de Lorraine, mademoiselle de Guise; and the 1608 marriage of César de Bourbon, duc de Vendôme (Henri IV's own natural son by his late mistress, Gabrielle d'Estrées) to the wealthy Françoise de Lorraine, duchesse de Mercoeur. The crown's involvement in all of these marital arrangements was designed to establish long-lasting bonds of obligation between the Bourbon dynasty and members of the kingdom's most powerful princely families, many of whom had previously taken leading roles in efforts by the Catholic League to resist Henri's accession, and many of whom held rival claims to the French throne.

The 1605 engagement of Henri II de Rohan to Sully's daughter was also useful as a way to help contain the potential for civil unrest among the kingdom's small but powerful Huguenot population. Marriages such as those of the prince de Conti with a prominent princess from the house of Guise were designed by the crown in part to help to stave off disloyalty among leading Catholics. But in the months leading up to Marie's January 1605 ballet Huguenot discontent was also being stoked by Henri de la Tour d'Auvergne, duc de Bouillon who, having been implicated in several Spanish-backed conspiracies against the king, had now established a stronghold in Sedan from which he posed a significant military and political threat to the Bourbon monarchy.[70] To address Huguenot concerns and thus defuse Bouillon's capacity to garner a greater following, the king in October 1604 had agreed to hold a Protestant assembly the following summer. Before this assembly could take place, however, Henri sought ways to strengthen the hand of Sully, his representative at the event, among the latter's more radical co-religionists. In fall 1604, Sully was not particularly well respected among large numbers of French Protestants due to the favour shown to him by the now-Catholic Henri IV, but also because of his brother Philippe de Béthune's devout Catholicism and position as French ambassador in Rome. Sully gained better standing among his fellow Protestants, though, by breaking off his daughter Marguerite's engagement to Guy de Laval, who had been flirting publicly with conversion to Catholicism and would in fact turn apostate in March 1605.[71] Moreover, through his daughter's marriage to the high-ranking, well-respected Henri II de Rohan, Sully further increased his credibility with his co-religionists, thereby helping to minimize their distrust for the crown based on Henri IV's now "favourable attitude" towards the Catholic church.[72] Ultimately, at the Protestant assembly in summer 1605, Sully as the crown's representative succeeded in limiting points of discussion to primarily procedural matters.

This context helps to clarify the political stakes informing Marie's public support for the Rohan-Béthune marriage through a ballet in her name honouring its announcement. Giovannini, the Florentine resident in Paris, expressed concern that such kinship arrangements would backfire on the king and his family:

> Il giuditio, che si faccia di questo parentado non è punto buono, parendo che non sia se non a disegno che Rosni si vadia così fortificando nella fattione Uganotta, con l'allianza anche del Duca di Dua Ponti marito della sorella di Roano; et il Re non ci ha pensato nonché preveduto, potendo questo Roano come herede del Regno di Navarra, in defetto di figlioli del Re, pigliar il pretesto che il Mariaggio della Regina Marg[heri]ta sia il vero et il buono, et in conseguenza questo della Regina nullo, et il Dolfino bastardo, come vuole anche pretender la Marchesa che il suo sia il buono, et nella disputa di questi mariaggi, fare con l'appoggio delli Ugonotti il fatto suo.

> [The opinion made of this marriage is not at all good, it being thought that this marriage is designed solely so that Rosny will thus be fortified in the Huguenot faction, with the alliance also of the duc of Deux-Ponts, husband of Rohan's sister. And the king neither had thought, nor had foreseen this, this Rohan being in the position as heir of the kingdom of Navarre, should the king not have a son, to take as pretext that the marriage of the Queen Marguerite is the true and valid one, and that in consequence this marriage of the queen [Marie de Médicis] is nothing, and the dauphin [is a] bastard, as also the marquise [de Verneuil, Henriette d'Entragues] wanted to claim that her marriage was the real one, and in the dispute of these marriages, to make his interest with the help of the Huguenots.][73]

Giovannini here expresses the fear that by strengthening Rohan through this marriage, Henri IV risked keeping alive challenges to dynastic stability ventured in the name of Henriette d'Entragues' son, Henri de Verneuil. Ultimately, however, his anxieties about Rohan would prove unfounded, for throughout Henri IV's reign, as well as in the moment of transition to Marie's regency, the duke remained loyal.[74] Honouring the Rohan-Béthune alliance by celebrating it with a *ballet de la reine*, therefore, the crown in winter 1605 not only strengthened its immediate capacity to put down Huguenot unrest but also helped to secure ties between the Rohan family and Marie, thereby further isolating d'Entragues and helping to secure Bourbon political stability.

A closer look at extant sources reveals how the queen herself shaped these and other aspects of this ballet through her selection of its highest-ranking women dancers. To be chosen to appear alongside a royal personage in a ballet was a particular mark of social and political favour, and in the case of Marie's ballets, as we have seen in chapter 1, such decisions were attributable to the queen herself. The women who danced under her direction in this particular 1605 *ballet de la reine* included Henri de Rohan's eldest sister Catherine, wife of the duc de Deux-Ponts mentioned by Giovannini in the letter quoted above. Catherine and her two sisters had been among the party chosen by the king to welcome his new wife upon her arrival at Marseille in December 1600, and thereafter they were often at court.[75] When their mother the duchesse de Rohan was taken ill after arriving in Paris in early January 1605, Marie de Médicis accompanied the king in a lengthy visit to her lodgings.[76] A *ballet de la reine* would have been an especially appropriate type of festivity by which to mark royal favour towards these particular families, since the Béthune and Rohan clans were well known for their interest in ballet per se. Sully and his wife often danced in royal ballets; indeed, several years later at the king's request they would build a special room for ballets at the Arsenal, their Paris residence, while in 1609 Sully's second wife Rachel de Cochefilet was chosen by the queen as one of the women to dance in her last, most magnificent ballet (discussed in chapters 4 and 5). The duchesse de Rohan and her children, too, had performed before the king in several ballets at the court of his sister Catherine de Bourbon in the early 1590s. Texts for these earlier productions, most likely authored by madame de Rohan herself, urged loyalty to the French crown and resistance to Spanish tyranny, some of the very goals that underpinned Henri IV's determination, a decade later, to match Henri de Rohan with Marguerite de Béthune.[77]

It was not only Protestant grands whom Marie honoured in 1605 through her choice of women dancers, however, for Marie also personally sought out participation by at least one young woman from a powerful Catholic house. In a January 1605 letter, Marie wrote to her "cousine" [female cousin], otherwise unnamed, to inform her that she was gathering all of the princesses present in Paris in order to make a ballet and that she wished this woman's daughter to be among them. Marie entreated her addressee to agree and also to ask the duc de Mayenne's permission on Marie's behalf; she hoped that the young lady would be allowed to depart for Paris with haste.[78] From this reference to Charles de Lorraine, duc de Mayenne, we may deduce that the queen's letter was addressed to Mayenne's wife Henriette de Savoie-Villars, marquise de Villars and duchesse de Mayenne, and that the princess in question was their youngest daughter Renée de Lorraine. Renée's elder sister Catherine de Lorraine, wife of Charles Gonzague, duc de Nevers, would not have required her parents' assent in order to travel to Paris, but Renée was unmarried in 1605, when the queen wrote this letter.[79] This was not the only honour Marie showed this young woman and close members of her family. Her father was entertained personally by the king and queen in Paris on the last day of February that same year, for example, when at the king's express command Mayenne heard Giulio Caccini and his family sing.[80] Renée's brother-in-law the duc de Nevers also appeared prominently in the 1605 *ballet de la reine*'s final entry, as we will see in chapter 3; Renée herself danced along with Sully's wife in Marie de Médicis' 1609 *ballet de la reine*; and in 1610, the king and queen honoured Renée's family by choosing her to accompany Marie at the latter's coronation.[81]

Marie may simply have wished to show Renée de Mayenne favour out of personal loyalty or friendship, or as part of her general duty to include young women of the highest ranks in her ballets as a form of socio-political patronage designed to help facilitate these women's marital prospects.[82] In choosing this young woman for her ballet, though, she also legitimized her own authority. Marie had to a certain extent demeaned her own social position in 1602 by choosing the king's mistress Henriette d'Entragues, marquise de Verneuil, to dance in her first French court ballet, as related in chapter 1. Moreover, she had undertaken this action out of loyalty to another woman of lower standing, Marie's childhood companion from Florence, Leonora Galigaï. By granting the marquise a position among the troupe of women who danced in her troupe on this earlier occasion, Marie had gained d'Entragues' help in convincing the king to give Galigaï, rather than a Frenchwoman of higher rank, a particularly influential position within the queen's household. Speaking of Marie's general efforts on behalf of Galigaï several months prior to this 1602 queen's ballet, however, Sully gave voice to a more general attitude at the French court condemning the queen's actions: as he remarked to the Florentine representative in Paris, if Henri IV's new consort refused as attendants and companions those *who could make her queen*, she would be neither taken nor esteemed as one.[83] Given this predominant view, combined with the lingering threats to Marie's position posed by the marquise's pretensions to queenship, it makes sense that on the occasion of her second major ballet in France Marie made sure to present herself on stage alongside Frenchwomen of the highest ranks: her letter to her "cousine," we will recall, announced her intention to gather around herself for this production all of the kingdom's *princesses*. Such strategies were especially important given the specificities of Marie's lineage as a Medici. The Medici dukes could claim only recent standing as princes relative to other European sovereigns; in fact, their line's power and wealth grew from their success as moneylenders, with the Medici being savagely disparaged on such grounds in polemics of the 1570s and 1580s. To undercut Marie's standing at the court of France, Henri IV's mistress Henriette d'Entragues reportedly called her a "fat banker." To promote her own socio-political authority as the king's wife and mother to the dauphin, therefore, Marie issued invitations to this ballet that enabled her to surround herself, on stage, with women of equal if not longer-standing noble lineage than her own.[84]

This cohort included two subgroups: the princesses of the blood and the *princesses étrangères*, or foreign princesses. The former included women from cadet (junior) branches of the house of Bourbon, whose male members (the princes of the blood) stood next in line for the throne should Henri IV die without legitimate male issue. Next in status were the *princesses étrangères*: women from the Lorraine-Guise-Mayenne, Gonzague-Nevers, Savoy-Nemours, and other noble families who held French territorial holdings and titles but whose standing as heads of cadet lines in foreign ruling dynasties also entitled them to independent, princely rank.[85] Having princesses of the blood and foreign princesses in her ballets brought honour to Marie.[86] Among this group, though, it was the foreign princely families that had the most to gain from Marie's friendship. As Jean-François Dubost notes, the Bourbon princes of the blood (Condé, Soissons, and to a lesser extent Conti) were a priori hostile to the new queen and her son, since the latter's legitimacy as heir to the throne weakened their own claims,[87] while families such as the Lorraine-Guise-Mayenne and Gonzague-Nevers, although they experienced the new queen as a lesser threat, stood to gain little from her: their own well-established rank internationally trumped that of the Medici (which was only centuries old). Additionally, the princes of Lorraine as well as Charles' father, Louis de Gonzague, first duc de Nevers, had in the 1590s converted from being key leaders and supporters of the Catholic League to being the French king's loyal allies; this shift had secured the access of these families to Henri IV, thereby making them less in need of Marie's interventions on their behalf.[88] Nonetheless, members of the house of Lorraine stood to lose a great deal should their ancient rivals, the Condé, come to rule France, and for this reason, the arrival of Marie and her son the dauphin was advantageous to them. The Guise also shared kinship ties with Marie by way of the Gonzaga-Nevers: in 1584 Marie's elder sister Eleonora de' Medici had married Vincenzo I Gonzaga, fourth duke of Mantua and Montferrat, while in 1599 Catherine and Henri de Lorraine, children of the duc and duchesse de Mayenne, had wed respectively Charles de Gonzague, duc de Nevers et Rethel, and his sister, Marie Henriette de Gonzague. It was towards the houses of Lorraine-Guise and Gonzague-Nevers, then – those princely families with whom she enjoyed the most obvious dynastic affinities yet who were as powerful if not more so than herself – that Marie launched an "offensive of charm" in hopes that by courting their friendship she would secure greater influence within French princely circles more broadly.[89]

The capacity to grant the privilege of appearing in a queen's ballet was an important tool in Marie's arsenal as she undertook such efforts. Honouring these families by extending to their female members the prestige that attended on-stage appearances in royal ballets, the queen elevated her own status while simultaneously fostering interpersonal bonds of connection with those noble families most likely to benefit from her legitimacy as queen – bonds which in turn could help to ameliorate the vulnerability she might otherwise face should her husband die and should she need to be confirmed as guardian for the dauphin and, potentially, as regent.[90]

Sovereign yet Subject

Thus far, I have outlined the king's symbolic enactment of royal authority as host of his wife's ballet in a set of actions that helped prepare the

Grand Salle du Louvre audience for the queen's entrance, accompanied by women dancers from the kingdom's most prominent families. By sponsoring and dancing in a ballet celebrating the announcement of a marriage arranged by the crown between two key Huguenot houses, and by ensuring that its performers also included Catholic princesses, Marie positioned herself as an active participant alongside her husband in the crown's efforts to bind the kingdom's most powerful nobles closer to itself and to put forward the image of a unified France no longer weakened internally by paralyzing religious and political factionalism. I now turn to additional elements of the on-stage action in which the queen's embodied personhood surrounded by these princesses, as well as other performers and objects, worked to ensure political stability by expressing, in ceremonial terms, her unique institutional position as both one with the king through marriage, and hence a participant in the king's majesty and dignity, and as separate from him, due to her gendered inferiority.

As queen consort, Marie de Médicis paradoxically occupied two mutually antithetical socio-juridical positionings. On the one hand, the queen as the king's wife shared in the majesty that pertained to sovereignty. Sovereignty was understood as indivisible and inalienable, given by God to the "Most Christian" king; increasingly, prerogatives of rule were positioned as inherent to the royal bloodline rather than being dependent on religious rituals, such as the *sacre*. But in accordance with the sacrament of Christian marriage, the king and queen as husband and wife became two beings in one. As a result, the female consort participated in her husband's sovereign dignity, and in this sense enjoyed with him a majesty enjoyed by no other person within the kingdom. Simultaneously, however, her presumed inferiority as a woman established the queen's fundamental difference from the king. Early modern practices of crown devolution in France precluded women – the "weaker sex" according to the law of nature – from rule. In addition, both canon law and Roman law positioned the husband as head of the family, requiring of the wife both submission and obedience to his power. In this sense, the French queen consort was simultaneously sovereign, equal to her husband in majesty and dignity, and subject, positioned as inferior to, and owing allegiance to, her husband.[91]

Cosandey, analysing the *sacres*, royal entries, and funerals organized for French consort queens of the late sixteenth and early seventeenth centuries, notes how these ceremonial presentations and representations of the queen took into account both her royal dignity, shared with the king, and the rules of crown devolution, which established a fundamental difference between queens and kings.[92] But even ceremonial occasions typically dismissed by political historians as frivolous entertainments could and did function analogously to the genres of royal ceremony Cosandey takes as her focus, I suggest. These aspects of Marie's January 1605 ballet, in fact, made it particularly useful to the Bourbon monarchy. On the one hand, the queen regnant could represent and model, in gestures signalling feminine submission to her husband, the obedience that the king's political subjects owed their prince. On the other hand, she could represent the king's dignity, thereby expanding the range of possible sites for the *mise en scène* of sovereign might while simultaneously advertising the authority on which rested her reassuring capacity to exercise royal power, if only temporarily, should her husband's death force her son's accession before he reached adulthood.

On stage, as we have seen, the queen and her female companions in the *grand ballet* wore carnation and white, as did the violins, lutes, singers, and pages. This uniformity of dress, in the colours of the royal livery, represented on a visual register the women's allegiance, as one collective body, to the crown. Coming back together after moving apart in the dance, their *grand ballet*'s choreographies underscored such images of unity and harmony, as did their earlier procession to the centre of the room followed by their collective salute to the king as the event's most honoured spectator. When these dancers arrived in the centre of the hall, moreover, the royal Music or chorus of voices sang Henri IV's praises.[93] In this way, the *grand ballet*'s costuming, movement, gesture, and music together registered its dancers' harmonious submission to the sovereign.

This was important because the king had to be the recipient, not the giver, in acts of submission both symbolic and material. For this reason, he himself could not model, in symbolic gestures, the obedience owed to him by even his highest-ranking subjects. But because of her gender, the queen consort could. As Henri IV's wife, Marie de Médicis enacted her status as a private juridical subject when immediately upon arriving at the centre of this ballet's performance space she saluted the king and then subjected her own movements to a pause while the ballet's choir echoed, vocally, the honour she had enacted via silent gesture. This moment of ceremonial homage exemplified, for other French subjects, the political virtue of obedience. Leading a troupe comprised of dancers from the kingdom's most socially elevated families, moreover,

Marie engineered their participation in this gesture along with her, thereby choreographing the movements and pauses through which they signalled their houses' shared submission to the monarch.

Bookending this moment, however, were elements of the queen's spatial and visual positioning that declared her unique share in the king's sovereign dignity. Of all the women dancers, it was Marie who entered the performance space first – a temporal arrangement that registered the priority of her royal status as consort over and above the kingdom's other high-ranking women. The fact that she alone among these dancers claimed the prerogative of seating herself, and in a specially decorated chair no less ("la reine ... sassit dans une cheze de satin incarnate toute couverte de clinquans" [seated herself in a chair of carnation satin all covered with tinsel]),[94] further marked the majesty that Marie alone shared with the king.

In a portrait that dates from 1606–7, now held at the Bilbao Fine Arts Museum, Frans Pourbus the Younger painted Marie de Médicis next to a chair richly decorated with embroidered crimson fabric (Figure 2.3). This portrait looks forward to the more famous 1609–10 portrait by Pourbus commemorating her coronation (reproduced on this book's dust jacket and as Figure 5.2), with its dais decorated in *velours cramoisy*.[95] Chairs "spoke very clearly of status in a period when benches and stools were the normal form of seating," Janette Dillon notes, while the elaborately constructed dais or throne "produce[d] and highlight[ed] the distance between the monarch and others by its framing structure (back, arms, and canopy)."[96] In early modern France, the provision of a chair for the queen in royal entries and a dais for her on the occasion of her *sacre* helped to register the exceptionalism of her standing as the king's divinely given consort.[97] So too did the chair, prepared for Marie on the occasion of her 1605 ballet, decorated in carnation-coloured satin covered with *clinquant*. Like the chair in Pourbus' portrait of the queen from this same time period, the ballet's decorated chair for Marie signalled through its similarity to the chair and dais in the royal entry and the *sacre* the queen's unique institutional position as representative of, and partner in, the majesty pertaining to sovereignty.

The queen's superiority along with the king, over and above his subjects, found further expression in this ballet's use of additional on-stage objects associated with dynastic exclusivity, in particular the dwarf and the female Italian singer who, as "luxurious accessories," helped to advertise the sovereignty invested in their royal patrons.[98] Henri IV, as France's first Bourbon monarch, claimed membership in an exclusive

82   Dancing Queen

Figure 2.3. Frans Pourbus the Younger (1569–1622), "Portrait of Marie de Médicis (Maria de' Medici) (1573–1642)," 1606–7. Oil on canvas, 214.7 × 124.5 cm. Museo de Bellas Artes, Bilbao, Spain. DeA Picture Library/ Art Resource, NY.

group of princes who, partly through marriages restricted to members of their own caste, asserted their distinction apart from, and above, the political subjects over whom they ruled. As Cosandey explains, kings in early modern France no longer married within the kingdom, for doing so might give the impression of suzerainty, rather than sovereignty. The families over whom France's modern monarchy ruled could not be allowed to hope that they would ever be elevated as peers and affines to the reigning dynasty. Rather, French nobles needed to remain under strict admission to royal authority. When the king married, therefore, his bride had to be chosen from outside the kingdom. To further enforce the gap between ruler and ruled, moreover, she would need to be the daughter of a foreign sovereign prince.[99] Had Henri married one of his own subjects, such as his late mistress Gabrielle d'Estrées or his current mistress Henriette d'Entragues, this union would have lessened the gap between his rank as sovereign and that of other high-ranking noble families, who owed him unquestioned obedience. By contrast, Henri IV's marriage to Marie, a princess from a foreign dynasty, helped to emphasize the new Bourbon dynasty's distinctiveness within the kingdom. "Objects" within the queen's ballet that in their foreignness embodied a type of cultural capital we might call "supra-national," either through exoticness or by means of their association with Medici dynastic prestige specifically, further marked the symbolic as well as political capital that accrued to the king and his legitimate progeny by means of this foreign dynastic marriage.

I have argued above that the queen's dwarf who toured the hall both looked back to the king in the audience and looked forward to Marie's on-stage entrance. In addition, the connotations of exoticness that this performer's unusual stature evoked underscored the singular status of his royal patrons. Prior to 1617, the dwarf Jean Mauderon (*dit* Maudricart) held the office of usher of the queen's cabinet, making him the most likely candidate to have performed in this 1605 ballet's first entry.[100] As a member of the queen's household, Maudricart's very presence signalled Marie's authority, since early modern dwarfs, because of their small size, were often viewed by contemporaries as "monsters" or "natural wonders."[101] In light of their rarity, dwarfs also functioned as "living, breathing luxury items" acquired by princes and nobles in order to "broadcast and even to create the illusion" of imperial power.[102] The early Bourbon court of France, like the Medici court in Florence, the Gonzaga court in Mantua, and the Habsburg courts in Spain and Austria, kept what David Loades has called "innocents" and "freaks" – including mutes, giants, and dwarfs.[103] Dwarfs and other novel "objects that speak," as Bernadette Andrea has noted, were also "requisite at the courts of the Ottoman sultan and the Holy Roman emperor."[104] An insider/outsider who represented courtliness in miniature but who also served as an exotic rarity to be consumed and patronized by the French crown, Maudricart's very being marked in multiple ways the alleged superiority of his female patron as a member of not only her natal dynasty, the Medici, but also the Bourbon dynasty into which she had married.[105]

This dwarf was not the only performer whose appearance in Marie's 1605 *ballet de la reine* marked the luxury and magnificence made possible thanks to the king's foreign marriage, however: also strikingly novel was the unnamed "Italienne" whose song so impressed the unnamed writer of the letter collected in Peiresc's *registres*. As we have seen, this Italian woman first arrived on stage among the musicians of the royal Music. Like this group of singers (and like the queen and princesses) she wore incarnat and white, the colours of the French livery. Yet she was also specially costumed: the letter's author states that she was "si bien atifée quil me seroyt impossible de vous la depeindre" [so remarkably dressed that it would be impossible for me to depict her].[106] This woman performed with the Music when this vocal ensemble sang the king's praises after the queen and her female companions had marched to the centre of the room and again when it accompanied, in song, the women's ballet. She also sang alone during the intermission in the queen's dancing.

Rather than a regular insider/outsider at the French court, as was the dwarf who danced the first entry, this singer must have been a member of the famous Caccini consort.[107] In August 1604, as is well known, Henri IV and Marie wrote letters to the Tuscan grand duke Ferdinando I de' Medici and grand duchess Christine of Lorraine, respectively, requesting that the vocal consort patronized by them, headed by the famous composer and singing teacher Giulio Caccini, be allowed to visit France. In late December 1604, Giulio, his second wife Margherita, son Pompeo, and daughters Francesca and Settimia arrived in Paris, where they remained until May 1605. The Caccini were thus present at the French court on 23 January 1605, when Marie's ballet was performed. On 16 January, Giulio wrote that his eldest daughter Francesca (known as "La Cecchina") had sung two French airs which so pleased the French king that he made her repeat them twice.[108] Then, in a letter dated 1 March, Guilio wrote that "tutto questo Carnovale dopo il ballo che fece la Regina nei primi giorni" [throughout carnival after the ballet made by the queen in the first days] the king and queen had constantly called on them to perform and had shown them great courtesy. Giulio does not explicitly state that one of "his" women sang in the ballet, but the royal couple's attentiveness to the Caccini in general and the king's response to La Cecchina's singing in particular indicate that the "Italienne" whose voice so charmed the Louvre audience during the queen's ballet that season was most likely Francesca herself, although she may also have been Settimia or Margherita, both of whom seem to have been greatly admired.[109]

This "Italienne" was not the first woman singer, or even the first Italian professional woman singer, to appear on the French court ballet stage. In 1581, the famous *Ballet comique de la royne* sponsored and danced by Louise de Lorraine-Vaudemont, wife of the last Valois king Henri III, had featured as the Cardinal Virtues two female lute players and two women singers, all unnamed, as well as a duet for Tethys and Glaucus sung by Violante Doria, the Genoese soprano, and her husband the composer and bass singer Girard de Beaulieu.[110] As early as 1572, Doria and Beaulieu had received remuneration as servants to Elisabeth d'Autriche, wife of Charles IX, and during the 1580s they garnered salaries and pensions from Queen Louise de Lorraine-Vaudemont and, to a lesser extent, Henri III.[111] Their duet for the *Ballet comique*, composed perhaps by Beaulieu himself, concluded with a "highly ornamented final strophe" which in its execution would have required from Doria a "vocal agility" that was "equal to or surpassing that displayed by Beaulieu, one of the most celebrated singers of the period."[112] The *ballet de la reine* performed in winter 1605 thus built on such famous precedents by featuring another professional Italian woman singer – one of arguably more renowned virtuosic capacity.

The precise musical qualities of female song for the 1605 ballet remain opaque. Since no extant evidence identifies this ballet's vocal music or its verse texts, we cannot know whether the celebrated "Italienne" sang in French, Italian, or even Spanish (although we do know that the Caccini women sang at the Louvre in all three languages before a French royal audience).[113] Nor do we (yet) know whether this woman's solo performance for the ballet was an *air de cour*, as would have been standard in French court ballets for this period, or whether she in fact performed a *récit*, that largely Italian innovation which came to be adopted in *ballet de cour* by the end of the decade. Either way, however, her solo musical interlude likely brought to *ballet de cour* some of the aesthetic qualities for which the Caccini women were so noted throughout Europe. According to Suzanne Cusick, these included a new, more nuanced relationship between music and text enabled by the singer's "constantly flexible dynamics and improvisation of manner," an emotional intensity and rhetorical power enabled by the female body's ability to produce its high voice naturally (as opposed to through falsetto), and last but not least a remarkable responsiveness to "the conceits that informed the song's words" enabled by the singer's virtuosic technique, most notably her "distinctive expressive use of ... breath control and *gorheggiando* (literally warbling)" designed to offer "extremely clear declamation of a song's words" and to imitate "the dynamic shape of speech."[114] By introducing to French court ballet the innovative performance values and virtuosic techniques for which the Caccini women were renowned across Europe, this 1605 ballet therefore contributed quite directly to an important shift in French court ballet music that occurred during the first decade of the seventeenth century.

According to Henri Prunières, this decade witnessed an important change in the *récits* for court ballet productions, which prior to 1605 were designed to be declaimed rather than sung. This shift towards sung *récits* in turn moved the genre away from the *ballet à entrées* towards *ballet mélodramatique* and eventually opera, in which music assumes for itself the dramatic task previously shared with poetry.[115] Prunières suggests that the initial shift towards expressive dramatic song within *ballet de cour* reflects the influence of Giulio Caccini and the poet Ottavio Rinuccini. Present in France between the years 1601 and 1605 thanks to the queen's patronage, Caccini and Rinuccini at this time stood as the two cultural figures most strongly associated with dramatic expression in Italian song.[116] If the "Italienne" who sang during the queen's 1605 ballet was Francesca, Settimia, or Margherita Caccini, however, this means that Marie's patronage had a more direct impact on French court ballet music than that for which scholars like Prunières have previously credited her. In fact, one of the queen's own productions featured as its chief musical highlight a diva-singer famously associated with the new *stile rappresentativo* developed in early opera.

As an aesthetic novelty incorporated within the most important genre of court entertainment in early seventeenth-century France, this much-coveted foreign visitor signalled the queen's elevated status as a powerful patron.[117] According to Dubost, one of the principal lessons Marie had learned at the Tuscan court concerned how secondary dynasties might gain prestige internationally via concerted policies and practices of artistic patronage, and once in France the new queen applied this lesson on a "grand" scale.[118] Building on Dubost's assertion, we can see how, with its inclusion of female monody, the 1605 *ballet de la reine* formed an important early moment in this concerted policy and practice of patronage. Moreover, such patronage advertised Marie's own dynastic prestige placed in service to that of her husband.

This was not Marie's first or only effort to champion professional female musicians of international fame; rather, it built on a pattern of concerted patronage that began prior to her departure from Florence. In 1589 and 1590, Marie along with Eleonora Orsini had taken up patronage of their own *concerto di donne* in Rome after her uncle Ferdinando I had dissolved the *concerto di donne* in Florence that had been instituted by Marie's father Francesco I de' Medici in part to rival the Este court's female consort.[119] Lucia Caccini, Giulio's first wife, had been one of the earlier Florentine group's members,[120] and in 1590, Lucia sang in Rinuccini's *Maschere di bergiere* in the role of a shepherdess who, fleeing civil war in France, sought the aid of Florence and of Marie's future husband, Henri de Bourbon. Marie would no doubt have been present at this performance (she may even have danced in it), and that same year, she commissioned madrigals by a female composer, Laura Guidiccioni, for a production of Tasso's *Aminta* in which she herself acted.[121] Then, in 1600, Lucia's eldest daughter Francesca made her professional debut in an opera performed as part of the Tuscan court's festivities for Marie's wedding. Five years later, when both Marie and Henri wrote to the queen's uncle Ferdinando I de' Medici requesting that the Caccini consort and its women be allowed to visit France, the queen's request arguably held equal if not greater weight than that of her husband: the Florentine court's majordomo Giovanni del Maestro, for example, noting the Caccini family's departure for France, specifies that they were called by ("chiamata dalla") the queen, while mentioning nothing about the French king.[122] For the carnival season 1605, then, the world's most famous women singers, in great demand across Europe, found themselves in France thanks in large part to Marie's sustained interest in virtuosic female song together with her Italian and specifically Florentine dynastic connections.

At the same time, admiration for the Caccini women also rested on their ability to sing in many languages and national styles. In this sense these singers paralleled the period's diva-actresses of *commedia* dell'arte, including Isabella Andreini. Renowned for her mimetic skill, versatility, humanist training, and linguistic lability, Isabella at the 1589 wedding celebrations for Ferdinando I de' Medici and Christine of Lorraine had charmed the new grand duchess by speaking and singing in Christine's native French, and during the earliest years of Marie de Médicis' queenship, Isabella and her troupe the Gelosi had sojourned in France at the royal couple's behest.[123] Like Isabella, Francesca Caccini possessed an admirable versatility, particularly in her skillful rendering of multiple languages: Henri IV himself praised Francesca's singing in the French language as excelling that of any musician resident in France. Francesca's status as an emblem of Italian cultural superiority certainly resonated strongly with international visitors, as we will see in chapter 5, while Giulio and Francesca Caccini (and I would argue Settimia and Margherita as well) symbolized Florentine cultural excellence per se and thus functioned, in a way, as "Medici propaganda."[124] At the same time, however, the Caccini women's stylistic and linguistic ecumenicism enabled them to exceed affiliation with any one princely court. Female monody within princely spectacle, in other words, formed an avant-garde aesthetic development that marked and distinguished elite patrons from across Europe in a shared sovereign status that transcended national and linguistic boundaries. In this way, the "cosmopolitan" qualities that overlaid their performances promoted the singularity of status that Henri IV shared, through marriage, with his consort.[125]

Ceremonial Expressions of Political Partnership: Abstract Theory, Embodied Practice

In thinking about these and other aspects of this ballet as represented in the document that Peiresc collected, this chapter has taken its cue in part from Malcolm Smuts and George Gorse's introduction to an important volume of collected essays on the politics of space in early modern European courts. Smuts and Gorse introduce this collection by noting how "the juxtaposition of human bodies and physical objects in space provided courts with a supple language through which hierarchical distinctions of rank and honor were defined and contested, and complex political messages conveyed. Focusing on spatial issues provides a way of decoding the mysteries of early modern court societies, by reconstructing the largely unwritten rules that shaped them from within."[126] In line with such understandings, this chapter has read the January 1605 *ballet de la reine*'s ceremonial placement of Marie de Médicis' body in relation to other performers and objects on stage as an important prompt concerning a larger "mystique" of queenly power at the court of Henri IV to which Marie herself contributed. Also helpful for analysing this ballet have been insights about performance and ceremonial outlined in Janette Dillon's *The Language of Space in Court Performance, 1400–1625*. The early modern English accounts of movements in and through royal and noble households that Dillon analyses register a "sense of ceremony" by means of their "heightened concern with spatial and kinetic protocols," "ostentatious display of wealth through rich objects and materials," and large numbers of "attendants."[127] Dillon's study does not take up ceremonial or court performance in early modern France. But the interest it shows English contemporaries to have taken in descriptions of kinetics and proxemics, in conspicuous consumption, and in a gravity that manifested itself through slowed pacing of movement on such occasions, also makes itself felt in the description of the 1605 queen's ballet archived in Peiresc's papers, for as this chapter has explored, this eye-witness account registers numerous signifying codes involving kinetics, proxemics, and opulent display, including the occasion's orderly placement of persons both on stage and off; the specific colors and fabrics worn by the queen, her female dancing companions, and the other performers; the ballet's use of rare or novel artists and objects; and the dancers' choreographed gestures and movements.

Among other methodologies, then, this chapter brings a hermeneutics of space together with attempts to consider more abstract principles of rule made visible in early modern French ceremonial. Building on work published by political historians associated with the so-called American "neo-ceremonialist" school,[128] it reads the January 1605 *ballet de la reine* in much the same way that contemporary scholars of French ceremonial read instances of ritualized royal performance: as a means of elucidating medieval and early modern political theory. Analysing Marie's ballet in this way involves examining a particular performance moment for what it can tell us about the queen's qualified participation in royal sovereignty and her structural importance to the perpetuation of monarchical rule in times of royal minorities. But while a given *ballet de cour* can be parsed in relation to the history of these and other intellectual, juridical, and theoretical concepts, individual performances enacted in particular court spaces by specific historical personages also link ideas about monarchy to topical and personal circumstances. The examination of royal ceremonial that this chapter has undertaken with respect to Marie de Médicis' January 1605 ballet, then, understands this production's political meanings as deriving from the production's engagement with theories of rule but also from its participants, both of which need to be interpreted with reference to embedded, local contexts.

One such context is the set of marriages Henry was arranging in the period, which in turn have meaning partly because of deeply rooted social and political structures in the French kingdom. Danced in celebration of one such marriage, this ballet reveals much about the structural role of queens within the French monarchy; it also makes visible the particular entourage that Marie was constructing in winter 1605 in connection with her occupation of that larger institutional role.

Another, related local context for this production was Marie's still questionable status as wife and queen and the fact that in the face of such ongoing uncertainties, made all the more threatening by continued conspiracies against the king, queen, and dauphin, no one could really be sure the Bourbon dynasty was going to last. At the time of this ballet's performance, the fallout from one such conspiracy – d'Auvergne's plot involving Henri IV's natural son born to Henriette d'Entragues, supported by Spain – had not yet been resolved. By November 1604, d'Auvergne lay imprisoned in the Bastille; in December, his sister Henriette d'Entragues was placed under house arrest in Paris, and their father, Charles Balzac d'Entragues, was also apprehended.[129] The Parlement of Paris would soon condemn to death the two men, while Henriette, having been found guilty of involvement in their scheme, would be sentenced to retirement at the convent of Beaumont-lez-Tours.[130] The first of these verdicts would not be announced until 1 February 1605, however, and in the meantime questions of how justice would be served, and how future threats to Bourbon stability would be contained, remained unanswered. Given this lack of closure, Marie's true status as wife and queen was still subject to dispute. While awaiting judgment and sentencing by the Parlement of Paris, for example, Henriette was rumoured to have declared that if she died, it would be said always that the king had put to death his own wife, and that she herself was queen before "the other," i.e., Marie de Médicis.[131]

It was in connection with the political pressures forged by such particular, contingent circumstances, therefore, that the queen's January 1605 ballet worked to link abstract, philosophical ideas about French sovereignty, and the place of consort queens in relation to such sovereignty, to contestable arguments about Marie's particular instantiation of the queen's institutional role. Foregrounding her official standing as the king's legal partner, the ballet flouted all rumours to the contrary. At the same time, by incorporating female members of major noble dynasties, the ballet actively showcased Marie's role, alongside Henri IV, in the work of building unity within the kingdom, and with it longevity for the new Bourbon regime.

Chapter Three

Alliances and Others

The 1602 ballet organized and performed by Marie de Médicis, as chapter 1 has discussed, combined verbal and visual adaptations of classical and Christian iconography to help promote the new queen's authority as Henri IV's legitimate consort and mother of the dauphin. The following year, the king while seriously ill announced his wish that Marie be designated the dauphin's guardian, and thereafter, as chapter 2 has outlined, the crown made a concerted effort to present her as worthy of a more central political role, including by way of the queen's January 1605 ballet with its incorporation of qualities found in French royal ceremonial and its choice of female dancers from powerful princely families capable of aiding Marie as regent, should the need arise. It was not only female casting choices in this 1605 *ballet de la reine* that helped to fashion powerful networks for the new queen while emphasizing her incipient political authority, however, for as this next chapter explores, the production also included several entries by male performers, including a surprise coda to the ballet initiated by the *prince étranger* Charles de Gonzague, duc de Nevers.

Typically, a royal ballet in France began with entries by lesser status members of the court – musicians, pages, the queen's *filles*, for example – and ended with the *grand ballet* or set of choreographed group dances performed by each production's highest ranking individuals. The dancers for this *grand ballet* then initiated a set of social dances, known in England as the revels, by choosing partners from the audience. In keeping with these expectations, Marie's January 1605 ballet featured a number of entries preceding the queen's, yet in contradistinction to received assumptions that royal women's ballets were exclusively decorous in tone, the entries on this occasion included a grimacing and leaping dwarf from Marie's household and a young royal male (César de Vendôme) *en travesti* (cross-dressed, in terms of gender). The production concluded, moreover, with an even less decorous entry following the queen's *grand ballet* during which a group of "Turks" and "Moors," a "Tartar," a dwarf, and several camels performed movements one contemporary eye-witness likened to a "cinq pas" danced by "beasts." With their fictional crossings of gendered and human-animal divides, these various antic episodes helped to set in relief the queen's grace, a quality viewed by contemporaries as embodied evidence of a social superiority granted by God and available only to elites. In these ways, the ballet supported Bourbon efforts to promote quasi-mystical reverence for the legitimate royal bloodline while highlighting Marie's worth as the king's domestic and political partner.

This production's final, surprise entry also forwarded a less straightforwardly recuperative political agenda, however. Its overarching fiction rehearsed a motif found in many European *divertissements* from this period: strange visitors arriving from far away lands in order to see for themselves the glorious attributes of a ruler whose fame had travelled throughout the world.[1] In this entry's particular rendering of the trope, figures representing regions designating the Ottoman empire's reach across North Africa, Central Asia, and the European Mediterranean bowed in submission before Henri IV. From one contemporary document we learn that such attempts at graceful civility failed miserably, with the "strangers" being laughed off stage as failed imitators of the courtier's arts. Anti-Ottoman sentiment embedded in this moment offered a barely veiled critique of official crown policy with respect to the French king's alliance with the Ottoman sultan. So did elements of crusading rhetoric embedded in Charles de Nevers' self-presentation as a knight of Thrace in texts for this final ballet entry and in an additional court entertainment that this entry set in motion.

The patronage relationship these entertainments helped to forge between Nevers and Marie de Médicis encompassed a series of texts authored in connection with the duke that praised the royal marriage, much as the crown's own representational programs did, as not only a domestic but also a political partnership. Nevers would ultimately prove an unreliable ally: less a loyal subject of the French crown than a sovereign *prince étranger* and pretender to the title of emperor of the East. In 1605, Nevers' entry for Marie's ballet mapped images of social and political disorderliness onto "beast-like" foreign bodies in ways that promoted his own but also the queen's nobility of race.

In the process, however, the French royal house's need to surround itself with the higher nobility and its aura of mystical authority in its attempt to achieve a smooth succession opened it not only to collaboration but also contestation.

Civility's (Islamic) Others

To explore such ambiguities as they played out in the ballet that Marie de Médicis danced on 23 January 1605, it is useful to reconsider the manuscript description of this production by a spectator at the Louvre performance, discussed in the previous chapter.[2] Read through the lens of Renaissance dance literature and civility discourse, this document helps to reveal how Marie's dignified comportments on this occasion, especially when set against the entries that framed her *grand ballet*, helped to promote the queen's grace, a quality closely defined in connection with early modern social racism, i.e., the belief that noble birth conferred social, moral, and even physical superiority.[3]

As dance historian Mark Franko explains, grace – understood as a "systemic form of [social] theatricality" – was the primary ideal for the Renaissance courtier. Renaissance theories of grace, Franko argues, were enacted and elaborated through kinesis in general and dance in particular.[4] "Profiling" the dancing body as the locus of such theories, Franko extracts from the period's dance literature a specific set of codes for noble pose and gesture, concluding that grace primarily reveals itself in gestures and postures against which it defines its own.[5] Rather than explicitly describing the qualities that define permitted gesture, in other words, early modern dance literature outlines the kinds of movement that grace prohibits. These movements are "fast, unexpected, brief, repetitive and suggestive or mimetic"; by deduction, desirable "permitted gestures" must be "by opposition slow, smooth and separated by pauses and halts."[6] Grace also reveals itself in dance through an upright carriage or posture which indicates prudence, understood as the ability to mediate between extremes. Elite social dance, known as the *basse danse*, showcases such mediation between extremes through the reverence or choreographed bow, followed by sober walking steps with a partner in simples and doubles, steps which Franko notes are indistinguishable, in dance literature descriptions, from everyday walking. In these ways, "the steps of the *basse danse* exhibit the dancer's probity to all present by circulating two or three times through a room."[7]

Such choreographies also coded what Franko calls "hyperbolically natural gesture," which like sprezzatura in civility literature marked aristocratic status.[8] The courtier's movement was by definition mimetic, a form of social performance. Yet affectation had to be eschewed since, in accordance with late sixteenth-century ideas of race, noble virtue, revealed via the capacities for excellence in dancing that theorized and enacted such virtue, required as its basis noble birth. In dance, obviously mimetic gesture or imitation of what one was not – gestures and movements that we might call extra-mimetic – carried associations of extremity and vice. By contrast, intra-mimetic gesture – gesture designed to heighten or enact hyperbolically one's true nature – encoded a form of virtue and prudence available only to elites. Pierre Charron, writing in 1601, suggests that this latter capacity for intra-mimetic kinesis which transcends distinctions between natural and acquired gesture is available only through god's grace. "[C]onceal[ing] coded behavior with a natural appearance," grace thus understood was both god-given and acquired.[9] Such notions, Franko suggests, partly explain why dance treatises from the period remain frustratingly vague regarding the technical qualities that defined the gestures permitted by civility: as inimitable inspirations of a god-given nature, noble movements "cannot be analysed."[10]

Such understandings provide a useful framework for parsing the onstage movements and gestures performed by Marie de Médicis and her female companions as described in the eye-witness account archived in the *registres* or collected papers of Nicolas-Claude Fabri de Peiresc. On initial glance, this document's lack of detail when recounting their *grand ballet* hampers any analysis of the women's dancing and its historical meanings. Taken in light of the period's theories of nobility as revealed in gesture and movement, however, this paucity of description proves paradoxically informative, a sign that the women's kinesis connoted divine ineffability. Moreover, the few choreographies this letter does mention in connection with the ballet's high-ranking women include precisely those which Renaissance dance literature associates with noble status. In elite social dance, we have seen, grace is most clearly demonstrated through the reverence followed by sober walking or marching. The queen's ballet merely reverses this order: first the women marched or walked gravely, making a little passage towards the centre of the hall ["la reine accompaignée de unze princesses marchant d'une façon grave faisant des petis pasages et comme elle feut au millieu de la sale"], then the queen along with the other women dancers saluted the king, presumably with a reverence or bow ["estant auprès du Roy ... la reine avec ses princesses sallua sa magesté"]. In their passage, moreover, the women "exhibit[ed] their probity to all present"[11] by moving through the Grande Salle du Louvre, their intra-mimetic or hyperbolically natural walking steps in upright posture signalling the very ability to mediate between extremes which, according to civility literature and dance theory, constituted graceful nobility.

This production further secured such connotations for the queen and princesses insofar as their movements conformed to strictures against vertical self-assertion: a conformity made visible through contrast with the leaps and jumps performed on stage, moments previously, by "un petit nain de la reyne" [a little dwarf belonging to the queen]. Following the entry and placement of the ballet's various musicians, we learn from the letter archived in Peiresc's collected papers, this dwarf appeared suddenly, dressed in a black taffeta cassock covered in *clinquant* and having two faces as one depicts Janus, making a thousand grimaces, leaps, and capers ["soudain entre un petit nain de la reyne avec une soutane de taphetas noier couverte de clinquans aiant deux visages comme on depeint Janus"]. After making two or three tours of the hall, this performer returned to the door from which he had entered. The reference by our unnamed spectator to this dwarf's "entrechat" – a jump during which the dancer's legs beat against each other rapidly; also a light jump or capriole – is to my knowledge the first known use of this specific dance term, preceding the 1609 reference cited in Le Robert's historical dictionary of the French language as well as its 1610 appearance in the *livret* for the *Ballet de Monsieur de Vendôme* as part of the description for a set of exuberant antic dances performed by eight dwarfs who served the Saracen sorceress Alcine.[12] In the 1605 *ballet de la reine*, therefore, it was likely not only this performer's unusually short height but also his innovative steps that helped to capture the audience's attention.[13]

The danced tour of the Grande Salle du Louvre performed by Marie's dwarf, moreover, encompassed precisely those qualities explicitly prohibited by civility. First, although fast and unexpected movements were frowned upon in the *basse danse*, the queen's dwarf entered "suddenly" – unexpectedly, quickly, or both. Second, his gestures involved suggestive imitation of an extra- as opposed to intra-mimetic quality: grimacing and wearing a masque with two faces, this performer signalled not only a hypocrisy and two-facedness linked to (professional) acting, but also the negative valences of courtly affectation that defined, through opposition, that more elevated social theatricality known as noble grace. Finally, the dwarf's "leaps and capers" would have indicated for contemporaries the vanity against which nobility sought to define itself. As Margaret McGowan notes, drawing on Jacques Tahureau's 1565 *Dialogues*, vanity or affectation defined for contemporaries the dark underside of skilfull courtly dance.[14] Jumps with leg beats, essential components of the *galliard* or *cinq pas*, encompassed improvisation and variety, and required considerable skill and practice to pull off well.[15] Excellence in executing such steps, in fact, marked the mastery in the art of dance necessary to the male courtier's enactment of noble virtue. But because this courtier's body "would seem to increase its height and volume" when undertaking such elevated movements, Franko notes, such jumps risked association with not only agitation and madness, in the sense of lack of measure, but also "the physical inflation of vanity or vainglory."[16] Danced by a dwarf, such choreographies would have connoted over-reaching in an even more obvious fashion, since the performer's shorter stature would visually have exaggerated his efforts to achieve vertical elevation via physical exertion. Such avant-garde choreographies danced by a member of the queen's household looked forward to Marie's own entrance. Her tour of the room as leader of the *grand ballet*'s female troupe, however, would have exhibited probity through grave, measured, and intra-mimetic walking steps. Like her dwarf, the queen would likely have been physically diminuitive in relation to the average male courtier, then, but her kinetic restriction to a primarily horizontal plane, contrasted with this dwarf's allegedly vicious affectation and over-reaching, signalled Marie's humble, virtuous conformity to a noble status that was divinely given and which appeared as grace.[17] In these ways, this production diverted its audience with daring agility as well as histrionic glances and gestures, while simultaneously placing the court's elite female dancers, led by the queen, at a moral distance from the demeaning connotations such burlesque comportments indicated.

Following the dwarf's entry, genuflections enacted by the duc de Vendôme dressed "en fille" [as a girl] performed a similar function. From the letter archived in Peiresc's papers, it seems that after the dwarf left the hall and immediately before the queen and princesses appeared, César de Vendôme, the king's eldest natural son by his late mistress Gabrielle d'Estrées, entered the playing space and, while cross-dressed, performed a reverence honouring his father. Franko has persuasively argued that all-male burlesque ballet of 1620s and

1630s provided a sanctioned forum through which disaffected nobles commented satirically on their diminished power under an increasingly absolutist monarchy.[18] Cross-dressing – whether of race, class, or gender – was a frequent means of enacting particularly pointed political satire of this kind; a noble dancer's feminized appearance on stage, for example, might figure his economic and political disempowerment before the king.[19] Franko's work does not trace such burlesque elements prior to ballets at the court of Louis XIII, but I read César de Vendôme's appearance in the 1605 *ballet de la reine* costumed "en fille" as an earlier instance of such *travesti* roles and their politically satiric function. Marie's 1602 *Ballet of the Sixteen Virtues*, discussed in chapter 1, had already symbolically assimilated and incorporated Vendôme, along with any political threat he may have posed to her authority as royal mother, by presenting him in the guise of Cupid walking before the queen as Venus. Three years later, Marie's ballet for carnival 1605 similarly honoured while nonetheless containing Vendôme, for in this production, too, he preceded Marie infantalized through his appearance: in this case not as the youthful Cupid but via a costume the gender of which returned Vendôme to the skirts he had left behind, along with childhood, after having been breeched several years earlier. On the one hand, Vendôme's appearance commented ironically on his own displacement within France's patrilineal dynastic system by his half-brother the future Louis XIII. At the same time, his extra-mimetic burlesquing of femininity, like the leaps and gestures enacted by Marie's dwarf prior to Vendôme's entry, helped to highlight through contrast the intra-mimetic grace claimed by this production's female troupe led by the queen. When Marie and her troupe entered the playing space after Vendôme, they literally followed in his footsteps by addressing the king in a salute, before proceeding to their figured dances. Vendôme's *travesti* role engaged exaggeratedly extra-mimetic qualities, thereby commenting ironically on his inferior status as the king's merely "natural," i.e., bastard, son. By contrast, the queen's own grave and solemn comportment and her intra-mimetic walking steps signalled a natural body perfected by grace. In this way the structuring of this ballet's entries, together with their choreographies, once again made use of non-verbal forms of embodied communication to promote Marie's legitimacy as the king's legal consort.

With this production's final entry or coda, such contrasts between performers whose postures and movements signalled grace and those whose comportments embodied its opposite became even more explicit. Contradictions among contemporary accounts make it difficult to reconstruct what precisely took place during this final entry. By reading extant sources side by side and thereby partially reconciling discrepancies between them, however, it is possible to devise a fairly reliable outline of the on-stage action and begin analysing its aesthetic and political implications.

According to the account of the queen's ballet archived in Peiresc's collected papers, once the queen and princesses had finished their dancing the audience heard at the door of the hall a sounding of trumpets, oboes, and drums: "enfin comme la Reine eut achevé de danser on entendit douze trompettes à la porte de la salle autant dhaubois et tambours." The king, not knowing what it was – "le Roy ne sçachent que s'estoyt" – placed the queen in her seat and dismissed the princesses who had danced with her, after which the duc de Nevers, having previously placed himself in a corner, came forward mounted on a *bidet* (a small, squat horse or pony) decorated with *clinquant*. Arriving at the centre of the room, Nevers played a lute passed to him by a monkey who served him as lackey. Next, there appeared on stage a number of camels with riders in exotic guise. The same letter found in Peiresc's *registres* mentions seven camels mounted by seven Turks; another French contemporary, Jacques Nompar, duc de La Force, describes how at the end of the queen's "magnificent" ballet two big camels entered with two "savages" on top, the trumpets marching before them ["deux grands chameaux avec deux sauvages dessus, les trompettes merchant devant eux"];[20] *Le romant des chevaliers de Thrace*, printed that year, states that the "savages" riding these two camels were a "Tartar" and a dwarf accompanied by "dix esclaves Turcs sonnans du haut bois" [ten Turkish slaves sounding oboes] and wearing golden chains at their necks, arms, and legs, together with eight well-dressed "Moors."[21] After entering the playing space, the full entourage – the camels and their "savage" riders, accompanied by "Moors" and "Turks" – got down on their knees before the king.[22]

Extant sources do not clarify whether these figures were actual foreigners or French performers wearing exotic costumes. A half century later during the reign of Louis XIV, the French crown would spend considerable sums on "real and figurative *esclaves turcs*," including individuals chosen to man a model flotilla used for pleasure cruises on the Grand Canal at Versailles.[23] Converted "Turks," too, were present at the court of Henri IV: Marie de Médicis herself had brought with her to France one Turkish captive, Madeleine Vernaccini, dite "Médicis," as one of her women of the queen's chamber, and continued to recruit potential converts with help from Savary de Brèves, Henri IV's ambassador to the Sublime Porte.[24] For the 1610 *Ballet de Monseigneur le duc de Vendôme*, though, it was not actual foreigners but European musicians wearing turbans and "masques basanés" (masks designed to represent their skin as dark) who performed as Turkish slaves.[25] During Marie's 1605 *ballet de la reine* the on-stage camels, too, may have been personated by French performers: Louis Battifol, who seems to have consulted François-Antoine Jolly's eighteenth-century transcription of the letter found among Peiresc's *registres*, assumes as much when describing their riders, who were mounted "on ne sait comment" [one knows not how].[26] Live camels could also be found in Paris at this time, however: the dauphin kept one prior to Henri IV's death, and in September 1604 Charles de Nevers was reported in court circles to have acquired several,[27] perhaps with the aim of building a menagerie to showcase his own dynastic ambitions (to be discussed below). Live camels that got down on their knees accompanied by "Turks" had previously appeared in at least one European court festivity, moreover: during a 1596 tournament in Stuttgart, the masquerade company led by duke Friedrich featured "five camels, each led by two lackeys in Turkish costume," and "[w]hile parading, the camels went down on their knees at the ladies' stand," after which "they were tethered out of sight to avoid frightening the horses."[28] Requiring restraint and capable of disturbing other creatures, these camels must have been real animals, even if the "Turks" who accompanied them on this occasion were court lackeys dressed *à la turque* rather than actual denizens from Ottoman territories. Describing Marie's 1605 ballet, *Le romant des chevaliers de Thrace* notes that the dwarf who kneeled at the king's feet had descended from a camel "qui s'agenouilla, *ayant esté ainsi dressé*" [who got down on its knees, *having thus been trained* (emphasis mine)].[29] The entry's exotic figures, therefore, seem to have been a mix of humans personated by European performers and actual animals from foreign locations.

After one of this entry's camels had performed its version of the courtly reverence, according to *Le romant*, the dwarf who had ridden it into the hall delivered a letter to Henri IV and then took from a basket carried in this same camel's mouth a cartel (a scroll on which was written a challenge to mock battle) for distribution to the princes and lords in the ballet's audience. This cartel defiantly challenged these spectators to participate, as armed knights, in a martial entertainment that would take place later that carnival season.[30] The audience's uproarious outburst in response to this entourage seems to have scuttled the troupe's original plan to deliver an additional spoken harangue, however: according to our letter writer, the entry's performers hearing drums, oboes, violins, lutes and other instruments making "un bruit, un tintamarre" [a great discordant din], and "voiant que les dames pissoient soubs elles et que la plupart des gentilhommes estoient disposés à couchier le balet de rire" [seeing that the ladies pissed themselves and that the majority of gentlemen were disposed to shit with laughter over the ballet], became so abashed that they soon wearied of their dance and found themselves unable to utter their "dict."[31] After their ridiculous "cinq pas," the entry's fictional entourage exited the room "bien mocqués et honteus" [well mocked and ashamed]. According to our letter writer, these "bestes" [beasts] sought to save at least partial face by departing in order to write out their planned speech addressing Henri IV; meanwhile, though, the ballet's other performers left in their coaches for the Arsenal, where the evening's second performance would take place, while the princes among the Louvre audience initiated the *bal* or social dancing that lasted until the king declared his departure from the Louvre with his retinue for the ballet's next performance venue.

When the ballet's final entry devolved to confusion, the audience's scornful laughter seems to have prompted, and have been prompted by, the strangers' failure to enact the complex codes and gestures that signified early modern civility. During the Renaissance and Baroque eras, royal courts became crucial sites for the production and reproduction of a noble class that increasingly defined itself in terms of excellence in not only arms but also letters.[32] Nobility remained rooted in birth, but virtue became increasingly important as well. Virtue, to be visible, required enactment, meaning that nobles, to demonstrate their allegedly innate status, sought multiple occasions through which to practice not only the arts of war but also the courtly arts of rhetoric, music, and dance, as well as to reveal their lettered taste and judgment through appreciation for and patronage of skilled professional artists. When visitors from the "imagined geographies" of the Ottoman empire arrived on the French court stage at the end of Marie's 1605 ballet, therefore, their failure to mimic the noble courtier's capacities with respect to military prowess but also music, dance, and verbal eloquence only confirmed their baseness.[33]

If the "highest souls" were made by God "in the image of the harmonious heavens," a particularly effective way to perform one's own noble perfection was through demonstrable appreciation of excellence in music, which in humanist thought enjoyed "a special place as the worldly manifestation of divine order."[34] Pierre Matthieu's praise for Marie de Médicis in his description of her 1600 entry at Lyon deploys just such notions when referencing her love of music as befitting such a magnanimous and "well born" soul.[35] Kings, too, demonstrated virtue by displaying musical appreciation: according to Ronsard's late sixteenth-century preface to the *Livre de meslanges*, for example, "all the most worthy persons of past centuries, whether monarchs, kings, philosophers, governors of provinces, or captains of renown, felt themselves especially gripped by the love of music … so that music has always been the sign and the mark of those who have shown themselves virtuous, magnanimous, and truly born to have nothing of the common herd about them."[36] During the queen's ballet for carnival 1605, as noted in chapter 2, Marie de Médicis and Henri IV seated themselves for performances of virtuosic female song. In so doing, they modelled for the entire Louvre audience such noble appreciation for musical excellence. The response to music by the troupe from Ottoman lands in the ballet's coda differed wildly from that of the royal couple, however, for rather than demonstrating appreciation for the soundings of royal lutes, violins, and trumpets, these camels and their riders seem to have produced their own discordant din.[37] In the sixteenth and early seventeenth centuries, powerful Ottoman military forces were especially known for their initial assaults, during which they made "a fearful impact upon their enemy to the blare of drums, tambourines, trumpets, and diverse other instruments."[38] Our letter writer metaphorically turns such strategies against the ballet's on-stage "Turks" and their companions, though, for in this ballet entry the forces unbalanced by musical soundings were not Christian soldiers confronted by menacing Muslim armies but *esclaves turcs* and other figures associated with Ottoman territories. Adding to this fantasy reversal, our letter writer registers confusion with regard to whether it was the "savage" riders or their exotic mounts who made the "cinq pas" and "tintamarre" on this occasion. Scholars working in animal studies have traced how the "human-animal divide … produce[s] and maintain[s] racial and other forms of cultural difference"; during the colonial period in particular, "representations of similarity" attempted to "link subaltern groups to animals and thereby dehumanize them."[39] Such mechanisms in the ballet's final entry were enhanced by casting a dwarf as one of the camel's riders, for as Yi-Fu Tuan has shown, early modern dwarfs (such as those who rode camels in this instance) often functioned at courts as "human pets."[40] But even this entry's elegantly dressed "Moors," according to this letter's author, found themselves reduced to the level of beasts whose unseemly vocal outbursts elicited from the French court audience not abject fear but laughter.

In a further revelation of their own closeness to unimproved, bestial nature, the entry's performers failed in the noble arts of dancing and verbal eloquence as well. The letter archived among Peiresc's *registres* likens this group's blundering movements to the male courtier's dance par excellence – the *cinq pas* – but in a highly sardonic vein, since in this instance, the corpus of would-be dancers exhibited movements connoting the opposite of grace, that mysterious kinetic quality reserved solely for God's chosen elite. The discrepancy between the movements this entourage attempted and the comportment it actually achieved signalled the strangers' affectation – affectation being the over-extension of oneself, in the attempt to impress, that according to contemporary civility literature revealed baseness of rank.[41] The audience's laughter at such foolishness seems to have caused these characters to fall short in the noble art of rhetoric, too, since when faced with the spectators' mockery, the coda's troupe became so ashamed ["si honteux"] that they couldn't say a thing ["sans pouvoir jamais dire un mot"]. Soon, we are told, they would be given the chance to save face by putting their "dict" to the king in writing; during the ballet performance itself, however, their only recourse was ignominious exit.

If the ballet's first entry performed by the queen's dwarf threatened an overly virtuosic and overreaching *basse danse*, then, its last entry raised an opposite but equally disturbing possibility: the courtly arts of music, dance, and rhetoric undertaken with no virtue at all. Bookended by this coda with its failed imitations of the decorous self-display deemed proper to royals and high-ranking nobles, on the one hand, and by antic burlesque entries by the queen's dwarf's and the duc de Vendôme, on the other, the *grand ballet* danced by Marie de Médicis, contrasted with what it was not, advanced embodied claims for the queen's own nobility of race.[42] The contemporary idea that certain bloodlines were said to carry an extraordinary propensity towards virtue, granted to them by god and by nature, gained increased purchase in France at this time partly as a way to compensate for the drop in exclusive access to noble privilege caused by the sale of royal offices, as I will explore in the next chapter, but also because of the Bourbon monarchy's continued dependence on the "traditional, charismatic legitimacy" that longstanding noble bloodlines ensured.[43] Marie's 1605 ballet cultivated such "charismatic legitimacy" for the queen through her leadership of the kingdom's highest ranking women in the *grand ballet*, chapter 2 argues, but also by setting in relief her performed nobility of race in that *grand ballet* through burlesque entries, one of which mobilized what might be called proto-Orientalist understandings of regionally specific ethnicity and of religio-cultural difference.

Restoring "the seat of his [Thracian] empire"

More favourable although still stereotyped representations of "Turks" were not unheard of in court ballets and related genres of entertainment from this period. For several centuries, the Ottoman empire had enjoyed vast territories, extensive trade networks, and formidable military capabilities, and this geopolitical reality meant that sustained derision towards the Ottomans and other Islamic powers simply was not possible.[44] This was especially the case in France given the alliance François Ier had entered into with Süleyman the Magnificent, in 1536, as a means of combatting the Holy Roman Emperor Charles V. This alliance had been renewed by subsequent Valois monarchs and, in 1604, by Henri IV himself. In late sixteenth- and seventeenth-century French fiction as a whole, then, including in this period's court entertainments, negative images of the cruel and amorous "Turk" appear alongside more positive views.

In 1541, for example, the Valois court's celebrations of the marriage arranged between François Ier's niece Jeanne d'Albret (Henri IV's mother) and William I, duc de Jülich et de Clèves, included a series of sumptuous entries the last of which featured a group of performers, one of which may have been François Ier himself, "vestuz à la mode des Turcs de vestemens de fin drap d'or" [costumed in the fashion of Turks in habits made from fine gold cloth] with exotic feathers decorating their hair and beards.[45] In this entry, admiration for Ottoman magnificence seems to have trumped more negative stereotypes, perhaps as a way of celebrating the recently achieved Franco-Ottoman alliance. François Ier's son Henri II followed in his father's footsteps not only by renewing the "capitulations" but also by performing in a 1559 carousel as a "Turk."[46] More temporally proximate to Marie de Médicis' 1605 ballet is the depiction of a troupe of Turks in Antoine de Nervèze's verses for a staged combat performed at the court of Henri IV. Trafficking in the "cruel Turk" stereotype, Nervèze's poem begrudgingly admits to the formidable military successes Ottoman armies continued to enjoy; according to this cartel, the fields of Mars are for this troupe of "Turks" beautiful gardens, moistened by the torrents of blood that their weapons make run from the flanks of those so unfortunate as to fight them ["Les campagnes de Mars, qui sont les beaux jardins / Où nous faisons souvent ... / Promener nos valeurs ... / Ne se mouillent james dans les pluyes de sang / Que lors que nostre main les fait couler du flanc / De ceux que leur mal-heur nous presente à la guerre"].[47]

In these entertainments, figures from the Ottoman empire exhibit admirable qualities such as magnificence or valor, but in other instances, they serve as objects of condemnation and derision. The year after the 1453 fall of Constantinople, for example, the "entremets de la Croisade turque" [course of the Turkish crusade] performed at the Burgundian court in Lille as part of the famous "Voeux de Faisan" [Pledge of the Pheasant] banquet featured a performer in the role of "Sainte-Église" [the Holy Church], mounted on a camel led by a man "habilliet en Sarasinois" [in Sarasin costume], complaining of "Turcks et mescreans" ["Turks" and miscreants].[48] Fifty years later, the 1501 banquet organized by Anne of Bretagne to entertain extraordinary ambassadors who had come to Louis XII's court to negotiate the marriage of Philip of Austria's son Charles to Anne and Louis' daughter, Claude of France, featured a mummer costumed "à la turque." Having invited the women of France to dance, and having been refused by each of them, this figure, "triste et despiteux" [saddened and aggrieved], threw his weapon to the floor before leaving the hall, "mal content desdites alyences ... contre luy" [discontented at the alliances against him].[49]

During the second half of the sixteenth century and afterwards, French subjects with proto-nationalist leanings might well have wished to forget the humiliating circumstances that had brought about François Ier's need to ally himself with the Ottoman sultan, rather than against him, as a way of countering the Holy Roman Emperor Charles V. Having been defeated in Pavia and imprisoned in Madrid, François was forced to petition the Ottoman sultan for aid.[50] Most Europeans both Protestant and Catholic viewed the Ottoman empire as a grave threat to Christendom, yet the shame of France's earlier humiliation lived on in the terms of the Franco-Ottoman alliance outlined in the contract that successively re-registered it, since these renewed "capitulations," like the original contract of 1536, were clearly delineated not as a treaty between equal partners but as an 'ahdname (unilateral grant) on the sultan's part.[51] For pragmatic reasons France's formal alliance with the Sublime Porte continued to hold throughout the sixteenth and seventeenth centuries. Throughout this period, though, crusading rhetoric experienced moments of concentrated revival, including via court entertainments. In response to Ottoman expansionism in the mid-1560s, for example, festivities staged during the Bayonne summit in June 1565 sought to strengthen France's relationship with a number of Protestant and Catholic states across Europe in part through "rhetorical demonization of the Turk," as Ellen Welch has argued.[52] Representations of "Turks" in French court entertainments were by no means uniformly negative, then, but they often voiced general resentments towards, and more topical anxieties about, the "Ottoman menace."

This larger pattern within French *divertissements* from the period helps to situate the rather puzzling account describing *esclaves turcs* and other fictional figures from Ottoman-held territories in Marie's 1605 *ballet de la reine*. Eye-witness descriptions of early modern performances are not always trustworthy, and in this case lack of information regarding our letter's author and addressee further vexes such questions of authority.[53] None of the other sources about this performance known to date substantiates this letter's testimony regarding the audience's derisive laughter and its consequence of forcing the entry's performers to bumble their way off stage. The unnamed writer of the 1605 ballet's description clearly attended this performance, however: no second-hand account could be this detailed and include so many unique specifics corroborated by other, reliable sources. Henri IV, moreover, is known to have taken great amusement when other court productions went unexpectedly astray: when pyrotechnics designed for a barriers at court accidentally set the hall on fire, for example, the king responded with great mirth, and in 1609, as chapter 5 will discuss, the king shared with the English ambassador a hearty laugh when recalling how a heated altercation between the Spanish extraordinary ambassador and the Venetian representative during the queen's ballet a week earlier had become so loud that Marie de Médicis herself heard the discourteously raised voices while dancing. Shaming of "Turks" and "Moors" by courtiers during staged entertainments was not without French precedent: witness the previously mentioned rejection of a "Turk" who wished to dance with French court women during the 1501 banquet at the court of Louis XII and Anne de Bretagne. Tensions regarding Ottoman incursions in Europe seem to have fueled negative depictions of "Turks" in subsequent court entertainments, moreover, and at the time of Marie de Médicis' second *ballet de la reine*, such tensions had been revived in

France by the Habsburg-Ottoman war (1593–1606) in which, as Péter Sahin-Toth has shown, many French subjects participated.[54] After 1603, moreover, when the young Ahmed I came to power and the Ottomans found themselves at war with not only the Austrian Habsburgs but also the Persian Safavid dynasty, many European Christians dared to hope that a crusade might have a reasonable chance of success.[55] Might such a confluence of forces have informed the final surprise entry for Marie de Médicis' ballet in which the audience at the Louvre directed derisive laughter at fictional figures from Ottoman territories?

Given what we know about this entry's chief impresario Charles de Nevers, it seems possible, even likely, that this coda's invitation to mock this group was planned rather than merely accidental. We learn of Nevers' involvement in the queen's ballet from the account of this performance archived in Peiresc's papers: according to this letter, as we have seen, the duke himself appeared on stage during this production's final entry. We also know from this same source that after camels had entered the playing space together with a group of "Turks" and "Moors," one of the camels' riders presented a letter to the king as well as a cartel or written challenge to princes and lords in the ballet's audience. According to the duc de la Force, who enclosed a copy of this cartel with the letter to his wife describing the queen's ballet, this text was "un défi de la part de M. de Nevers, pour combattre à la barrière, d'une partie qu'il a faite de quatre tenants, pour recevoir et soutenir contre tous ceux qui viendront" [a challenge from M. de Nevers to fight at the barricade a party that he has made of four defenders that he will receive and support against all those who come].[56] The term "barrière" indicates a stylized combat involving "small-scale chivalric battles between opposing squads of costumed "knights" who were separated by a barricade erected across the performance space."[57] From other sources, we know that a combat at the barricade indeed took place in Paris, on 25 February 1605, and that the troupe Nevers led during this combat styled themselves the "Chevaliers de Thrace" [Knights of Thrace]. *Le romant des chevaliers de Thrace* tells us, in fact, that it was in order to propose this very combat that Nevers designed his entry for the queen's ballet on 23 January.[58]

In 1602, Nevers had travelled to Hungary to engage in military action against the Ottomans by joining one of the troupes in service to the Holy Roman Emperor Ferdinand II. This decision, together with Nevers' spectacular demonstration of courage during that action, at the siege of Buda, "marked him out as an individual prepared to put his enthusiasm [for crusading ideals] into practice."[59] The idea of a crusade is not directly stated in the letter and cartel given out during the final entry for Marie's January 1605 ballet, yet these texts elaborate on the fictional persona Nevers adopted as a knight from Thrace. By calling on Greek and Roman mythology to comment allegorically on his worth as a warrior and courtier, the texts also define Nevers, and his troupe of Thracians, in contradistinction to the fictional Asians and Muslims who had been sent to deliver messages to Henri IV from this troupe in the final entry for the ballet. According to the letter presented to Henri IV by the camel-riding dwarf in this entry, for example, Nevers and his Thracian companions had arrived in France in order humbly to ask Henri IV's permission to challenge at the pike and the sword the bravest knights of his court, since by undertaking this combat they would be able to live up to the advantage the god of war had given to the Thracians by establishing in their lands the seat of his empire ["ils supplient tres-humblement vostre Majesté de leur permettre de deffier au combat de la picque, & de l'espée, les plus braves de voz Chevaliers pour leur faire paroistre que ce n'est sans raison, que le Dieu de la Guerre à [sic] donné c'est advantage aux Thraciens d'establir en leurs terres le siege de son Empire"].[60] In Greek myth, Ares was said to reside in Thrace and served as its patron, and so by designating themselves Thracian knights Nevers and his companions proclaimed a military prowess that inhabitants of Thrace had legendarily enjoyed, as a gift from the gods, since ancient times. In two cartels for this same Thracian troupe, this bellicose aspect of the knights' identity appears prominently, yet these texts also emphasize other qualities that, according to civility literature, were essential to the ideal courtier. The first of these cartels, addressed to the "Palladins de France," explains how these Thracian knights, having been "nourris dans les hazars de Mars" [nourished in the hazards of Mars (the Roman Ares)], have arrived in France in order to show that when armed they know well how to battle. But since Thracians are also brought up in the delights of love ["les delices d'amour"] and serve equally the god of war and the god of love, the cartel further explains, this troupe also seeks opportunities for proving how well they can love and serve women ["aymer & servir les Dames"].[61] The Thracians' second cartel, issued in the voice of Victory for the combat that took place on 25 February 1605, builds on the first when explaining the arrival of performers costumed as Mars and Love. Mars comes with these Thracian warriors to France, this cartel explains, in order to prostrate himself at the feet of Henri IV, the world's greatest military leader, but also so that Henri will take seriously the troupe's memorable valor. Meanwhile Love, who accompanies Mars on this occasion, presents his arrows to the queen, ceding to her rare virtue all honours that he himself receives throughout the world.[62] Contextualizing such motifs, the anonymous narrator of *Le romant des chevaliers de Thrace* notes a discrepancy between the way these Thracian challengers present themselves in their cartels and the way that Thracians are typically depicted. Nevers and his troupe, *Le romant*'s narrator admits, know full well that Love is not at all adored in Thrace, since the bellicose denizens of this region are given only to arms; Mars, their only god, is so firmly associated with this region, in fact, that he himself is called Thracian. Nevers and his companions have decided to give Love as a companion to Mars in order to sweeten the latter's rudeness, however, since in "polite souls" the flames of love always accompany the desire for glory.[63] These texts draw on Greco-Roman mythology, then, to emphasize Nevers' service to both Henri IV and Marie de Médicis, but also to associate Nevers and his companions with an ancient civilization here evoked as the pinnacle of both military prowess and courtly civility.

If our eye-witness account of Nevers' appearance in his own person at the start of the ballet's final surprise entry is accurate, the duke's onstage actions similarly called up the glories of Thrace's Greco-Roman past. According to this document, as we have seen, the duke entered the playing space from a corner of the hall mounted on a *bidet* before playing a lute passed to him by a monkey. This moment in the performance may have figured Nevers as another Orpheus, the lyre-playing Thracian king/priest, but it also drew on the "new model of the ideal warrior prince" derived from Homeric epic. This ideal had arisen in late sixteenth-century France in association with Charles' own father, Louis de Gonzague, as well as with the house of Guise.[64] Uniting qualities of military valor with musical sensibility, this new image of the princely warrior arose partly in response to pressures on the aristocracy that had led to prescriptions of education, particularly musical education, as a way to revive noble prestige. Outlining these aspects of the ideal, Brooks traces this image of musically gifted warrior princes in connection with Catholic grandees who, under the pressures noted above, came to represent themselves as exemplars of military competence but also musical sensibility. In this effort, comparisons to Achilles proved particularly useful, since in a famous moment from Homer's *Iliad* this formidable Greek warrior had played the lyre as a form of respite from the cares of battle. When in 1605 Nevers appeared on the French court stage playing a plucked string instrument in imitation of the ancient lyre, then, he seems to have modelled his on-stage persona in connection with Orpheus but also Achilles, thereby claiming the combined identities of feudal lord and cultivated courtier through which leading Catholic princes in late sixteenth-century France asserted their superior social standing as worthy *nobles de race*.

Comparisons to the Greek warrior Achilles and hence with the legendary victory of the Greeks in the Trojan war would have enhanced the allusion to Nevers' descent from the Paleologues that I read as central to his fictional persona as a Thracian knight. Originally, "Thrace" was a Greek term broadly designating areas north of Thessaly inhabited by indigenous tribes known as Thracians. Geographically, however, ancient Thrace seems also to have included the Balkans, especially the region now called Bulgaria and parts of eastern Serbia, northeastern Greece, the eastern republic of Macedonia, and the Bosphorus and Dardenelles.[65] Ancient Thrace, then, seems to have encompassed the situation of Constantinople/Istanbul but also that of Troy. Prior to its occupations by the Ottomans, Thrace was conquered first by the Franks and then by the Byzantines,[66] while the last Byzantine kings to rule Thrace were Nevers' direct ancestors, the Paleologues. Indeed, thanks to the 1531 marriage of his paternal grandfather Federico Gonzaga to Margherita Paleologus, Nevers asserted a "lineal connection" to this "last dynasty of Eastern Roman Emperors."[67] Sounding a lyre in a ballet entry the fiction of which centred on messages delivered from Thracian knights, Nevers thus fashioned a fictional persona for himself that drew on the mythic stature of Orpheus as Thracian prince and of Achilles as Greek prince, but also the legendary status of ancient Thrace itself as home to Troy, precursor to the western Roman empire, and Byzantium, seat of the eastern Roman empire.

Because of his Paleologue lineage, no doubt, as well as the reputation for crusading zeal that Nevers gained internationally thanks to his stint with the Imperial army against the Ottomans in Hungary in 1602, the duke would soon be approached by a group of Greek Christians requesting his help in founding a military order to liberate, from Ottoman "tyranny," Christians living in the Morea.[68] This specific project did not ultimately materialize, yet beginning in 1613 Nevers would throw himself behind Père Joseph's vision of mounting a new international order of knights known as the *milice chrétienne* dedicated to the delivery of Christians from Ottoman rule.[69] As David Parrott notes, the duke's motives in these instances were certainly pious, yet Nevers' "crusading ambitions were [also] intimately linked with the territorial claims that his Paleologus ancestry would give him over most of the potential reconquests,"[70] since "[e]ven regaining a small part of the Byzantine Empire would open up dazzling prospects to Charles, who could thus lay claim to status and prerogatives as titular emperor of the East."[71]

In keeping with Nevers' pretensions to the Byzantine throne, two printed texts published in the years immediately preceding and following the queen's 1605 ballet sought to convince Henri IV to lead a crusade that would liberate Thrace from the "Infidel." One year following the queen's ballet, the 1606 *Discours parénétique sur les choses turques*, edited by Jean Aimé de Chavigny, proposed the benefit to Christendom should the French king join with other princes to take up common arms in Greece and Thrace, thereby defeating the Ottomans and alleviating the suffering of those enslaved by them.[72] Similarly, an earlier text by Chavigny printed in 1603 predicted that Constantinople, "*la grande cité de Thrace*," would one day be liberated from the "turban" by the king of France who, having chased away Arabs, "Moors," "Turks," and others in order to return the Catholic church to its position of supremacy, would both live up to his name of most Christian king and, by retaking Constantinople, achieve a beautiful and useful location "pour dominer à tout le monde."[73] Messianic, universalist visions of the French king had identified him as the true savior of the East. In one particular version of this claim, the prophet Daniel's vision of four great empires came to support a reading of history in which the Assyrians, Medes, Persians, Macedonians, and Byzantine Greeks would ultimately give way to the last great emperor: the king of France.[74] This idea of *translatio imperii a Græcis in Francos* provided one means through which Valois and Bourbon kings of France could attempt to rival, discursively at least, the prestige enjoyed by the Habsburgs thanks to their monopoly on the position of Holy Roman Emperor.[75] When printed texts in the years closely preceding and following the queen's 1605 ballet urged Henri IV to join in a crusade against the Ottomans, they called up such messianic visions. So, more loosely, did the final entry to Marie's ballet in which figures from Greco-Roman and Christian Thrace acknowledged the French king's greatness while simultaneously hinting that Henri IV, in recognition of this loyal service, should join with the true, lineal descendant of the Paleologues to retake his lost homeland for the good of all Christendom.[76]

The Thracian knights' letter presented to the king during Marie's ballet alludes to this hoped-for alliance when it explains why this troupe has sent a group of messengers – the dwarf and "Tartar" on camels, the "Moors," and the "Turks" – to petition Henri IV on the Thracians' behalf. Since Mars has taken on mortal guise as the French king himself, the letter states, these knights dare not show themselves until they have won from Henri the opportunity to prove themselves in mock battle as worthy of this god's gaze. Knowing that no other court could afford them a better opportunity for acquiring glory, the Thracians humbly request, through their vassal messengers, the king's permission to offer sacrifices to Mars during the stylized combat to come.[77] "Give us the field and the day," this letter continues, "and look at the knights of your court with those eyes through which you were accustomed to animate their courage in combat, so that each one will run to arms without excuse or else show himself unworthy of your generous inspirations and of the inimitable examples of your valor" ["Nous la supplions aussi nous donner le camp & le jour, & regarder les Chevaliers de vostre Cour de ces yeux dequoy vous avez accoustumé d'animer leurs courages au combat, afin que chacun coure aux armes sans excuse, ou se monster indigne de vos genereuses inspirations, & des inimitables exemples de vostre valeur"].[78] This passage emphasizes the king's authority as both model for the combatants and material sponsor of the barriers: Henri IV has not only inspired the knights of Thrace to challenge his courtiers but will also fulfil the role of patron to them, since it is he who will determine the date for the event ("the day") and provide the "field." Most obviously, this field was the Salle du Bourbon that on 25 February 1605 would be transformed into the performance space for the combat at the barricade. On another level, though, this text together with Nevers' self-designation as leader of the Thracian troupe hints that the field of battle in question should be the Balkans or the Levant, with Henri IV offering material as well as ideological support for the duke's effort to retake the ancient seat of his Paleologue forebearers. Rather than allying with "Moors," "Tartars," and Turkish slaves, whose attempts at civility this ballet's entry showed could never amount to more than ridiculous affectation, the king of France would be much better off joining forces with Nevers, who, thanks to Henri's help, would finally succeed in restoring Thrace to the civil and military greatness it had formerly exhibited under first Greco-Roman and then Byzantine Christian rule.

This message reflected Nevers' own dynastic pretensions, I have suggested, but it was also perfectly congruent with the underlying policy goals that had informed Clement VIII's decision to accept Henri IV's reconciliation with Rome, in 1595, and to annul the king's first marriage, in 1599, so that Henri could wed Clement's niece, Marie de Médicis. As Tadhg Ó hAnnracháin has shown, throughout the Clementine pontificate "an integral part of papal policy as spiritual leader of the Republica Christiana" involved "assist[ing] and participat[ing] in the Christian struggle against Islam, with particular reference to the Ottoman empire."[79] Having accepted Henri IV's conversion to Catholicism, and having paved the way for his marriage to the devoutly Catholic Marie de Médicis, Rome hoped that this first Bourbon king of France would break with his Valois predecessors by agreeing to join the Catholic rulers of Italy and Spain in a crusade to retake Ottoman territory.[80] After 1603, when the young Ahmed I became sultan and entered into a costly military conflict with the Persian empire, papal hopes that a league of Christian rulers might finally unite in a crusade received an important boost.[81] Just one week following Marie's 1605 *ballet de la reine*, the new papal nuncio to France, Maffeo Barberini, conveyed such hopes in his first royal audience, urging France's involvement in a league of Christian princes that would join together in support of Catholics and potential converts to Catholicism in Hungary and Thrace.[82] The nuncio also sought to impress on Henri IV his duty as "Most Christian King" to support the Spanish king Philip III's naval efforts against a "Turkish infidel" weakened by its war against the Safavid dynasty's forces in Persia and by an alleged "lack of obedience" on the part of Ottoman military forces; this was a golden opportunity, Barberini stressed, for liberating Christians from "Turkish tyranny."[83]

As Clement VIII together with popes before and after him knew well, "the perceived best interests of individual states was, almost invariably, the strongest factor in determining the foreign policy pursued. At times this could cut directly across papal ambitions."[84] To combat this tendency, Ó hAnnracháin explains, Rome "attempt[ed] to harness and channel dynastic ambition towards the perceived interest of the church in a cognate fashion to its attempts to inflect the noble martial culture of Europe towards war on behalf of religion."[85] In relation to such diplomatic efforts by the Holy See, Nevers' ancestral ties to the Paleologues could prove highly useful, since the dynastic ambitions this lineage prompted, when presented as consonant with Henri IV's own, emphasized the very message that Clement VIII wanted to convey: the benefits to the Bourbon monarchy of concerted military action against the Ottoman empire.

Like other early modern rulers, of course, the king of France had to balance religious commitments against other state interests; in Henri IV's particular case, this calculation included awareness not only of the economic advantages gained from France's status as a privileged trading partner with the Ottomans, whose networks extended throughout the Mediterranean and Balkan regions as well as into Russia and the Far East, but also of the benefits of Ottoman challenges to Habsburg domination on the Italian peninsula and elsewhere.[86] At this time Habsburg ambition remained France's greatest challenge in the international arena, and because ongoing Ottoman military action against the Austrian Habsburgs in Hungary helped to reduce Spanish threats to France, even a weakened Ottoman ally could not be dispensed with. In February 1603, therefore, Henri IV refused to receive an embassy from the Persian shah Abbas I the Great concerning an alliance against the Ottomans,[87] and instead in 1604 formally renewed his kingdom's commitment to the Franco-Ottoman alliance initiated by François Ier.[88] Because the Ottomans were struggling politically and militarily at this time, however, and because England under James I was now pursuing its own peace with Spain (to be discussed in chapter 5), France found itself having to support the United Provinces in their war against the Habsburgs without the help England had formerly provided. In the weeks leading up to Marie de Médicis' January 1605 ballet, in fact, Henri IV seems to have been actively flirting with deploying official French regiments in Flanders in support of Protestant "rebels." The possibility of outright action against the Habsburgs sparked a vigorous pamphlet debate in Paris and became a topic of heated discussion among diplomatic circles.[89] Henri's threat to move against the archdukes in the Spanish Netherlands gained further traction through the kind of unity showcased before foreign ambassadors through court entertainments such as Marie's January 1605 ballet which, as chapter 2 has shown, featured displays of intimacy between the monarchy and France's most prominent grands both Protestant and Catholic. And yet Charles de Nevers' own contributions to the queen's ballet in its final, surprise entry partially undercut such messages. Rather than joining the war in Flanders against Spain and the archdukes, Henri IV would be better off forging an "imperial" alliance with the living descendant of the Paleologues, a would-be emperor in his own right whose valor and civility, joined with Henri IV's own, could finally defeat the "Ottoman menace."

Collaboration ... and Contestation

As a duke within France, Nevers owed juridical allegiance to the French king. As a Gonzaga, however, he belonged to one of early modern

Europe's most prestigious and long-standing dynasties, currently ruling in Mantua and Montferrat, and as head of this ducal line's cadet branch Nevers enjoyed sovereign status in his own right – a ranking that within France gave him the title of *prince étranger*.[90] As a Gonzaga, moreover, Nevers claimed descent from the Paleologues, and in this last respect entertained dynastic and territorial aspirations that met and arguably exceeded Henri IV's own. Giving voice to these extraordinary ambitions, Nevers presented himself during the queen's January 1605 ballet and the combat that followed as a knight from Thrace, a region in Asia Minor formerly controlled by the Paleologues in their capacity as the last emperors of Byzantium. This fiction of fearsome yet civilized Thracian warriors seeking to prove themselves before the great warrior Henri IV flattered the French king, but it also hinted that the potential alliance Nevers offered him was a military one designed to take back a region previously ruled by the Franks and Byzantines. When in 1604 Henri IV had renewed his kingdom's commitment to the Franco-Ottoman alliance, this action proved unpopular with many French subjects both Protestant and Catholic. But it must have been especially frustrating for Nevers, whose possible standing as emperor of the East by right of inheritance would be greatly aided by a successful crusade uniting the *Republica Christiana* against the Ottomans. By mounting an unexpected final entry for the French queen's 1605 ballet, therefore, Nevers quite literally staged an implied critique of Henri IV's policy with respect to the Franco-Ottoman alliance, one that was veiled enough to be tactful yet hinted at broadly enough to hit its mark.[91] On one level, anti-Ottoman rhetoric in this instance undermined the king's interests. On another level, though, it may have served those interests: after all, the Bourbon monarchy at this time and in the future would need to avoid overtly refusing Rome's urgings regarding the Ottomans. While the crown would never commit to actually endangering the Franco-Ottoman alliance and the check to Habsburg dominance it provided, then, hints in public that someday France might reverse its policies towards the "Turk" may well have served Bourbon purposes.

This reading of the ballet's final entry has thus far begged the question of Marie de Médicis' own involvement in, and support for, the crusading rhetoric Nevers' entry for her ballet put in motion. *Le romant des chevaliers de Thrace* ascribes to Nevers and several male companions, without explicitly mentioning the queen's involvement, the design to initiate the February 1605 combat via this coda to Marie's production.[92] As we have seen, the sound of martial instruments at the end of Marie's *grand ballet* seems to have caught Henri IV off guard. According to the eye-witness spectator at the Louvre whose description of the ballet is archived in Peiresc's *registres*, "when the queen had finished dancing, one heard twelve trumpets at the door of the room [and] as many oboes and drums, and the king *not knowing what it was*, seated the queen ... and ... behold Monsieur de Nevers enters the room ..." (emphasis mine). Did this final entry at the end of Marie's ballet, with its anti-Ottoman messages, also come as a surprise to the queen? At present we lack sufficient evidence to answer this question decisively. But while the extent to which Marie de Médicis took part in planning the final entry for her own ballet remains unclear, we can begin to ascertain the ways the entry's inclusion in her production laid the groundwork for the queen's alliance with Nevers, an alliance aligned with not only the queen's own commitments to international Catholicism but also the larger representational program, undertaken by the ballet as a whole, to promote Marie as the king's worthy political partner.

Queens' ballets, this book's previous chapters have shown, functioned as prestigious symbolic spaces over which their chief patron-performer presided, and Marie's choice of high-ranking performers made use of this space to help build a network of clients who could strengthen her own political position. When arranging rehearsals for this particular ballet, for example, as we have seen in chapter 2, Marie had personally invited to dance alongside her a princess of the Mayenne clan. The Mayenne, a cadet branch of the house of Lorraine, were aligned, through double marriage, with the house of Gonzague-Nevers. More specifically, the eldest daughter of the duc de Mayenne, Catherine de Lorraine, was Charles de Nevers' wife. The appearance in Marie's ballet of Catherine's sister Renée de Mayenne, along with the kingdom's other princesses, lent legitimacy to the latter's contested authority as royal consort, I have argued, since by surrounding herself on the French court stage with this woman and other female members of the kingdom's most powerful houses, rather than women of lesser social standing such as Henriette d'Entragues, the new queen secured greater influence for herself within French princely circles more broadly. At the same time, the queen's invitation to this woman constituted a mark of favour towards the entire Guise-Lorraine clan along with their affines the Gonzague-Nevers. With the ballet's final entry featuring the duc de Nevers, then, Marie's production extended to a male prince from this same dynastic grouping the practice of publicly honouring as the queen's particular companions the kingdom's highest-ranking women.

The relationships with members of this group that such actions helped to build underscored Marie's resolutely Catholic credentials, including her commitment to crusading ideals. France's foreign princes, and especially the Mayenne-Gonzague princes, formed a coherent unit characterized by intermarriage but also devotion to international Catholicism.[93] Charles de Nevers' father-in-law Charles de Lorraine-Mayenne, to take just one example, had been one of the main leaders of the Catholic League, and only Mayenne's poor health had precluded him from following in the footsteps of his kinsman, Philippe Emmanuel Lorraine, duc de Mercoeur, who after the League's defeat sought to rescuscitate his reputation through military service in the Imperial army against the Ottomans.[94] When Marie used her 1605 ballet as part of a larger "offensive of charm" meant to woo members of this clan, then, and when Nevers placed himself on her court ballet stage in an entry with strong anti-Ottoman messages, the queen's own commitments to Catholic reform and revival, but also a broader struggle against Islam, came into sharper focus.

Courtly spectacle in Tuscany at the time of Marie's marriage had already fashioned the new queen as an important agent in securing her husband's commitment to a crusade. Celebrations in Florence, for example, took up this theme in two separate entertainments.[95] On the evening of Marie's wedding, the magnificent banquet in the Salone dei Cinquecento at the Palazzo Vecchio had concluded with a *Dialogo di Giunone e Minerva* (Dialogue of Juno and Minerva) in which the two goddesses, after some dispute, agreed to join forces in honour of the new French queen whose child would "conquer the Orient, recover the lost empire, and extend the boundaries of the French kingdom" ["Da te sorga un famoso / domator d'Oriente, che l'impero / perduto acquisti e spieghi il regno augusto"].[96] Three days later, during a festivity performed in the Riccardi Palace garden, the goddess Diana had compared the queen's beauty to that of Aurora, proclaimed that she embodied the (military) virtues of Bellona and Minerva, and predicted that her union with Henri IV would result in "illustrious offspring" whose military victories would "extend the glory of Tuscany and France from north to south, and east to west, while also ... seeking to tame the Ottoman Empire and recover Jerusalem for the Christians."[97]

In France, too, first at the time of her arrival and then again during her regency, Marie was proclaimed in court panegyric as central to Bourbon efforts against the Ottomans. François de Malherbe's "Ode to the Queen," for example, which was delivered aloud in Marie's presence during her 16 November 1600 entry at Aix and circulated more widely in two printings (1601 and 1603), evoked similar imagery when predicting the arrival of a dauphin who would in future win glory for his people by defeating in battle the Ottoman sultan:

> Par vous un Daufin nous va naistre,
> Que vous-mesmes verrez un jour
> De la terre entiere le maistre,
> Ou par armes ou par amour;
> ....
> O combien lors aura de veuves
> La gent qui porte le Turban!
> Que de sang rougira les fleuves
> Qui lavent les pieds du Liban!
> Que le Bosphore en ses deux rives
> Aura de Sultanes captives![98]

[Through you a dauphin is born to us whom you yourself will see one day master of the whole earth through either war or love ... Oh, how many then will be the widows of the people who wear the Turban! Blood will make red the rivers that wash the feet of Lebanon! The Bosphorus in its two banks will have captive Sultans!]

This vision, of course, was never achieved, yet ballet productions organized by Marie during her regency continued to mobilize similar tropes. The 1615 *Ballet du Triomphe de Minerve* (also known as the *Ballet de Madame*), which celebrated the double Bourbon-Habsburg marriage arranged by Marie and her advisors, for example, included printed verses that prophesied Louis XIII's victory in the Levant and his role in ensuring "la ruine du turban." Thrown into the air by a group of Sibyls, these verses also predicted the birth of another dauphin (the future Louis XIV) who would wield the French king's scepter over both land and sea.[99] Discussing this and other moments in the 1615 ballet, a lengthy allegorical explication that circulated in print and was dedicated to Marie emphasized at even greater length the Bourbon dynasty's future defeat of the "Turkish tyrant."[100]

Scholars have long noted that Marie's commitment to crusading ideals took concrete shape in 1616, the year she subscribed to the *milice chrétienne* organized by Père Joseph together with Nevers; indeed, her financial donation of 1,200,000 *livres* was by far the largest given to this order.[101] And yet Marie's involvement in Catholic crusading culture far preceded this moment, as Brian Sandberg has recently shown: she undertook efforts to convert Muslims to Catholicism both during Henri IV's lifetime and following his death; she offered sustained patronage to missionary orders, such as the Mercedarians, dedicated to freeing European slaves in Muslim-held territories; in 1606 she in all likelihood supported her cousin Don Giovanni de' Medici's commission of a galleon in Marseille sent to attack the Ottomans in the Eastern Mediterranean; and during the 1600s and 1610s Marie together with members of her household frequently recommended French nobles and other mariners for service on Maltese and Tuscan galleys charged with raids on Muslim ships.[102] Marie as regent would follow in her late husband's footsteps by firmly resisting Rome's pressures to officially register the Council of Trent and revoke the Edict of Nantes. The actions noted above, though, suggest that she would likely have encouraged as more than empty rhetoric the challenge to Franco-Ottoman relations mounted by Charles de Nevers during his entry for her 1605 ballet.

Marie's religious commitments were not the only reason she may have sanctioned – or perhaps approved if only in retrospect – the duke's involvement in her ballet, since elements of that involvement also helped to underscore the mystique of queenly authority rooted in partnership with the king that chapter 2 has argued animated this entertainment as a whole. We have seen how texts delivered during the ballet's final entry lauded the inspiration to love and service provided by the queen as well as the king. Extending this imagery, a second cartel authored on behalf of Nevers and his companions for the February 1605 combat praised the queen's capacity to channel the love of French subjects to Henri IV's heir, the future Louis XIII. In this set of verses, Victory explains to the king how Mars and Love, arriving in the combat's performance space, had of their own volition left the skies in order to honour Henri's successes. Astonished by the sight of Henri IV, Mars prostrates himself and renders his own sword to the French king, for just as the sun inspires warmth, so Henri's looks inspire valor. Meanwhile, Love, who worships the Beauties of the queen, gives up his own weapons to her. Love humbles himself before Marie in this way, Victory asserts, because this god is indebted to her: her rare virtue has wounded the greatest heart of all, that of the king, and in this way the French queen has given Love himself a power beyond sea and land ["L'amour qui de la Reine adore les beautez, / Luy prese[n]te ses traits, da[n]s le Ciel redoutez, / Et luy cede l'hon[n]eur qu'il avoit par le mo[n]de: / Car sa rare vertu, qui vous a peu charmer, / Blessant un coeur plus grand que la terre & la mer, / Rend son pouvoir plus grand que la terre & que l'onde"].[103] Two verse texts sung during the 1605 combat by La Renommée (the goddess Fame) go further by crediting Marie's success at winning not only the king's love but also that of his loyal subjects. In one of these poems, addressed to court ladies ["Aux Dames"], Fame asserts that Mars is captivated by the beautiful women of Henri IV's court and above all by that chaste Cypris (Venus) who has captured all of France.[104] Then, in a another song addressed directly to the queen, Fame clarifies that by means of this affective victory Marie has ensured not only the kingdom's internal stability but also its eventual expansion outward, in imperial fashion: because Marie has captured the soul of the indomitable warrior Henri IV, Mars can do no better than to worship Marie, the greatest queen who lives ["Mars qui defere le laurier / A cest indomptable Guerrier / Dont vous tenez l'ame captive / Venant ce grand Prince honorer / Ne peut mieux faire qu'adorer / La plus grande Royne qui vive"]. Addressing Marie as princess of Florence ["Princesse, honneur des Florentins"] but also as the ornament of France ["L'ornement de toute la France"], Fame tells the queen that her "happiness goes hand in hand with his courage" ["vostre bon-heur / Marche à l'esgal de sa vaillance"], for if this generous prince through his valorous exploits gathers the sweet fruit of his palms, she "make[s] taste the sweetness of a legitimate successor by whom storms are calmed" ["Vous faictes gouster la douceur / D'un legitime Successeur, / Par qui les orages sont calmes"].[105] French subjects thus owe their kingdom's internal peace not only to the king's warrior greatness but also to Marie's virtuous fecundity. The happy impact of the royal marriage also reaches further, however. Thanks to Marie's divine perfections, Fame sings, all the great hearts of war – i.e., the princes and lords who perform in this combat – will until their dying days assist her dauphin in the conquest of the earth ["Au Ciel de vos perfections / S'embrazent les affections / De tous les grands coeurs de la guerre, / Qui jusqu'à leur derniere fin / Assisteront vostre Dauphin / En la conqueste de la Terre"].[106] Having won the love of not only the king but also his warrior grands, Marie will go on to channel such affections towards the dauphin. In the present moment, her influence helps to maintain the peace at home that Henri IV has achieved. In the future, though, her capacity to attract devotion to Henri's heir will secure Bourbon dynastic continuity, and with it France's glorious reach outward so as to achieve, under the future Louis XIII, world domination.[107]

Thanks to Nevers' contributions to the occasion of Marie's ballet, which initiated this combat and its texts, the Bourbon monarchy therefore gained another rhetorical platform for its own discursive legitimation. In this textual rhetoric, moreover, Marie's political contributions as Henri IV's wife and the dauphin's mother received decisively positive emphasis. As I will now explore, however, the costs to the regime included Nevers' access to a highly prominent platform from which to agitate for forms of recognition within France and internationally that could end up fostering, rather than containing, his potentially dangerous independence.

Although printed sources lauding the duke's heroic actions in Hungary squarely located the motivation behind his trip as a desire for glory in service to Christianity, Péter Sahin-Toth has shown, Henri IV and his advisors were less firmly convinced, for although the king seems to have sanctioned Nevers' travel to London and Holland, and possibly his plans for military action in Hungary, the French government's discovery of the Biron conspiracy that year seems to have made Henri think better of this: in July 1602, according to Villeroy, the king now wished that Nevers would return to France, presumably so that he could keep a closer eye on him.[108] Diplomatic correspondence reveals no formal recall, but does show that after the duke was wounded at Buda, Henri IV and his counselors feared that news of his injury would draw Ottoman attention to Nevers' engagement in the Imperial camp.[109] After Nevers returned to convalesce in France, moreover, he continued negotiating with the Imperial government for a return to the Hungarian front. A March 1603 missive from Henri IV to the French ambassador at the Sublime Porte, Savary de Brèves, reveals that while the king intended to do everything he could to retain the duke in France so as not to cause further diplomatic difficulties with the Porte, Henri could not forbid this action outright, presumably because Nevers' independent status as a *prince étranger* meant that any outright command to this effect would likely cause its own significant political difficulties.[110]

Ultimately Nevers relinquished his hopes of returning to Hungary, even rejecting the duc de Bouillon's efforts in Strasbourg to recruit him to revolt against Henri IV,[111] but in return he seems to have expected rewards that would ensure ceremonial recognition of his rank, about which he was known to be notoriously sensitive. One such reward may have been appointment to the royal *Ordre de Saint-Esprit* or Order of the Holy Spirit. Founded by Henri III, the *Saint-Esprit* was used by the king of France as an outward demonstration of his religious credentials but also to draw prominent Catholic nobles and princes in greater loyalty to the crown.[112] Recruitment to this royal order was arguably "the ultimate accolade" for French courtiers within the period's lively "commerce in the currency of courtly honour."[113] Knights were appointed to the order each January, and in November 1604, the papal nuncio's secretary Agostino Gioioso reports, talks had begun regarding Henri IV's impending choice of new appointees. When Henri IV retired to Saint-Germain for his private devotions just days before the order's annual induction was to take place, however, he had not yet officially named its new members, and according to Gioioso, this (in)action had left many malcontented courtiers ("qua malcontenti") still hoping to be chosen for this honour.[114] Henri IV's retirement to Saint-Germain asserted his unquestioned prerogatives as sovereign by emphasizing the fact that access to the *Saint-Esprit* and its ceremonial honours could be achieved through him alone, on his personal timeline, as dictated by his personal (and privileged) spiritual state. For Nevers, a *prince étranger* and hence sovereign in his own right, this must have rankled, especially since the very first noble inducted to the *Saint-Esprit* had been his father, Louis de Gonzague.[115] As chief knight of this order, Louis enjoyed a ranking above that of all other members. This ceremonial honour, David Parrott indicates, was useful to Louis' son Charles in the latter's own assertions of courtly status, helping him to claim precedence over members of the house of Guise, for example.[116] Even more useful, though, would have been Charles' *own* appointment to this order.[117] "Other nobles," Brian Sandberg has noted, "carefully conserved their letters and commissions related to their crusading experiences to use as proofs for their induction into the Order of the Holy Spirit."[118] Was Nevers one of the "malcontents" to whom the nuncio's secretary referred approximately one month prior to the queen's January 1605 ballet? If so, the duke's fictional request for his king's support in reviving the glories of Greco-Roman and Christian Thrace, by reminding both French courtiers and foreign ambassadors in the ballet's audience of Nevers' own crusading credentials in Hungary, may have sent a not so subtle message that he, like his father before him, merited greater consideration and reward. Henri IV, shortly after this ballet, would promote the Huguenot duc de Rohan to the office of colonel general of his Swiss guards. After having been reminded by the final entry to the queen's ballet that Catholic grands, too, deserved appeasing, the king may not have appointed Nevers to the *Saint-Esprit* but he did name him colonel general of the light cavalry.[119]

Honourific appointments within France could only partially appease Charles de Nevers' ambitions, however, and the international nature of his claims often posed potential difficulties for the Bourbon regime both at home and abroad. In fall 1604, for example, Nevers had begun actively pressing territorial rights through his mother to the duchies of Clèves and Jülich, should they end up being partitioned after the death without heirs of duc Johann Wilhelm. Nevers' claims posed a threat to Henri's German Protestant allies, and so the king refused his request for letters of introduction to a number of German princes. Henri could perhaps have fostered in Nevers a sense of obligation to the French crown by supporting his actions with respect to Clèves and Jülich; by doing so, though, he would have risked "reinforcing Charles' own sovereign status and independence, thus ensuring that Charles might prove an even less compliant client of France in future."[120]

This potentially dangerous independence was something Marie de Médicis would have to contend with, as regent, since despite her own crusading aspirations she too would need to uphold a guarded approach to the Ottoman alliance, one that was visibly consistent with her late husband's. In 1613, for example, she would refuse Nevers the permission he requested to lead an attack against the "Turks," even though in response the duke would end up joining forces with other princes in a rebellion against the French crown.[121] In 1616, Marie did sign on as the first financial donor to the registry for Nevers' Christian Militia, as noted above; yet as Albert Cremer cautions, this action needs to be understood as part of the arrangement that Richelieu, Marie's chief advisor at the time, brokered with Nevers in exchange for the duke's concessions following the prince de Condé's arrest: Nevers would abandon his fellow rebels, transferring his loyalties back to the crown, and in return Marie would favour his engagements, including the plan for a Christian Militia that Nevers had concocted along with Père Joseph.[122] Like Henri IV before her, then, Marie would need to juggle relationships with powerful grandees, the implications of which involved both collaboration and contestation.

On the one hand, then, the queen's ballet for carnival 1605 along with its unexpected coda worked to stave off disorder and discontent within the kingdom, at least temporarily, by favouring ambitious grands and by gaining, in exchange for that favour, an entourage for the queen that helped to promote the crown's own program supporting her incipient political authority. The queen and her particular ally in this instance, the *prince étranger* Charles de Gonzague, duc de Nevers, registered such claims in part by defining Marie, like Nevers himself, in contradistinction to an entourage of fictional visitors from the Islamic world. Through this fantasy of encounter, the final entry for this queen's ballet mapped images of social and political disorderliness onto "beast-like" foreign bodies. In the process, though, the French royal house's need to surround itself with higher nobility and its aura of mystical authority, in order to achieve a smooth succession, opened new avenues for political contestation.

Overall, this analysis suggests that significant complexities are lost when we continue to assume that court entertainments, including women's court entertainments, served as univocal expressions of royal policy or propaganda. Royal women's ballet at the court of Henri IV, this chapter shows, encompassed actors with competing agendas, some of whom might find ways to insinuate their own messages even when these countered official royal policy. Such contradictory gestures, to the extent that they kept audiences guessing regarding the crown's own stance in the realm of foreign relations, may in the end have served the king's interests. Yet his collusion in promoting such ambiguity, by means of this performance, cannot be claimed with any real certainty. In the end, the possibility of dissident voices remains an open one.

Chapter Four

Eros and "Absolutism"

Marie de Médicis' ballets, I have suggested, offered spaces for royal legitimation but also political contest, sometimes even working at crosspurposes to official Bourbon policy. Nuancing this argument further, the current chapter turns to the queen's final production as dancer, *The Ballet of Diana and her Nymphs* performed in January 1609, alongside the *Ballet de Madame*, performed in April of that same year by Marie's eldest daughter Elisabeth. Engaging contemporary debates regarding virtue, virility, and the racial superiority of noble and royal bloodlines, these ballets in their verse texts as well as casting choices underscored Bourbon dynastic efforts to assure social, political, and moral ascendancy for Henri IV and his consort. In doing so, however, both productions also navigated the serious challenge to royal authority set in motion by Henri IV's last great *amour*: his pursuit of the young Charlotte de Montmorency.

Support for dynastic monarchy in general depended on the notion that royal and noble bloodlines carried an extraordinary propensity towards virtue, granted to them by god and by nature.[1] The Catholic League, arguing that heresy was "a form of derogation that extinguished nobility,"[2] had sought to use Henri IV's confessional waverings as justification for his exclusion from the succession. In response, the king's supporters had championed the principle of inalienable hereditary rights of succession as well as the notion of racially based superiority, on the basis of noble bloodline, on which his claim to the throne rested. Because noble virtue was also frequently associated with virility, especially in the case of kings, royal propaganda supporting Henri's hereditary claims also emphasized his sexual prowess, made evident through his siring of male offspring.[3] But this need to advertise Henri

IV's sexual exploits, combined with the crown's reliance on new robe families and the sale of offices, complicated the Bourbon monarchy's efforts to appropriate for itself the sacred, mystical aura that attended the higher nobility's exclusive assertions of moral elevation. The sale of offices, regularized in late 1604 by a new tax on hereditary office known as the *paulette*, gave late Valois monarchs and their Bourbon successors an important measure of financial and political leverage with respect to the grands by raising much-needed funds for the royal treasury and by fostering loyalty to the crown among the group of families who rose to noble rank through such practices. And yet, the seeming ease with which commoners rapidly secured upward mobility into the noble ranks could be seen to place in question the higher nobility's mystical claims to divinely sanctioned superiority based on longstanding bloodlines and, by extension, the "traditional, charismatic legitimacy" of hereditary monarchy itself.[4] Emphasis on Henri IV's virility caused a related set of problems.[5] The evidence of masculine self-control that Henri IV's prowess on the battlefield provided helped to offset his history of apostacy. So, at one level, did the king's prodigious sexual energies: as Katherine Crawford has noted, Henri IV's ability to produce issue with his various mistresses, particularly during his childless marriage to Queen Marguerite de Valois, provided much-needed evidence for his reproductive capacity, thereby distinguishing his successes from Henri III's spectacular failures in this regard. And yet the king's philandering also posed serious problems, since royal children born to Henri's mistresses muddied efforts to clearly distinguish the true, virtuous royal line from other, illegitimate lines that Henri had sired – thereby resulting in the crown's increased vulnerability to faction and rebellion. Equally problematically, given contemporary notions of racial degeneration through vice, Henri IV's extramarital sexual relationships complicated royalist efforts to craft in connection with his reign the image of virtuous self-control on which the authority of dynastic kingship depended.[6] On one level, the king's *amours* could prove politically advantageous, then. But when these same exploits seemed to threaten the coherence of Henri's claims to political authority on the basis of noble, masculine virtue and its capacity for self-governance as well as governance of the political nation, the king's womanizing became a worrisome political liability.

This chapter traces how the *Ballet of Diana and her Nymphs* and the *Ballet de Madame* confronted such challenges. Drawing on proto-feminist defenses of noblewomen's worth adapted from early modern civility literature, poetic verses for the queen's *Ballet of Diana* insisted on Marie's ordered soul or mind and framed her physical beauty on stage as the visible manifestation of spiritual virtue. At the same time, by harnessing to her embodied personhood the erotic frisson roused by female song in the moments preceding her danced entry, this ballet claimed for Marie an erotic pull capable of wresting the king's amorous attentions away from vice towards the legitimate royal bloodline. As events immediately following this ballet's performance indicate, such attempts to catch the king's heart for the purposes of avoiding racial degeneration through vice proved only partly successful: for while this ballet's verse texts exalted the queen and the high-ranking members of her all-female dance troupe as virtuous beauties capable of reforming even the most dissolute (male) hearts, the king remained stubbornly resistant to such reformative efforts. In the end, Marie's 1609 *Ballet of Diana* failed to contain politically damaging rumours about the king's lack of masculine self-control. But royal women's ballet under her aegis did not give up the fight, for shortly following the queen's *Ballet of Diana*, the *Ballet de Madame*, danced by Henri's six-year-old daughter Elisabeth, revisited tropes and iconographies from her mother's January 1609 production in a new epideictic register, one in which the balance between praise and blame leaned significantly more heavily towards the latter.

**Marie's *Ballet of Diana and her Nymphs*:
The On-stage Action and Its "Directrice Absolue"**

Although we lack printed *recueils* for Marie's other ballet productions, verses for three songs performed during her January 1609 *Ballet of Diana and her Nymphs* circulated in print soon after they had been performed at court, while music for these same songs (adapted for lute accompaniment) appeared in print that same year.[7] Two of these songs – a "Récit de la naiade portée sur un dauphin" ["*Récit* of the Naiad Carried on a Dolphin"] and an "Air: pour le balet de la Reyne, La Renommée au Roy" ["Air: For the Queen's Ballet, [Sung by] Fame to the King"] – have led scholars to deduce that this production featured a naiad or water nymph as well as the goddess Fame. From the third set of verses, entitled "Vers masculins pour la chaisne du mesme balet" ["Masculine verses for the chain of the same ballet"], we also know that this ballet featured a *chaîne* or hay: a dance form made up of interlacing lines and serpentine patterns.[8] All three songs reference Marie's role leading a troupe of women costumed as nymphs of the forest, while the "Récit de la naiade portée sur un dauphin" specifies that these nymphs were accompanied by their goddess Diana.[9] For this reason, scholars and biographers typically refer to this production as *Le ballet de Diane et ses nymphes* [*The Ballet of Diana and her Nymphs*]. (For full transcriptions of this ballet's verses, with English translations, see Appendix 2).

Despite these poetic and musical fragments, as well as numerous contemporary references to this ballet's magnificence, scholars to date have lacked sufficient evidence with which to map this ballet's subject matter and action.[10] Two manuscript letters held in Mantua and recently discovered by Janie Cole, however, offer lengthy eye-witness descriptions of the ballet's first performance on the evening of 31 January 1609. One of these letters, authored by Traiano Guiscardi, secretary to the Mantuan ambassador in France, is addressed to Vincenzo I Gonzaga, duke of Mantua; the other was written by Traiano's wife, Vittoria Dalla Valle Guiscardi, to Vincenzo's wife, Eleonora de' Medici (Marie's sister).[11] From these reports alongside the printed verses mentioned above, it is now possible to outline the first detailed account of what took place on stage.

According to both letters, the ballet's action began when a curtain in the performance space fell to reveal "un gran monte" [a great mountain][12] at the foot of which appeared two "strade" [paths or entrance ways][13] through which entered "12 paggi, sei per banda et un' infinità de' sonatori colle viuole dolcissimamente sonando con habiti pomposi, et tutti di concerto" [twelve pages, six per troupe, and an infinity of players with viols very sweetly playing in magnificent habits and all in harmony].[14] When the violas stopped playing, "Cantò poi la Fama alcuni versi in lodi lode di Sua Maestà et delle ninfe del balletto" [Fame sang some verses in praise of His Majesty and of the nymphs of the ballet].[15] This song was the air for the goddess Fame reproduced in the printed music and *recueil*, with poetic verses written by François de Malherbe. After Fame's entry, eight "ombre" [shades] appeared from the same paths at the base of the mountain from which the pages and viols had entered, and "danzando a due, a due et finalmente tutte insieme fecero un leggiadro balletto" [came dancing two by two and finally all together, making a graceful ballet].[16] After these shades vanished, all of the other performers retired in order to make room for the mountain, now revealed to be a moving set machine. Having advanced nearly to the room's centre, this device opened to reveal a sea in which appeared a dolphin, moving as if on the water. On this dolphin sat a naiad or sea nymph who, "accompagnata da gran numero di voci, et di liuti" [accompanied by a great number of voices, and by lutes], made "una rarissima musica" [a music most rare].[17] After singing her "soavissima melodia" [very sweet melody], which Vittoria Guiscardi notes was "accompagnata da gran moltitudine di musici con i liuti" [accompanied by a great multitude of musicians with the lutes], the nymph then sang alone, accompanying herself on the "ghitarrone" (a term synonymous by this time with the theorbo) "divinissimanente" [most divinely], in Vittoria's words, "leggiadramente" [charmingly, gracefully], according to Traiano's phrasing.[18] This solo song was the "Récit de la naiade portée sur un dauphin" found in the print sources mentioned above. Coming to the end of her *récit*, the naiad with "la sua machina" [her machine] retired, at which point "un bel giardino" [a beautiful garden] revealed itself at the other extremity of the hall.[19] Seated in this garden were "la Reina con l'altre dame del balletto" [the Queen with the other ladies of the ballet], "tutte in habito di ninfe di colore incarnato et celesto con argento, con dardi in mano et con tanta quantità di diamanti che abbagliavano la vista" [all in nymphs' costumes in the colours carnation and sky blue with silver, with arrows in [their] hand[s] and with such a [large] quantity of diamonds that [the dancers] blinded the [audience's] sight].[20] Marie de Médicis stood first and came forward to begin the dancing with "gratia stupenda" [stupendous grace].[21] Next came the other women, two by two. When they rejoined as a group, the women together danced their ballet, which as we have seen from the print sources included a "chaisne" described in "vers masculins." This ballet, Vittoria Guiscardi writes, was "nuovo, bello et ben danzato, et massime da Sua Maestà che ben pareva fra l'altre il sole fra le stelle" [new, beautiful, and well danced, and most of all by Her Majesty who well appeared among the others [like] the sun among the stars]. After this *grand ballet* had thus "riuscì vago et bello" [succeeded, beautiful and charming], the formal dancing ended quite literally with a bang: according to Traiano, the assembly heard several artillery shots, while Vittoria similarly mentions that "si spararono molti pezzi d'artiglieria" [many pieces of artillery were discharged] – most likely loud guns such as arquebuses or muskets. Thereafter, the social dancing began, during which the queen and her companions performed a "brando" or *branle* (a popular courtly dance from the period) partnered by princes and lords from the audience.

As this summary suggests, the Guiscardi letters provide a wealth of valuable new information about this ballet performance; they also emphasize Marie's investment, as this production's primary patron, in ensuring that details of the performance and its on-stage action would be conveyed to her sister Eleonora de' Medici and brother-in-law Vincenzo I Gonzaga at the court of Mantua. Vittoria's letter, addressed to Eleonora, begins by explaining that she had found herself in the audience for Marie's 1609 ballet "thanks to Her Majesty" ["Essendomi ~~hanata~~ trovata al balletto della Reina per gratia di Sua Maestà"]; more baldly, Vittoria's husband Traiano prefaces his detailed description of the ballet in his letter to Vincenzo by stating that "La Reina m'ha *comandato* di dar parte a Vostra Altezza del *suo* balletto" [the queen *commanded* me to share [news] of *her* ballet with Your Highness (emphasis mine)]. This effort on Marie's part to seek out Traiano and Vittoria's presence at the performance so that they could convey its specifics in significant detail suggests her personal investment in those specifics.

Noting a similar level of involvement on Marie's part, Hector de la Ferrière wrote in 1885 that it was she who organized and directed this entertainment ("la reine en était l'organisatrice et la directrice absolue") with "la reine Marguerite" adding an important "esprit inventif."[22] In 1905, though, Charles Merki paraphrased Ferrière incorrectly as having claimed for Marguerite the entire credit for this ballet's organization.[23] From this point forward, scholarly tradition has let stand the claim that Marguerite, rather than Marie, took primary responsibility for directing this ballet as a whole, including its aesthetic and thematic dimensions.[24] This assumption fits with a larger narrative according to which the greatness of late Valois courtly spectacle was evacuated thanks to the brutal coarseness of Henri IV combined with the alleged cultural inexperience of his second wife. On this view, only after Queen Marguerite's 1605 return to Paris could the famous tradition of ballet, inaugurated by her mother Catherine de Médicis, begin to revive.[25] Marguerite's learned refinement and first hand experience with elaborate *divertissements* were indeed assets for the French court, and Marie would no doubt have welcomed her ideas and input. And yet Marie's considerable activity prior to winter 1609, as a performer and organizer of court entertainments, indicates that she would not have *required* help from Henri IV's first wife in order to mount a production of this nature.

French contemporaries, in fact, directly credit Marie, rather than Marguerite, with having invented and organized the *Ballet of Diana and her Nymphs*. Pierre de L'Estoile, for example, writes that "Le samedi 31ᵉ et dernier de ce mois [janvier 1609] *la reine* fit, à Paris, *son* ballet magnifique, dès longtemps *pourpensé par elle et dessiné*" [On Saturday the 31st and last of this month [January 1609] *the queen* made in Paris *her* magnificent ballet *for a long time planned and designed by her* (emphasis mine)]. L'Estoile also writes that this ballet was performed only in two places, at the Arsenal and Queen Marguerite's, and that at the latter, their Majesties found a magnificent and sumptuous collation (a light meal or repast) that their host had made ready for them, complete with marvellously designed miniature fruitseller figures placed on three silver plates made specially for the occasion.[26] In this passage (and indeed throughout his journal), L'Estoile clearly differentiates between Marie de Médicis and Marguerite de Valois by referring to Marie as "the queen" while designating the king's first, cast-off wife as "Queen Marguerite." L'Estoile certainly credits Marguerite for the artfully designed collation at her *hôtel* following the ballet's second performance there (one wonders if it was this passage that prompted Ferrière to suggest that Marguerite lent to this ballet occasion an "esprit inventif"). But it is the reigning queen Marie whom L'Estoile clearly designates as having directed and devised the ballet proper.

Marie de Médicis, therefore, took a direct role in organizing and arranging "suo balletto" (to use the phrasing offered by both L'Estoile and the Guiscardis), not least the dances in which she herself performed. How, though, did the structure of this ballet's on-stage action as outlined in the Guiscardi letters intersect with the iconographies and verbal images found in the three printed verse texts, and to what aesthetic and political ends?

(Dance) Lessons from a Queen: New Bourbon "Methodologies of Authority"

In taking up such questions, it is important to specify the order in which this ballet's songs were performed. Relying on the ballet's *recueil* and Bataille's volume, previous discussions of Marie's *Ballet of Diana and her Nymphs* have positioned the naiad's *récit*, placed first among this ballet's verses and music in these sources, as the first sung text in performance.[27] The Guiscardi letters discussed above clarify, however, that the first words spectators encountered in performance were those of Fame's air, authored by François de Malherbe. Malherbe's poem begins with the goddess Fame announcing her own arrival in France after having broadcast throughout the world her praise for Henri IV's incomparable greatness in peace and war.[28] In keeping with this stanza, McGowan asserts that this ballet's overarching theme was the glorification of Henri IV.[29] By Fame's second stanza, however, her air's focus has already shifted to the ballet's troupe of beautiful nymphs, led by the queen.[30] Not only this air but the verses for this production's two other printed songs, in fact, place primary emphasis on the ballet's chief patron-performer, proclaiming what Marie de Médicis can do for the court of France and for her husband once her merit is duly recognized.[31]

Anticipating the queen's arrival on stage with her troupe, Fame explains in direct address to Henri IV that Diana's nymphs have travelled with her to the court of France because they wish to judge for themselves whether this "miracle des Roys" [miracle of kings] merits the renown that Fame has spread on his behalf. These nymphs "[t]irent un cueur [sic] à leur service" [attract hearts to their service] through their superiority of rank, manifested in "les titres ambitieux" [the ambitious titles] "de leur ayeux" [of their ancestors] and an advantage of bloodline ["sang"] so great that "on ne leur peut faire quitter / Sans estre yssu du parentage / Ou de vous, ou de Jupiter" [no one can make them yield without being of the lineage of you or of Jupiter]. In keeping with the pastoral topos whereby true beauty is found in the woods and forests while false beauty and affectation reign at court, as well as the early modern argument in defence of women's nobility that God places together in women everything in the world that is beautiful, Fame declares that in this troupe of dancing women all the treasures that nature assembles when fashioning bodies have come together without artifice ["Tout ce qu'à façonner un cors / Nature assemble de trésors / Est en elle[s] sans artifice"].[32] Graced with "dignes qualitez" [qualities of rare worth] that only the heavens can provide, these nymphs from the woods and forests prove superior not only socially, via their elevated rank, and aesthetically, via their exceptional beauty, but also morally, through their demandingly virtuous conduct:

> Loin des vaines impressions
> De toutes folles passions
> La vertu leur apprend à vivre:
> Et dans la Cour leur fait des lois
> Que Diane auroit peine à suivre
> Au plus grand silence des bois.

> [Virtue teaches them to live
> Far from the vain impressions
> Of all mad passions:
> And in the Court makes laws for them

That [even] Diana would have difficulty following
In the deepest silence of the woods.]

Having emphasized the dancers' immunity to passion as well as their incomparable beauty and social status, Fame next focuses her encomiastic lens on the queen, who guides them ["Une Reyne, qui les conduit"]. Leading this troupe of nymphs in dance as well as rank, this royal beauty "reluit" [glitters] with "tant de merveilles" [so many marvels] that even the sun who overcomes all things would, if he were sensitive to shame, hide in seeing her ["le soleil qui tout surmonte, / Quand mesme il est plus flamboyant, / S'il estoit sensible à la honte, / Se cacheroit en la voyant"]. Faced with the queen's luminous beauty and the divinely sanctioned superiority it evidences, Fame "la feray tousjours fleurir / Au rang des choses eternelles" [will make her flourish always among the rank of eternal beings] by immortalizing Marie in song: "Tant que mon dos aura des ailes, / Son image aura des autels" [As long as I have wings to fly, so her image, no less than the images of the gods, will have altars (i.e., be worshipped)]. To initiate such universal adoration now and in the future, Henri IV should welcome and exalt these proud beauties who humble themselves by appearing before him. If he does so, they will in turn lend him their favourable judgment ["Grand Roy, faites-leur bon accueil: / Louez leur magnanime orgueil, / Que vous seul aurez fait ployable: / Et vous acquérez sagement, / Afin de me rendre croyable, / La faveur de leur jugement"]. Until now your glorious feats have had envious detractors, Fame sings, but what souls so insolent will dare to doubt my reliability when they see these nymphs' lovely lips telling your greatness with me? ["Jusqu'icy vos faits glorieux / Peuvent avoir des envieux: / Mais quelles âmes si farouches / Ozeront douter de ma foy, / Quand on verra leurs belles bouches / Les raconter avecques moy"]. By duly honouring the queen's preeminence, Henri IV can win his consort's good opinion and that of her closest female companions, such that Fame's praise of him will become believable even to the most savage souls and his glory will spread, justly, to all corners of the world.

According to Fame, it is these women's virtuous souls or minds, in conjunction with their superiority of rank, which makes them eminently worthy of both the king's regard and that of posterity. The dancers led by the queen on this occasion, the duc de La Force reports, included all of the princesses and a number of ladies.[33] Based on the Guiscardi letters, both of which name these eleven women in order from highest to lowest rank, we now know that, of the troupe as a whole, four dancers were princesses, while the remaining seven came from families of well-established noble standing going back at least four generations – an important consideration given the prevailing understanding at this time that "nobility is the more perfect in proportion to length of ancestry."[34] In keeping with such notions, Fame's song draws on what Jeroen Duindam calls the higher nobility's "belief or feigned belief in the physical and moral superiority of their own race ... proven by deeds of their forefathers" and "passed to the descendants through blood and seed."[35] Malherbe, in conjuction with his emphasis on the "ambitious titles" and "advantages" of "blood" these dancers have inherited from their "ancestors," stresses the women's incomparable corporeal beauty. He also emphasizes a consonance between their physical perfection and a moral perfection that reveals itself as light and brightness. Fame, as we have seen, anticipates the sun's shame at the moment of Marie's glittering arrival on stage. Henricus Agrippa's treatise on the nobility of women had argued that female beauty "itself is nothing other than the refulgence of the divine countenance and light which is found in things and shines through a beautiful body."[36] Like Agrippa's defence of women, André Du Chesne's 1605 *Figures mystiques du riche et précieux cabinet des dames* adapts Neoplatonism for the purposes of proto-feminism when it defines women's excellence of soul or mind as the material cause of women's corporeal beauty, and claims that the beauty of a woman's body not only depicts the beauty of her own soul but also participates in the divine spirit when that woman's soul, by perfecting and mastering matter, has rendered that body more receptive to the imprint of divine beauty's quality and force. For Du Chesne, the light of beauty that shines through and surmounts the shades of matter in virtuous women constitutes a ray of spiritual beauty, passing through matter, which encases brilliant light and allows us to discover the immortal.[37]

In keeping with such notions, Fame's song emphasizes qualities of brightness and light in connection with the queen's on-stage appearance and proclaims that such luminous beauty exists hand in hand with Marie's noble beauty of mind or soul – a spiritual beauty that in turn manifests as immunity to eros. The nymphs that the queen leads on stage may allow Love to create through them daily new proofs of his charms ["Elles souffrent bien que l'Amour / Par elles face chaque jour / Nouvelles preuves de ses charmes"], Fame sings, but as Cupid quickly finds out, he possesses no weapons they themselves cannot block ["Mais si tost qu'il les veut toucher, / Il reconnoist qu'il n'a point d'armes / Qu'elles ne facent reboucher"]. This stanza acknowledges the dancers' erotic allure, the fact that their corporeal beauty arouses desire in the less perfected beings among their audience. The nymphs themselves, however, have no trouble fending off the arrows with which Cupid wounds their own admirers: "Et la force de leurs esprits / D'où jamais n'ap[p]roche le vice / Fait encore accroistre leur pris" [And the strength of their minds, where vice never approaches, makes them still more meritorious]. Indeed, virtue has provided "lois" [laws] for these nymphs so exacting, Fame tells us, that even the goddess of chastity herself would find it difficult to uphold their codes of comportment "[a]u plus grand silence des bois" [in the deepest silence of the woods]. As denizens of such forests, these nymphs have situated themselves "[l]oin des vaines impressions / De toutes folles passions" [far from the vain impressions of all mad passions], such that their souls ["âmes"], upholding virtue's rigorous laws, remain free from passion and its sufferings.

The next sung text after Fame's air, according to the Guiscardi letters, was performed by a naiad (or water nymph). This *récit* expands on the connections between noble rank, beauty, and virtue implied by Fame; it emphasizes further the contrast Fame draws between the virtue these nymphs embody and the ballet audience's susceptibility to cupidity; and it fills out, in greater detail, the claims Fame hints at regarding this troupe's capacity to benefit Henri IV and his court.

According to this naiad, the nymphs of this ballet, supremely confident in their own beauty, feel only disdain towards men in the audience ["Les hommes les ayment en vain, / Et la fierté d'estre si belles / Est la cause de tout leur dedain"]. And rightly so, since "le juste orgueil de se voir / Si parfaites dans leur miroir / Endurcit si fort leur courage, / Qu'il faut croire que leur Beauté, / Qui tient vos ames en servage, / Maintient les leurs en liberté" [the just pride of seeing themselves so perfect in their mirrors so greatly strengthens their courage that one must believe their beauty, while holding your souls in servitude, maintains theirs in liberty]. This depiction of the queen and her female companions achieving tranquility and freedom through a beauty that they gaze at proudly, in their own mirrors, recalls the image on Du Chesne's title page (see Figure 4.1), in which a noblewoman wearing a mirror hanging from her waist is framed by the verbal explanation that "Cette Beauté est de Dieu, et ses ornemens sont ornemens de vertu" [this Beauty if from God, and her ornaments are ornaments of virtue]. It also recalls the engraving for the 1604 edition of Pierre Charron's treatise *De la sagesse* in which Wisdom appears as a beautiful woman looking at herself in a mirror (see Figure 4.2). This second title page engraving expresses allegorically

Figure 4.1. Title page, André Du Chesne, *Figures mystiques du riche et précieux cabinet des dames: ou sont represantées au vif tant les beautez, parures, et pompes du corps feminin que les perfections ornemens et atours spirituels de l'âme*. Paris: Chez Toussaintz Du Bray au Palais en la gallérie des Prisonniers, 1605. Folger Shakespeare Library.

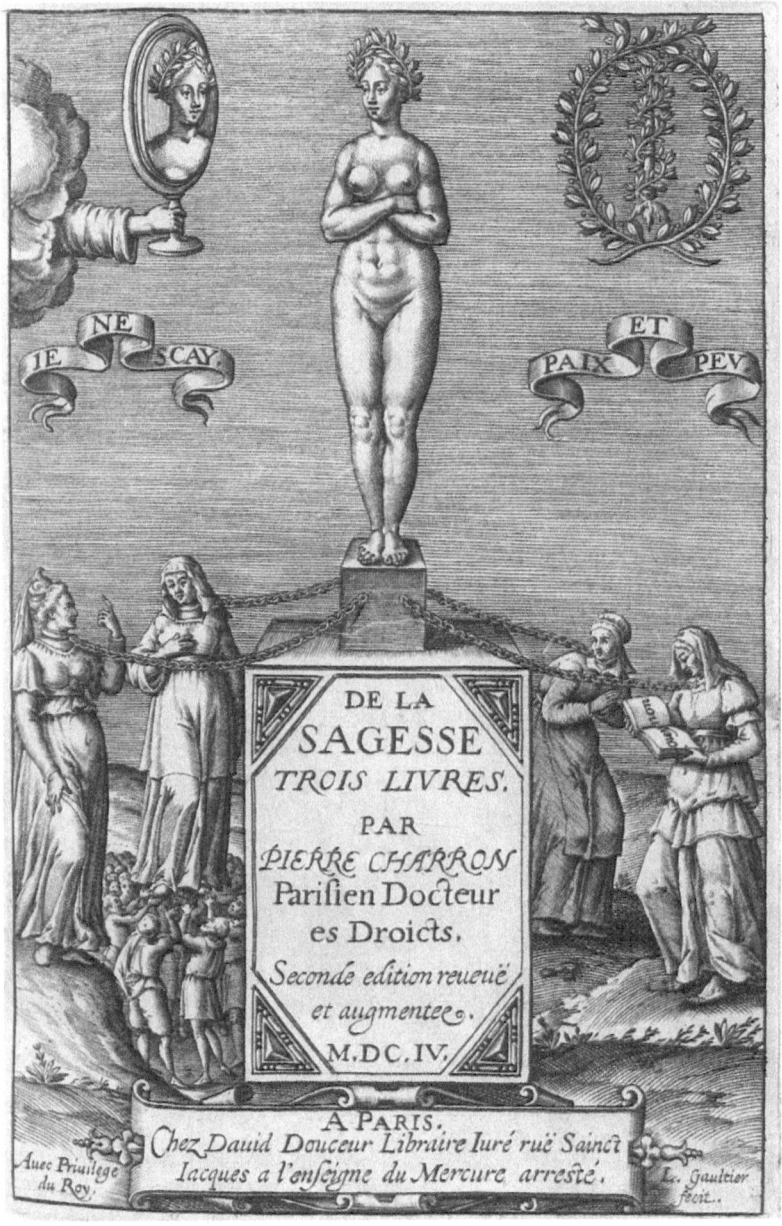

Figure 4.2. Title page, Pierre Charron, *De la sagesse*. Paris: Chez David Douceur Libraire, 1604. Rare Books and Special Collections, the University of Sydney Library.

Charron's definition of wisdom as the self-knowledge that inheres in virtue and his argument that such knowledge – and the liberty and repose it enables – can be acquired only through a practice of self-mastery in which reason maintains control over the passions.[38] Like the images from Du Chesne and Charron, the naiad's song from the *Ballet of Diana and her Nymphs* merges neostoic with Neoplatonic motifs when describing the troupe of nymphs whose physical beauty, which they regard proudly in their mirrors, marks externally the self-knowledge and practices of mental self-control through which they achieve virtue as well as freedom.

The naiad tells us, however, that these dancing nymphs present a vivid contrast to their spectators, audience members who only irritate the dancers by pursuing a reward that even the gods dare not wish for ["rien ne les irrite tant / Que de voir qu'on s'a[i]lle flattant / En sa vaine persérvérance, / Et qu'un homme puisse espérer, / Par ses pleurs, une recompense / Que les Dieux n'osoient desirer"]. Addressing these very audience members, the naiad tells them that they must learn to "Réglez doncq si bien vos soupirs, / Que mesme en vos plus grands désirs / Votre cœur demeure insensible, / Et cessant de vous enflâmer, / Si c'est quelque chose possible, / Adorez-les sans les aymer" [control your sighing so well that even in your deepest desires your heart remains unmoved and, ceasing to impassion yourselves, if such a thing is possible, adore them without loving them]. But because they have little practice in the arts of stoic self-mastery, these same spectators will require the nymphs' help. Extending Fame's earlier claim that Diana's nymphs have no trouble blocking Love's assaults, the naiad tells her audience that these dancers will strike "un coup ... glorieux" [a glorious blow] by destroying the god who seduces them; they will fashion Cupid's tomb, the naiad promises, by causing this god to burn again in the fire of his own torch on the same altar where he is adored ["elles iront détruisant / Ce Dieu qui vous va séduisant, / Et le faisant brusler encore / Au feu de son propre flambeau, / De l'Autel mesme où l'on l'adore, / Elles en feront son Tombeau"]. Courtiers in the ballet hall, like the lovesick shepherds who populate Honoré d'Urfé's prose romance *L'Astrée*, exhibit in their sighs and tears signs of weakness typically associated with femininity. Like d'Urfé's shepherds, the ballet's spectators also erect temples and build altars where their impassioned souls, burning in profane ardor, make adoring sacrifices to Love.[39] Soon, however, "Les coeurs qui ne sçavent qu'aymer / Apprendront de se reformer / Avec de si chastes exemples, / Et désormais, dedans la Cour, / On ne trouvera plus de Temples / Où l'on sacrifie à l'Amour" [hearts that know only to love will learn to reform themselves with the help of such chaste models, and henceforth within the court one will not find any more temples where one makes sacrifices to Love]. The queen and her women, in other words, will model for these courtiers the wise self-knowledge that, according to Charron's *De la sagesse*, constitutes virtuous self-mastery. By following the nymphs' example, the naiad proclaims, such "pauvres Espri[t]s" [poor souls] may finally leave off inflaming themselves with passion ["cessant de vous enflâmer"].

The central means by which this troupe of nymphs enacted such pedagogical modelling was dance itself, the next set of ballet verses informs us. This third song, entitled "Vers Masculins Pour La Chaisne du Mesme Balet" [Masculine Verses for the Chain of the Same Ballet], ventriloquizes the queen and her ladies in the present tense as if they were singing while dancing. Here the nymphs boast that "la neige de notre sein" [the snow of our breast] has given them victory over Cupid. This trope references a whiteness of skin tone associated with otium or leisure (possible only for those of higher rank) and hence elite social status; in line with Petrarchan discourse as well as its adaptation in pastoral drama and literature, snowy breasts also signalled a virtuous noblewoman's emotional coldness when confronted by her loving servant's verbal blandishments. The third set of sung verses for Marie's *Ballet of Diana and her Nymphs*, though, adds to such connotations a specific emphasis on dance as the means by which these nymphs achieve such chastity of heart and mind.

The poem begins with the ventriloquized dancers declaring that "Nos esprits libres & contens / Vivent en ces doux passe-temps, / Et par de si chastes plaisirs, / Bannissent tous autres désirs" [Our minds, free and happy, live in these gentle pastimes and by such chaste pleasures banish all other desires].[40] Elaborating further, it explains that such gentle pastimes include the dance, the hunt, and other innocent, pastoral activities, and that it is these pastimes which ensure the nymphs' immunity to the laws and sufferings which Love inflicts on those at court ["La dance, la chasse, & les bois / Nous rendent exemptes des lois / Et des misères, dont l'Amour / Afflige les coeurs de la Cour"]. Having emphasized that the women's virtue takes a specifically mental form and how this elevated mental state embodied outwardly in their dancing allows them to escape the miseries of passion, the verses explain further that "c'est plustost avec cet art / Qu'avec la pointe de ce dard, / Que cette trouppe se deffant / Des traits de ce cruel Enfant. // Car, en changeant tousjours de lieu, / Nous empeschons si bien ce

Dieu, / Qu'il ne peut s'asseurer des coups / Qu'il pense tirer contre nous" [It is more with this art than with the point of this spear that this troupe defends itself against the arrows of this cruel child because, in always changing places, we thwart this God so well that he cannot be sure of the shots he thinks of aiming at us]. Referencing "ce dard," these lines gesture to the arrows that the queen and her companions held in their hands as they rose from their seated positions in the recessed garden setting at the far side of the performance space and came forward to dance their *grand ballet*, according to the Guiscardi eye-witness accounts. "[C]et art" in the lines above, however, refers to the ordered beauty of their figured choreographies, in particular the *chaîne* or hay mentioned in this song's title.

The *chaîne*, as noted earlier, was a dance comprising interlacing lines and serpentine patterns; in court ballets it was used frequently as a vehicle through which dancers transitioned from one geometrical or figured dance pattern to the next.[41] Describing this ballet's *chaîne*, the verses in masculine rhyme emphasize how the troupe's fluid yet closely coordinated movements as a collective functioned as a highly disciplined tactic through which to escape Love's onslaughts. It is by "changeant tousjours de lieu" [always changing places] – in other words, dancing with repeated weaving motions – that the queen and her companions in the guise of Diana and her nymphs avoid the darts of desire that Cupid aims at them.[42] Although this god seeks to incite their passions, his fire will not ignite ["Qu'alors qu'il nous pense enflamer, / Son feu ne se peut allumer"]. Rather, by occupying themselves without boredom in such virtuous pastimes, the nymphs rob from this tyrannical god the glory of enslaving them ["Ainsi nous défendans de luy / Et passans nos jours sans ennuy, / Nous essayons de luy ravir / La gloire de nous asservir"].

This virtuous state of mind and its achievement through rigorous corporeal control in the dance can be learned even by dissolute courtiers, however. In developing this message, the *Ballet of Diana and her Nymphs* draws on the humanist belief that cosmic order, when replicated and represented in architectural and artistic projects, can make humans virtuous. More specifically, the ballet takes up the notion, articulated in humanist dance treatises, whereby beauty and order in noble dance both reflects and inculcates virtue.[43] The naiad, we will recall, tells this ballet's spectators that the nymphs they will soon see on stage are determined to bring better laws to "you" ["Ces Ninfes pleines de mespris, / Voyant tant de pauvres Espri[t]s / Qui bruslent d'une ardeur profane, / Quittent leurs antres & leurs bois, / Et viennent avec leur Diane / Vous donner de meilleures loix"]. These laws, presumably, are the codes and rules that Fame has said are given to the nymphs by Virtue. The ballet's third song clarifies that the "meilleures loix" brought by these virtuous nymphs consist in the exacting rules of courtly dance manifested in their *grand ballet* as highly controlled kinesis, and specifically as the ability to move as a collective in motions that mirror cosmic harmony as well as more local political harmony and order.[44] This idea that the laws or rules of dance could inculate virtue was not new: we see it in dancing master Fabrizio Caroso's introduction to the first book of his *Nobiltà di dame* (1600), described by its author as a text "In Which are Taught the Rules Whereby May Be Learnt Those Fine Ways, Graceful Movements, and Courtly Manners ... When [Practising] the Art of Dancing ... Adapted to the Fundamental Law and Made Perfect in Theory." This first section of the text, Caroso explains, treats "the art of dancing ... and also of proper deportment therein, not previously set forth by anyone – those highly praiseworthy and necessary VIRTUES which render beautiful (and are capable of so rendering) any prince or princess, lord or lady, knight or noblewoman, gentleman or lady, or any other well-born and -bred man, woman, youth, or maiden."[45] As we have seen from the Guiscardi letters, the queen and her ladies not only danced their *grand ballet* but at the end of this ballet proper moved out into the audience to take up high-ranking courtiers in the audience as their partners in the revels. In this way Marie de Médicis and her troupe not only modelled virtue in their orderly *chaîne* but also helped facilitate for those in the audience who witnessed them an opportunity to practice similarly artful self-mastery in mixed-gender social dancing.

When read together, this production's three songs outline a thematics of virtue with strong ties to neostoicism. "[E]specially in the France of Henry IV and the Netherlands" following the 1599 publication of Justus Lipsius' *Politica*, Gerhard Oestreich notes, revived stoic principles "became the ideology, almost the religion, of educated men."[46] According to late sixteenth-century French political theory, the king as divinely chosen sovereign presided over a just, harmiously ordered kingdom in part thanks to his own virtue. This virtue inhered in the monarch's capacity for self-control, understood as right reason unimpeded by the passions and their disorders.[47] Thinkers such as Michel de L'Hôpital insisted that this virtuous ruler, who exhibited an order in his own soul or mind that paralleled the order of God's creation, both was law and made law – rules and patterns of behaviour that he exemplified in himself and also dictated to his subjects through ordinances that regulated the kingdom.[48] This legislative power in turn constituted the prince as sovereign, no longer limited by reciprocal relations of obligation to vassals (as he had been under feudal models of government) but chosen by God to rule over his subjects justly, with unquestioned sway.

In neostoic thought and the late sixteenth- and early seventeenth-century French political writings it influenced, virtue of the type exemplified by sovereign princes was not available to women. Lipsius had developed a theory of wisdom in which truth might be discovered through an ethics that transcended confessional controversy rather than through divisive religious doctrine, but in keeping with the "explicitly masculinist" ethos of ancient stoicism, his *Politica* also followed Aristotle in denying women a role in public life due to their inherently lascivious nature.[49] *Politique* writers in France such as Guillaume Du Vair had drawn on neostoic thought when promoting Henri IV's settlement as a means of avoiding continued religious wars, on the one hand, and dominance by foreign powers, on the other; simultaneously, they appealed to familiar understandings of women's inherent weakness as taken up in the so-called Salic law. Du Vair's argument in support of Henri IV's claim to the throne over that of the Spanish Infanta Isabel Clara Eugenia proposed by members of the Catholic League, as Rebecca M. Wilkin has shown, associated Leaguer sedition – and its support of a foreign female candidate to the throne of France – with disorderly vulnerability to passion and lack of self-control merely masquerading as religious zeal.[50] Such notions resonated with the "theory of legislative sovereignty" developed by Jean Bodin, the "architect of political absolutism," whose 1576 *Six livres de la république* "identified the subordination of women to men as the defining feature of political order" and whose 1580 *De la démonomanie des sorciers* "attacked women's foibles, particularly their ostensibly insatiable lust."[51] In the "modern" monarchy outlined by these and other French political theorists, the sovereign's inalienable, God-given power to command found legitimation in the king's capacity to uphold natural law – the laws or codes of virtue – in his own comportment. In accordance with nature's rendering of women as weak and vicious, however, only men could be chosen by God to fulfil the role of sovereign; therefore, only a male king whose virtuous sovereignty was recognized by his subjects could put an end to decades of disorder and civil war unhampered by the political weakness of the late Valois dynasty or the Catholic church's inability, in the face of unrelenting confessional schism, to unite the kingdom in one body of believers.

The verse texts for Marie's 1609 *Ballet of Diana and her Nymphs* analysed above give voice to certain aspects of neostoic thought in their emphasis on virtue rooted in a set of laws or codes of comportment found in nature that, when followed, ordered the soul and controlled the passions so as to bring happiness and liberty. In a twist on the overt masculinism of neostoicism and its development in absolutist political thought, however, the 1609 queen's ballet suggested that Henri IV's court could acquire virtue, and the king could achieve lasting glory, only thanks to women. Via their dancing, the women of this ballet, led by the queen, were said to bring to the court of France a beauty and virtue that their audience otherwise lacked. According to this ballet's verse texts, the ordered, harmonious court on which the first Bourbon monarch's glory rested required the "better laws" of mental self-control that the queen and her ladies had been given by virtue and which they were said to model so admirably on this court ballet's own stage.[52]

In this sense, the production that Marie de Médicis organized and danced in January 1609 made a concerted bid for an extension of royal authority, rooted in the virtuous sovereign's capacity to make and uphold just laws, to his female consort. Sharing in the king's sovereignty through Christian marriage, in which the husband and wife's two bodies and souls become one, the queen of France occupied a unique institutional position. In contemporary juridical and political theory, the king's wife, though subject to him in accordance with her gender, nonetheless participated in the sovereign virtue her husband had been chosen by God to embody. This aspect of the queen's position could be used by the crown to its advantage. To govern a well-ordered polity, the sovereign needed to reveal his own virtue – in the work of reasoned statecraft but also in his domestic affairs, as husband and father – so as to provide an inspiring model for his subjects. Yet this ruler needed to inculcate awe in order to command his subjects' strict obedience, and this second mandate required the king to distance himself from his subjects, appearing before them only rarely.[53] Marie's 1609 ballet, I suggest, exploited such contradictions within theories of sovereignty and in the process negotiated for the consort queen an enlarged space of activity within monarchical governance. The king needed to represent virtuous sovereignty, but he also needed to hold back in making such representations immediately visible in his own person in order to achieve the distancing effect that would ensure his subjects' submission. As the king's wife, the queen consort was the only person besides the king himself who embodied sovereignty. Through dynastic marriage, therefore, the crown could both withdraw itself (in the person of the king) and reveal itself (in the person of the queen). In public appearances such as this 1609 *Ballet of Diana and her Nymphs*, therefore, the queen usefully represented and modelled for the king's subjects, through her dancing, the virtue necessary to render legitimate her husband's sovereign authority as divinely sanctioned law-maker.

The *Ballet of Diana and her Nymphs* thus offered an innovative contribution to the "methodology of authority" that Henri IV's reign adapted from neostoic thinkers such as Lipsius.[54] According to Michel Sénellart, this methodology engaged a dialectic between force and example as well as complex mechanisms of opinion management. In keeping with Lipsius' ideas regarding princely rule, Fame's air tells Henri IV that the rumours of his miraculous kingship which she has been trumpeting throughout the world have until this point been questioned by some, but that even such "savage" minds would no longer dare to doubt her reliability once this ballet's women dancers, having been welcomed and honoured by the king, added their praise for him to Fame's own. "Jusqu'icy vos faits glorieux / Peuvent avoir des envieux" [Until now your glorious feats have had envious detractors], Fame sings to Henri, but if he welcomes them and honours their greatness ["Grand Roy, faites-leur bon accueil: / Louëz leur magnanime orgueil"], the nymphs' lips, too, will join Fame in telling Henri's greatness, and what soul, then, could be so insolent as to dare to doubt Fame's reliability? ["Mais quelles âmes si farouches / Ozeront douter de ma foy, / Quand on verra leurs belles bouches / Les raconter avecques moy"]. Drawing on notions of silent noble dance as a form of mute rhetoric, this stanza stresses the troupe's capacity to represent and teach virtue and, in so doing, to change the minds of even the most hardened sceptics regarding Henri IV's virtuous kingship.[55] In this division of labour within the royal marriage, the king commands with sovereign force at a distance from his subjects while his wife, appearing publicly on the court ballet stage, legitimates his legislative authority through her virtuous example and its contribution to Bourbon "opinion management." In conjunction with my own argument elsewhere that this ballet told "a story of queenly beauty and its contribution to statecraft," therefore, it seems that Fame's final stanza leveraged contemporary understandings of glory as the reward of virtue as part of a larger message regarding Marie's contributions to Bourbon dynastic consolidation.[56]

Dance and/vs Song: Angélique Paulet and the Limits of Marie's (Proto)feminism

Drawing on late sixteenth-century notions of kingship influenced by neostoic theory, this ballet's verses insist that without the aid and intervention provided by Marie, Henri IV's court lacks orderly virtue. The king's glory and renown, based on his reign's capacity to instil virtuous order, could not be assured without her. In negotiating this space of political authority for Marie, however, the January 1609 *ballet de la reine* engaged surprisingly edgy qualities of eroticism by means of the naiad's entry performed by Angélique Paulet.[57]

Paulet's ballet entry seems to have been primarily responsible for the notoriety and attention this production gained among contemporaries and, by extension, for the preservation of the ballet's verse texts via print. Writing immediately after the performance, Pierre de L'Estoile proclaims that Paulet herself "emporta l'honneur du ballet" [stole the show].[58] A few weeks later, on 21 February 1609, L'Estoile notes in addition that he paid five *sols* for a printed *Recueil des vers du balet de la Reyne* along with two other "fadaises," or trifles.[59] During the ballet's performance, we now know from the Guiscardi letters, Fame's air came first, followed by the nymph's *récit* sung by Paulet. In the pamphlet that L'Estoile purchased as well as the identical *recueil* published by a different printer, however, the naiad's *récit* appears first. Given the timing of L'Estoile's purchase (subsequent to the ballet performance) and the fact that two rival printers issued this pamphlet, it seems plausible that this *recueil*, rather than being a *livret* or booklet available for distribution among the ballet's audience at the time of performance, was issued after the event with a new ordering of sung texts, one that was designed to capitalize on the notoriety within Paris circles that rumours of Paulet's performance had immediately generated.[60] The second book of court airs arranged by Gabriel Bataille (royal lutenist, composer, and future master of the queen's music during Marie's regency) and issued by Pierre Ballard (printer of the king's music) keeps the ordering of texts found in the *recueil* in its rendition of the ballet's three songs adapted for lute accompaniment. To capture the interest of potential purchasers, it seems, all of these printed sources led with the ballet's most famous sung entry. This performance proved so sensational, in fact, that when Madeleine de Scudéry wrote about it forty years later in her historical novel *Artamène, ou Le Grand Cyrus*, she expected her readers to know and recognize it. According to Scudéry, "Elise" (Paulet's fictional name in this account of Henri IV's reign) had been admired throughout the court from the age of five thanks to her beauty, wit, spirit, pride, and especially her gifts in song, dance, and lute-playing,[61] but only with her appearance singing and playing the lute on a dolphin in a *ballet de la reine* – Marie's 1609 production – did Paulet's fame spread throughout France and beyond.[62]

One factor explaining the notoriety Paulet's performance achieved is the specific aesthetic qualities of its music, to be discussed in chapter 5. Another important factor was Paulet's parentage. Angélique's father, Charles Paulet, sieur de Coubéron, was early seventeenth-century France's most infamous financier, reviled especially for his association with the *droit annuel*, a new tax on venal office instituted in late 1604.[63] The *droit annuel* was notorious in part because although all nobles in early modern France were equal juridicially speaking, not all were socially equal. Hierarchies within this group included those between nobles of the sword and the robe (though this division was arguably less fixed than historians have traditionally assumed) as well as divisions based on longevity of noble lineage. The most prestigious nobles were those whose ancestry "had never included a commoner": those whose nobility was seemingly so ancient that dependence for that noble title on its giver, the king himself, could conveniently be forgotten. The least prestigious nobles were persons whose common ancestors had been ennobled by the sovereign within three or fewer past generations.[64] Ennoblement by the king rewarded royal service, but it also became the basis for venal office: the creation, buying, and selling of offices in service to the monarch.[65] The *droit annuel*, given the informal title of *la paulette* in acknowledgment of Charles Paulet's alleged role in its authorship, turned venal office into a more stable source of profit for both the king and his officeholders, in part by giving those officeholders hereditary rights to their positions. The *paulette* thus anchored the growth of a centralized state administration and decreased the court's reliance on higher-ranking nobles, while aiding and abetting a much larger transformation of the social elite in which noble status – along with those economic, legal, and social privileges previously available only to those who occupied the pinnacle of French society by virtue of birth, or through generations of royal service – could be attained through wealth alone.[66] Seeking to maintain the exclusiveness of their estate, many nobles resented the relative ease of access to the lowest noble echelons now regularized by the *droit annuel*, voicing this discontent in part through frequent, disdainful verbal attacks on financiers:

those who held the offices responsible for farming the collection of royal revenues, collecting those revenues, and/or making payments from the royal treasury.[67] Financiers attracted contempt in part because the remarkable and highly visible success of several individual financiers, who had bought their way into tax farming offices in the first place, meant that the group as a whole appeared to have risen "in one or two generations" to a status the sword claimed to have earned only through merit – a quality they understood as being rooted in birth combined with length of (military) service, as Jay Smith has shown – and which even fairly new magistrates of the sovereign courts believed they had achieved only after much longer terms of service.[68]

Such anxieties about social mobility help to explain the rumours about Angélique Paulet that spread throughout the French capital shortly following her appearance in the queen's *Ballet of Diana and her Nymphs*. One of these rumours circulated as the refrain for a *vaudeville* or popular satirical song. In response to the rhetorical question "Qui fit le mieux du ballet?" [Who made the best of the ballet?], this refrain offered the following reply: "Ce fut la petite Paulet, / Montée sur le Dauphin / Qui montera sur elle enfin" [It was the little Paulet, mounted on the Dauphin, who will mount her in the end].[69] This *vaudeville*'s satiric edge relies on the pun whereby "dauphin" means both dolphin and the French heir apparent. In January 1609 the actual dauphin was only seven years old, yet this inconvenient detail did not stand in the way of those who authored this ditty; nor did it deter Tallemant des Réaux, who quotes its refrain several decades later. Tallemant's *Les Historiettes*, immediately after referencing these lines, explains that "monsieur le Dauphin" was a "pauvre monteur" [poor mounter] (here Tallemant calls up Louis XIII's reputation for sexual abstemiousness) and so his father "y monta au lieu de luy" [mounted there in place of him]. Apparently, Henri IV so desired Angélique Paulet sexually that he invited her to "sing under him," and "everyone agrees that he fulfilled his desire" ["Henry IV, a ce ballet, eut envie de coucher avec la belle chanteuse pour la faire chanter sous l'homme; tout le monde tombe d'accord qu'il en passa son envie"].[70] Tallemant adds that Henri IV was assassinated while travelling to Paulet's house, accompanied by the dauphin's halfbrother César de Vendôme; perhaps the king had already discovered that Vendôme did "not like women," Tallemant smirks, and hoped to "rendre ce prince gallant" by exposing his bastard son to Paulet's (sexual) charms.[71] Tallemant's propensity for calumny (J.M.H. Salmon has called him a "scandal-monger"), combined with his heightened sensationalism when gossiping about women performers, suggests that we should hesitate to take such anecdotes at face value.[72] Nonetheless, Tallemant was not alone in his insinuations about Angélique's promiscuity – as several other satirical references to her erotic enticements as a performer in the years closely following her 1609 ballet performance make clear.[73]

This pattern of response to the naiad's sung entry stemmed in part from early modern notions that afforded to women's vocal music a special power to arouse men sexually while also signalling the female singer's own potential arousal. Describing Paulet's performance, L'Estoile's diary draws on such assumptions in the following passage, for example: "cette petite chair blanche, polie et délicate, couverte d'un simple crêpe fort délié, au travers duquel paraissaient les linéaments d'une partie secrète encore plus déliée, mettait en goût et appétit plusieurs personnes" [this little white flesh, polished and delicate, was covered in a plain crepe, very loose fitting, through which appeared the outline of an even looser secret part, stimulating and giving appetite to many people].[74] L'Estoile's use of the term "délier," in the sense of to come undone, to loosen or free, punningly conveys how Paulet's costume, which allowed relatively unrestricted visual access to the singer's "even looser secret part" (her genitalia), signified concomitant ease of sexual access. This young woman's particular social identity as a financier's daughter, I wish to suggest, compounded the vulnerability to scandal put in motion by contemporary assumptions concerning the hypersexualized nature of women's public song. Notably, the same commentators who besmeared Paulet's sexual reputation also made malicious statements about financiers: L'Estoile, for example, not only describes how this young woman stimulated the erotic appetites of spectators thanks to her revealing ballet costume, in the passage just discussed, but also rails against Charles Paulet and his fellow *partisans*, whom he labels "true thieves and leeches."[75]

To contemporaries such as these, Paulet's musicianship on display during the queen's 1609 ballet seems to have signalled sexual looseness but also a viciousness tied to rapid social climbing. Contempt for financiers centred on the ways that these speculators, lenders, and farmers for taxes on venal office made their money, but also encompassed disdain for the ways they (conspicuously) spent that money: on extravagances such as buildings, expensive clothing, and other kinds of cultured practices or objects previously available as forms of self-designation only to a smaller set of French elites. Paulet's graceful accomplishments during the naiad's ballet entry represented the status recently acquired by her father, who as one of the king's secretaries in the Paris *chambre des comptes* had been ennobled and had gained the right to pass noble title to his children after twenty years of service.[76] These same "bonnes grâces," however, could also signal her family's (sordid) investment in further social mobility, since Angélique, it was rumoured, had come to garner the attention of noble lovers from the highest social ranks in part through extensive (and expensive) training in the arts of song, lute-playing, and dance. The *vaudeville* refrain noted above pithily voices such resentments: answering the rhetorical question of which performer profited most from this ballet, it names Angélique, who found herself "mounted" by the dauphin, the kingdom's highest ranking individual after the reigning king. This young woman displayed the same arts of music which noblewomen of the highest ranks themselves practiced in more enclosed, private social spaces. Yet for many, Paulet's courtly skills marked not innate nobility – understood as pertaining to qualities of blood and hereditary transmission and carrying with it both physical and moral perfection, as we have seen earlier in this chapter – but its dark double: the "inauthentic" imitation of a conspicuous consumption deemed proper and even virtuous for "true" nobles, but which to many proved unseemly and (sexually) vicious when taken up by those at the margins of France's newly expanded elite.[77]

Through her skills as a musician, Paulet had by 1609 gained privileged access to court circles.[78] Her prominent inclusion in the queen's ballet, as a form of social patronage, honoured Paulet's family. By extension, it also underscored the French crown's determination to expand the nobility through venal office despite resentment by those who wished to maintain greater exclusivity and power for their own group. Insofar as Marie's ballets favoured roles for women singers such as Paulet, they might initially seem to have anticipated efforts by later women-led Paris salons to champion greater public influence for female elites as a group across social stratifications within that group. These salons would defend, while simultaneously embodying through the social makeup of their own female membership, the very expansion of the nobility brought about through venality of office. The *précieuses* named by contemporaries in connection with seventeenth-century Paris salons, as Carolyn Lougee has shown, included not only three French queens and numerous women from the kingdom's noble families of highest standing but also significant numbers of women whose male relatives had been recently ennobled, including wives and daughters of financiers.[79] Vittoria and Traiano Guiscardi include among the list of dancers chosen by Marie to appear alongside her in this 1609 ballet three women who later presided over or took up membership in such salons: Catherine de Vivonne, vidame de Mans and future marquise de Rambouillet, who formed the famous *salon bleu* at the *hôtel de Rambouillet*;[80] Charlotte-Marguerite de Montmorency, one of the *précieuses* named in connection with Rambouillet's salon;[81] and Louise-Marguerite de Guise-Lorraine, princesse de Conti, who, following Marie's exile by Richelieu and Louis XIII in 1631, would go on to create a salon-in-exile at her château in Eu.[82] During the 1620s, Rambouillet would take concrete steps to rescue Paulet from the sexual scandals her performance in Marie's 1609 ballet had catalyzed, inviting her to join the *salon bleu* where Paulet again sang and accompanied herself on the theorbo for occasions such as the *intermedii* performed during the 1629 *La Sophonisbe* acted by Rambouillet's daughter Julie.[83] Madeleine de Scudéry – another member of Rambouillet's circle and a salon organizer in her own right – would literally rewrite the story of Paulet's participation in Marie de Médicis' ballet. Insisting on Paulet's sexual innocence, her *Artamène, ou le Grand Cyrus* narrates how the remarkable performance "Elise" (Paulet) gave during the queen's ballet caused the king of Phénicie (Henri IV) to be "transporté d'admiration" [transported with admiration] of the most elevated kind. At first, the king saw her only as a miracle and not as a mistress ["il ne la regarda sans doute en ce temps-là, que comme un Miracle, et non pas comme sa Maistresse"]; when some years later he, like Elise's other admirers, became a "slave" to her beauty, she firmly (though politely) resisted his advances.[84] As we have seen, verses for the ballet production organized and danced by Marie de Médicis powerfully emphasize for the queen and the women she led in dancing during this production's *grand ballet* the kind of social and moral respectability that Scudéry attributes here to Paulet. But the ballet itself failed to extend such defenses of female virtue to this lower-ranking woman performer: rather this production grounded the queen's authority in part through distinctions between public female song – associated with sexual availability as well as lower social rank – and (silent) women's dance, linked by contrast with noble virtue.

Such a limited defence of elite women across social stratifications stemmed in part from the crown's continued dependence on the "traditional, charismatic legitimacy" that longstanding noble bloodlines ensured.[85] Discourses concerning nobility of race gained purchase in seventeenth-century France in part as a way to compensate for the diluted exclusivity in access to noble privilege caused by increased proportions of new members at lower echelons, but also because such discourses supported the basis for dynastic monarchy itself.[86] Moreover, patterns of imagery promoting the queen's nobility of race held particular political utility given the specificities of Marie's lineage as a Medici. The Medici dukes could claim only recent standing as princes relative to other European sovereigns; in fact, their line's power and wealth grew from their success as moneylenders, with the Medici being savagely disparaged on such grounds in polemics from the 1570s and 1580s. Henri IV's mistress Henriette d'Entragues, as we have seen, reportedly called Marie a "fat banker," and indeed, the unequal status between Marie and Henri on the basis of relative princely rank resembled, on a certain level, the "misalliances" between high-ranking male nobles and women from wealthy financier families within France, women whose fathers had acquired noble status only recently by purchasing offices in the king's (financial) courts using wealth acquired through practices such as moneylending and tax collection.

To promote Marie's socio-political authority as the king's wife and mother to the dauphin, therefore, the crown needed to de-emphasize these inauspicious aspects of the royal marriage while similarly creating for the queen charismatic images of divinely sanctioned preeminence. Not surprisingly, therefore, the *Ballet of Diana and her Nymphs* reserved its textual emphasis on female virtue for the queen and the higher-ranking noblewomen with whom she danced. This ballet's verses praising its women dancers worked to distance the beauty of their silent dancing – associated with virtue – from vocality of the type offered by Angélique Paulet's performance. Fame's air, sung first in actual performance, establishes this distinction by predicting that no one will fail to believe this goddess's accounts of Henri IV's great deeds when they see these nymphs' lovely lips telling them with her ["Quand on verra leurs belles bouches / Les raconter avecques moy"]. To literally speak or sing with open throats in such a public fashion would risk publishing the dancers' alleged whoredom, as it did Paulet's. The ballet ingeniously navigated this dilemma for the queen and her ladies, however, through a strategy Fame's final lines hint at: the audience, rather than *hearing* these "twelve rare beauties" praise Henri IV, is given the opportunity to "*see* these nymphs' lovely lips telling" that "greatness" (emphasis mine). This phrasing situates the nymphs' powerful rhetoric of royal praise in a visual rather than aural register. As we have seen in previous chapters, *basse danse* when performed by persons belonging to families of longstanding noble rank was thought to instantiate noble grace. In these ways, the nymphs' silent figured dances, especially when set against vocal performance by the lower-ranking noblewoman Angélique Paulet, marked for Marie de Médicis and her female companions in the *grand ballet* a superior moral, social, and even physical standing that members of the French upper nobility and royalty claimed for themselves alone.

Eros Channeled to (Sovereign) Virtue: Marie Dances Diana

Fame's air initially proffered the tantalizingly erotic possibility of literal singing or speaking by this ballet's high-ranking dancers. The ballet ultimately withdrew this possibility when the queen and her ladies performed their dance in silence. Before their entry, however, the ballet's next sung entry offered the erotic qualities of female song performed by Angélique Paulet. Lacking textual references to Paulet's virtue, the ballet went out of its way to generate through her entry a powerful sexual response. L'Estoile records how Paulet's costume, with its semi-transparent fabric, roused the appetites of spectators, as we have seen, while a closer look at Paulet's verses shows that this audience-effect was likely stimulated further through textual suggestion. As soon as Diana and her nymphs (the queen and her ladies) arrived on stage, Paulet sang, they would destroy "this god who goes around seducing you," "mak[ing] his tomb" by causing Cupid to "burn again in the fire of his own torch on the same altar where he is adored." The naiad's reference in the present tense to "Cupid's" seduction of "you" suggests that the spectators being enticed by Love were this singer's own auditors at this very moment she voiced these words. The naiad's sung text, in other words, drew attention to the erotic pleasure its audience experienced when hearing her lines declaimed musically on stage. The most privileged member of this same audience, of course, was Henri IV himself. But why would Marie de Médicis stage for her husband this highly erotic entry starring not herself but another woman?

Fame's air, we have seen, represents the queen and her ladies as enticing yet virtuous orators whose persuasive power, as silent dancers, can only enhance the king's own reputation. Fame's song concludes by calling on Henri IV to do his part – the king must acknowledge their beauty "sans artifice" [without artifice] – and warns that "leur souhaiter plus d'appas, / C'est vouloir, avec injustice, / Plus que les Cieux ne peuvent pas" [to wish greater charms than these women provide is to desire, unjustly, more than the heavens can provide]. As epideisis, these lines combine praise and blame – blame directed at those who harbor "unjust" desires for women whose beauty relies on artifice and affectation, praise for those who recognize this troupe's authentic, divinely given "charms." The textual emphasis on Paulet's erotic appeal in the nymph's *récit* seems to contradict such efforts to direct the king's amorous attentions toward higher-ranking noblewomen and in particular toward their leader, the queen. Yet Paulet's ability to arouse Henri IV may ultimately have proved advantageous to Marie, given her husband's ongoing enchantment with Henriette d'Entragues, the marquise de Verneuil.

During the period leading up to this ballet's rehearsals, d'Entragues was the only woman whose hold on the king's affections posed any real challenge to Marie's authority as Henri IV's wife and mother to his heir. Writing that same year, the English ambassador to France, George Carew, reported that Marie's "main and sole opposition [was] against the marquise de Verneuil, who being of an excellent, pleasant, and witty entertainment, maintaineth still a strong hold in the king's affections ... For the rest of those, who have the name of the king's mistresses, she [Marie] carrieth herself with great aequanimity, being not only content, but rather desirous, that by directing the king's affections touching that point to many others, they may be the more weakened towards the marquise."[87] In 1602 and then in 1604, as we have seen in previous chapters, the marquise had been at the centre of schemes that, had they succeeded, would have done away with the king while elevating as the "true dauphin," under Spanish protection, Henriette's own son to Henri. In early 1605 the Parlement of Paris had found the marquise guilty of knowing involvement in the second of these conspiracies, yet almost immediately following the publication of this judgment, the king pardoned his mistress. Soon thereafter, he began writing her intimate letters. In 1606, for example, Henri complained in letters that he loved Henriette more than she loved him, while during the period 1606–8, after she asked to break off their liaison, Henri begged her not to. Acknowledging Henriette's "ingratitude," the king by the end of 1608 admitted even to himself that she found his attentions boring, perhaps even repellent, yet still he requested her company.[88] Marie's standing within France certainly trumped Henriette's based on her status as mother of the king's legal heir, but Henri IV's son by this mistress, Gaston Henri de Verneuil, continued to prove threatening enough that even as late at 1608 the queen sought to stop the marquise from bringing the child with her when she visited the king.[89]

On 25 November 1608, the Florentine representative reported that Henriette had almost succeeded in using her influence with the king to have the queen's close companion and supporter Louise-Marguerite de Guise, princesse de Conti, exiled from court.[90] Since this woman was a powerful member of the house of Guise, and it was the Guise whom Marie most needed to support her worth as the king's named guardian of the dauphin and, potentially, as future regent, the marquise's action also menaced Marie. In the end, the Guise made known their serious resentment and Henriette was forced to reverse her request. Two months later, the queen advertised this triumph over Henriette by prominently honouring the princesse de Conti among the troupe of women dancers who performed in her *Ballet of Diana and her Nymphs*.[91]

In light of this ongoing enmity between the queen and the marquise, it seems plausible that the eroticized positioning of Paulet within this same ballet may have been prompted in part by one of Marie's aims at this time as reported by Carew: promotion of the king's philandering with other women as a way to divert his attentions away from Henriette d'Entragues. But Paulet's enticing performance riding a dolphin may also have proved useful for the queen through its indirect attack on Henriette's claims to have mothered the true "dauphin." Shortly prior to this ballet, the future Louis XIII had finally reached the age when he could be breeched – dressed in male attire – and removed from the royal children's quarters at Saint-Germain-en-Laye to reside in Paris with his parents.[92] One of his first public appearances in the capital, in fact, was as a spectator at this ballet, at Marie's own behest.[93] Juxtaposed with the literal dauphin's presence in the performance hall, the otherwise puzzling appearance of a titillating young woman riding a machine in the shape of a dolphin gains topical import. Seated on her mechanical dolphin, the social-climber Paulet recalled the "counterfeit" claims to royal authority that Henriette d'Entragues had long persisted in making for herself along with her son, the equally "artificial" would-be dauphin. In 1602, as we saw in chapter 1, the marquise had danced in Marie's first ballet, but never again would she gain from the queen such an "unbecoming concession."[94] Rather, winter 1609 saw d'Entragues replaced on the court ballet stage by another erotically enticing yet much less politically powerful young woman of the lower nobility. Angélique Paulet's tantalizing appearance singing and riding her own dolphin/dauphin thus simultaneously represented, debunked, and displaced key elements of Henriette's threat to Marie.

Containing this mistress's power at least rhetorically, the ballet promoted the queen's authority to the extent that the image of a naiad riding a dolphin figured Marie's own fertility as necessary to French political stability. According to the Guiscardi letters, the moving mountain out of which this dolphin and its rider appeared came onto the stage after a ballet danced by eight shades. Shades – shadowy images of night or death – represented danger or evil, while flowing water placed alongside naiads and dolphins connoted the fertility, understood as the ability to bear healthy male children, through which French queens claimed socio-political authority.[95] It seems plausible, therefore, that the dolphin in this instance might also have evoked the true dauphin born to Henri IV thanks to Marie: he through whom France would overcome the dark shadows of unrest and civil war that had haunted the kingdom under the spectacularly infertile late Valois monarchy.

Ordering its entries so that the queen's dancing immediately followed Paulet's performance, the ballet further displaced Henriette by channeling towards Marie's allegorical role as Diana the erotic impact that Paulet's sung entry set in motion. Paulet's entry, I have suggested, generated palpable sexual tension. In a song addressed to the ballet's spectators, Paulet noted how Cupid was seducing them in the present tense, as we have seen. Her throat opening in song offered notions of incipient sexual arousal, moreover, and this, alongside her scantily clothed visual appearance and association with "vicious" social climbing as Charles Paulet's daughter, evoked tantalizing images of "looseness" and hence sexual availability. Neither Paulet's *récit* nor any other extant verse for this ballet speaks of her virtue, and indeed, no known feature of the production suggested that spectators might be frustrated should they wish to approach Paulet sexually, such that the only thing that stood in their way, it must have seemed, was Paulet's exit from the stage. The queen, by contrast, did not sing publicly during her ballet; in this way she avoided the damage to social reputation that Paulet's public singing risked. Instead, her production's patronage of song performed by another woman enhanced the queen's reputation for superior musical taste while simultaneously putting in motion an erotic frisson that presumably lingered in the moments after Paulet had retired from the performance space, when Marie herself appeared.

In this way, the sexual tension generated by Paulet's entry would have carried forward to inflect her dancing, a less socially risky performance mode which both revealed the grace inherent in elevated noble status and marked the enhanced moral capacity such noble status was seen (naturally) to confer. Dancing as Diana, the erotically appealing yet chaste goddess of nature, the moon, and the hunt, Marie in this ballet called up a rich iconographic tradition developed by numerous highranking Frenchwomen before her, including several powerful royal mistresses. Her ballet deployed this iconography to a new end, however: that of proclaiming Marie's position as legal participant in the king's sovereignty, beloved object of his intimate regard, and rightful partner in his prerogatives of rule.

Paulet's own words on stage drew attention to this powerful combination of moral and social elevation with erotic appeal embodied by Marie in her allegorical role as the goddess Diana. Describing the queen and her troupe, the naiad performed by Paulet explains how "tant s'en faut qu'en vous blessant, / Elles s'aillent esjouissant / De ce que leur trait vous surmonte; / Qu'au contraire, en blasmant leurs coups / Leurs beaux yeux semblent avoir honte / D'user leurs armes contre vous" [far from going around, as they wound you, rejoicing that their arrows have overcome you, on the contrary, while condemning their blows, their beautiful eyes seem ashamed to use their weapons against you]. We know from the Guiscardi letters that the queen and her women danced with darts or arrows in their hands. Costuming and gesture thus reinforced this troupe's allegorical identification as Diana, goddess of the hunt, with her nymphs. Yet as the naiad's song indicates, these darts also encompassed the looks or glances the dancers threw to members of the audience. "Enjouer," a hunting term, means to cock one's gun, while "trait" means any weapon that is thrown. Supplementing the visual image of darts or arrows in the dancers' hands, the naiad's words claim that even these women's eyes throw looks – another set of darts which Cupid, against the nymphs' own intentions, added to his arsenal of weapons.

Relevant to this passage is the Neoplatonic idea that the lover's contemplation of physical beauty, which starts with desire, can either remain there or can lead the viewer towards love of divine beauty understood as light and brightness. Ficino voices this concept as follows: "The appearance of a man, which because of an interior goodness graciously given him by God is beautiful to see, frequently *shoots a ray of his splendor*, through the eyes of those looking at him, into their souls. Drawn by this spark like a fish on a hook, the souls hasten toward the one who is attracting them. This attraction, which is love, since it derives from the beautiful good, and happy, and is attracted to the same things, we do not hesitate to call Goodness, Beauty, Blessedness, and a God" (emphasis mine).[96] We see similar Neoplatonic ideas, with the locus of beauty shifting from male to female bodies, in Book Four of Castiglione's *Book of the Courtier* as well as in French pastoral drama and literature including d'Urfé's *L'Astrée*, where women's beauty appeals first to men's sensual desires but ultimately leads true lovers towards spiritual love, the pursuit of which results in more purified emotions as well as the lover's spiritual elevation.[97] Later woman-led salons, with their emphasis on *politesse* and *civilité*, built on such ideas to powerfully forward the idea that women, as agents of love and its capacity for spiritual and intellectual elevation, played a necessary and beneficial role in civil society. In a similar kind of argument, the 1609 queen's ballet suggests that Marie de Médicis and her ladies can teach virtue to men in the audience by themselves modelling immunity to passion at the same time that this teaching only works through these women's initial capacity – even against their own will – to draw men through physical desirability.[98] The *Ballet of Diana and her Nymphs*, I have argued, emphasized textually its male spectators' enslavement to profane ardor. Arousing spectators with female song, it reinforced this idea viscerally. The sexual tension left lingering after Paulet's sung entry next haunted the on-stage dancing performed by the kingdom's highest-ranking women. The ballet's texts describe these dancers as taking up the elevating public role ascribed to them by civility literature not despite but through the erotic force that accrued to their self-display. According to courtly dialogues such as Castiglione's *Book of the Courtier*, the desire that noble ladies evoked in men through their beauty and witty conversation was essential to civil society: male nobles, defined primarily through their preeminence as warriors, could only be convinced to practice the refined arts of courtesy thanks to the erotic motivation provided by women's enticements. Verses for the *Ballet of Diana and her Nymphs* offer a twist on this notion: unwittingly enslaving male spectators with desire yet purposefully modelling for those same spectators the solution to that enslavement, Marie de Médicis and her dancing companions enacted a mixed-gender "conversation" directed towards elevating, civilizing ends.

In keeping with this idea, we can read this ballet's metaphor of "darts" thrown from the eyes of the queen and her dancing companions in connection with gendered postural codes as forms of enticing yet prudent conversation in Renaissance *basse danse*. As Mark Franko explains, in *basse danse* the dancer's eyes and glance ideally form a modest look which is nonetheless directed outward, towards others; this "ostensibly passive gaze ... stages the body to be viewed" by other courtiers who thereby become the dancer's interlocutors.[99] In Thoinot Arbeau's dance treatise, young women dancers in particular embody this paradoxical combination of passive modesty with provocative conversation: keeping their eyes lowered ["les yeulx baissez"] and maintaining a humble countenance ["avec une contenance humble"], *demoiselles* of the court are instructed to occasionally glance, with virginal coyness, at those watching them ["regardans quelquefois les assistans avec une pudeur virginale"].[100] Noblewomen's dance is here imagined as passive yet powerful enough to stage itself before others whose gazing attention it attracts and engages, all while exhibiting the strictest "pudeur" or modesty. According to the naiad's *récit*, the queen and her female companions in the dance could not help but provoke desire in spectators through the "darts" that their glances "thr[e]w." In this way, they engaged "interlocutors" in their audience. Building on the concept of dance as mute rhetoric put forward in the final stanzas sung by Fame, the words of this naiad's *récit* render textually explicit the idea that Marie de Médicis and her troupe, rather than literally speaking or singing, entered into a similarly provocative yet much more elevating conversation with the men before whom they silently danced.

Depictions of Diana's capacity to elevate and civilize kings through her erotic yet virtuous qualities had accrued previously in connection with the official position of French royal mistress, starting with Diane de Poitiers.[101] Diana iconography associated with Diane de Poitiers frequently gave positive political emphasis to this mistress's amorous influence over Henri II.[102] As Henri Zerner notes, for example, on the reverse of one mid-sixteenth-century medal Diane appears in modest dress as the young and pleasing goddess of the hunt, leaning on her bow and stamping on Love, who cowers on the ground beneath her. Context, according to Zerner, lends this image a productive ambiguity: rather than representing a simple triumph of chastity, a reduction of Love to powerlessness, the medal marks Diane's submission of eros to her own service.[103] In keeping with this imagery, contemporaries frequently extolled Diane's erotic influence over Henri II as a beneficial force, capable of transforming this warrior king into a just, and cultured, ruler of his people.[104]

Henri IV's mistress Gabrielle d'Estrées, too, had frequently been pictured as Diana, first in highly erotic portraiture and later, as her political importance grew, in ways that emphasized her participation in sovereign rule. It was through Henri's relationship with Gabrielle, Kathleen Wellman has shown, that the king seems to have first promoted the idea that erotic partnership with the sovereign might coincide with political partnership.[105] Gabrielle, according to Wellman, enjoyed "more significant and extensive roles ... in the political arena than that played by other mistresses or by virtually any queen"; she was also "the only woman to keep Henri IV even remotely faithful."[106] It is striking, therefore, that at the zenith of Gabrielle's power Henri commissioned a set of tapestries depicting her as Diana, partner to the king-Apollo, along lines originally pioneered by and for Diane de Poitiers.[107]

Gabrielle died before her hoped-for wedding to the king and thus never attained the status of queen. Soon after her passing, though, and during the period of his engagement to Marie de Médicis, Henri commissioned a new set of galleries designed to enclose the queen's garden at Fontainebleau, one of which – the Gallery of Diana – featured on its walls images of Henri as Apollo-Mars juxtaposed with his new consort and political partner Marie as Diana-Virtue.[108] The king's depiction as Sol-Apollo with his wife as Diana featured also in royal entries at Rouen (1603) and Metz (1610), which praised the royal marriage as a partnership securing peace for the kingdom as a whole.[109]

The 1609 *Ballet of Diana and her Nymphs*, too, represents Marie-Diana as the king's personal and political partner. Malherbe's verses for Fame's air allude to the queen's allegorical role as Diana the moon goddess, a beauty who "[d]e tant de merveilles reluit" [glitters with so many marvels] that even the sun "qui tout surmonte" [who overcomes all things] should hide before her presence. Vittoria Guiscardi's letter, we will recall, states that the troupe of women led by Marie de Médicis all wore nymphs' costumes decorated with silver and with so many diamonds that the audience found itself blinded. From the English ambassador George Carew's report, discussed in more detail in chapter 5, we know that among the diamonds Marie sported on this occasion was one of Europe's largest and most precious gems, the Beau Sancy. Malherbe's reference to the queen's glittering marvels comments directly on the effects of candlelight in the performance hall caught and reflected back out into the audience by this jewel and others, and translates such wealth into evidence of Marie's moral and spiritual superiority. More than any other material facet of royal culture in early modern Europe, according to Luc Duerloo, jewellery represented "the exceptional state of grace that was royal power."[110] Precious gems, due to their indestructibility as well as their unparalleled capacity for reflecting or refracting light, also signalled royal invincibility. Drawing on such connotations, Malherbe's verses insist that Marie, bedecked in gems such as the Beau Sancy, shared in the king's own luminous, divinely sanctioned authority.[111]

The queen's participation in the king's sovereign power also found representation through her allegorical role as the goddess of the hunt. In classical Rome, women such as the empresses Julia and Faustina had appeared on official medals as Diana, mother of the gods surrounded by animals, including animals of the hunt, in ways that proclaimed the authority of empire itself.[112] The hunt also hinted at sovereign force, as Nicola Courtright notes, given that in times of peace kings, who were also first warriors of their realms, signalled their incipient military authority through prowess in hunting. When queens and royal mistresses appeared as Diana in her guise as huntress, then, such representations figured them as partners in the political authority that pertained to kingship.[113] Courtright makes this point with respect to the ordering of royal spaces and the visual art that decorated them, but by extending her insight to this 1609 ballet we can see that Marie's allegorical role in this instance similarly proclaimed her share in the power and force of Henri IV's sovereignty.

Emphasizing the queen's Diana-like immunity to desire as part of her claims to political agency, the ballet also recalls the precedent set by Henri IV's sister, Catherine de Bourbon. In 1593, Catherine had organized a ballet danced before Henri IV in which she appeared as Diana. This ballet's plot, as Éliane Viennot notes, centred on Diana's victory over Cupid, whom Catherine then brought, enslaved, before her brother. Allegorically, this ballet proclaimed Catherine's mastery over her own passions in loyal submission to the king's order that she relinquish her true love, the comte de Soissons, in order to consolidate Henri's political position.[114] Like this earlier ballet performance by her sister-in-law, Marie de Médicis' appearance dancing the role of Diana figured not only the queen's self-mastery over her passions but also her worthiness as the king's political ally.

The April 1609 *Ballet de Madame* and the Limits of (Patriarchal) Absolutism

Above, I have outlined how Marie's January 1609 production adapted to its chief patron-performer's purposes, and to the purposes of hereditary monarchy, a powerful pattern of self-authorizing Diana imagery previously associated with powerful women from the ancient and recent past. In this chapter's final section, I turn to the period immediately following this production, when such allegories together with the casting choices that informed them took on pointed topical implications in light of Henri IV's seemingly unbridled infatuation with Charlotte-Marguerite de Montmorency, the future princesse de Condé.

It was while attending a rehearsal at the Louvre for Marie's January 1609 *Ballet of Diana and her Nymphs*, rumour has it, that the king first became enamoured of the fifteen-year-old Charlotte. Court ballet scholars have often followed Paul Henrard in asserting that Charlotte in this production danced the role of Diana.[115] The Guiscardi letters confirm that this young woman was among the troupe who danced under Marie's direction, on this occasion, but the close reading of this ballet's verse texts offered earlier in this chapter indicates that Marie herself, rather than Charlotte-Marguerite, personated Diana on stage. According to this ballet's verses, the king, like others in the ballet's audience, was to learn from Marie and her companions in the dance how to quell Cupid's unruly passions; honouring their greatness, his glory would be secured, by Fame, throughout the world. In reality, however, the king's pursuit of Charlotte following the queen's ballet only ended up highlighting for contemporaries Henri's dangerous susceptibility to the "vaines impressions / De ... folles passions" [vain impressions of foolish passions].

Among those who expressed alarm at the king's latest *amour* was the court poet François de Malherbe, the author of Fame's verses for Marie's January 1609 *Ballet of Diana*. Malherbe's correspondence notes that he was called by the queen to the ballet's performance at the Louvre and that at the spectacle's conclusion, the king separately charged him with a new commission: a cycle of poems praising Henri's love not for his wife but for the young Montmorency princess. As Malherbe explains, "Je vous viens de dire que la Reine m'avoit commandé de voir son ballet: à cette heure meme, Leurs Majestés m'ont envoyé querir pour m'en demander mon avis ... Le Roi m'a entretenu de quelque autre galanterie dépendante du ballet, qui étoit la vraie occasion pourquoi il m'a envoyé querir exprès par un garcon de la chambre, et le ballet n'a servi que de prétexte" [I was telling you that the Queen commanded me to see her ballet: at that same hour, their Majesties fetched me in order to ask my opinion of it ... The king conversed with me about some other gallantry dependant on the ballet, which was the real occasion why he sent to fetch me immediately ... and the ballet only served as pretext].[116] Malherbe's phrase "quelque autre galanterie," scholars agree, references Henri IV's erotic pursuit of Charlotte-Marguerite de Montmorency; it was on the very occasion of Marie's *Ballet of Diana and her Nymphs*, in other words, that the king first commissioned Malherbe's cycle of poems celebrating "Alcandre's" love for "Oranthe."[117] Rather than immediately complying with the king's directive for a set of poems honouring Henri's passion for Charlotte-Marguerite, however, Malherbe waited over four months, until June 1609, to begin composing the first poem in the cycle. Malherbe's biographer René Fromilhague reads this gap in time as evidence for the poet's allegiance to the queen, his primary royal patron.[118] I find this conjecture to be plausible, especially when we consider that the first composition to which Malherbe turned, following his commission by the king, was a set of verses for another royal women's ballet, verses that rather than exalting Henri's new passion boldly caution against it on moral but also political grounds.

This second set of verses was composed for the 2 April 1609 *Ballet de Madame* performed at Saint-Germaine-en-Laye by Henri and Marie's six-year-old daughter Elisabeth. Later, these verses appeared in print under the title "De petites Nymphes qui mènent l'Amour prisonnier. Au Roi" [Verses of the Little Nymphs who Take Love Prisoner. To the king].[119] (Readers will find a full transcription of the poem, with English translation, in Appendix 3.) Malherbe's poem begins with a joyful announcement: finally those poor souls who suffer from Cupid's darts will see their pains turned back on their author and will be consoled at the expense of Love ["À la fin tant d'amants dont les âmes blessées / Languissent nuit et jour, / Verront sur leur auteur leurs peines renversées, / Et seront consolés aux dépens de l'Amour"]. Such poetic justice is possible, the ventriloquized dancing nymphs explain, because "Ce public ennemi, cette peste du monde, / Que l'erreur des humains / Fait le maître absolu de la terre et de l'onde, / Se treuve à la merci de nos petites mains" [this public enemy, this plague to all the world, whom the error of humans makes absolute master over land and sea, [now] finds himself at the mercy of our little hands]. Presenting a Cupid "dépouillé de ses armes" [deprived of his weapons], the nymphs implore Henri IV to abandon his generosity, mock Cupid's tears, and make him feel the rigor of the king's laws: "Quittez votre bonté, moquez-vous de ses larmes, / Et lui faites sentir la rigueur de vos lois." Command that Cupid receive justice without amnesty ["Commandez que sans grâce on lui fasse justice"], the nymphs cry, for though Cupid's passions are always amusing, "c'est un bruit commun que dans tout votre empire / Il n'est point de malheur qui ne vienne de lui" [it is a common rumour that throughout your empire there is not a single misfortune that does not come from him]. This Cupid, whom human error makes "maître absolu" [an absolute master], is more dangerous in Peace than Mars is treacherous in war; will not the king's own valor, having felt the outrage of Love's impudence, furnish the king with a just anguish? ["Votre seule valeur, / Qui de son impudence a ressenti l'outrage, / Vous fournit-elle pas une juste douleur?"]. Europe already trembles under the shadow of Henri's laurels, the nymphs conclude, and once he has similarly subdued this monstrous Cupid, nothing will be capable of troubling his glorious rule: "Attachez bien ce monstre, ou le privez de vie, / Vous n'aurez jamais rien qui vous puisse troubler."

This poem's depiction of the king's own valor subjected to Love's impudence, scholars note, offers a thinly veiled reference to Henri IV's infatuation with the young Montmorency princess, while the poem's demand for rigorous justice on the king's part calls on Henri IV to master an ardor which risked troubling his soul as well as his reign.[120] In support of such readings, critics cite a letter to Malherbe dated 12 May 1609 in which the poet's friend Nicolas-Claude Fabri de Peiresc writes that "Nous avons veu ces beaux vers du ballet de Madame, que nous avons admiré pour leur perfection, et encores plus pour la genereuse liberté dont vous y avez usé" [We have seen those beautiful verses for the ballet of Madame, which we admired for their perfection, and still more for the generous liberty which you used in them].[121] According to Antoine Adam, Peiresc's letter shows that Malherbe's critical intention was both understood and admired by contemporaries; as Raymond Lebègue further clarifies, if Peiresc and his colleagues wished to congratulate Malherbe for his generous liberty, it is because this poem for the April 1609 *Ballet de Madame* exhorted Henri IV to triumph over his passions, in particular his lovesickness for the young Charlotte-Marguerite.[122] What about this particular *amour* would have prompted such a warning, however? To explore this question, further contextualization is needed regarding the marriage Henri IV arranged for Charlotte de Montmorency with his own nephew Henri II de Bourbon, prince de Condé.

At the time of the *Ballet of Diana and her Nymphs*, Charlotte was engaged to one of the king's most honoured companions, François de Bassompierre, but once the king decided to pursue her, he broke off this engagement and set about arranging the young woman's union with Condé. As Katherine Crawford explains in another context, the seeming "symmetry of illicit extramarital behavior" achieved when a royal mistress was also commiting adultery against her own husband had the potential to "dampen ... moral criticism of the king"; to lessen criticism of Henri's culpability in taking Charlotte as his new mistress, it was important that she not remain unmarried.[123] In choosing Condé for Charlotte's husband, however, Henri seems to have entertained two additional motivations. First, the king seems to have believed that this union, unlike the planned marriage with Bassompierre, would ensure for the girl a husband unlikely to rival Henri for her affections. Just days after the ballet, when announcing to Bassompierre that he would break off his engagement to Charlotte, the king voiced the worry that his friend's likely success in winning Charlotte's love (Bassompierre was known as a ladies' man) would have brought about Henri's hatred of him; for this reason, he explained, he wished to marry off the young girl to Condé, whom he was sure loved hunting far more than ladies.[124] Yet the arrangement of Charlotte's marriage to Condé was also prompted by a more obviously political motivation: by uniting this first prince of the blood with the Montmorency clan – a family known for its longstanding loyalty to the crown – the king hoped to secure access to Charlotte for himself while simultaneously constraining Condé's potential for rebellion. According to Bassompierre, the Montmorency-Condé marriage was suggested to the king by the duc de Bouillon, who argued that the only other unmarried woman at court suitable for Condé on the basis of rank was Renée de Lorraine and that since this marriage would effect an alliance for Condé with Renée's powerful father the duc de Mayenne, former head of the Catholic League, it was too politically dangerous.[125] In marrying Condé to Charlotte, therefore, the king believed that he would retain his homosocial relationship with Bassompierre, secure Charlotte's affections for himself, and provide a suitably elevated match for Condé that would simultaneously foreclose other, more politically dangerous marital alliances for his nephew.

As first prince of the blood, Condé was de facto leader of the Bourbon line's cadet branches, Conti and Soissons. It was these Bourbon princes of the blood who posed the greatest threat to efforts promoting Marie de Médicis' worthiness to serve as regent, in the event of a royal minority. Actions that might contain Condé's ambitions were thus useful to the king, queen, and dauphin alike. Nonetheless, the particular means through which the king sought to limit Condé's power carried its own negative consequences for the Bourbon regime. Condé was a member of the *maison royale* (the royal house) of France, which consisted not only of the royal family (the king, queen, and their legitimate children, known as the *enfants de France*) but also the princes of the blood, who were Bourbons of the legitimate male line in their own right. In attempting to humiliate Condé by cuckolding him, the king brought into question the (masculine) virtue of a member of his own immediate bloodline. Initially, it seems, Condé showed enthusiasm for the match, most likely taking into account the dowry Charlotte would bring as well as the still positive consequences for his status at court stemming from marital alliance with one of the kingdom's great princely houses. But after the engagement papers were signed on 2 March and the king's amorous designs became more widely known, Henri IV's plans to demean his nephew by seducing Condé's wife became the talk of Paris.[126] Diplomatic circles, too, were aflutter with rumours regarding Condé's anticipated humiliation: the Florentine ambassador reported, for example, that when Condé begged the king to break off the marriage, Henri's only reply had been that a good subject obeyed his king in all things.[127] Such "absolutist" demands provoked from Condé a series of outbursts, but the prince was not the only one who grew troubled, for the king, in forcing his nephew into this marriage with the express purpose of cuckolding him, and thus undermining the claims to virility of another legitimate Bourbon male, threatened to call into question the very noble virtue, in the sense of superiority rooted in bloodline, on which his own political authority as head of the French royal house depended.

After Condé's marriage went forward, on 17 May 1609, the political dangers set in motion by Henri's pursuit of Charlotte-Marguerite increased. In April, Condé had begun planning his escape from France with help from the Spanish government, and in late June he fled the realm, Charlotte in tow, seeking refuge first in Flanders and then Milan, both territorial possessions of Spain.[128] Under pressure from Philip III, the archdukes Albert and Isabel refused Henri's demands that Condé be returned to France; in response, the French king took visible steps to raise an army designed to march on Flanders with the aim of retrieving Charlotte while striking back at Spain.[129] The king's desire to recover the young princess – and make an example of his rebellious nephew Condé – was not the sole motivation behind these threats, of course. By passing through the archdukes' territories, he also sought to influence the succession to the duchy of Clèves, a territory of significant strategic import in the European struggle to limit Hapsburg power. Before these plans could be fully realized, however, Henri IV was assassinated, on 14 May 1610. Only the king's death, it appears, saved France from entering into a costly war against the Habsburgs precipitated at least in part by his obsession with Charlotte.

After Condé's engagement to Charlotte had been arranged but prior to their wedding, Elisabeth de France danced her 2 April 1609 *Ballet de Madame*. Composed for this production, Malherbe's verses "De petites Nymphes qui mènent l'Amour prisonnier. Au Roi" warned of Henri's need to conquer Cupid's dangerous passions. In so doing, the poem gave voice to concerns prompted by the king's pursuit of the future princesse de Condé but also by a more sustained set of behaviours on the king's part. Henri, we have seen, had failed to follow through with the punishments the Parlement of Paris had imposed on Henriette d'Entragues, marquise de Verneuil, following her conviction for treason in 1605. Instead, he released the marquise almost immediately and then resumed his amorous exploits with her, to the chagrin of Marie de Médicis but also a great many royal councilors. The *Ballet de Madame*'s call for Henri IV to undertake rigorous justice rather than leniency towards Cupid may allude not only to Henri's infatuation with Charlotte-Marguerite de Montmorency, therefore, but also to his continued weakness in relation to his treasonous mistress. Malherbe's verses for the *Ballet de Madame*, in other words, arguably gestured beyond the king's affection for any one woman to encompass a larger pattern of action whereby Henri IV, asserting the absolute authority of an inscrutable and resolutely personal judgment, nonetheless failed to demonstrate the self-control over one's own passions that contemporary juridico-political discourse upheld as the basis for "absolutist" royal male authority. In this sense, Malherbe's poem for the *Ballet de Madame* appears even more bold, politically, than has been previously noted.

In performance, the *Ballet de Madame* conveyed such messages not only verbally, through Malherbe's text, but also by recasting, quite literally, roles and iconographies familiar to the king (and other members of his court) from Marie de Médicis' *Ballet of Diana and her Nymphs* performed two months previously. In one contemporary manuscript version, Malherbe's text for Elisabeth's ballet appears under the title "Pour le ballet de Madame *habillée en Diane* menant l'Amour prisonnier au Roi" [For the ballet of Madame *in the guise of Diana* bringing Love as prisoner to the king (emphasis mine)].[130] From this title, we learn that "Madame" – the young Elisabeth – appeared on stage during this ballet personating Diana. Goddess of chastity and of the hunt, Diana had been evoked in the queen's January 1609 ballet visually, by Marie and her troupe of dancers in their garden or woods dressed as nymphs holding arrows, as well as textually, when Fame's air placed these dancers under the rigorous control of Virtue and presented them as models for this ballet's audience, including the king. That ballet's verses had promised that the French court, though presently overrun by Cupid, might soon be subject to the "better laws" given to Diana and her nymphs by Virtue, and that those who suffered Love's wounds could, on the example of the queen and her companions, learn to reform themselves. Two months later, however, Henri had yet to check Love's unruly dominance, at the expense of not only his nephew Condé but also the Bourbon dynasty's own reputation for virtue. As if seeking to rectify this problem, the *Ballet de Madame* gave the earlier ballet's role of Diana to the pre-pubescent Elisabeth. Elisabeth's age offered an indirect yet still legible commentary on Henri's pursuit of Charlotte-Marguerite, for the latter's youth, contrasted with Henri IV's now advanced age, was part of what made the king's actions appear so foolish, and hence so threatening, to the very basis of French monarchical authority. Even more strikingly, the *Ballet de Madame*'s casting of Elisabeth placed the call to resist Cupid's tyrannies in the mouths of children – Henri IV's own daughter along with a troupe of young girls in the guise of little nymphs. In this way, the production shadowed under the guise of disarming, youthful innocence a thread of moral and political advice that might otherwise seem frankly accusatory.

If the *Ballet de Madame* boldly cautioned Henri against unchecked sexual indulgence, then, it took these rhetorical liberties by way of iconographies familiar to and approved by Marie de Médicis on the occasion of the queen's ballet two months previously. What are we to conclude, then, about the queen's own position with respect to Malherbe's verses on this second occasion? Although numerous sources have conflated this small-scale *Ballet de Madame* with Marie's earlier *Ballet of Diana and her Nymphs*, these ballets were clearly separate events, the one being danced by Marie in Paris on 31 January and the other by her daughter at Saint-Germaine-en-Laye, the royal children's residence, two months later. That being said, the *Ballet de Madame* may have adapted its verses from entries originally designed for a second *ballet de la reine* that Marie herself was to have performed during carnival that same year. We learn of this other ballet from George Carew, the English ambassador. Carew's letters indicate that immediately following the 31 January performance of Marie's *Ballet of Diana and her Nymphs*, Henri IV's secretary of state Nicolas de Neufville, seigneur de Villeroy, told him that this event was in fact "but her petit Ballet, and the grand Ballet should be on Shrove tewsday."[131] When Carew visited Marie herself, several weeks later, both she and Henri IV also mentioned to him that she was "busy" with "her second Ballet, which she had purposed to have shewed the first Sunday in Lent."[132] Throughout that day, Carew reports, this ballet was put on and off again several times, but performances seem finally to have been thwarted in earnest when news reached Paris that evening that Marie's uncle, Ferdinando I de' Medici, had died: the entire French court went into mourning, such that the planned ballet as well as several other entertainments could not appropriately be performed.[133] Might the *Ballet de Madame*, more appropriate than a queen's ballet during a period of official mourning because performed by children and only as a private entertainment, have taken up where Marie's *Ballet of Diana and her Nymphs* and its planned successor entertainment left off, extending the earlier ballet's themes of chaste self-control toward more pointed critique?[134]

No contemporary diplomatic correspondence, to my knowledge, describes the *Ballet de Madame*'s performance at the royal children's residence; nor do contemporary diaries by courtiers or Parisians. The *Ballet de Madame* was thus likely staged as an informal affair for the king, queen, and their immediate entourage. The ballet's publishing history is also informative in this respect. Whereas Malherbe's poem for the queen's *Ballet of Diana and her Nymphs* appeared in print almost immediately after the performance (though not by Malherbe himself), by contrast his verses for the *Ballet de Madame* (although they circulated in manuscript) were not published until the 1620s. This temporal gap between the ballet occasion and the publication of Malherbe's poem for it suggests that the harsher rhetoric of blame specific to the *Ballet de Madame* seems to have been kept close, whereas the more obviously encomiastic rhetoric found in the *Ballet of Diana and her Nymphs* circulated more immediately and widely. Whereas the much more public *ballet de la reine* sticks fairly closely to the genre's panegyrical functions, then, the more private court performance could afford greater political risks.

This shift in Malherbe's ballet verses from an epideictic balance that leans towards praise to one that privileges blame places royal women's ballet for winter 1609 in good (literary) company. Analysing contemporary and near-contemporary depictions of Henri IV's earlier entanglements with Gabrielle d'Estrées, duchesse de Beaufort, Kathleen Wine notes that although the king successfully reunited France after the wars of religion in part thanks to policies of clemency rooted in affection for his rebellious subjects, positive seventeenth-century myths of Henri IV as king of hearts had a darker side in novelized histories such as d'Urfé's *L'Astrée* (1610) and the anonymous *Histoire des amours du Grand Alcandre* (1651).[135] The *Alcandre*'s originating author is most frequently identified as Louise-Marguerite de Lorraine, princesse de Conti, who herself danced alongside the queen in the 1609 *Ballet of Diana and her Nymphs*.[136] Conti's *roman à clef* concludes by evoking the image of Henri IV worshipped after death by his subjects "jusqu'à l'adoration" [to the point of adoration], yet throughout the text the king's promiscuity proves a liability. In *Alcandre*, as Wine notes, Henri's infatuation with Gabrielle d'Estrées blinds him to his mistress's faults, including her lack of sexual fidelity to him; it also brings into question the king's own loyalty to the true church and to his subjects. Henri's final obsession with "Florise" (Charlotte-Marguerite de Montmorency), moreover, is prompted not only by her dancing "un dard a la main (comme par figure de Ballet)" [an arrow in hand (as had been the case for her ballet character)] but also by erotic instabilities internal to "Alcandre" himself, who "ne pouvoit vivre sans quelque amour nouvelle" [could not live without some new love].[137] A politicized language of blame focused on the king's *amours*, then, features prominently in such novelistic prose histories. As Wine notes, other near contemporaries such as Mézeray and Péréfixe inscribe positive images of the king-seducer yet also "bluntly condemn a politically dangerous 'folie,' which made the king seem 'rien moins qu'Henry le Grand'."[138] Looking closely at poetic texts produced directly for royal women's court ballets from the year 1609, we see that panegyric for these ballets anticipates such later assessments, for these productions, too, both flattered the king and warned him against an excessive clemency which extended not only to former Catholic Leaguers and to the Jesuits, recalled to France in 1603, but also to Cupid, a less obvious but still monstrous enemy within.

On this reading, royal women's ballet at the court of Henri IV commented critically on elements of the king's personal prerogative (his notorious philandering) that seemed poised to damage, perhaps irreparably, the assertions of orderly self-governance on which Bourbon dynastic monarchy based its most "absolute" sovereign claims. This finding, like the argument outlined in chapter 3, leads to a rethinking of royal women's French court ballet as a vehicle for political rhetoric. I have argued that the queen's 1609 *Ballet of Diana and her Nymphs* self-reflexively champions women's vocal and dance performance as a vehicle through which to arouse but also control bodily and political unmanageability – that of the French court as a whole but also the king himself. Verses for this production as well as the 1609 *Ballet de Madame* also mix praise with blame: the king is warned by Fame in the first instance to respect his wife if he knows what is good for him and when he fails in mutual fidelity to her, two months later, he is chastised by a troupe of youthful nymphs who, in the vacuum left by his susceptibility to unruly passion, themselves bind Cupid, thereby modelling for Henri how to save his kingdom from the single misfortune that troubles it. Even court ballet sponsored and danced by members of the French royal house itself, therefore, held the potential for topical critique. Royal women, by means of performances they directed and danced in, could thus deploy *divertissements de cour* not only to promote "absolutist" kingship but also to challenge – if only rhetorically – some of its privileges.

Chapter Five

Dances of Diplomacy: London, Valladolid, Paris

This book's previous chapters have analysed some of the ways in which the ballets danced and organized by Marie de Médicis navigated domestic politics, whether of the French royal house or of the French political nation. Additionally, as this final chapter will explore, the queen's ballets offered highly subtle opportunities for negotiating France's position within a larger geopolitical nexus. Historians and biographers have had little if anything to say about Marie's contributions to early Bourbon diplomacy during her husband's lifetime. Yet as events of state attended by ambassadors from neighbouring courts, Marie's ballets were by definition occasions of pan-European political importance. Considered in light of the multiple, intersecting levels on which court entertainments could navigate diplomatic exchanges between monarchical states, the queen's productions come into relief as complex dances of diplomatic ceremonial.

One level on which such diplomatic exchanges occurred involved the use of visual and textual allegories derived from Greco-Roman literature and mythology. Because foreign diplomats made up an important segment of the audiences for these entertainments, and because the humanist training of these ambassadors gave them familiarity with the literature of classical antiquity, allusions to a shared cultural repertoire from the antique past could speak across vernacular linguistic differences that might otherwise impede the transmission and reception of messages between one European court and another.[1] Arguably, though, courtly magnificence was an equally if not more effective tool for navigating international political relationships than was mythological content. For while "court entertainments functioned as strategic or ideologically driven displays" designed to "'impress' domestic spectators with the prince's overwhelming authority," as Ellen Welch has recently argued, "early modern commentators more often described court entertainments as a means to dazzle *foreign* observers."[2] Productions such as these provided crucial opportunities to show off before representatives of foreign rulers the host court's wealth, but also its appreciation for virtuosity in various media, including music, dance, and scenic design. When early modern ambassadors described court entertainments in official correspondence, in fact, their accounts often neglected discussions of dramatic, i.e., representational, content, instead privileging reports of significant expenditure or magnificence. These reports often centred on details such as rare gems or costly fabrics, as well as other production values that signalled the exclusiveness of sovereign rank – such as innovative instances of artistry or the involvement of artisans particularly sought after at other princely courts.

As this chapter will explore, however, entertainments in this genre also navigated international relations through qualities of organization and execution that enabled particularly subtle forms of diplomatic communication. Marie's productions specifically, I will suggest, succeeded in conveying favour to certain foreign governments while slighting others, and in ways that could not easily be pinned down, through the "mute diplomacy" they put in motion through non-verbal social codes pertaining to the relative temporal and spatial positioning of ambassadors.[3] Speaking without overtly saying a word, these aspects of Marie's ballets participated, in ways not previously understood, in the "poetics of diplomatic appeasement" that scholars such as Nathalie Rivère de Carles have traced in early modern theatre more broadly.[4]

The availability of such forms of international political engagement became especially important to the French crown beginning in 1603, after James I acceded to the English throne. Prior to this point, as this book's introduction has outlined, France had benefited from Spain's war against Elizabethan England as well as Habsburg military entanglements in the Netherlands because these conflicts, by tying up Spain's financial and military resources, helped to diminish its capacity for aggressive action elsewhere. But the new English king's commitment to international peacemaking wherever possible led to an about-face in Anglo-Spanish relations, and France was now excluded from meaningful alliance with England, on behalf of the United Provinces, against the Habsburgs.[5] In the months leading up to Spain's ratification of the peace with England, in summer 1605, the Bourbon monarchy also found itself excluded from a mutual exchange of ceremonial favours between the Stuart and Habsburg dynasties enacted by means of two masques, in England, and a *sarao*, in Spain. As Mark Hutchings and Berta Cano-Echevarría explain, "The word *sarao* is an old-fashioned Spanish term denoting a social event or celebration involving music, dance, and entertainment."[6] These entertainments placed on display each host court's magnificence and dynastic might. Through the active participation of the English and Spanish consort queens and their children, moreover, court spectacle on these occasions also helped the two powers to communicate their mutual interest in a lasting peace to be secured through dynastic marriage.

In response, the French turned to equivalent entertainments of their own, starting with the ballet Marie de Médicis danced at the Louvre on 23 January 1605. By means of the occasion it celebrated – a Protestant marriage alliance designed to help strengthen two high-ranking Huguenot families known for military expertise and political loyalty to the French king – this ballet signalled French readiness for armed intervention on behalf of the United Provinces, even without English aid. At the same time, careful arrangement of ambassadors in the audience attempted to offset the damage to Henri IV's already shaky religious credentials caused by his support for the Protestant States against Catholic Spain. Such efforts were nearly scuttled thanks to an unanticipated challenge to Henri IV's authority as host. From this incident combined with close attentiveness to ceremonies of diplomacy in London and Valladolid, however, the French learned several valuable lessons, the fruits of which they mobilized at the final ballet that Marie danced as consort queen, in January 1609.

Advertising Bourbon magnificence to domestic as well as foreign audiences, this production displayed material wealth in the form of costly gems and demonstrated European cultural leadership by combining Italian vocal innovations with native French stylistic excellence. By delaying the ballet's timing so as not to conflict with the *Masque of Queens* danced in London by James I's consort Queen Anna of Denmark and by introducing important innovations regarding the ballet's performance locations, moreover, the French successfully navigated rivalries with Spain for influence over the English in ways that helped to shift balances of power among the three kingdoms and beyond.

Two Queen's Masques, a *Sarao*, and the Treaty of London, 1604–5

As we saw in chapter 1, Marie de Médicis had danced her 1602 *Ballet of the Sixteen Virtues* shortly following the birth of a dauphin, and by celebrating the promise of dynastic continuity that this birth made possible, this ballet contributed to a larger political program seeking to re-sacralize the monarchy for French subjects. This entertainment conveyed this message internationally as well, however, since Marie together with Henri IV had made a point of inviting to the performance every foreign representative in France at the time.[7] Advertising the royal couple's fertility before this international segment of the ballet's audience, the queen's production thus drew attention to the possibility of alliances with foreign powers that might be secured via dynastic marriages.

A tentative suggestion for one such match formed part of the proposal Henri IV's extraordinary ambassador Maximilien de Béthune, marquis de Rosny (the future duc de Sully), made to James I shortly after the latter's accession to the English throne in 1603. The larger aim of Sully's embassy to James' court was to convince the new English government to unite with France in an offensive alliance on behalf of the United Provinces, against Spain. To sweeten the proposal, Sully raised the idea of a Stuart-Bourbon dynastic marriage.[8] James did agree to a defensive league and to secretly allowing the Dutch to recruit soldiers in England to be paid for by France.[9] Yet his significantly greater interest in diplomacies of appeasement with Spain soon revealed itself through two court masques danced by his wife, Anna of Denmark.

Throughout Elizabeth I's reign, no Spanish ambassador had been present in England to vie for the first place of honour among foreign representatives at the year's most important court festivities.[10] Shortly after Sully's visit to London, however, Philip III had sent his own extraordinary ambassador, Juan de Tassis y Peralta, first count of Villamediana. At Queen Anna's 1604 *Masque of the Twelve Goddesses*, Villamediana was placed under the canopy of state on James' right, a mark of great honour. During the revels, moreover, he was taken out by Anna's favourite, Lucy Russell, countess of Bedford, and thereafter was joined in the social dancing by Queen Anna and her son, Henry, prince of Wales. For these revels, Anna sported a red sash or belt, and because red was Villamediana's colour, this costuming choice advertised her favour towards Spain.[11] That summer, James signed the treaty declaring peace with Spain, and while preparations were underway for this treaty's ratification in Valladolid the following May, the Stuarts used Anna's *Masque of Blackness*, performed on 6 January 1605, to signal their interest in a dynastic marriage that would be designed to cement the peace.[12] At this masque, foreign representatives in the audience again saw Spain publicly honoured: not only was Villamediana seated at the right hand of the king (the most privileged location for ambassadors) but he was even taken out by the queen herself as her dance partner during the revels. Not surprisingly, rumours of an Anglo-Spanish match began to circulate almost immediately following this production in diplomatic reports written by ambassadors stationed in London.[13]

Reciprocating such gestures, celebrations of the treaty's June 1605 ratification in Valladolid included a *sarao* through which the Spanish Habsburgs indicated their own interest in such a marriage. During the social dancing that concluded this *sarao*, Philip's consort Queen Margarita de Austria publicly favoured James' representative the earl of Nottingham by inviting him to dance with her, thereby returning the January 1604 gesture in which Anna of Denmark's favourite, the countess of Bedford, had taken out Villamediana in the revels at the *Masque of the Twelve Goddesses* as well as the January 1605 occasion when Anna herself danced with him during the revels for her *Masque of Blackness*. When in the Valladolid *sarao* the Infanta Aña appeared as a performer, moreover, her parents reciprocated the honour shown to Spain in January 1604 when, as we have seen, Prince Henry presented himself during the social dancing for his mother's *Masque of the Twelve Goddesses* at which Villamediana had been so fêted. Appearing in the Valladolid *sarao* seated in a chariot that moved across the performance space, Aña participated in an emblematic procession signifying the power and continuity of the Habsburg dynasty; in this way, her conspicuous appearance made this occasion a powerful vehicle for "dynastic wooing."[14] The Spanish crown devolved to male offspring in the first instance, but should something happen to Aña's younger brother and should Philip III sire no other living son, Aña would inherit the throne. The power this inheritance would give her future husband made the idea of a Spanish match particularly attractive to other dynastic monarchies. So did the rumour that Aña might come to possess the Low Countries, destined to revert to Spain should the archdukes Albert and Isabel die without issue. Aña's on-stage appearance in 1605 in Valladolid had advertised to English representatives in the audience Spanish interest in a match between Aña and Henry, then, but also the potential benefits to England of such a prestigious union.[15]

The English had managed to convince the Spanish of their sincere interest in the peace as well as in such a dynastic match in part because Anna's masques, by honouring the Spanish ambassador, constituted an "orchestrated humiliation" of his French equivalent. In 1604,

Henri IV's ambassador Christophe de Harlay, comte de Beaumont, had been invited not to the *Masque of the Twelve Goddesses*, as was Villamediana, but to the less prestigious *Masque of the Knights of India and China* (also known as *The Orient Knights*) organized and danced by Ludovic Stuart, duke of Lennox.[16] Because Lennox's masque was danced by a mere courtier, rather than a queen, and because it was scheduled for an occasion that was less prestigious than Twelfth Night, the most important of England's Christmas festival dates at court, Beaumont's invitation to the *Masque of the Knights of India and China* signalled, without stating overtly, England's preference for friendship with Spain over the honour it had previously reserved for France under Elizabeth I.[17] Beaumont sought to change the course of affairs by complaining directly to James that his exclusion from the *Masque of the Twelve Goddesses* would directly contravene the tradition by which France enjoyed precedence at the English celebrations for Twelfth Night. In response, the English made two moves that caught the French off guard but which they would learn from and eventually put in motion themselves in 1609, as I will explore below. First, the English dealt with the French ambassador's complaint by manipulating the timing of the queen's production: moving forward, by two days, the date for Anna's performance, and therefore giving no actual Twelfth Night masque, they could satisfy the letter of Beaumont's complaint that no other ambassador should have precedence over the French at a Twelfth Night performance, while still showing preference for Spain by inviting them to a masque that was more prestigious because danced by the queen, just on another day. Second, the English manipulated ambiguities inherent in the nature of royal marriage in order to have their cake and eat it when it came to claiming responsibility for honouring the Spanish at France's expense. On the one hand, when confronted by the French ambassador, James responded by claiming that his wife, without consulting him, had invited Villamediana, but that because he could not reasonably rescind Anna's invitation without causing international scandal and grave insult to the Spanish, nothing could now be done. This response fobbed off responsibility onto Anna. To the Spanish, however, the English sent another message, for the story Villamediana reported back to Spain was that "although the [English] council [had] proposed to the King that to resolve inconveniences and differences the Queen's masque should not be performed, the King [had] answered that the Queen's will was his will and as she had gone with it thus far he wanted it to be performed in the presence of those whom she chose."[18] The following year, the situation only got worse for the French when Beaumont, in an attempt to regain some of his master's lost dignity, declined on the pretext of illness the invitation he received to the English court's first masque of the 1604–5 season.[19] The French ambassador feared that should he attend this event he would again be excluded from the more prestigious production, Queen Anna's masque for Twelfth Night 1605. Beaumont's strategy ended up working against him, however, for it gave the English a convenient excuse to invite Villamediana in his public capacity as ambassador on the basis that Henri IV's representative, due to ill health, could not be present.

The English, then, deployed ambiguities in the meaning attached to the timing of Anna's *Masque of the Twelve Goddesses*, as well as ambiguities in the meaning attached to responsibilities for issuing invitations to this same masque, to convey messages of wished-for friendship, or lack thereof, internationally. Diplomatic correspondence between Beaumont and Henri IV, and between Beaumont and Henri's counsellors, shows just how seriously the French took such matters. Because England had slighted France without stating so outright, however, this gave France wiggle room to continue seeking English friendship against Spain. Because the French continued to need the English, in fact, official royal propaganda, when it commented on celebrations of the Anglo-Spanish peace, placed the blame for France's difficulties on Habsburg Spain, rather than on Stuart England. We find such rhetoric in an account of the Valladolid *sarao* that circulated widely, within France, via the *Mercure françois* – the official government newspaper inaugurated that year. This description outlines the production's allegorical iconographies, names the production's royal performers, and ascribes an estimated value to the jewels worn by the Spanish queen during the performance. It also recounts the numerous marks of intimacy and regard given by the Spanish to James I's representative, the earl of Nottingham, during and immediately following the entertainment. Reminding its readers that until recently Spain, under the pretext of religion, had succeeded in keeping France internally divided (an allusion to the French civil wars and the long history of Spanish support for the Catholic League, first against the late Valois monarchs and then against Henri IV himself), the *Mercure françois* condemns as hypocritical not England's use of Anna's masques but instead Spain's seeming prioritization of state over religion in its declaration of peace with England, a Protestant monarchical state. The Spanish may have succeeded in winning over the English, the *Mercure françois* concludes, but only by hoodwinking France's former ally into an alliance that would ultimately work against England's own interests to the detriment of the United Provinces.[20]

"Hostipitality" at France's 1605 *ballet de la reine*

Behind such complaints lay a very real fear that the United Provinces might settle for peace on terms that would enable the Habsburgs to recuperate and then resume, from a strengthened position, outright aggression against France. Additionally, the *Mercure françois* account registers awareness that the French could not really hope to compete with the Spanish Habsburgs for England's friendship, and hence secure English support for the Dutch against Spain, via dynastic wooing at magnificent royal entertainments. The problem was that no Bourbon gesture toward dynastic marriage could match that which the Habsburgs were offering the Stuarts via the 1605 Valladolid *sarao*: only Spain enjoyed reversionary rights to sovereignty in the Low Countries, to be offered as dowry, and while a Spanish infanta could inherit the throne if no male heir was living, no French princess could claim her father's crown thanks to early modern interpretations of Salic law, which mandated rights of succession through the male line.[21]

Staged after Anna's 1604 *Masque of the Twelve Goddesses* and 1605 *Masque of Blackness* but prior to Philip and Margarita's *sarao*, Marie de Médicis' January 1605 ballet registers such disadvantages. On this occasion, the French seem to have made no particular effort to compete with Spain by giving special treatment to English representatives present in Paris. Instead, the French queen's 1605 ballet seems to have sent a defiant message, through its casting choices, regarding France's continued commitment to supporting the United Provinces even in the face of England's reluctance to continue sharing in this commitment.

As noted in chapter 2, this ballet was danced in celebration of Henri II de Rohan's engagement to Marguerite de Béthune, daughter of the future duc de Sully. The French crown had arranged this marriage as a way to help reign in Huguenot unrest, we have seen, but news of the Béthune-Rohan match also aided the crown insofar as sustained loyalty from the house of Rohan, a family of great military leaders, would be necessary should Henri IV need to undertake greater efforts against Spain on behalf of the United Provinces.[22] By the 1604–5 carnival season, the king had begun gathering three new regiments for possible deployment in Flanders. These troupes were to be led by members of the kingdom's greatest Protestant families, including Henri II de Rohan's brother Benjamin, seigneur de Soubise.[23] Ultimately these regiments were never mobilized, for while Henri IV remained actively committed to undermining Spain, he was not willing to risk what the Spanish ambassador swore would be Philip III's full declaration of war should the regiments be deployed. The mere threat represented by such military preparations sent a message of French strength, however. So did the queen's choice of dancers for her ballet that January: performed by herself along with women from the Rohan family, this production indicated, to visiting diplomats from across Europe, the French monarchy's commitment to Protestant allies both at home and abroad.[24]

At the same time, however, the new Bourbon dynasty required the support of powerful Catholic nobles within France, as well as the papacy. To gain the throne, Henri IV had needed the pope to acknowledge his abjuration of Protestantism. He also required papal annulment of his childless marriage to Marguerite de Valois so that he could produce a legitimate heir. Thereafter, to repay the symbolic debt he owed Clement VIII and to successfully compete with Spain for influence in Rome as well as at other Catholic European courts, Henri had needed to fulfil the assurance he had given at the time of his absolution to actively "show in words and deeds" the faith appropriate to the French king's role as "eldest and devoted son of the Catholic church."[25] His 1600 marriage to Marie de Médicis, a devout Catholic princess, helped in this regard; so did the king's action of recalling the Jesuits to France in 1603.[26] By 1605, however, France's need to prolong war in the Netherlands in order to weaken Habsburg Spain required actions in support of Huguenot grands, such as the crown's arrangement of the Béthune-Rohan marriage discussed in chapter 2, that might seem to place in question the sincerity of Henri IV's Catholicism.

To balance out the message this ballet sent regarding crown support for Protestants at home and in the Low Countries, therefore, the French deployed a strategy used previously for Marie's 1602 *Ballet of the Sixteen Virtues*: choreographing the audience so as to preserve precedence for the papal nuncio followed by other Catholic powers.[27] As chapter 2 has noted, for the queen's 1605 ballet Henri IV entered the Grande Salle du Louvre just before the performance began in order to put the assembly to order ["pour faire ranger tout le monde"], first arranging the ambassadors so that the English representatives were placed on one side and the papal nuncio and representatives of Catholic rulers on the other.[28] The French secretary of state responsible for foreign affairs,

Nicolas de Neufville, seigneur de Villeroy, specifies in a letter to Beaumont, Henri IV's ambassador in England, that James I's newly arrived extraordinary ambassador, the duke of Lennox, "was invited to be at the queen's ballet" and that "the nuncio and the other ambassadors were then in a separate scaffold, and the said duke in another accompanied by the English and Scottish lords and gentlemen that were with him."[29] According to Baccio Giovannini, the Florentine representative to France, this arrangement specified that the English would be seated on the king's left, leaving for the nuncio as well as the ambassadors of Spain, Venice, and Flanders the scaffold to Henri IV's right.[30] These seating arrangements made use of "diplomatic ambiguation" – the strategy of "cultivating ambiguity" by giving a particular act "a second meaning" designed to "undermine the negative effects of the first."[31] In this case, the organization of visiting diplomats in the ballet's audience, which reserved the most prestigious spatial positioning for the pope's representative while still accommodating the English, sent a second message regarding the French crown's religious and political commitments, one that, in undermining the message sent by the production's honouring of Huguenot nobles within the kingdom, rendered the ballet's overarching political meaning less easy to pin down with certainty.

Before the performance proper could begin, however, these careful arrangements were subjected to serious challenge. Describing these circumstances in an official missive to the Medici court, Giovannini writes:

> La Regina fece il suo balletto, et essendo state messe le seggiole per li Amba[sciato]ri ... intervenne che essendo entrati nella sala p[rim]a che vi fusse il Re et che la festa si cominciasse, li Inglesi si messono a sedere ne' luoghi destinati per il Nuntio et per li Amb[asciato]ri Catt[oli]ci senza che vi fusse chi dicesse lor nulla. Et venendo il Re a veder la sala, et trovando q[uest]o disordine, fece lor destramente dire che quello non era il lor luogo, ma essi fecero orecchie di mercante; et intanto il Nuntio et li altri Amb[asciato]ri che si trovavano in camera, sentendo ch'era stato lor usurpato il lor luogo, si lasciavano intendere di non voler altrim[en]ti intervenirvi; onde il Re di nuovo hebbe sino a tre volte a farli pregar che se ne levassero, come poi alla fine fecero et si messero nella parte destinata per loro, et il Nuntio poi et li Amb[asciato]ri si messero nella loro.[32]

> [The queen made her ballet, and the ambassadors' seating having been arranged ... it came about that the English, having entered the room before the king was there and prior to the start of the festivities, seated

themselves in the places arranged for the nuncio and the Catholic ambassadors without anyone saying anything to them, and the king coming to see the room, and finding these disorders, skillfully made to tell them that that was not their place; but these [the English] pretended not to hear, and in the meanwhile the nuncio and the other ambassadors that were in the room, perceiving their places to be usurped, let it be understood that they would not attend unless they were given their proper seats. Whence again the king had to entreat the English three times to get up from where they were seated, as finally they did, and put themselves in the place arranged for them, and then the nuncio and the [Catholic] ambassadors put themselves in theirs.]

For this ballet as for other similar occasions, ambassadors of foreign states rivaled one another for coveted invitations and for seats in proximity to the hosting monarch; in this way, court entertainments as forms of diplomatic ceremonial negotiated the relative status of rival European powers. The privilege of being placed nearest to the king, on his right, indicated great honour.[33] When Lennox and his troupe seated themselves on the scaffold to the right of where Henri IV would sit, therefore, they "usurped" both the physical position that the French crown had assigned to visiting Catholic representatives and the visible, ceremonial marker of Bourbon friendship that this position coded. The French could not afford to entirely alienate Lennox and his master, given how important England's support for the United Provinces was to their own foreign policy interests. But neither could they afford the damage to Henri IV's reputation as eldest son of the church should Lennox's presumption – and its slight to the new papal nuncio Maffeo Barberini – be allowed to stand. Canceling the ballet entirely would have been one way out of this predicament. In order to save face after the humiliation France had suffered at Anna of Denmark's 1605 *Masque of Blackness* performed just two weeks earlier, however, and to hint at defiance towards Spain through a ballet honouring Protestants who might lead regiments against Habsburg forces in the Spanish Netherlands, France needed its own queen's ballet to go forward as planned.

When confronted with Lennox's unanticipated actions in the performance hall, therefore, Henri IV mobilized the "conditional codes" outlined in Jacques Derrida's theory of "hostipitality." According to Derrida, hospitality requires of hosts a measure of control over their guests, an enforcing of limits upon where foreign others can trespass.[34]

Derrida (following Kant) discusses primarily post-Enlightenment laws and practices of hospitality in modern nation states. Nonetheless, his theories regarding the boundary limits of households, countries, and nations, the ways in which hospitality "fold[s] the foreign other into the internal laws of the host," and the extent to which host and guest "negotiate the reciprocal identities that shape hospitable encounters" can prove useful for our understanding of early modern guest-host relations, including those involving foreign diplomats at court ballets and masques.

The motives behind Lennox's extraordinary embassy were not clear to other foreign representatives in Paris: puzzling over the meaning of his visit, most ambassadors concluded that it was merely designed to reassure the French of English friendship, despite the Anglo-Spanish peace.[35] To have arrived in time for Marie's 23 January ballet, though, Lennox would have had to begin his journey not long after Beaumont had written to France with word of his own exclusion from Anna's *Masque of Blackness*, and this timing, together with the nature of Lennox's actions in the audience for Marie's ballet, suggest that when he came to Paris armed with "words of compliment" (Giovannini's phrase), this extraordinary ambassador also carried a mandate of ensuring that English prestige would not be flouted at the French court's seasonal festivities in retaliation for the treatment Beaumont had just received at Anna's masque.[36] When Lennox seated himself among the audience for Marie's 1605 ballet, he seized for his master a sign of prestige that was properly the host court's to give. Intentional or not, his contravention of this ceremonial code constituted a "diplomatic incident" – the term Lucien Bély uses to describe an event that crosses the usually impassable line dividing external, ceremonial workings of diplomacy from the internal, hidden negotiations through which diplomatic relationships and strategies are played out, thereby revealing the "underground tensions" that invisibly structure diplomatic culture.[37]

Reading this encounter through the lens of Derridean "hostipitality," moreover, we can see that Lennox's actions tested, on a symbolic level, French willingness to enforce limits in the face of foreign trespass. Giovannini writes that the French king "cleverly" ("destramente") rectified the "disorder" ("disordine") that Lennox had put in motion by firmly yet courteously insisting that the English remove themselves to the seats his government had assigned to them. The Florentine ambassador does not indicate with any specificity the content of Henri IV's remarks to Lennox at this moment. One of Villeroy's letters to Beaumont, however, reports that during this same ballet the king informed the English extraordinary ambassador of his serious resentment regarding the assault on French dignity that Beaumont's (mis)treatment at Anna's masques represented.[38] The French could not force the English to honour them above the Spanish at Anna's performances. Lennox's precipitous actions on the occasion of Marie's 1605 ballet, though, provided an unexpectedly useful opportunity for Henri IV to reassert his own sovereign dignity before an audience that included, by royal design, all of the foreign ambassadors in Paris.[39] For in this remarkable performance of "hostipitality" at his own wife's ballet, Henri IV responded to Lennox's challenge by successfully folding the English visitors into the laws or regulations of an entertainment occasion and place over which he presided as sovereign.

A Queen's Ballet, a Queen's Masque, and the Truce of Antwerp, 1609

This show of royal authority indicated that on its own turf, at least, the Bourbon monarchy could only be pushed so far. And yet the "diplomatic incident" in the audience for Marie's 1605 ballet involving the papal legate and the duke of Lennox had forced Henri IV to navigate precedence openly, under threat of public challenge. In hopes of achieving a more seamless promotion of Bourbon authority at the next major production danced by Marie de Médicis four years later, the crown made better use of several resources at its disposal, including the queen consort herself but also the king's former wife, Marguerite de Valois. Through interventions by these two women combined, the French displayed a magnificence designed to compete in splendour with the London and Valladolid entertainments discussed above. These two queens, moreover, enabled the crown to choreograph this ballet's audience in ways that advertised and cemented France's recent success in shifting England's position on the Dutch to coincide more closely with its own.

At the time of Marie's 1605 ballet, France had hoped to keep alive Spain's war in the Netherlands. But when in 1606 Henri IV marched against the rebellious duc de Bouillon, the costs of this military campaign necessitated a temporary reduction in French payments to the Dutch and so the latter, lacking consistent financial support, agreed to an eight-month truce.[40] Forced to change tack, France next sought to ensure that any future agreement between Spain and the United Provinces would be made on terms least beneficial to the former. Toward this end, the French put pressure on the English to join with them in a defensive league designed to guarantee for the Dutch the terms of any peace treaty. James I's government demurred, however, and when Queen Anna of Denmark again invited the Spanish ambassador to her winter 1608 *Masque of Blackness* (an action that James determined to support, should the French complain, by demanding repayment of French debts to England incurred during Elizabeth I's reign), France finally went it alone, signing a bilateral agreement with the United Provinces.

By entering into this defensive league, Henri IV elevated himself to a position James wished for himself: that of preeminent mediator in efforts towards peace on the larger European geopolitical stage. Meanwhile, France's continuing commitment to Dutch sovereignty weakened Spain's position, as did the archdukes' strong desire to put an end to the war even if this meant recognizing independence for the United Provinces. In hopes of delaying the peace negotiations, Philip III sent an extraordinary ambassador to France in June 1608 armed with a proposal for a triple marriage between the houses of Austria and Bourbon. According to this scheme, the French dauphin (the future Louis XIII) would marry the Infanta Aña; Elisabeth, eldest daughter of Henri IV and Marie de Médicis, would wed the Infante Philip, heir to the Spanish throne; and Christine, Henri and Marie's second daughter, would marry Don Carlos, the Spanish king and queen's second son. Christine's dowry, moreover, would include sovereign control of the Low Countries to be passed to her and her husband when the archdukes died without issue.[41]

Henri IV may have well have been inclined toward dynastic marriage with Spain at this point in time: a short while earlier, he had arranged to have the dauphin send a letter to the Infanta Aña and had given the impression in Rome that he wished for his heir a marriage that would assure close ties with the Spanish crown.[42] After the arrival of Spain's extraordinary ambassador Don Pedro de Toledo, however, the king stood firm in his profession of support for the Dutch, at Spain's expense. Expressing surprise that Spain and the pope would think him capable of pursuing control of the United Provinces for his own "private interest," Henri insisted that by staying true to the Dutch and thus gaining credit with them, he would be in a much better position, after a peace had been signed, to help obtain good conditions for Catholics in the United Provinces. With this response, and by agreeing to let Queen Marie de Médicis hold a separate audience with Don Pedro to discuss possibilities for a marriage between her daughter Elisabeth and Philip III's heir, the king held firm in his position regarding Dutch sovereignty while simultaneously keeping open possibilities for a future Habsburg-Bourbon marriage alliance.

This strategy helped pave the way for the double marriages with Spain that Marie's regency government would go on to negotiate shortly after Henri IV's assassination in 1610.[43] In the more immediate term, it also gave France maximum leverage with the English. In late spring 1608, even prior to Don Pedro's arrival in France, rumours concerning this extraordinary ambassador's mission had begun to circulate amongst the diplomatic community in London. Within a short time, the English asked Henri IV's ambassador there how Spain's marriage proposals might be received, and in response, the latter heightened rather than downplayed English suspicions.[44] These anxieties, combined with James' wish to be seen as a peacemaker, helped to turn the tide against Spain in June 1608, when the English finally agreed to a defensive league with the Dutch that matched in duration the earlier agreement France had signed with them.[45]

Thereafter, French representatives at The Hague needed their English counterparts to stand firm with them on what course the States should pursue during negotiations for their truce with Spain. These negotiations eventually resulted in the Truce of Antwerp, ratified in late May 1609, by which military action between the United Provinces, the Spanish Habsburgs, and the archdukes would cease for a period of twelve years. The French favoured a truce such as this rather than a full declaration of peace since the former, being limited in duration, would make resumption of war more likely; they also wanted to ensure that any agreement would include Spain's acknowledgment of Dutch sovereignty, since this proviso would help to ensure independence for the United Provinces even after the truce had expired. English commitment to these same objectives would aid France significantly. Mere speculation about Don Pedro's mission, we have seen, had helped convince James I to sign his own June 1608 defensive alliance with the Dutch. Several months later, therefore, the French government organized the occasion of Marie's ballet for carnival 1609 in ways that allowed them to wield in relation to the English both a carrot and a stick simultaneously. This ballet, we will see, sent messages of favour to the English. At the same time, it helped to maintain courteous relations with the Holy See and with Spain, thereby keeping open the possibility of Bourbon rapprochement with the Habsburgs.

Ever since the Anglo-Spanish peace had been registered with the Treaty of London's ratification in 1604–5, the French had been seeking to weaken James and Anna's pro-Spanish stance; they had also sought a public advertisement of this shift in English foreign policy at one of Anna's masques. After Beaumont had been humiliatingly excluded from Anna's 1604 *Masque of the Twelve Goddesses* and 1605 *Masque of Blackness*, he was replaced as ambassador to the Stuart court by Antoine Le Fèvre de la Boderie who, together with his wife Jeanne le Prévost, established improved relations with both James and Anna.[46] By winter 1608, when Anna performed her *Masque of Beauty*, Boderie still had not succeeded in securing an invitation from the English king and queen. During this performance and the collation that followed it, however, the English queen pointedly refused to exchange words with the wife of the archdukes' ambassador (this woman had also been seated at an insulting distance from Anna and James' daughter, the princess Elizabeth), while also ignoring the Spanish ambassador – a treatment that allegedly caused him to confess his wish not to have been present at all.[47] In the months leading up to Anna's 1609 *Masque of Queens*, moreover, Spain's advantage over France in relation to England's favour at Anna's entertainments became increasingly unclear, not only because the previous summer James under pressure from the French had entered into a bilateral defensive league with the Dutch, but also because France had (profitably) changed tactics in relation to James' consort.

Previously, the French had registered irritation when faced with evidence of Anna's agency in foreign affairs by means of the masques she organized and danced. After her 1604 *Masque of the Twelve Goddesses*, for example, Henri IV had voiced to Boderie his distrust of Anna and his wish that James, for whom he had little personal respect, would act with more prudence in future so as to restrain and counteract his wife's power, which if left unchecked might threaten to undo what from Henri's perspective was England's best interest: friendship with France.[48] In 1608, when the Spanish ambassador was invited by Anna to her *Masque of Beauty*, Henri had instructed the English ambassador in Paris, George Carew, to inform his queen that the king of France cared nothing for her opinion, while Boderie advised the English secretary of state Robert Cecil, earl of Salisbury, that James should more carefully contain his wife, since even the rumour of Anna's control over such an important matter as invitations to a royal masque constituted a manifest insult to James, who "doit etre le maître en sa maison" [should be the master in his own house].[49]

These efforts to shame the English on the grounds of their queen's "meddling" in international affairs mobilized a larger set of anxieties concerning women's suitability for political responsibility.[50] And yet Anna of Denmark's role as a diplomatic actor was hardly unique within the framework of early modern dynastic political culture. As feminist scholars working in "the new diplomatic history" have recently articulated, at the "origins of [modern] diplomacy ... women acted as agents of cross-state and cross-cultural information gathering, alliance-building and networking and as political negotiators, even if this was sometimes controversial."[51] Women's participation in diplomatic culture was especially marked in the realm of dynastic marriage negotiation; as Silvia Z. Mitchell notes, "the indispensable function royal marriages played in forging alliances and devising strategies was axiomatic to early modern rulers and diplomats," and such matrimonial alliances, rather than "revolv[ing] exclusively on the actions of male rulers," also involved royal mothers, whose "brokerage, patronage and adjudication" made them "leading figures in negotiations concerning their children's marriages."[52] Contemporary notions of maternal nature legitimated such interventions by providing a discursive frame according to which royal women's involvement in arranging dynastic marriages was considered an extension of women's "natural" concern for their own offspring. As we have seen, female organizers, patrons, and performers in royal entertainments surrounding the Treaty of London in 1604–5 were crucial to the hints these occasions offered regarding dynastic marriage possibilities, and hence to the gestures of mutual sincerity and regard between monarchical states that these occasions put in motion. When the French grumbled about the influence Anna exercised in the realm of foreign affairs through the masques that she organized and danced, therefore, their complaints registered, if only begrudgingly, just how important James' consort was to England's geopolitical positioning as it intersected with France's own.

Faced with indisputable evidence of Anna's considerable sway in international relations, and having failed in their attempts to pressure James to contain this influence in ways that would benefit them, the French finally set in motion a more successful course of action. In May 1608, Henri IV sent word through Boderie as well as less official channels that any rumours the English queen might have heard about his enmity towards her were false; rather, he held Anna in very high esteem and only wished to do her service. Once he learned that she had received this gesture positively, the king asked Anna to serve as godmother to his recently born son Gaston, duc d'Orléans.[53] In response to these indications that Henri IV wished to put all ill will and misunderstandings behind them, Anna took preliminary steps towards honouring France at her next masque. Already, at her January 1608 *Masque of Beauty*, she had indicated a position of greater neutrality: although Anna had invited the Spanish ambassador rather than the French, at the event itself she ignored the Spanish representative as well as the wife of the archdukes' ambassador, as we have seen. To further mitigate the insult to France implied by having invited the Spanish ambassador, Anna sought Boderie's permission to honour his wife, the French "ambassadress," as a guest at the production (a gesture that Boderie refused to accept).[54] A year later, Spain sent to London an extraordinary ambassador, Don Fernando de Giron, charged with securing an invitation to Anna's upcoming masque for winter 1609. In late December 1608, however, Anna excused herself from giving the regular Spanish ambassador an audience; moreover, she made a point of informing Boderie's wife that she had refused this request because she knew the Spanish representative's objective had been to gain an invitation for Giron and for himself to her masque – an invitation she had no desire to extend.[55] Anna, it seems, purposefully sought ways to sidestep Spanish expectations, though not overtly. Additionally, she went out of her way to convey this information to the French, through unofficial female channels. By means of informal women's networks associated with yet technically separate from professional modern diplomacy, therefore, the English queen consort sent an early signal to Henri IV's government that an important door had been opened to them.[56]

In response, the French manipulated the timing, location, and guest list for their own queen's entertainment in Paris that season so as to flatter the English without giving Catholic powers overt cause for offence. We learn much about such maneuverings – including how closely they intersected with arrangements for Anna's *Masque of Queens* across the channel – from Carew. In early January 1609, Carew reported to James I's secretary of state Robert Cecil, earl of Salisbury, that the prince de Joinville and Villeroy had sounded him out for further news of Anna's masque while refusing to state outright what was at stake. When Carew inquired whether anything specific depended on events surrounding Anna's masque, Villeroy dodged the question, indicating instead that "this Queene [Marie de Médicis] also would make a Maske this Shrovetide, wherein there should be fifty gentlewomen, and Ladies." In the English ambassador's view, this "awnswere did the rather confirme unto me, that they had taken some allarme at our Maske."[57] The French could not yet be sure that they would finally avoid humiliation at

Anna's upcoming *Masque of Queens*, but Villeroy's response to Carew's question indicated that should this occur, France would have at the ready its own prestige weapon: a queen's ballet, the social and political importance of which Villeroy hinted at through his seemingly casual reference to its extraordinarily large number of high-ranking women performers.

The English were now in a bind. Any overt steps to exclude the Spanish ambassadors from Anna's upcoming masque would announce a break with the Habsburgs at a time when openly severing this relationship might prove precipitous. And yet the French had made clear their determination to secure an invitation to Anna's production – so much so that should Boderie be excluded, he was instructed to defend his master's dignity by removing himself from England entirely.[58] To avoid overtly declaring sides, therefore, the English postponed the date of Anna's masque, originally planned for Twelfth Night, in hopes that Giron would be forced to depart before the performance.

Meanwhile, the French, too, had been delaying the date for their own queen's ballet in hopes that prior to its performance they would gain a more sure sign of English favour toward them at Anna's equivalent production. In a missive dated the day following Marie's *ballet de la reine*, Carew outlines the back story. Several weeks previously, Carew explains, the French queen had spoken to him "doubtfully of her owne maske," saying "that if she made any [such performance], it should not be shewed at Court but in the towne."[59] Shortly thereafter, Carew writes, the French had received confirmation from persons recently in England that "her M[ajes]ties maske was put of[f], till Ferdinando Girone should be gone, and that then the French Ambassad[o]r should be invited to yt."[60] At this point, Carew was invited to Marie's ballet by the duc de Sully, at whose Paris residence, the Arsenal, the ballet was to be danced, while Carew's wife Thomasine was invited by Marie de Médicis (in a gesture carefully calibrated to reciprocate the invitation to Anna's masque that the English queen had extended, the previous year, to Boderie's wife).[61] Marie's ballet, Carew was told, would take place on 25 January. The production was not danced until 31 January, however, immediately prior to which Henri IV personally invited Carew to the ballet as well. Explaining this further postponement, Carew describes conversations with both the king and queen during the actual performance. At the ballet, Henri informed Carew that he had received a letter from Boderie the previous day. Then, at the end of the performance, Marie told Carew that she understood Anna of Denmark's masque would take place the next day, i.e., on Candlemas. (The *Masque of Queens* would indeed be performed on Candlemas, although in England this feast fell ten days later than it did in France.)[62] The French queen's comment, Carew writes, "made me conceave, that the Ballet was procrastinated, upon attending newes out of England, of the proceeding of her Ma[jes]ties maske."[63] Marie would not openly admit that the postponement of her ballet was dependent on the English, while Villeroy, too, hedged his response to Carew's question on this point.[64] But clearly, the French had delayed the performance date of their own *ballet de la reine* in order to ensure that any gesture this production put forward honouring the English would be reciprocated via Boderie's treatment at Anna's *Masque of Queens*.

Having improvised regarding the timing of Marie's ballet in order to influence events in London, the French then capitalized on the presence of two queens at Henri IV's court in order to organize the ballet's invitations in ways designed to court the English while avoiding the political fallout from any obvious breach of protocol regarding the nuncio and Don Pedro. Starting in fifteenth-century Italy, as Garrett Mattingly has established, relations between European states became more centrally regulated in part through the creation of resident ambassadors,[65] yet as Carolyn James notes, women's "chameleon-like flexibility" with respect to these and other officially recognized structures of foreign relations made them "useful, even formidable diplomatic actors."[66] Since James I's accession, the English in their interactions with visiting ambassadors had actively capitalized on this flexibility via Anna of Denmark's masques. After Beaumont had been excluded from her 1604 *Masque of the Twelve Goddesses*, for example, James had declared to the Spanish ambassador that in this, the queen's will was his will, while to the French ambassador he had proclaimed the opposite: that it was his wife, not he, who had invited Villamediana at Beaumont's expense. Because Anna's actions could be interpreted as identical with James' or as separate from them, depending on the context, her control over invitations to her own masque allowed the English to woo the Spanish while disavowing responsibility for doing so. This maneuvering had placed France at a disadvantage, but on the occasion of Marie de Médicis' ballet in winter 1609, the French regained strategic ground by seizing on the even more "chameleon-like flexibility" available to them thanks to the presence at court of not only the king's current wife Marie but also his first, cast-off wife, Marguerite de Valois.

For some time, Queen Marguerite had presented a liability for the new Bourbon dynasty: not only had she failed to produce an heir, but in

1604–5, in connection with the conspiracy against the crown discussed in chapter 2, various discontented nobles had used doubts about the annulment of her marriage to the king in order to question the legitimacy of the dauphin born to his new wife Marie de Médicis. In summer 1605, partly to contain such threats, Henri IV recalled Marguerite to court from exile in Usson. The next year, Marguerite "authenticate[d] the marriage" of Henri IV and Marie de Médicis by making the dauphin her heir.[67] She also helped to bolster the Bourbon monarchy's foreign policy goals when, on 31 January 1609, she hosted a performance of Marie's ballet at her new Paris residence across from the Louvre.

Because Philip III's extraordinary ambassador Don Pedro was still in Paris, the French could not fail to invite him to this royal entertainment; nor could they neglect to honour the pope's representative to Henri IV's court, Roberto Ubaldini, if they wished to compete with Spain for influence in Rome while simultaneously promoting, both at home and abroad, Henri's reputation as a sincere Catholic. Ubaldini had made known his refusal to attend the queen's ballet alongside the English ambassador on account of religious differences.[68] And indeed, in 1605 the French had experienced first hand the difficulty of adequately controlling an audience for Marie's ballets that included representatives of both England and the Catholic powers, even when separate scaffolds had been constructed in order to create clear spatial divisions between them. In 1609, therefore, rather than inviting all of the ambassadors to the ballet's first performance at the Louvre, France enforced temporal as well as spatial separation between visiting representatives by dividing them between performances at two different locations: the Arsenal, the Paris residence of the duc de Sully, a prominent Huguenot, and the newly constructed *hôtel* of Queen Marguerite, a devoted Catholic.

Had this ballet been danced at the Louvre and had one set of ambassadors been invited there, the other set could legitimately take umbrage at being excluded from a performance hosted by the king and his consort in their own palace. Neither the Arsenal nor Marguerite's *hôtel* was a palace of the reigning monarch, however; rather, as Marie de Médicis had been careful to stress when discussing her production with the English ambassador, these were private residences "in the town." Carew could thus be invited to the performance hosted by Sully while the nuncio and Don Pedro could be invited to the one hosted by Queen Marguerite, with neither side being given obvious cause for offence.

By having both Marguerite and Marie issue their own invitations to these performances, moreover, the French used to their advantage an important plasticity inherent to queenship as it was defined and practiced in early modern France. We learn from Carew that Marie de Médicis invited his wife Thomasine to attend her ballet's first performance at the Arsenal, while Marguerite issued the nuncio's invitation to this same ballet's second performance at her *hôtel*.[69] In the audience for Marie's ballet at the Arsenal, the king explained to Carew that later he would attend the production's second performance where the nuncio and the Spanish extraordinary ambassador would be present, but that it was Queen Marguerite, not he, who had invited the nuncio, and that although Henri IV had invited the Spanish and Venetian ambassadors there, just as he had invited Carew to the Arsenal performance, he would make the excuse of having a headache in order to leave early.[70] Carew notes that in reality Henri IV did not depart early from Marguerite's; instead, the king "caused the ballet" to be danced there twice. What is more, the ballet at Marguerite's residence was supplemented with a collation, which Carew admits "was more than we had at the Arsenal." But as the English ambassador reports reassuringly, and as Villeroy noted in his own letter to Boderie, such gestures meant little when weighed against the fact that Queen Marie de Médicis had invited the English to the Arsenal, while Marguerite, who hosted the Spanish and other Catholic powers, was a queen "de moindre qualité" [of lesser quality].[71]

When unpacking the complex calibrations of prestige attached to these invitations as contemporaries reported them, it is helpful to remember that as the French king's consort, the queen shared in the majesty proper to sovereignty through her husband's communication of this dignity to her via marital union. And yet she, unlike the king, remained a private person subject to the law in ways that he was not. This aspect of the French queen's positioning – the "duality of personhood" inherent in her status as both a participant in the royal dignity and a juridical subject or subordinate – meant that she both represented the state and existed separately from it.[72] When Marie de Médicis issued a ballet invitation to the English ambassador's wife, her share in the king's sovereign majesty as legitimate consort gave this gesture official weight, as an action undertaken by the French crown. At the same time, however, the queen's gender defined her as separate from her husband, and at this additional level, her invitation could be presented as private and hence only semiofficial, in ways that an invitation from the king himself could never have been. Further adding to this ambiguity, Marie proffered her invitation not to the English ambassador himself but to his wife, whose standing in relation to official diplomacy was even less clear than the queen's own. After a temporal delay allowing for sufficient confirmation that events in London were going their way, however, the French no longer needed to hedge their bets quite so carefully. They therefore rendered irreversible the gesture of honour they had at first only tentatively extended to England through Marie's invitation to Thomasine Carew: this was the moment when Henri IV invited Carew to his wife's ballet at the Arsenal. Thereafter, because Marguerite's queenship was of a "lesser quality" than Marie's, the Bourbon regime made sure that the honour extended to the Stuarts through Marie's invitation to Carew's wife, as unofficial as this was, could still be viewed by the English as exceeding that which the Spanish received by being hosted at Queen Marguerite's.

At the same time, Marguerite's own standing meant that her actions in inviting the nuncio and in hosting him and Don Pedro could partially offset the insult to the pope and Philip III implied by their representatives' exclusion from this ballet's first performance. After 1599, when Marguerite's marriage to Henri IV was annulled, she was released from the public function that union with the king had assigned to her. No longer occupying the institutional position of royal consort, Marguerite in 1609 embodied a lower status than that enjoyed by Henri IV's new wife, Marie. As reflected in her retention of the title "Queen Marguerite," however, she continued to represent the king's dignity – much as a dowager queen in France retained the royal dignity, and the title of queen that signified this, even though her status was now subordinate to that of her daughter-in-law, the new queen regnant.[73] Through Marguerite's invitation to Ubaldini, the French honoured the letter of the nuncio's demand that he not attend the ballet alongside the English ambassador. Moreover, because the French had muddied the issue of precedence by ensuring that the ballet performance to which both the nuncio and Don Pedro had been invited was hosted at the *hôtel* of a queen, the Spanish extraordinary ambassador, too, found it difficult to complain.[74] Initially, Carew reports, "Don Pedro construed the inviting of me to the Arsenal where the Ballet was first to be shewed, to be a geuing of precedence to great Brittayne, and that he gave out thereupon, that he cared not for those sights." The Spanish extraordinary ambassador, in other words, knowing full well that the French had slighted Philip III by inviting his representative to the second performance rather than the first, initially threatened to boycott Marie's ballet under the pretense that "shows" such as these were beneath him. Ultimately, however, the risk to Habsburg prestige that Don Pedro would have incurred by publicly absenting himself from this important diplomatic occasion seems to have outweighed the potential damage involved in accepting the invitation.[75]

Still, diplomatic reports of what transpired in the audience at Queen Marguerite's residence indicate just how decisively the tide had turned in favour of alliance between France and England, at Spain's expense. When at this performance the Venetian ambassador refused to address Don Pedro as "His Excellency" (in keeping with Venice's claims of parity in status with Spain), the irate Don Pedro loudly insulted him and threatened to use physical violence. Even Ubaldini (who for some time had been trying to intervene with Henri IV on Spain's behalf) seems to have found this behaviour objectionable, finally interrupting Don Pedro's angry tirade with the interjection, "Eh per l'amor di Dio che basta" [Oh, for the love of God, enough].[76] Henri IV, whose ability to compete with Philip III for influence in Rome had been hampered by his own refusal to abandon the United Provinces at the pope's urging, seems to have found this incident highly amusing; so did Carew, who reports that Don Pedro apparently "spoke so loudly as the Queene heard these words plainly though shee were dancing. The king hath been mer[r]y at it since, saying 'La Farce valoit bien le Balet' [the farce made the ballet well worth it], for there was never better Rodomontade [Don Pedro], nor Pantalonade (who ever seemeth fearfull) [the Venetian], acted in any Comedy."[77] Among the insults Don Pedro had hurled at the Venetian ambassador was the term "Pantalone"; with this slur, he had likened Venice's presumption of parity with Spain to the ridiculous self-importance of this cowardly would-be suitor from Italian *commedia dell'arte*. Carew's missive builds on this metaphor, as well as on Henri IV's comparison of the Spanish-Venetian altercation to a "farce," when it likens events in the ballet's audience at Queen Marguerite's to a play in which Don Pedro, too, performed the role of a fool – "Rodomontade" being, by the late sixteenth century, a derisive epithet meaning an insolent boast associated with Spanish variants of the *miles gloriosus* or braggart soldier character type.[78]

At the royal court in London, Spanish efforts to secure ceremonial signs of English favour were similarly ineffective. Having received communications from Carew regarding Marie's ballet in Paris, the English remained firm in their resolve to defer Anna's *Masque of Queens* until the Spanish extraordinary ambassador, finally admitting defeat, took his leave. Directly thereafter, the French ambassador to James I's court received an invitation to Anna's masque and with it, the advertisement of English friendship that had been denied to France ever since Anna's 1604 *Vision of the Twelve Goddesses*. Boderie's letters to members of Henri IV's council record at length his favourable treatment at Anna's production. Having been escorted to the royal palace, Boderie and his wife supped with the English royal family, while at the performance James I placed Boderie next to himself and entertained him personally throughout, just as Henri IV had done with Carew at Marie's ballet at the Arsenal. As part of their conversation during the masque, James carefully explained to Boderie that all along he had wanted France to be invited to his wife's masque as a sign of particular honour; in this way, the English reciprocated Henri IV's gesture when insisting to Carew, during the Arsenal performance of Marie's ballet, that his attendance at the ballet's second performance later that evening would be perfunctory. Then, during the revels that followed the masque's choreographed dances, Prince Charles (the future Charles I, then duke of York) honoured France by taking Boderie's daughter out as his partner in the social dancing.[79] Because Boderie represented Henri IV, Boderie's daughter could stand in unofficially for one of the French king's daughters; the English monarchy's gesture in having a son of James and Anna select the French ambassador's daughter as his dance partner thus enhanced the signs of friendship with France that this occasion put in motion by hinting at England's interest in a possible Stuart-Bourbon marriage in which James and Anna's second son, Charles, would wed a daughter of France.

In Paris, meanwhile, Henri IV had sought to ensure that all of the ambassadors present in Paris would attend Marie de Médicis' ballet – presumably so that representatives from across Europe could report on this occasion's political implications in missives sent to their own masters.[80] These implications included the signals this ballet sent regarding Anglo-French friendship, by means of Carew's invitation to the Arsenal performance, as well as the performance values this occasion demonstrated thanks to additional interventions by Marie and Marguerite: these aspects of the production, as I will now explore, indicated the Bourbon monarchy's capacity to rival in cultural patronage and material splendour the magnificence used previously, by the Stuart and Habsburg dynasties, when these powers had "wooed" one another at two masques and a *sarao* in 1604–5.

During the performance at Marguerite's *hôtel*, we know from Carew's letters, the nuncio and Spanish extraordinary ambassador along with Henri IV and Marie de Médicis were fêted with a collation. From one contemporary French source we learn that this feast was not only remarkably costly but also noteworthy for its artful inventiveness: according to Pierre de L'Estoile, "at Queen Marguerite's their Majesties found a magnificent and sumptuous collation which this lady had prepared for them (rumoured to have cost 4,000 écus)," the "singularities" of which included three silver plates displaying figures selling pomegranates, oranges, and lemons, the artifice of which was so remarkable that all present seem to have taken them for objects of nature.[81] These aspects of Marguerite's contribution to the occasion helped to mitigate any offence to Rome and Spain resulting from the fact that their representatives had been invited to the second rather than first of Marie's performances that same evening. But Marguerite de Valois' collation also forwarded the crown's diplomatic goals by placing on display before representatives of numerous Catholic powers the new Bourbon dynasty's success in harnessing to itself a conspicuous consumption and an excellence in artistic patronage for which her natal family, the late Valois dynasty, had long been admired.

At this same ballet, moreover, on-stage production values showcased a capacity for magnificence newly available to the Bourbon dynasty thanks to the experience with opulent courtly spectacle and privileged access to exclusive patronage networks that Henri IV's second wife Marie enjoyed in her own right, as a Medici princess. Describing the Arsenal performance of the ballet in his official report to the English court, Carew writes that the queen's "masque ... was rich in apparaile" and "plentifull of fayre Laides, of excellent musike, and of other actors, so as there were above fowerscore persons used in the performing of it, besides certayne motions and shewes, of rockes, seas, and woods."[82] Chapter 4 has provided additional details regarding the innovations in scenography and stage machinery referenced briefly here in Carew's phrase describing this ballet's "motions and shewes, of rockes, seas, and woods"; for the purposes of this chapter's focus on international diplomacy, it is Carew's references to the ballet's "excellent musike" and "rich[ness] in apparaile" that require additional contextualization and analysis.

The performers in Marie's ballet for carnival 1605, we saw in chapter 2, had included an Italian woman singer from the Caccini consort who "charmed the ears of the company by her voice more divine than human." This instance of solo female song within court ballet had introduced for the first time in France a musical trend admired across

Europe: female monody within representational, dramatic spectacle. It had also demonstrated the French king and queen's standing as (temporary) patrons to Europe's most famous vocal performers. Marie de Médicis had for some time sought to patronize accomplished women singers such as these: in a letter from the early 1600s to Archduchess Isabel Clara Eugenia, for example, the queen referenced the pleasure she had received at hearing Isabel de Camere, a Spanish singer who had passed through France on her way to Flanders, and expressed regret at not having been able to detain this woman longer from returning to the archduchess's service.[83] Marie's letter flatters her addressee as the more powerful cultural patron while simultaneously fostering connections between herself and the archduchess through the implication she, Marie, shared Isabel Clara Eugenia's elevated appreciation for excellence in women's courtly song. In winter 1605, Marie finally got her chance to demonstrate this shared sensibility and the royal virtue it connoted by bringing the even more famous Caccini women to France for several months. Given France's exclusion from the reciprocal gestures of "stroking" by means of diplomatic ceremonial in London and Valladolid that year and the previous one, the international prestige that accrued to the French monarchy through this patronage coup would have been particularly useful. One of Guilio Caccini's letters from this period reveals as much in its report that James I's extraordinary ambassador the duke of Lennox expressed great admiration for Francesca's singing, confessing that his own queen, due to her love of Italian culture, would receive no greater pleasure than to have Francesca on loan from Marie de Médicis for a month.[84] Of course no such sharing occurred: despite her best efforts Marie herself was only able to borrow the Caccini women's services for a short time.[85] Giulio's hoped-for scenario is telling, though, for the capacity to patronize these avant-garde women singers from Italy, even temporarily, was indeed a much sought-after privilege, one for which the Bourbon court, thanks to Marie's dynastic connections, would have been envied and admired.

Four years later, when Marie danced her January 1609 ballet, female monody within courtly spectacle was still in vogue: multiple women singers – including Ippolita Recupito and Vittoria Archilei as well as Francesca, Margherita, and Settimia Caccini – had performed during the *intermedii* for the October 1608 *Il giudizio di Paride* mounted in Florence for the wedding of Marie's cousin the crown prince Cosimo de' Medici to Maria Maddalena of Austria, for example.[86] France no longer had at its disposal Italian women performers of such fame, but the 1609 *ballet de la reine* continued to harness the prestige associated with such musical trends through the *récit* performed by Angélique Paulet.[87] At the centre of this production's efforts to shape images of royal power worthy of being reported abroad, I believe, was the entry during which a "moving mountain" opened to reveal a seascape in which appeared Paulet, costumed as a nymph seated on a dolphin moving, as if swimming, on the waves.[88] As discussed in chapter 4, a primary function of Paulet's song was deictic, introducing and describing the nymphs who next appeared on stage personated by the queen and her eleven female companions. In this way, Paulet's vocal performance exemplified an important shift in French court ballet towards sung *récits* in imitation of Italian models, for although sung airs had become quite standard in ballet at the court of France, *récits*, which functioned primarily as epideictic interludes, prior to 1605 had been spoken rather than sung.[89] When this musician accompanied herself in solo song with the "chitarrone," or theorbo, moreover, her entry reproduced a musical practice firmly associated with Giulio Caccini, whose 1602 manifesto for the new *stile rappresentativo* had declared the "chitarrone" to be "più atto ad accompagnare la voce … che qualcunque altro" [better for accompanying the voice … than any other instrument].[90]

Through the elevated appreciation for avant-garde musical developments from Italy which the Bourbon monarchy thus modelled, Paulet's performance during Marie's ballet heightened the French court's standing as a site of cultural excellence equal to that of its political rivals. But the nationally specific aesthetic qualities French contemporaries ascribed to Angélique Paulet's singing, too, aided Bourbon efforts in this regard. Thus far, I have emphasized the Italianate aspects of Paulet's *récit*, but a closer look at its printed music indicates additional qualities typically associated with French court song per se. Writing in his diary about this "ballet magnifique," L'Estoile reports that "La petite Paulette emporta l'honneur du ballet, tant par ses bonnes grâces que par sa voix harmonieuse et délicate (qu'on disait, au jugement même du roi, surpasser en bonté et douceur celle du sieur de Vaumesnil)" [the little Paulet stole the show as much by her good graces as by her harmonious and delicate voice which, it is said, even in the judgment of the king, surpasses in goodness and sweetness that of Monsieur de Vaumesnil].[91] Guillaume de Boulanger, sieur de Vaumesnil, was much admired within France as a lute player, singer, and composer of solo lute music, and he performed frequently at the late Valois and early Bourbon royal courts.[92] Remarkably, according to

Henri IV's own assessment, Paulet's "harmonious and delicate" voice exceeded in "goodness" and "sweetness" even that of the great Vaumesnil.[93] Paulet's music teacher, according to Madeleine de Scudéry, was Pierre Guédron,[94] perhaps the period's most noted singer-composer of *airs de cour*. And in this most popular genre of French secular vocal music, sweetness and delicacy were especially valued as performance qualities. Paulet's *récit* thus seems to have skillfully adapted Italianate musical trends to specifically French vocal stylings. A brief look at the printed music for the *récit* sung by Paulet supports this suggestion. Musically, "Ces Ninfes pleines de mespris" is not particularly dramatic, nor would its execution have required especially showy expressivity. The extant print rendition does not necessarily match what was performed on stage: the only musical notation that remains, like that for other *ballet de cour* songs, has been adapted for amateur vocal performance. Nonetheless, the relative lack of conspicuous virtuosity required of the singer for "Ces Ninfes pleines de mespris" stands in marked contrast to the vocal qualities for which the women trained by Giulio Caccini were famous. Paulet's music also contrasts strikingly with Fame's song for this same ballet. Théodore Gérold, rightly I think, describes Fame's song as a typical ballet air sung in praise of the monarch, of a "pompous character, in which the singer could also validate [faire valoir] his art and his virtuosity."[95] These qualities are evident even in its extant version adapted for amateurs. Compared to Fame's air, the nymph's *récit* evinces a more restricted vocal range and requires no particularly demanding leaps in pitch within a given musical phrase. It also includes few trills, especially when compared to Fame's use of marked and extended melismas (at least one of which ranges over an octave). Overall, Paulet's *récit* might be described as relatively declamatory, particularly in the first four lines of each strophe or verse, which move step-wise strictly within the tonic key (G-). The last two lines of each strophe move to the dominant; they also rise in pitch significantly, creating a more stirring effect that would have drawn the audience's attention to the concluding words of each verse's sixth and final line. Text, rather than rhythm, seems to drive this song's movement. The considerable aesthetic appeal that contemporaries ascribed to Paulet's *récit* for this ballet, therefore, must have been tied to the goal of making all of the words understood – though rendered in that most Italianate of musical forms, the sung *récit* – through the very "sweetness" and "delicacy" that the French themselves claimed characterized the distinctive excellence of their own language.

Marie's ballet thus deployed a form of cultural capital associated most strongly with the queen's natal dynastic court – female monody embedded within representational court spectacle – while simultaneously pleasing French members of its audience with musical stylings they would have recognized as specific to their own culture. This combination of form with style would also have rendered the Bourbon monarchy's excellence in cultural patronage more easily recognizable to foreign diplomats familiar with the prestige of Italian musical trends. The strategy seems to have worked. According to Madeleine de Scudéry, as we have seen, the appearance of "Elise" in this *ballet de la reine* immediately caused Paulet's fame to spread throughout France and beyond, to all of the other kingdoms whose ambassadors attended this occasion.[96] Extant diplomatic correspondence does not name the singer who performed this role, perhaps because ambassadors did not know her identity or did not think this information would hold particular resonance for their foreign addressees.[97] Carew, as we have seen, made note of this ballet's "excellent musike," however, while Traiano Guiscardi (Vincenzo I Gonzaga's ambassador to France) noted with approbation the "most rare music" sung by this ballet's naiad (Paulet) who accompanied herself "most divinely."[98] Even Don Pedro de Toledo, who left France almost immediately following his outburst during Marie's ballet, made arrangements to take with him a "plan" of the production's music "to send to the archduke to have the tablature engraved in copperplate and printed in Spain," Pierre de L'Estoile writes.[99] I have not been able to determine whether the music for this ballet actually made its way to the courts of Albert and Isabel and/or Philip III and Margarita de Austria. The very existence of rumours that it would do so as reported by L'Estoile, however, indicates the contemporary belief that this production's music could not fail to generate appreciation not only in France but also at other powerful European courts.

Also noted with admiration by this ballet's audiences both foreign and domestic was what Carew calls its "rich[ness] in apparaile," and in this, too, Marie's interventions as patron-performer were influential.[100] Letters written by Jacques Nompar, duc de la Force at the time of this ballet's rehearsals report that the upcoming production "sera fort magnifique et la Cour fort parée" [will be very magnificent and the court greatly decorated] and that the ballet will be performed "avec grand apparat" [with much pomp].[101] Particularly striking in this regard was the bejeweled habit worn by Marie de Médicis, most notably her headdress on which was mounted the Beau Sancy diamond.

Figure 5.1. King James I of England and VI of Scotland, after John De Critz the Elder. Early seventeenth century, based on a work of c. 1606 (oil on panel). National Portrait Gallery, London.

Figure 5.2. Frans Pourbus II (1569–1622), Marie de Médicis (1573–1642) in coronation robes, c. 1610 (oil on canvas). Musée du Louvre, Paris, France. Bridgeman Images.

At this time Europe's most sought-after stones included the Grand Sancy diamond and its smaller cousin, the Petit or Beau Sancy, named after their owner the French courtier Nicolas Harlay, seigneur de Sancy.[102] On several earlier occasions, Henri IV had borrowed both Sancy diamonds and had desired that Harlay "give" them to him for the crown jewel collection, since the king's depleted treasury made it impossible for him to purchase these gems.[103] Elizabeth I had sought both diamonds for the English crown jewel collection; so had Marie de Médicis' brother-in-law Vincenzo I Gonzaga, duke of Mantua, although the latter, despite his reputation as a lover of fine jewels, ultimately declined to pay the exorbitant price Harlay was asking.[104] When Harlay approached Marie herself as a potential purchaser she responded with great interest – unsurprisingly, given her trained appreciation in precious stones – but in Henri IV's view Harlay's asking price remained too high.[105] In March 1604, therefore, Harlay's brother Christophe, comte de Beaumont, then France's ambassador in England, arranged to sell the Grand Sancy to James I for the sum of 60,000 écus (approximately $4.2 million in today's currency).[106] In time for his 1605 coronation procession, the new English king had the Grand Sancy mounted on an extravagant hat ornament known as the Mirror of Great Britain; he then memorialized this event by commissioning two portraits in which the Mirror of Great Britain appears prominently (for one of these, see Figure 5.1). This loss of the Grand Sancy to the Stuarts struck a considerable blow to Bourbon prestige and in response Henri IV quickly took action to acquire the smaller Beau Sancy for Marie at a price of 25,000 écus, so that at least this lesser of the two diamonds would remain within the kingdom as a sign of French wealth and power.[107]

In an instance of rivalrous self-display with the Stuarts, Marie's regalia for her May 1610 coronation included the Beau Sancy mounted on her crown, as captured in Frans Pourbus the Younger's famous portrait of the queen in her coronation habit painted some time during 1609–10 for the Petite Galerie of the Louvre (Figure 5.2).[108] Even earlier, Marie had been painted by Pourbus with the Beau Sancy in her hair, in a portrait emphasizing her royal majesty executed in 1606–7, shortly after the diamond's purchase, copies of which had been commissioned by Vincenzo I Gonzaga himself (Figure 2.3).[109] In January 1609, moreover, Marie wore the Beau Sancy among the precious gems that adorned her costume for her ballet in Paris. Our knowledge that Marie sported this particular diamond on this occasion comes from Carew, who reports that during the ballet's performance Henri IV made him "survey the diamonds on the Queenes head, of w[hi]ch the greatest, was one w[hi]ch he called le petit Sancy, and sayd we had in England the great Sancy, speaking of it, as if he would fayne compasse that stone agayn."[110] When Henri pointed out this aspect of his wife's performance to the English ambassador, he was making sure that Carew could not fail to note the new Bourbon dynasty's discernment in the same kinds of cultural patronage that James had recently undertaken by acquiring, and conspicuously displaying as part of his own regal attire, the other Sancy diamond.

Possession of gems like these signalled not only the aesthetic acumen found among powerful patrons but also other important political qualities. Invincibility, for example, inhered in the stones' indestructibility as well as their unparalleled capacity for reflecting or refracting light. Often brought to Europe by adventurers or diplomats with connections in trade or diplomacy with the Far East or Asia, gems such as the Sancy diamonds implicitly marked the would-be imperial reach of their sovereign owners. Diamonds and other rare stones were also among the period's most readily transportable forms of wealth, easily pawned, for example, in order to raise ready cash for paying mercenary armies.[111] These features meant that the Beau Sancy, put on view as part of the French queen's ballet habit, would have coded for Carew and other diplomats in the audience not only Bourbon magnificence but also its imperial ambitions and ready military and political strength as an enemy or ally.

Earlier, the Spanish monarchy had sought to woo the English at the 1605 *sarao* in Valladolid, during which Margarita de Austria's sumptuously bejeweled dress displayed both Habsburg wealth and imperial aspirations (a fact that the *Mercure françois*'s print description of this occasion reported with some pique, as we have seen). Ambassadorial descriptions of Anna of Denmark's masques from this same period, too, typically noted the new Stuart dynasty's prosperity as reflected in precious gems decorating the queen's costumes: in 1608, for example, the Venetian ambassador reported of Anna's *Masque of Beauty* that "[t]he apparatus and the cunning of the stage machinery was a miracle, the abundance and the beauty of the lights immense, and the music and the dance most sumptuous. But what beggared all else and possibly exceeded the public expectation was the wealth of pearls and jewels that adorned the Queen and her ladies."[112] French ambassadors had not been favoured at the 1605 *sarao*, nor at the English *Masque of Beauty* or any queen's masque preceding it. But in 1609 the Bourbon dynasty made sure that visiting diplomats from both sides of the confessional divide would have no excuse but to attend one of its two *ballet de la reine* performances, where they could not help but witness evidence of French strength and prosperity.

The ambassadors who reported admiration for this and other elements of the ballet's magnificence were many: Marie along with Henri IV had invited the Florentine representative, for example, and although Guidi himself did not attend, his correspondence reports the opinion, of those who did, that it was "very beautiful and very superb."[113] Through Guidi's secretary Giovanni delli Effetti, news reached Cardinal Maffeo Barberini, former extraordinary nuncio to France and future pope, that Marie's "very beautiful and magnificent" ballet had cost no less than "15,000 scudi."[114] According to Guidi, moreover, Marie had personally made efforts to detain "Ambassador Malaspina" in Paris long enough to witness her ballet.[115] As noted in chapter 4, the queen also personally intervened to ensure that detailed descriptions of her 1609 ballet would reach her sister Eleonora de' Medici and brother-in-law Vincenzo I Gonzaga. Prefacing her letter to Eleonora, Vittoria Guiscardi reports that she found herself in the audience for Marie's ballet at the Arsenal "thanks to Her Majesty"; more baldly, Vittoria's husband Traiano informs Vincenzo that "the queen *commanded* me to share [news] with Your Highness of her ballet" (emphasis mine).[116] Through these visitors, then, Marie ensured that reports of her opulent ballet reached the court of Mantua. Vincenzo had not been willing to pay Harlay's requested price for the Sancy diamonds, and though the French had lost the Grand Sancy to James I, they had acquired the Beau Sancy, in this sense besting Mantua if not England. This context of rivalrous acquisition helps to clarify why Vittoria made sure to report to the duchess of Mantua details of the costly diamonds worn by this ballet's women dancers – "most of all Her Majesty, who it was said had on her [jewels of] a half million in value, so much that it made of her a wondrous show" – and why Traiano, commanded by Marie herself to report the details of her ballet to his master, similarly noted that she and her ladies wore "so many diamonds on their habits that it was a marvel … the most beautiful sight in the world."[117]

Faced with such signs of France's increasing wealth and power, as well as the subtle yet unmistakable messages of friendship between France and England conveyed by means of audience arrangements at this queen's ballet and the *Masque of Queens* danced by Anna of Denmark ten days later, Spain had little choice but to admit defeat. Don

Pedro's mission, we will recall, had been to drive a wedge between France and England, at the expense of the United Provinces, by means of a proposed triple Habsburg-Bourbon dynastic marriage. Reciprocity between the entertainments danced by Anna of Denmark and Marie de Médicis during the final weeks of his embassy, however, advertised the extent to which such efforts had failed. In March 1609, Spain finally acknowledged Dutch sovereignty as part of the terms set out in the Truce of Antwerp announcing a twelve-year cessation in military action against the United Provinces. Meanwhile France, having succeeded in obtaining its sought-after alliance with England in support of the Dutch Protestants, nonetheless maintained good relations with Rome and kept open longer-term possibilities for Habsburg-Bourbon rapprochement to be secured through dynastic marriage(s). To achieve all of these aims, however, the French government had needed to implement teamwork in its navigation of foreign policy by means of diplomatic ceremonial: teamwork that required the agential political involvement not only of Henri IV, his ministers, and his ambassadors sent to foreign courts, but also of queens and ambassadors' wives.

Conclusion

Following Henri IV's assassination in 1610, Marie de Médicis no longer danced in court ballets. But as regent for the young Louis XIII she organized several entertainments in this genre performed by her children.[1] Immediately following the declaration of Louis XIII's majority, moreover, Marie served as impresario for the *Ballet du Triomphe de Minerve* (also known as the *Ballet de Madame*) danced by her eldest daughter Elisabeth, future consort of Philip IV of Spain. This March 1615 production championed Marie's continued importance to orderly governance within France and celebrated her success in keeping the kingdom free from costly military engagements abroad by means of the Bourbon-Habsburg double marriage.[2] After the 1619–20 wars of mother and son and prior to Marie's exile from France in 1631, moreover, numerous ballets danced by Louis XIII, his wife Anne d'Autriche, and Marie's younger daughters Christine and Henriette Marie included verses addressed to Marie in the audience, and at one of these ballets in particular – the 1624 *Ballet de la reine, dansé par les nymphes des jardins* – Marie together with her daughter-in-law Anne d'Autriche participated actively, behind the scenes, in conversations with the English extraordinary ambassador that would help to set in motion negotiations for Henriette Marie's engagement to the future king of England, Charles I.[3]

Scholars are now beginning to recognize Marie's savvy use of court ballets for political purposes.[4] But as this book's analysis of the earlier ballets Marie herself danced suggests, her later successes on this front did not arise *ex nihilo*. Focused on the period leading up to Marie's regency, this book's analysis of Marie's cultural activities in France offers significant new findings regarding the ways that she was positioned representationally as well as the ways that she herself contributed to this positioning. The evidence this book offers regarding Marie's sustained engagement in court ballet and related genres leading up to and throughout her marriage shows that the entertainments she organized and performed in the face of sustained anxieties about dynastic continuity during her husband's lifetime gave her direct training in the performing arts as subtle vehicles for political legitimation and negotiation. These earlier productions consistently defended and maintained Marie's own position, I have argued, as part of a larger governmental program that promoted the French consort queen's political authority not in its own right but as a means of maintaining the new Bourbon regime's stability in the event of Henri IV's untimely death. In the process, however, Marie's ballets opened politically significant spaces for negative commentary on official royal policy, such as the Franco-Ottoman alliance, as well as for critiques of Henri IV's philandering and its adverse impacts on Marie personally and on Bourbon authority more broadly. Exploring these aspects of her productions, the book nuances the view, still evident in recent scholarship, that it was only beginning with her regency that Marie gained a modicum of political independence, including via her use of the courtly arts.[5]

In taking up this argument, *Dancing Queen*'s microanalysis of particular ballets asks us to rethink previous assumptions regarding the exclusively elevated tone proper to women's entertainments in this genre. Overall, *ballet de cour* research tends to focus on productions sponsored and performed by men, particularly during the reigns of Louis XIII and XIV. Those women's ballets that have received significant scholarly attention, such as the 1581 *Ballet comique de la royne*, typically belong to the late Valois period and seem to have featured decorous choreographies. When scholars map and theorize productions that take up more burlesque elements, their focus has been all-male ballets, primarily from a later period; according to Mark Franko, for example, in burlesque ballet ca. 1620–36, the sub-genre he most values for its "playful resistance" to "absolutist" forms of rule, no women danced. "Unlike Valois court ballet," Franko writes, "burlesque ballets under Louis XIII were performed by all-male casts."[6] My own work, however, shows that during the period immediately following the last Valois reign but prior to Louis XIII's kingship, elements of the strange, the exotic, and the edgily erotic could feature prominently in royal women's ballet, as could performers of both sexes. Even when royal women did not adopt in their own bodily comportment the antic, the grotesquely strange, or the lascivious, royal women's ballet itself could – and did.

In this line of argument as well as others, this book aligns with other recent efforts to nuance an "arts of power" approach to early modern court culture more generally and court entertainments more specifically. Influenced by the Warburg Institute, scholarship on court ballets often reads such entertainments as univocal expressions of royal propaganda. And yet, Giora Sternberg's work on the court of Louis XIV makes the case that "status interaction" as negotiated by means of ceremonial necessarily "involved multiple meanings, protagonists, and agendas, practical as well as ideological."[7] Sternberg's own microanalyses reveal, rather than smooth over, the uneven and often unpredictable ways in which rival claims to social rank and power materialized at the level of concrete interactions.[8] Applying such insights to considerations of gender, rank, and foreignness at the first Bourbon court of Henri IV, my own work suggests that the ballets danced by Marie de Médicis engaged similar complexities.

If these entertainments did not function as blunt expressions of royal propaganda in relation to a French court audience, neither did they do so in relation to an international, pan-European courtly audience.[9] Rather, by engaging multifaceted modes of communication and political intervention, including approaches that drew on women's "semi-official" status as political agents, Marie's ballets manipulated the subtle social and cultural codes of international courtly society in order to more deftly navigate the often unpredictable vicissitudes of rivalry and alliance that characterized relations between early modern dynastic monarchical states. In particular, within the space for royal women's agency opened up by France's position with respect to England and Spain, the flexibilities available to the French crown through its employment of a cross-gender cast of political actors provided Henri IV's government with a breadth of manoeuvre in foreign policy not adequately recognized in previous studies. Scholars such as Magdalena Sánchez, working on Spain, have helped to complicate notions of court space by looking at the ways in which royal women managed to carve out spheres of significant political influence, including in the realm of foreign policy, through their own dynastic connections as well as their own separate households or residences, including royal nunneries.[10] Indeed, as Jeroen Duindam insists, early modern courts were almost always polycentric institutions comprising the households of several members of a dynasty.[11] Under patriarchal dynastic monarchy, it is true, "[p]ower was vested first and foremost in a single ruler." And yet this "unipolar picture" was necessarily "complicated" by a number of factors, including "the imperatives of dynastic reproduction and succession." The "structural characteristics of dynastic power," and in particular the need for male heirs birthed by women from prestigious ruling families whose natal bloodlines complemented in their social distinctiveness the status enjoyed by their husbands' own family lines, meant that queens and their entourages, even in dynastic courts where power revolved first and foremost around ruling males, constituted "alternative centers."[12] Duindam does not draw out the implications of this insight for court entertainments, but this study's final chapter – and indeed, the book as a whole – suggests the usefulness of doing so.

The first Bourbon court of France saw the birth of personal "absolutist" monarchy, in which the male sovereign became one with the state – a development which would gain full force during the reign of Henri IV and Marie de Médicis' grandson, Louis XIV.[13] And yet premodern statecraft, including but not only in the arena of international diplomacy, could benefit significantly from female members of ruling dynasties, even – or perhaps especially – when these women's gender precluded them from rule in their own right, as was the case in early modern France where queenly authority was officially limited by notions of Salic law. This book's detailed study of the French court ballets organized and danced by Marie de Médicis suggests that, particularly after Queen Marguerite's return from exile in 1605, the even less "unipolar" centre of power at Henri IV's court, with its multiple queens and their "royal" households, not only gave the French government greater opportunities for (dissimulative) manoeuvre in its navigations of foreign policy but also opened new spaces for women's (semi-official) political influence.

It is beyond the scope of the present study to consider in detail the legacy Marie's contributions as ballet patron-performer offered for future queens at seventeenth-century French and European courts. Nonetheless, it is my hope that by mapping the innovations both aesthetic and political that Marie's own ballets set in motion, this book will encourage future work on this topic. One focused starting point for such research might involve the court entertainments danced and organized in France by Marie's daughter-in-law Anne d'Autriche; another might be the considerable performance activity that Marie's own daughters initiated, thanks to dynastic marriages arranged by their mother, at the courts of Spain (Elisabeth), Savoy (Christine), and England (Henriette Marie). These women's activities as performers followed literally in Marie's footsteps. It was no doubt as a result of these literal footsteps, too, that the value of courtly spectacle more generally and of dancing queens in ballets or masques in particular gained increased purchase, in France but also across Europe, as a vehicle for dynastic legitimation, consolidation, and negotiation.

Appendices

1 Verse Texts for the *Ballet of the Sixteen Virtues,* performed 19 February 1602

2 Verse Texts for the *Ballet of Diana and her Nymphs,* performed 31 January 1609

3 Verse Texts for the *Ballet de Madame,* performed 2 April 1609

Please see pp. 234–5 for a list of primary sources for all three appendices.

Appendix 1

Verse Texts for the *Ballet of the Sixteen Virtues*

MAINTENANT LES VERTUS SACRÉES

Au Roi

    Maintenant les Vertus Sacrées
    Quittant leur céleste séjour
    Viennent offrir[1] en ces contrées
    Leurs clartés[2] comme un[3] nouveau jour.
    Il faut que tout vous rende[4] hommage,
    Grand Roi, merveille[5] de nostre age.   6

    L'équité, la foi, la clémence,
    Qui sont vos divins ornemens,
    Ores[6] font gouter[7] à la France
    Mille divers contentemens.
    Il faut que &c.[8]   11–12

    Dessous ces figures mortelles
    Se présentent ces déitées[9]
    Qui font marcher au devant d'elles
    Les jeux, les ris, les gaietés.[10]
    Il faut que &c.   17–18

---

1 1608D: "porter."
2 Clarté: flambeau, torche, lumière du jour; figurative: éclat, caractère illustre.
3 1608A: "com[m]'un."
4 Matthieu: "fasse"; Malingre: "face."
5 Matthieu, Malingre: "miracle."
6 Ores: or, ore, i.e., maintenant.
7 1608A, 1608D: "gouster."
8 Mss, Fr. 24352: "Il faut &c."
9 1608A, 1608D: "se presente ces deitez."
10 Mss, Fr. 24352: "gayetés."

NOW THE SACRED VIRTUES

To the King

Now the Sacred Virtues
Leaving their celestial dwelling place
Come to offer in these lands
Their pure illumination like a new dawning.
Everyone must pay tribute to you,
Great King, marvel of our age.   6

Equity, faith, clemency,
Which are your divine ornaments,
Now cause France to taste
A thousand diverse happinesses.
Everyone must etc.   11–12

Beneath these human shapes
These deities present themselves
And bring in, marching before them,
Pastimes, Laughter, and Delights.
Everyone must etc.   17–18

Ces Muses viennent pour offrande
Vous donner le plus beau des lieux,[11]
Et les Nymphes d'une autre bande
Leurs plaisirs plus délicieux.
Il faut que &c.   23–24

Recevez, Monarque invincible[12]
Ces délices et ces ebats,[13]
Au lieu[14] de ce glaive[15] terrible
Qui vous faisoit craindre aux combats.
Il faut que &c.   29–30

POUR LE BALLET DE SEIZE DAMES REPRESENTANT LES VERTUS, DONT LA ROYNE ESTOIT L'UNE

Jean Bertaut

Voyant la douce Paix et la divine Astrée
Habiter maintenant ceste belle contrée,
Et sembler y promettre un second âge d'or,
La Foy, la Pieté, la Bonté, la Clemence,
L'Equité, la Raison, la Douceur, l'Innocence,
Bref, toutes les Vertuz y retournent encore.   6

Les voicy qui s'ornant de figures mortelles
Font, à pas mesurez, cheminer devant elles
La Richesse, et la Joye, et les chastes Esbats:
Afin[16] qu'il se remarque en ces ombres parlantes,
Que les seules Vertus par la paix fleurissantes
Font fleurir la richesse et la joye icy bas.   12

Grand Monarque François, l'heur de nos destinées,
C'est par vous qu'elles sont en France retournées:

---

11 1608A, 1608D: "cieux."
12 1608A and 1608D: "invinsible."
13 1608A and 1608D: "ses delices et ses ébats"; ébats: divertissements, jeux folâtres.
14 Mss, Fr. 24352: "Lieu."
15 Royster: "glaine" [sic].
16 In early sources, "Afin" is rendered "A fin" (with space, and no accent), but it clearly means "afin," i.e., in order.

These Muses have come to give you,
As an offering, the most beautiful of places
And the nymphs, from another country,
Their most delicious pleasures.
Everyone must etc. 23–24

Receive, invincible monarch,
These delights and these frolics
In place of this terrifying two-edged sword
Which caused you to be feared in battle.
Everyone must etc. 29–30

FOR THE BALLET OF THE SIXTEEN LADIES REPRESENTING THE VIRTUES, OF WHICH THE QUEEN WAS THE FIRST

Jean Bertaut

Seeing gentle Peace and divine Astraea
Now inhabiting this beautiful country
And seeming to promise here a second Golden Age,
Faith, Piety, Generosity,[17] Clemency,
Equity, Reason, Gentleness, Innocence,
In Brief – all of the Virtues return here again. 6

Behold them, who adorning themselves with mortal appearance[18]
Make Plenitude, Joy, and chaste Pastimes
Walk in measured steps before them:
So that, through these talking shadows, it may be known
That only Virtues, when flourishing through Peace,
Make Abundance and Joy flourish here below. 12

Great French Monarch, good fortune of our destinies,
It is through you that they have returned to France.

---

17 Benevolence, bounty.
18 Alternatively, "mortal faces."

Vous en avez chassé leurs mortels ennemis:
Aussi, c'est pres de vous qu'elles se viennent rendre,
Saçhant que de vous seul elles doivent attendre
Le permanent sejour qu'elles s'y sont promis. 18

Vous les verrez venir superbement parées,
Et non comme Platon les auroit desirées
Pour charmer tout d'amour à les voir seulement:
Mais, ny leur riche habit n'empesche point leurs charmes
Ny ce n'est point de honte à vos heureuses armes,
Qu'en France la Vertu s'habille richement. 24

Ce ne sont que beautez, qu'attraits, que mignardises
Dignes d'assujettir les plus libres franchises,[19]
Et dont mesme les Dieux se sentent combatus.
Amour les accompagne, et dans ses vives flames
Fait pour elles bruler les plus celestes ames:
Mais est-il rien si beau que l'amour des Vertus? 30

L'amour en est divin, la flamme en est louable,
Et digne de bruler d'une ardeur perdurable
Dans les plus beaux esprits jusqu'au point du trépas:
Car tant s'en-faut qu'aimer (mesme avec violence)
Leurs celestes beautez ce puisse estre une offence,
Que ce seroit peché de ne les aimer pas. 36

Mais quand quelque inhumain les voudroit prendre en haine,
Encor ne sçauroit-il qu'il n'en aime la Reine,
Tant elle semble aimable aux coeurs moins amoureux.
La reine des Vertus les a toutes en elle:
Aussi, vous la donnant pour compagne eternelle,
Les cieux vous ont rendu contant & bienheureux. 42

---

19 Franchises: those who are not enslaved by love (literary sense).

You chased away their deadly enemies:
Therefore,[20] it is to be near you that they have come,
Knowing that from you alone can they expect
The everlasting sojourn that they have been promised here.   18

You will see them coming superbly[21] arrayed
And not as Plato would have desired them
To charm everyone with love at the mere sight of them.
But their luxurious dress does not hinder their charms,
Nor is there any shame to your fortunate arms
That in France Virtue dresses herself richly.   24

They are nothing but beauty, charms, daintiness
Worthy of subduing the freest resistant hearts[22]
And by whom even the Gods feel assailed.
Love accompanies them and, in his ardent flames,
Makes even the most celestial souls burn for them:
But is anything so beautiful as the love of the Virtues?   30

To love them is divine, to desire them admirable
And worthy of burning with an eternal flame
In the most beautiful of minds[23] until the point of demise:
Because, rather than it being an offence to love
(Even with violence) their celestial beauties,
It would be a sin not to love them.   36

But should some cruel person[24] decide to hate them
Still he would know that he loves their queen
So worthy of love she seems, even to the least amorous heart.
The queen of the Virtues contains them all within herself:
Therefore,[25] in giving her to you as eternal companion,
The heavens have made you happy and blessed.   42

---

20 In literary style, "aussi" at the start of a clause usually has this meaning; see, similarly, line 41 below.
21 In the sense of "proudly."
22 "Franchise" in the poetic sense: a heart not yet or no longer in love – one not "asservi par l'amour."
23 Alternatively, for "esprits": spirits, mindsets.
24 Literary sense of "inhumain": barbarous or cruel person.
25 In literary style, "aussi" at the start of a clause usually has this meaning; see, similarly, line 16 above.

Appendix 2

Verse Texts for the *Ballet of Diana and her Nymphs*

LA RENOMMÉE AU ROY POUR LE BALET DE LA REYNE

<blockquote>

Pleine de langues & de voix,
O Roy, le miracle des Roys,
Je viens de voir toute la terre,[1]
Et publier, en ses deux bouts,
Que pour la paix ny pour la guerre
Il n'est rien de pareil à vous.   6

Par ce bruit je vous ay[2] donné
Un renom qui n'est terminé
Ny de fleuve ny de montagne:
Et par luy j'ay fait[3] désirer
À la troupe que j'accompagne,
De vous voir & vous adorer.   12

Ce sont douze rares beautez,
Qui de si dignes qualitez
Tirent un cueur[4] à leur service:
Que leur souhaiter plus d'appas,
C'est vouloir, avec injustice,
Plus que les Cieux ne peuvent pas.   18

L'Orient qui de leur ayeux
Sçait les titres ambitieux,
Donne à leur sang un advantage
Qu'on ne leur peut faire quitter

</blockquote>

---

1 Lacroix: la terre.
2 Lacroix: ai.
3 Lacroix: faict.
4 Coeur.

FAME TO THE KING FOR THE QUEEN'S BALLET

Full of tongues and voices
O king, miracle of kings,
I come from seeing all the earth
And from announcing at both ends of it
That, for peace and for war,
Nothing is comparable to you.   6

Through this report I have given you
A renown that is not bounded
By rivers, nor by mountains,
And through it I have caused the desire
In the troupe that I accompany
To see you and to worship you.   12

These are twelve rare beauties
Who with such distinguished qualities
Attract hearts to serve them
That to wish them more charms
Is to want, unjustly,
More than the heavens can provide.   18

The Orient,[5] that knows
The ambitious titles of their ancestors,
Gives to their bloodline an advantage
That no one can make them yield

---

5 The East.

Sans estre yssu[6] du parentage
Ou de vous, ou de Jupiter.   24

Tout ce qu'à façonner un cors[7]
Nature assemble de trésors
Est en elle sans artifice:
Et la force de leurs esprits
D'où jamais n'ap[p]roche le vice
Fait encore accroistre leur pris.[8]   30

Elles souffrent bien que l'Amour
Par elles face chaque jour
Nouvelles preuves de ses charmes:
Mais si tost[9] qu'il les veut toucher,
Il reconnoist qu'il n'a point d'armes
Qu'elles ne facent reboucher.   36

Loin des vaines impressions
De toutes folles passions
La vertu leur apprend à vivre:
Et dans la Cour leur fait des lois
Que Diane auroit peine à suivre
Au plus grand silence des bois.   42

Une Reyne, qui les conduit,
De tant de merveilles reluit,
Que le soleil qui tout surmonte,
Quand mesme il est plus flamboyant,
S'il estoit sensible à la honte,
Se cacheroit en la voyant.   48

Aussi le temps a beau courir,
Je la feray tousjours fleurir
Au rang des choses eternelles:
Et non moins que les immortels,

---

6 Issu.
7 Corps.
8 Prix.
9 Sitôt.

Without being of the lineage
Either of you or of Jupiter.   24

All the treasures that nature assembles
When fashioning bodies
Exist in these ladies without artifice;[10]
And the strength of their minds,
Where vice never approaches,
Makes them still more meritorious.   30

They indeed allow Love
To make through them, each day,
A new proof of his charms;
But as soon as he wants to touch them,
He realizes that he has no weapons
They cannot block.   36

Virtue teaches them to live
Far from the vain impressions
Of all mad passions,
And in the court makes laws for them
That Diana would have difficulty following
In the deepest silence of the woods.   42

A queen, who guides them,
Glitters with so many marvels
That the sun who overcomes all things,
Even when his rays are most intense
Would, were he sensitive to shame,
Hide himself upon seeing her.   48

Therefore, it is to no avail that time runs fast;
I will make this queen flourish always
Among the rank of eternal beings:[11]
And so long as I have wings to fly,

---

10 That is, the physical beauty of these women is completely natural, not artificial.
11 The speaker, Fame, will make the queen live on eternally in poetic song.

Tant que mon dos aura des ailes,
Son image aura des autels.   54

Grand Roy, faites-leur bon accueil:
Louez leur magnanime orgueil,
Que vous seul aurez fait ployable:
Et vous acquérez sagement,
Afin de me rendre croyable,
La faveur de leur jugement.   60

Jusqu'icy vos faits glorieux
Peuvent avoir des envieux:
Mais quelles âmes si farouches
Ozeront douter de ma foy,
Quand on verra leurs belles bouches
Les raconter avecques moy.   66

RÉCIT DE LA NAIADE PORTÉE SUR UN DAUPHIN

Ces Ninfes pleines de mespris,
Voyant tant de pauvres Espri[t]s
Qui bruslent d'une ardeur profane,
Quittent leurs antres & leurs bois,
Et viennent avec leur Diane
Vous donner de meilleures loix.   6

Les coeurs qui ne sçavent qu'aymer
Apprendront de[12] se reformer
Avec de si chastes exemples,
Et désormais, dedans la Cour,
On ne trouvera plus de Temples
Où l'on sacrifie à l'Amour.   12

Car elles iront détruisant
Ce Dieu qui vous va séduisant,
Et le faisant brusler encore

---

12 Lacroix: Apprendront à.

Her image, no less than those of the gods,
Will be worshipped.¹³   54

Great king, make them welcome:
Exalt their great-spirited pride
That you alone have made to bend,
And you will wisely acquire,
In order to make my praise of you believable,
The favour of their judgment.   60

Until now your glorious feats
Have had envious detractors,
But what souls so insolent
Will dare to doubt my reliability
When they see these nymphs' lovely lips
Telling your greatness with me.   66

RÉCIT OF THE NAIAD CARRIED ON A DOLPHIN

These nymphs full of contempt,
Seeing so many poor souls
Who burn in profane ardor,
Leave their lairs and their woods
And come with their Diana
To give you better laws.   6

Hearts that know only to love
Will learn to reform themselves
With such chaste examples,
And henceforth within the court
One will not find any more temples
Where one makes sacrifices to Love.   12

For they [these nymphs] will destroy
This god¹⁴ who goes around seducing you¹⁵
And by making him burn again

---

13 Literally: "And not less than the immortals, just as my back will have wings, so her image will have altars."
14 Cupid, referred to in this ballet's second set of verses as an infant.
15 Alternative translation: "who is seducing you."

Au feu de son propre flambeau,
De l'Autel[16] mesme où l'on l'adore,
Elles en feront son Tombeau.   18

Après un coup si glorieux,
Elles s'en iront dans les Cieux,
Pour commencer une autre guerre,
Et ne croy pas que les mortels
Les puissent retenir en terre,
Si ce n'est avec des autels.[17]   24

Aussi bien, ne voyons-nous pas
Qu'elles puissent rien icy-bas
De toutes les choses mortelles;
Les hommes les ayment en vain,
Et la fierté d'estre si belles
Est cause de tout leur dedain.   30

Car le juste orgueil de se voir
Si parfaites dans leur miroir
Endurcit si fort leur courage,
Qu'il faut croire que leur Beauté,
Qui tient vos âmes en servage,
Maintient les leurs en liberté.   36

Et tant s'en faut qu'en vous blessant,
Elles s'aillent esjouissant
De ce que leur trait vous surmonte;
Qu'au contraire, en blasmant leurs coups
Leurs beaux yeux semblent avoir honte
D'user leurs armes contre vous.   42

Mais rien ne les irrite tant
Que de voir qu'on s'a[i]lle flattant
En sa vaine persévérance,

---

16 Lacroix: l'autel.
17 Lacroix: Autels.

In the fire of his own torch
On the same altar where he is adored,
The nymphs will make his tomb.   18

After striking so glorious a blow,
They will fly up into the heavens
To take up another battle;
And do not believe that mortals
Can keep them here on earth
If it is not by worshipping them.[18]   24

Therefore we do not see
That they can do anything here below
With any mortal beings;
Men love them in vain
And their pride at being so beautiful
Is the reason for their disdain.   30

For the just pride of seeing
Themselves so perfect in their mirrors
So greatly strengthens their courage
That one must believe their beauty,
While holding your souls in servitude,
Maintains theirs in liberty.   36

And far from going around,
As they wound you, rejoicing
That their arrows have overcome you,
On the contrary, while condemning their blows,
Their beautiful eyes seem ashamed
To use their weapons against you.[19]   40

But nothing irritates them so much
As to see someone flattering himself
In his vain perseverance,

---

18 Literally: "if it is not with altars," that is, by making sacrifices to them.
19 "Enjouer" is a hunting term, meaning to cock one's gun; "trait" means any weapon that is thrown.

Et qu'un homme puisse espérer,
Par ses pleurs, une recompense
Que les Dieux n'osoient desirer.   48

Réglez doncq.[20] si bien vos soupirs,
Que mesme en vos plus grands désirs
Votre cœur demeure insensible,
Et cessant de vous enflâmer,[21]
Si c'est quelque chose possible,
Adorez-les sans les aymer.   54

VERS MASCULINS POUR LA CHAISNE[22] DU MESME BALLET

Nos esprits libres & contens
Vivent en ces doux passe-temps,
Et par de si chastes plaisirs,
Bannissent tous autres désirs.   4

La dance, la chasse, & les bois
Nous rendent exemptes des lois
Et des misères, dont l'Amour
Afflige les coeurs de la Cour.   8

Et c'est plustost avec cet art
Qu'avec la pointe de ce dard,
Que cette[23] trouppe se deffant
Des traits de ce cruel Enfant.   12

---

20 Abbreviation for "doncque." Lacroix: donc.
21 Enflammer.
22 "Verses in masculine rhyme," i.e., with verse lines ending on a stressed syllable ("rime féminine" being when an uncounted syllable, the vowel of which must be a mute "e," concludes the verse line). Sixteenth-century poets had devised and implemented the principle of alternating masculine and feminine rhymes. This alternation rule had been universally followed since the time of La Pléiade, and therefore its deliberate violation here requires an announcement to that effect. On the alternation principle and French versification more generally, see Grammont, *Petit traité de versification française*, 356. On the "chaîne" or "hay" dance, see chapter 4, especially n.8.
23 Lacroix: ceste.

Or being able to hope to attain,
By his tears, a reward
That even the gods dare not wish for. 46

Therefore, control your sighing so well
That even in your deepest desires
Your heart remains unmoved
And, ceasing to impassion yourselves,
If such a thing is possible,
Adore them without loving them. 54

MASCULINE VERSES FOR THE CHAIN OF THE SAME BALLET

Our minds, free and happy,
Live in these gentle pastimes
And by such chaste pleasures
Banish all other desires. 4

The dance, the hunt, and the woods
Render us exempt from the rules
And miseries with which
Love afflicts the hearts of the court. 8

It is more with this art[24]
Than with the point of this spear
That this troupe defends itself against
The arrows of this cruel child[25] 12

---

24 The arts of "gentle-pastimes," such as dancing.
25 Cupid.

Car, en changeant tousjours de lieu,
Nous empeschons[26] si bien ce Dieu,
Qu'il ne peut s'asseurer des coups
Qu'il pense tirer contre nous. 16

Ainsi nous défendans de luy
Et passans nos jours sans ennuy,
Nous essayons de luy ravir
La gloire de nous asservir. 20

Il est bien vray qu'en nous sauvant,
Il nous va tousjours pour suyvant,[27]
Et nous poursuit en tant de lieux,
Qu'enfin il entre dans nos yeux. 24

Mais encor[e] qu'on puisse penser
Qu'alors il nous doivent[28] offencer,
Pourtant nous n'avons point de peur
Qu'il nous puisse enflâmer le coeur. 28

Car la neige de notre sein
Empesche si bien son dessein,
Qu'alors qu'il nous pense enflamer,[29]
Son feu ne se peut allumer. 32

---

26 Lacroix: Nous n'empeschons.
27 Lacroix: poursuyvant.
28 Lacroix: doive.
29 Lacroix: enflâmer.

Because, in always changing places
We thwart this god so well
That he cannot be sure of the shots
He thinks of aiming at us.   16

Thus by defending ourselves against him
And spending our days without boredom
We try to rob from him
The glory of enslaving us.   20

It is quite true that though he spares us
He is always chasing us
And pursues us in so many places
That finally he enters through our eyes.   24

But although one might think
That then he must injure us,
Still we are not at all afraid
That he could inflame our passions.   28

For the snow of our breast
Prevents his designs so well
That when he thinks to incite our passions
His fire will not ignite.   32

Appendix 3

Verse Texts for the *Ballet de Madame*

DE PETITES NYMPHES QUI MÈNENT L'AMOUR PRISONNIER.
Au Roi[1]

À la fin tant d'amants dont les âmes blessées
Languissent nuit et jour,
Verront sur leur auteur leurs peines renversées,
Et seront consolés aux dépens de l'Amour.   4

Ce public ennemi, cette peste du monde,
Que l'erreur des humains
Fait le maître absolu de la terre et de l'onde,
Se treuve[2] à la merci de nos petites mains.   8

Nous le vous amenons dépouillé de ses armes,
O Roi, l'astre des rois;
Quittez votre bonté, moquez-vous de ses larmes,
Et lui faites sentir la rigueur de vos lois.   12

Commandez que sans grâce on lui fasse justice;
Il sera malaisé
Que sa vaine éloquence ait assez d'artifice
Pour démentir les faits dont il est accusé.   16

Jamais ses passions, par qui chacun soupire
Ne nous ont fait d'ennui:
Mais c'est un bruit commun que dans tout votre empire
Il n'est point de malheur qui ne vienne de lui.   20

---

1 Mss, Fr. 9543: "Pour le Ballet de Madame habillée en Diane menant l'Amour prisonnier au Roi."
2 Trouve.

VERSES OF THE LITTLE NYMPHS WHO BRING LOVE AS PRISONER.

To the King[3]

Finally all the lovers with wounded souls,
Languishing night and day,
Will see their pains turned back on their author
And will be consoled at the expense of Love. 4

This public enemy, this plague to all the world,
Whom the error of humans
Makes absolute master over land and sea,
Finds himself at the mercy of our little hands. 8

We bring him to you deprived of his weapons,
O king, star of kings;
Leave off your generosity, mock his tears,
And make him feel the rigor of your laws. 12

Command that he receive justice without amnesty;
It will be difficult
For his [futile] eloquence has artifice enough
To contradict the doings of which he is accused. 16

His passions, which cause everyone to sigh,
Have never caused us trouble:
But it is a common rumour that throughout your empire
There is not a single misfortune that comes not from him. 20

---

3 Alternative title in Mss, Fr. 9543: "For the Ballet of Madame in the guise of Diana bringing Love as prisoner to the King."

Mars, qui met sa louange à déserter la terre
Par des meurtres épais,
N'a rien de si tragique aux fureurs de la guerre,
Comme ce déloyal aux douceurs de la paix. 24

Mais sans qu'il soit besoin d'en parler davantage,
Votre seule valeur,
Qui de son impudence a ressenti l'outrage,
Vous fournit-elle pas une juste douleur? 28

Ne mêlez rien de lâche à vos hautes pensées;
Et par quelques appas
Qu'il demande merci de ses fautes passées,
Imitez son exemple à ne pardonner pas. 32

L'ombre de vos lauriers admirés de l'envie
Fait l'Europe trembler;
Attachez bien ce monstre, ou le privez de vie,
Vous n'aurez jamais rien qui vous puisse troubler. 36

Mars, whose praise rests in ravaging the earth
With bloody murders,
Contributes nothing so damaging in the rages of war
As this traitor does in the sweetness of peacetime. 24

But without needing to speak more about it,[4]
Your valor alone,
Which has felt the outrage of his impudence,
Will it not provide a just anguish? 28

Mingle no weakness[5] among your high thoughts;
And by some charms
That he demands mercy on his past faults,
Imitate his example in pardoning nothing. 32

The shade of your laurels, admired and envied,
Makes Europe tremble;
Tie up, then, this monster, or take from him his life,
Nothing will remain, then, capable of troubling you. 36

---

4 I.e., it is unnecessary to give the details of it. Although "it" ("en") could refer in general to all of the disasters caused by Love, it more likely refers to the particular circumstances in which the king found himself subject to Love's impudence (the topic of this stanza). Malherbe here draws attention to the fact that he will not give the details of the outrage done to Henri IV's valor (probably for reasons of appropriateness).
5 Alternatively, "cowardice."

PRIMARY SOURCES FOR THE APPENDICES

For the *Ballet of the Sixteen Virtues*

Poetic Texts

Mss, Fr. 24352, f. 331r.
Bertaut, Jean. *Recueil des quelques vers amoureux*. Edited by Louis Terreaux. Paris: Librarie Marcel Didier, 1970. 241–3.
Royster, Don Lee. "Pierre Guédron and the Air de Cour 1600–1620." PhD diss., Yale University, 1973. 349.

Music with Verse Texts for "Maintenant les Vertus Sacrées"

1608A: Bataille, Gabriel. *Airs de différents autheurs mis en tablature de luth*. Paris: Pierre Ballard, 1608. ff. 40v–41r.
1608D: Guédron, Pierre. *Airs de cour, à quatre et cinq parties*. Paris: Pierre Ballard, 1608. ff. 56v–r.
Guédron, Pierre. *Les airs de cour*. Edited by Georgie Durosoir, with lute tablature transcription by Éric Bellocq. Versailles: Éditions du Centre de Musique Baroque de Versailles, 2009. 403–5.
Royster, Don Lee. "Pierre Guédron and the Air de Cour 1600–1620." PhD dissertation, Yale University, 1973. 283–4.

Contemporary Accounts that Reference These Verse Texts

Malingre, Claude. *Annales générales de la ville de Paris*. Paris: P. Rocolet, 1640. 481.
Matthieu, Pierre. *Histoire de France & des choses memorables advenues aux provinces estrangeres durant sept années de paix, du regne du roy Henri IIII...* 7 vols. Paris: Chez Pierre Metayer, Imprimeur du Roy ..., 1605. Volume 2, book 5, first narration, ff. 88v–89r.

For the *Ballet of Diana and Her Nymphs*

Verse Texts

Recueil des vers du balet de la Royne. Paris: Jean Nigaut, 1609. Bibliothèque Mazarine, 8° 35262-22.

Recueil des vers du balet de la Reyne. Paris: Toussaincts [sic] Du Bray, 1609. BNF, RES-YE-3026.

Lacroix, Paul. *Ballets et mascarades de cour de Henri III à Louis XIV (1581–1652), recueillis et publiés, d'après les éditions originales* ... 6 vols. Turin: J. Gay & Fils, 1868–70. 1: 171–9. Also available in facsimile reprint: Geneva: Slatkine Reprints, 1968.

Malherbe, François de. "La Renommée au Roi." In *Œuvres*, edited by Antoine Adam, 74–6, 820–1. Paris: Éditions Gallimard, 1971.

– "La Renommée au Roi." In *Œuvres de Malherbe*, edited by Ludovic Lalanne, 1: 146–8. 5 vols. Paris: Librairie Hachette, 1862.

Music with Verse Texts

Bataille, Gabriel. *Airs de différents autheurs mis en tablature de luth. Second livre*. Paris: Pierre Ballard, 1609. ff. 5v–8r. Also available in facsimile reprint: Bataille, Gabriel. *Airs de différents autheurs mis en tablature de luth*. Vol. 2. Geneva: Minkhoff Reprints, 1980.

For the *Ballet de Madame*

Verse Texts

Mss, Fr. 9543.

Malherbe, François de. "Ballet de Madame, de petites nymphes qui mènent l'Amour prisonnier." In *Œuvres*, edited by Antoine Adam. Paris: Éditions Gallimard, 1971. 76–7, 821–2.

– "De petites Nymphes qui mènent l'Amour prisonnier. Au Roi." In *Œuvres de Malherbe*, edited by Ludovic Lalanne. 5 vols. Paris: Librairie Hachette, 1862. 1: 149–50.

Notes

Introduction

1 Following the eighteenth-century scholar Pierre François Godard de Beauchamps, who in turn relied on Michel Henry's early seventeenth-century table of court ballet music (Beauchamps, *Recherches sur les théâtres de France*, 3: 48–9; see also Mss, Fr. 24357 f. 132r), scholars have typically attributed to Marie de Médicis three major ballets performed in 1601, 1605, and 1609; see, for example, Ciseri, "Ballets et carrousels," 138; Paquot, *Les étrangers*, 55 n1. For more detailed discussion regarding the 1602 performance date for Marie's first major production, rather than 1601 as is typically asserted, please see chapter 1. Undoubtedly, additional productions took place under Marie's sponsorship. In October 1608, for example, Marie is reported to have been planning and rehearsing a ballet to be danced at Fontainebleau in honour of her visiting brother-in-law Vincenzo I Gonzaga, duke of Mantua (*avviso* from Brussels to Florence, 18 October 1608, ASF, Mediceo del Principato, filza 4256, f. 461ff); to date I have found no further information regarding this production, however. Another possibility is an entertainment entitled *La felicité de l'âge d'or* (referenced as a 1610 ballet organized and danced by Marie in Kermina, *Marie de Médicis*, 103; see also Britland, "An Under-Stated Mother-in-Law," 206–7). Neither Henry nor Beauchamps cites a ballet in connection with Marie de Médicis with this title or a similar one, for 1610 or any other year, however, and to my knowledge we lack additional corroborating evidence regarding such a production.

2 For an accessible overview of Huguenot resistance theory in connection with notions of elective monarchy, as well as the Catholic League's subsequent recourse to such theories, see Kingdon, "Calvinism and Resistance Theory" and Salmon, "Catholic Resistance Theory." For more

detailed analysis, see Crouzet, *Guerriers de Dieu*; Baumgartner, *Radical Reactionaries*; Skinner, *Origins of Modern Political Thought*.

3 Prieto, "Isabel Clara Eugenia of Austria," 139–45; Duerloo, "Marriage, Power and Politics," 159; Mousset, "Les droits de l'infante Isabelle-Claire-Eugénie."

4 On the Salic law in relation to property rights and the exclusion of women from hereditary rule, see Hanley, "Engendering the State"; Hanley, "The Monarchic State"; Hanley, ed., *Les droits des femmes et la loi salique*; Hanley, "Configuring the Political Authority of Queens." Additional useful discussions include Giesey, "The Juristic Basis of Dynastic Right"; Giesey, *Le rôle méconnu de la loi salique*; Cosandey, *La reine de France*; Crawford, *Perilous Performances*; Conroy, *Ruling Women*, 1: 15–44.

5 Courtright, "A Garden and a Gallery," 59.

6 Ibid.; Cosandey, *La reine de France*, 27–52 (esp. 43), 296–332; Crawford, *Perilous Performances*, 13–21, 20. For a discussion of such ideas in relation to earlier regencies, see McCartney, "The King's Mother and Royal Prerogative."

7 McIlvenna, *Scandal and Reputation*, 10; Courtright, "A New Place for Queens," 278–9.

8 Kelly, "Murd'rous Machiavel." Smears directed against Catherine de Médicis and her Florentine origins included the claim that the Medici, who allegedly started out as coal merchants, excelled in "beastly whoredoms and lechery, dissimulation and treason"; see Etienne, *Ane Marvellous discourse*, 6–8, translated from [Etienne], *Discours merveilleux*.

9 Nordera, "Ballet de cour," 19.

10 Scholarly literature on the 1589 celebrations is extensive; for a now classic study, see Saslow, *The Medici Wedding of 1589*.

11 Solerti, *Gli albori del melodramma*, 1: 51; Bartoli Bacherini, "Musiche e danze," 143. Both Solerti and Bartoli Bacherini cite a letter dated 3 February 1590 in which Caterina Guidiccioni, mother of the composer Laura Guidiccioni, states that "Le principesse con le dame di palazzo fan loro stesse la pastorale del Tassino questo carnevale, e voglion madrigali per musiche" [The princesses with the ladies of the palace arrange their own production of the pastoral play by Tasso the younger, this carnival, and want madrigals for [the production's] music].

12 Carter and Goldthwaite, *Orpheus in the Marketplace*, 112–14. For additional instances of Christine of Lorraine's interactions with Marie, see Strunck, *Christiane von Lothringen am Hof der Medici*.

13 ffolliott, "Catherine de' Medici as Artemisia"; Crawford, *Perilous Performances*, 24–58.

14 On Catherine de Bourbon's ballets, see, most recently, Dorothée, "Le mécénat de Catherine de Bourbon."
15 My thinking about the ways that Marie's ballets merge classical with Christian imagery for the purposes of authorizing the queen's political agency takes inspiration from Cosandey's analysis of Rubens' cycle in "Représenter une reine de France." Earlier, pioneering work on Marie's patronage of Rubens includes Marrow, *The Art Patronage of Maria de' Medici*; Millen and Wolf, *Heroic Deeds and Mystic Figures*. More recent studies of Marie's artistic and architectural patronage include Courtright, "A Garden and a Gallery," "A New Place for Queens," and "The King's Sculptures in the Queen's Garden"; Dubost, *Marie de Médicis*; Cohen, "Rubens's France"; Galletti, *Marie de Medicis et le Palais du Luxembourg*; Graziani and Solinas, eds., *Le 'siècle' de Marie de Médicis*; Bassani Pacht, ed., *Marie de Médicis: un gouvernement par les arts*; Caneva and Solinas, ed., *Maria de' Medici (1573–1642) una principessa fiorentina sul trono di Francia*.
16 See, for example, *Les arts au temps d'Henri IV*; Nativel, ed., *Henri IV: Art et pouvoir*.
17 Courtright, "A Garden and a Gallery," "A New Place for Queens," and "The King's Sculptures in the Queen's Garden."
18 For ballets and related entertainments at the courts of Charles IX and Henri III, organized by Catherine de Médicis, see, for example, Yates's work from the 1940s (*The French Academies* and *Astraea*), book-length studies by McGowan (*Le ballet de cour en France*, her edition of the 1581 *Ballet comique de la royne*, and *Dance in the Renaissance*), Van Orden's *Music, Discipline, and Arms*, as well as essays by Thomas Greene ("The King's One Body"), Ewa Kociszewska ("War and Seduction"), Julia Prest ("Performing Violence"), and Ellen Welch ("Rethinking the Politics of Court Spectacle"). Studies of ballet at the court of Louis XIII and Louis XIV are also extensive; see, for example, Christout, "The Court Ballet in France: 1615–1641," Franko, *Dance as Text*, Cohen, *Art, Dance, and the Body*, and Prest, *Theatre Under Louis XIV*.
19 Fogel, *Les cérémonies de l'information*.
20 Prunières notes this problem when he touches on Marie's 1609 ballet, noting its musical innovations but lamenting the lack of full primary documentation that includes details of plot and theme (*Le ballet de cour en France*, 108–9).
21 McGowan, *L'art du ballet de cour*, 63–7, 85–99, Hoogleviet, "The *Balet de la Reyne* (1609)," and Lecomte, *Entre cours et jardins d'illusion*, 113 n25.
22 Jouanna, *L'idée de race*. For the concept of "social racism" in this period, see Kane with Smuts, "Politics of Race."

23 Although there is no such actual "school," the studies by Ralph Giesey, Sarah Hanley, and Lawrence Bryant cited in this book's bibliography together offer a set of sustained inquiries regarding the history of political symbolism in *ancien régime* France. Cosandey's *La reine de France* builds on this work by studying how individual queens are represented in coronations, entries, and funerals in order to elucidate larger developments in the function of queenship under systems of dynastic monarchy. Studies of royal entries under Henri IV's rule, led by Marie-France Wagner and Marie-Claude Canova-Green, enhance yet further what we know about Marie de Médicis' institutional role: see Canova-Green, *La politique-spectacle*; Canova-Green et al., eds., *Writing Royal Entries*; Wagner et al., eds., *Les jeux de l'échange*; *Les entrées royales … du règne d'Henri IV*, ed. Wagner, tome 2.

24 Cosandey, *La reine de France*, 124.

25 Dillon, *The Language of Space in Court Performance*.

26 Nicola Courtright discusses these challenges to the French queen consort's political authority in her unpublished paper, "A New Place for Queens in the Art and Political Imagination of 17th-Century France."

27 Franko, *Dance as Text*, 66, 86. Franko's research does consider women in relation to burlesque ballets during this period but only as members of the audience, analysing addresses to women spectators, for example, as vehicles whereby a courtier's political submission to his king might playfully be figured as erotic submission to a lady or mistress.

28 This phrase is Ellen McClure's (*Sun Spots and the Sun King*, 102). The past three decades have seen a considerable shift in how scholars understand early modern state formation and the transition from a medieval, feudal monarchy to the institution of modern dynastic monarchy. Beginning with William Beik's 1985 study *Absolutism and Society in Seventeenth-Century France: State Power and Provincial Aristocracy in Languedoc*, the notion of the 'absolutist' modern state has undergone compelling revisionist critique. For a useful summary of this debate within French historiography, see Cosandey and Descimon, *L'absolutisme en France*. Other helpful discussions for my book's purposes include Duindam, *Myths of Power*; Adamson, "The Making of the Ancien-Régime Court"; Nelson, *The Jesuits and the Monarchy: Catholic Reform and Political Authority in France (1590–1615)*. Beam, in *Laughing Matters*, offers a nuanced analysis of the "discourse of absolutism" as a "way of addressing the monarch that flatters and cajoles him by apparently accepting his view of himself" out of recognition that "acceding to the Bourbon monarchy's absolutist aims," or even appearing to do so, might result in personal gain (87).

29 Paster, "Eschewing Politeness."
30 Brooks, *Courtly Song*, 35–41, 117–254; McManus, *Women on the Renaissance Stage*, 1–59. Other feminist literary scholars who consider women's contributions to civility include Jones, *The Currency of Eros*, 11–20; Larson, *Early Modern Women in Conversation*.
31 For recent discussions of Catherine de Médicis' use of court ballets for navigating foreign relations, see Kociszewka, "War and Seduction," and Welch, "Rethinking the Politics of Court Spectacle." On the international diplomatic contexts for the 1615 *Ballet de Madame* and other court entertainments organized by Marie during her regency, see Mamone, *Paris et Florence*, and McGowan, ed., *Dynastic Marriages 1612/15*. With the exception of Welch's important discussion regarding the queen's January 1609 ballet in *A Theater of Diplomacy*, 33–57, Marie's contributions to foreign relations during her husband's lifetime have not garnered scholarly attention.
32 Smuts and Duerloo, "Occasio's Lock of Hair," 7. On this point, see also Colantuono, *Guido Reni's Abduction of Helen*, and Colantuono, "High Quality Copies and the Art of the Thirty Years War."
33 Welch, *Theater of Diplomacy*, 4.
34 Hosting court ballets could be a way of signaling to foreign rulers the monarch's political clout and financial solvency, while failing to host elaborate divertissements of this type could signal weakness. To give one example: although the English privy council prior to the Christmas festivities for 1604–5 had voiced concern about the cost involved in underwriting the masque Queen Anna of Denmark had planned for that season, the council ultimately decided that the negative political costs of canceling the queen's masque would outweigh the benefit of any financial savings. As Barroll explains, "[A]bandoning the idea of a Christmas masque merely 'for the saving of £4,000 would be more pernicious than the expense of four times the value.' For if foreign ambassadors noted that an event at the English court had been cancelled merely because it cost the sum of £4,000, then 'the judgment that will follow will be neither safe nor honorable.' That is to say, opinions might be formed regarding either a hidden financial weakness in the kingdom that might tempt aggressive international exploitation, or a lack of appropriate 'greatness' – of magnanimity in the quality of England's monarch himself" (*Anna of Denmark*, 99–100).
35 Morselli, "Rubens and the Spell of the Gonzaga Collections," offers an intriguing analysis of this competition, although she does not touch on court entertainments per se. On competition over artisans in relation to

court theatre, see Smuts and Duerloo, "Occasio's Lock," 6, and in France under Louis XIV in particular, see Welch, *Theater of Diplomacy*, 4.

36 As Sullivan explains, "when invitations to the masques were issued to them [ambassadors], it was stipulated that these invitations had for their purpose the honoring of the kings their masters, and when the ambassadors accepted such invitations it was in the name of their sovereigns" (*Court Masques of James I*, 17). Sullivan outlines in convincing detail how such productions, as public events to which the representatives of foreign monarchs were invited or from which they were excluded, enacted "the business of State" (2). For a more recent discussion see Butler, *The Stuart Court Masque and Political Culture*, 2–3, 49–50. On the politically significant arrangement of ambassadors in ballet audiences at the court of France, see Canova-Green, "Dance and Ritual," 403.

37 Colantuono, "The Mute Diplomat."

38 Rivère de Carles, "The Poetics of Diplomatic Appeasement," 7.

39 For a recent set of essays that makes evident the benefits of this methodological approach, which refuses as anachronistic to the study of early modern consort queens prior tendencies to strictly divide "hard" from "soft" power (or "high" politics from "cultural influence"), see Watanabe-O'Kelly and Morton, eds., *Queens Consort, Cultural Transfer, and European Politics*, esp. Morton, "Introduction: Politics, Culture and Queens Consort," 1–2.

40 Important monographs and essay collections on Anna of Denmark and Henrietta Maria include McManus, *Women and Renaissance Drama*; McManus, ed., *Women and Culture at the Courts of the Stuart Queens*; Tomlinson, *Women on Stage in Stuart Drama*; Britland, *Drama at the Courts of Queen Henrietta Maria*. Work on early modern women and performance that brings research on England together with transnational perspectives includes Brown and Parolin, eds., *Women Players in England, 1500–1660*; Parolin, ed., "Access and Contestation"; and the forum of short essays, entitled "Transnational Mobility and Female Performance in Early Modern Europe," edited by Gough and McManus and published in *Renaissance Drama* 44.2 (2016): 187–275.

1 Magnificence, Mistresses, and Marie's Dance of Maternity

1 "L'Année commença à la Cour de France par des fêtes, & par des bals, que la reine aimoit extrêmement, il s'en donna un entr'autres où cette Princesse dansa la premiére [sic] en masque, en présence des ambassadeurs des Princes étrangers, & du Legat même." Thou, *Histoire universelle*, 14: 61.

2 The last time a dauphin had been born was in 1518, when François Ier's wife Claude bore her eldest son (also named François). When this prince died in 1536, his younger brother (the future Henri II) became dauphin at the age of 17. When the future Louis XIII was born to Henri IV and Marie de Médicis in 1601, therefore, France had waited eighty-one years for such an event.

3 Matthieu, *Histoire de France*, vol. 2, book 5, first narration, 88v.

4 Guédron, *Airs de cour, à 4 et 5 parties* [Ier livre]; Bataille, *Airs de différents autheurs* (1608), 40v–41r. For a comprehensive transcription of Guédron's polyphonic version, see Royster, "Pierre Guédron," 283–4. The air's lyrics are also transcribed separately in Royster, 349, and in Mss, Fr. 24352, f. 331r. This air is composed in ternary rhythm, and the poetic text – largely identical for both versions – consists of five quatrains in *abab* rhyme pattern, each of which is completed with a rhyming couplet; each line (the refrain included) is seven or eight syllables in length. In these formal aspects, "Maintenant les Vertus Sacrées" matches the typical structure of *airs de cour* composed by Guédron at this stage in his career as outlined in Royster, 64.

5 Durosoir's edition of Guédron's *airs de cour* assigns "Maintenant les Vertus Sacrées" to the *Ballet des bacchantes* performed on 4 February 1608. It is certainly possible that the verse text of "Maintenant les Vertus Sacrées" as set to music by Guédron was used for this 1608 ballet (although Durosoir's edition gives no explanation in support of this claim), but if so, my argument based on Matthieu's quotation of this air's refrain indicates that its text was also used in Marie's 1602 *Ballet of the Sixteen Virtues*. Matthieu's text was printed in 1605, three years prior to the date Durosoir gives for the *Ballet des bacchantes*. Given this timing, it is not possible that he mistook the later ballet for the earlier one.

6 Mamone identifies as a key theme of the royal entry prepared for Marie de Médicis at Lyon in 1600 a similar emphasis on virtue as the basis for legitimate power (*Paris et Florence*, 117).

7 On clemency in relation to royal mystique, see Davis, *Fiction in the Archives*, 52–3. On Henri IV's use of clemency in relation to Catholic Leaguers as well as the Jesuits and this virtue's role in the development of royal absolutism, see Nelson, *Jesuits and the Monarchy*.

8 Musicologists rightly caution that the printed music for court ballet songs represents the latter's adaptation for amateur performance, rather than matching with any exactitude the music as it was written and performed for the ballets themselves. This being said, it is quite plausible that Guédron composed the musical setting for this air as performed in the 1602 ballet, even though the printed version was not

published until 1608. At Henri IV's court, Guédron had served as *maitre des enfants de la musique de la chambre* and was promoted in 1601 to the position of *compositeur en musique de la chambre du roy* (Babelon, "Avant-propos" and "Forward," Guédron, *Les airs de cour*, v, vii). He had also composed the music for "Secour mes dames," with verses by Honorat Laugier de Porchères, for the *Ballet des indiens*, a danced entry performed as part of the 1598 *Ballet des étrangers* (Guédron, *Les airs de cour*, 714).
9   Royster, "Pierre Guédron," 105 n3.
10 Van Orden, *Music*, 176–82.
11 Mamone, *Paris et Florence*, 88. On this entry in relation to numerous other instances of the pastoral Apollo in Medici court festivity, see Hanning, "Glorious Apollo," 507–8.
12 On the "Odellette," see Guichard, "L'Entrée de la reine," 30. On the arch dedicated to Henri IV as Apollo, see Vivanti, "Henri IV, the Gallic Hercules," 186, and Strong, *Art and Power*, 51. On the objectives of the Avignon royal entry as a whole, see Frappier, "Construction de la figure monarchique" and McGowan, "Les Jésuites à Avignon."
13 La Roque, *Hymne*, 9.
14 Ibid., 9–10.
15 Guillo refers to Marie de Médicis' first French ballet as the *Ballet de la reine femme d'Henry IV dansé à la grande salle de l'Evesché de Paris le dimanche gras 1601* and assigns to this production Jean Bertaut's "Beautés vivants portraits de la divinité" (*Pierre I Ballard et Robert III Ballard*, 2: 124–6). The 1602 and 1620 editions of Bertaut's poems indicate that this text was a "Récit pour une mascarade"; see Bertaut, *Recueil des quelques vers amoureux*, ed. Terreaux, 235–6, and *Les œuvres poétiques de M. Bertaut*, 421. Yet this information is not sufficient to determine the specific ballet or mascarade for which this Bertaut poem was composed. In private correspondence, Jeanice Brooks has helpfully clarified that the music to which "Beautés vivants portraits de la divinité" was set existed "well before 1600": as she points out, Charles Tessier included it in his manuscript circa 1597 and it also appears in the 1597 Le Roy/Ballard print. On the Tessier manuscript *recueil* and its inclusion of this *récit*, see Dobbins, "The Lute Airs of Charles Tessier," 29, and Dobbins, "Les airs pour luth de Charles Tessier," 171, 175. On the Le Roy/Ballard print, see *Airs de cour mis en musique à 4 et 5 parties de plusieurs autheurs* (Paris: Adrian Le Roy et la veufve de R. Ballard, 1597) as indexed in Lesure and Thibault, *Bibliographie*, 247. Bertaut's "Beautés vivants portraits de la divinité" could well have been used as an additional verse text for the ballet that Henry describes but which was danced not in 1601 but in

February 1602, as I argue. More evidence would be needed, however, to adequately support this claim.

16 Bertaut, *Recueil des quelques vers amoureux*, ed. Terreaux, 241–3. Battifol, *Le Louvre*, 112, unhesitatingly ascribes this same *récit* by Bertaut to Marie's 1602 ballet, but provides no information supporting his assertion.

17 Beauchamps identifies the performance date for the ballet featuring Bertaut's "Voyant la douce Paix et la divine Astrée" as Fat Sunday (i.e., Quinquagesimina Sunday or the Sunday before Ash Wednesday), 1601; see his *Recherches*, 3: 48–9. Beauchamps assumes that the ballet featuring this *récit* by Bertaut had to have been danced before 1602 when Bertaut's octavo volume of collected poems was printed. Royal privilege for this publication, however, was dated 25 February of that year (Bertaut, *Recueil des quelques vers amoureux*, ed. Terreaux, xviii), and Marie de Médicis' *Ballet of the Sixteen Virtues* was performed on 19 February 1602 – six days prior to this date. The *recueil*'s inclusion of Bertaut's *récit* "Pour le Ballet de seize Dames representant les Vertus, dont la Royne estoit l'une" does not preclude this same *récit*'s use in Marie's *Ballet of the Sixteen Virtues*, therefore. On the general need for caution regarding dates cited in Beauchamps, see Lancaster, "Errors," rpt. in Lancaster, *Adventures*, 349–52.

18 On these functions, see Durosoir, *Les ballets*, 15, and Durosoir, *L'air de cour en France 1571–1655*, 106–7.

19 "Récit. Pour le Ballet de seize Dames representant les Vertus, dont la Royne estoit l'une," in Bertaut, *Recueil des quelques vers amoureux*, ed. Terreaux, 41–3. Bertaut's poem is also reprinted in Lacroix, *Ballet et mascarades*, 1: 149–50.

20 *Les œuvres morales ... par Simon Goularrt* [sic]. During Henri IV's reign, multiple editions appeared in print starting as early as 1590; the fourth edition appeared in 1606.

21 Crouzet, "King of Reason." See also Nelson, "Royal Authority," 113, for a helpful summary of Crouzet's argument.

22 Caroso, *Courtly Dance of the Renaissance*, 89.

23 Ficino, *Commentary*, Speech II, chapters 2 and 5, esp. 51–2.

24 Ibid., Speech II, chapter 6, 52. For the influence of Florentine Neoplatonic thought throughout early modern Europe, see Kristeller, "European Significance." For discussions of Ficino's influence and adaptation in Renaissance France as a means for imagining the state and nation in heterosexually normative terms, see Crawford, *Sexual Culture*, esp. 109–51, and Reeser, *Setting Plato Straight*.

25 Ficino, *Book of the Sun*, chapter 11.

26 Matthieu, *Histoire de France*, vol. 2, book 5, first narration, 88r–89v.
27 Ovid, *Metamorphoses*, v. 346–84. I am grateful to Rebecca Laroche for suggesting this connection.
28 Matthieu, *Histoire de France*, vol. 2, book 5, first narration, 88r.
29 Bartolomeo Prosperi, the Este court's ambassador to Florence, qtd. in Solerti, *Gli albori*, 2: 56. Prosperi, referencing this production, writes that the grand duchess Christine of Lorraine has shown his own wife favour by inviting her to it. Solerti notes that in one manuscript collection (Magliabechiano II, IX, 45) this *ballo* is listed as having been performed by the principessa Leonora but that the same *ballo* appears in Palatino manuscript 249, n400, with the title *Mascherata di stelle, ballo danzato dalla Principessa Maria M[edici]*. That Marie was its principal dancer and impresario is confirmed by Prosperi's letter dated 8 March 1596, in which he describes his wife's invitation to "un ballo della signora Principessa Maria."
30 Solerti, *Gli albori*, 2: 57.
31 Rinuccini lists these six in three pairs: Elettra and Alcinoe; Celeno and Maya; Asterope and Taigete. He then adds a sentence explaining the "lost" seventh Pleiade, Merope.
32 Solerti, *Gli albori*, 2: 58.
33 Ibid. The dancers no doubt wore costumes *à l'antique*.
34 Ibid.
35 Ciseri, "Ballets et carrousels," 137; Bartoli Bacherini, "Musiche," 144. The *Mascherata di stelle* also takes up Dante's trope, in *Paradiso* X, 64–81, whereby celestial lights prove too powerful for human eyes. More specifically, Rinuccini adopts Dante's simile comparing the dancing stars of the highest spheres, usually invisible to human eyes, to women performing a *ballata* or dance song. On the women dancing in Dante's poem, see Singleton's useful commentary in Dante Alighieri, *Divine Comedy*, 182–3.
36 Chiabrera, "Canzone in lode della reina," 258. For this performance date, see Mamone, *Paris et Florence*, 35. This event and others celebrating Marie's wedding were attended by Cardinal Pietro Aldobrandini, cardinal nephew of pope Clement VIII, as well as many other ambassadors; see Mamone, "Feste." When likening Marie's graceful dancing to that of Venus, Chiabrera places his subject in a long line of illustrious Medici dancers going back to Lorenzo "il Magnifico," who sponsored *mascherate* and authored two courtly dances, one of which was named "Venus." On Lorenzo il Magnifico's authorship of two *basse danses*, "Venus" and "Laurus," found in a fifteenth-century Florentine manuscript collection containing the *Arte della danza* by Guglielmo da Pesaro, see Bartoli Bacherini, "Musiche," 144.

37 Mamone, *Paris et Florence*, 59.
38 Solerti claims that this *heroide* describes Marie de Médicis dancing sometime in the early 1600s (*Gli albori*, 1: 28–9). Internal evidence indicates Marie in her role as queen: the "inclita donna" of this poem wears a crown, for example, and her pure white pearl necklace strikingly recalls the famous pearl necklace that Henri IV gave her as a wedding gift. On the value of this collar (reputed to be "one hundred and fifty thousand crowns"), see Battifol, *Marie de Médicis*, 224. Solerti states that this poem depicts Marie dancing at the Tuscan court, but if the *heroide* is from early 1600s, as Solerti indicates, the poem could just as likely describe her dancing at the court of France. The possibility that Rinuccini's *heroide* depicts the 1602 ballet danced in Paris by Marie may not have occurred to Solerti because elsewhere he suggests that Rinuccini, who had come to France just after Marie arrived there, left Paris for Florence in the summer of 1601 and did not return until May 1602 (Solerti, "Un viaggio," 707; on Rinuccini's dates in Paris, see also Solerti, review of Raccamadoro-Ramelli, 403–4, and Masera, "La Familia Caccini," 481). Solerti's proposed trajectory for Rinuccini is hypothetical, for when exactly he left Paris is not known; on Rinuccini's activities in Paris, see also Prunières, *Le ballet de cour en France*, 106–8, and Prunières, *L'Opéra italien en France*, xxvi. Even if Rinuccini was not present in Paris for February 1602, his *heroide* may still allude if only loosely to Marie's first French court ballet, for Rinuccini could certainly have learned about the performance second hand, perhaps through Bertaut's *récit* which was printed as early as 1602, as we have seen, or even directly from the queen, with whom Rinuccini was intimate. Ultimately we cannot be sure when – or even if – the dancing nostalgically recalled by Rinuccini's speaker actually took place; the poem may instead describe a composite fictional *ballo* based on several different Florentine *mascherate* and/or French ballets, real or imagined. For my purposes, its interest rests less on its depiction of any actual historical event and more on its contribution to a larger set of Franco-Florentine intertexts that praise Marie's dancing in Neoplatonic terms.
39 All passages from this poem (in the Italian) are quoted from Solerti, *Gli albori*, 1: 28–30.
40 Bertaut, *Recueil des quelques vers amoureux*, ed. Terreaux, 242.
41 Yates, *French Academies*, 236–74; McGowan, *Dance in the Renaissance*, 87–90, 151–73; Le Roux, "Politics of Festivals," 101–17. For a more recent discussion of Catherine de Médicis' larger political program and emphasis on civic peace, see Crouzet, *Le haut coeur*.

42 "Leurs chefs estoyent parez & ornez de petits petits triangles enrichis de diamans, rubis, perles, & autres pierreries exquises & précieuses, comme estoyent leurs cols & bras garnis de colier, carquans & bracelets: & tous leurs vestements cou[v]erts & estoffez de pierreries, qui brilloyent & estinceloyent tout ainsi qu'on voit la nuict les estoiles paroistre au manteau azuré du firmament. Aussi ceste parure a esté estimée la plus superbe, riche & pompeuse, qui se soit jamais veue porter en masquarade." McGowan, ed., *Le ballet comique*, 15v–16r.
43 Greene, "The King's One Body," 76. See also McGowan, *Dance in the Renaissance*, 172–3.
44 Le Roux, *La faveur du roi*, 9.
45 Fenlon, "Origins," 20.
46 On Medici magnificence, see in particular Burke, *Historical Anthropology of Early Modern Italy*, 132–49.
47 Nelson, "Royal Authority," 111–15.
48 On performances of piety in Henri IV's royal entries, see Crouzet, *Les Guerriers de Dieu*, 2: 541–603; Finley-Croswhite, *Henri IV and the Towns*, 47–62; and Ramsey, "Ritual Meaning." See also Nelson, "*Religion Royale*."
49 Crépin-Leblond, "Le développement," 226. On Marie's trousseau and her collection of pearls and diamonds, see Landini, "Lo stile fiorentino alla corte di Francia," and Sframeli, "Perle e diamanti per la Regina." Cf. Battifol's dismissal of Marie's penchant for precious stones and jewelry as mere frivolity (*Marie de Médicis*, 28).
50 One of these spectators in the Grande Salle du Louvre was fatally injured. For details of this accident and the ballet's various Paris locations, see L'Estoile, *Journal*, 2: 65. See also Battifol, *Le Louvre*, 112.
51 Sully, *Mémoires*, 4: 93, emphasis mine. McGowan cites an excerpt from Sully's memoirs for the year 1601 as evidence for the "relative austerity which seems to have been the king's cautious approach to fêtes," yet notes that this caution "was to be modified somewhat by his marriage to Marie de Médicis who was accustomed to splendid spectacles and adored dancing" (*Dance in the Renaissance*, 177).
52 Baccio Giovannini, letter dated 2 March 1602 from Paris, ASF, Mediceo del Principato filza 4615a, ff. 192r–193r. The ballet is mentioned on f. 192v, where Giovannini also asserts that a full report will be given shortly by "Monsr. Marchesani" upon the latter's return to Florence.
53 Innocenzo del Bufalo to Cardinal Pietro Aldobrandini, Paris, 26 February 1602, BAV, Barb. lat. 5831, ff. 78v–79r, emphasis mine.
54 Innocenzo del Bufalo to his brother Muzio del Bufalo, Paris, postscript to a letter dated 26 February, ASR, Archivio Santacroce, busta 796, unpaginated.

55 Malingre repeats this information and adds to it the detail found in the left margin in Matthieu's printed history that this ballet was danced in "trois stations, la premiere au Louvre, la seconde en l'hostel de Guise, & la troisiesme en la gra[nde] sal[l]e de l'Archevesché" (Matthieu, *Histoire de France*, 89r). Malingre's version reads: "Ceste nuict valut à la Royne une journée, car en tous les lieux où le Balet fut veu & admiré, sçauoir en trois stations, la premiere au Louvre, la seconde en l'hostel de Guise, la troisiesme en la grande sal[l]e de L'Archevesché" (*Annales générales*, 481).
56 Agrippa, *Declamation*, 54.
57 Du Chesne, *Figures mystiques*, 26r.
58 Ibid., 52v–53v.
59 Rubin, "Heroic Image," 41–2.
60 Yates, *Astraea*.
61 See Vivanti, "Gallic Hercules," esp. 192, on medals and poems from the period 1598–1608 that take up the Astraea theme. On d'Urfé, see Rubin, "Heroic Image," 45; Yates, *Astraea*, 210.
62 Cosandey, *La reine de France*, 278–83.
63 Ibid., 282–3; Lecoq, *François Ier imaginaire*, 336; McCartney, "The King's Mother."
64 For such imagery in connection with François Ier and Henri II, in particular the latter's 1549 Paris entry, see Bryant, "*Parlementaire* Political Theory in the Parisian Royal Entry Ceremony" and "Politics, Ceremonies, and Embodiments of Majesty in Henry II's France," in his *Ritual, Ceremony and the Changing Monarchy in France*, 21–30, 127–54; on this imagery in connection with later Valois kings, see Yates, *Astraea*, 123.
65 Cosandey, *La reine de France*, 278.
66 Ibid., 285–9; Rodier, "Marie de Médicis et le culte marial."
67 In Cosandey's reading (*La reine de France*, 334–60, 339–44), numerous panels in Rubens' cycle portray the queen using both the traits of the Virgin and heroic traits taken from classical mythology. This layering, Cosandey suggests, makes Marie's identification with the Virgin both unmistakable and yet simultaneously only one possible reading among others. See also Cosandey, "Représenter."
68 See notes 15–17 above.
69 Michel Henry was one of the twenty-four *violons du roi* and a player for the city of Paris (McGowan, *L'art du ballet de cour*, 50). Henry seems to have composed the dance music for Marie's first French court ballet; his table also indicates the involvement of "M. Fransignes" – most likely Pierre Francisque [Fransigne, Fransignes] Caroubel, who according to Dobbins, "Caroubel," held the post of *violon ordinaire de la chambre du roi* under Henri III and Henri IV.

250   Notes to pages 44–5

70 Henry specifies further that the entry danced by Marie's *filles* culminated in a "branle gay" and indicates that the ballet as a whole featured four airs, the third and fourth being a galliard and a courante respectively. Margaret McGowan, in private correspondence, has suggested that Henry's apparent confusion may derive from his use of Old Style (herafter O.S.) dating.
71 http://palluy.fr/index.php?page=1601-a-1700-avant-paques. Accessed 15 November 2016.
72 Baschet, *Les comédiens italiens*, 113.
73 "Le jour de Carême-prenant, la reine joua son ballet magnifique au Louvre, premièrement devant le roi, puis chez madame de Retz, à l'Évêché et autres lieux, où Sa Majesté avait commandé d'assembler la compagnie pour le recevoir, et où plusieurs curieux de le voir se trouvèrent fort incommodés et mal à leur aise." L'Estoile, *Journal*, 2: 65. On possible connections between Marie's 1609 *Ballet of Diana* and literature associated with Mme de Retz's *salon vert*, see chapter 4.
74 See note 1 above.
75 Innocenzo del Bufalo to Cardinal Pietro Aldobrandini, Paris, 26 February 1602, BAV, Barb. lat. 5831, ff. 78v–79r; del Bufalo to his brother Muzio del Bufalo, postscript to a letter dated 26 February from Paris, ASR, Archivio Santacroce, busta 796, unpaginated. For a partial summary of del Bufalo's 26 February letter to Aldobrandini, see *Correspondance du nonce*, ed. Barbiche, 251 (Letter #135). Correspondence of the archducal ambassador to the French court also identifies a masked ballet danced on the last day of carnival 1602 by the queen of France accompanied by twenty-four princesses, ladies, and damsels very richly and honestly dressed and adorned ("Le dernier jour du quaresme prenant la Royne fist ung ballet en masquerade accompaignée de vingt et quatre princesses dames et damoyselles fort richement et proprement habillées et parées"). Philippe d'Ayala, Paris, 24 February 1602, HHS, Belgien PC 18-1.
76 Cosandey, *La reine de France*, 55–64.
77 Buisseret, *Henry IV*, 109, citing Ralph Winwood, *Negotiations*, 1: 288–9. According to Buisseret, Winwood also reports Marie's statement on another occasion that if she gave birth to a daughter, "she wished her bed might be her tombe" (*Henry IV*, 182, citing Winwood, *Negotiations*, 1: 293).
78 *Histoire des amours du Grand Alcandre*, 271; see also *Les amours du Grand Alcandre*, 89, and *Histoire des amours de Henry IV*, 338. Cf. the anonymously authored *Amours de Henri IV*, according to which the queen prepared two ballets, not just one: "La naissance du Dauphin fut célébrée par plusieurs réjouissances tant à la cour que dans les Provinces. La Reine fit préparer

deux ballets, qu'on étudia pendant deux ou trois mois" (*Les amours de Henri IV*, 1: 203).
79 Pardoe, *Life*, 1: 133.
80 Durosoir, "L'allégorie," 80.
81 For the period of lying in time following the dauphin's birth, along with that of Henriette d'Entragues' son, see Merki, *La marquise*, 97–8.
82 Cosandey, *La reine de France*, 284.
83 On these developments, see this book's introduction, n2.
84 Matthieu, *Histoire de France*, Book 4, 50v.
85 On such racial concepts in relation to the nobility and monarchy during the early modern period, see Jouanna, *L'idée de race*, as well as Kane with Smuts, "Politics of Race." For more extensive discussion of this mystique of bloodline during Henri IV's reign, see chapters 3 and 4.
86 On these celebrations, see L'Estoile, *Journal*, 2: 41. For a more detailed discussion of the Te Deum performance, see Van Orden, *Music*, 147–52, 174–6. Freer (Robinson), *Henry IV and Marie de Medici*, 2: 295, also mentions cannon shots and fireworks.
87 "[A]fin que le people le peust veoir en passant par la ville, la Nourrice le tenoit à la mammelle. Cest veue augmenta les actions de grace que l'on rendoit à Dieu de l'accroisement de ces faveurs sur cet Estat." Matthieu, *Histoire de France*, Book 3, 59v–60r.
88 On Henri IV's efforts to position Gabrielle symbolically as future queen, see Crawford, "Politics of Promiscuity," 223–4; Wellman, *Queens and Mistresses*, 323–56.
89 Buisseret, *Henry IV*, 78.
90 "Le dimanche 4e de ce mois [Novembre 1601], le roi étant arrivé, le jour de devant, à Verneuil, madame la Marquise y accoucha d'un fils, que le roi baisa et mignarda fort, l'appelant son fils et le disant plus beau que celui de sa femme, qu'il disait ressembler aux Médicis, étant noir et gros comme eux. De quoi on dit que la reine, étant avertie, pleura fort." L'Estoile, *Journal*, 2: 48; see also Chaussinand-Nogaret, *La vie quotidienne*, 47.
91 In his letters to the grand duke's secretary, the Florentine resident in Paris Baccio Giovannini describes at length the marquise's designs and actions, including her verbal insults towards the dauphin as another of the king's bastards. See in particular two letters partly in cipher dated 17 February 1602 (two days prior to Marie's ballet performance): ASF, Mediceo del Principato, filza 4615a, ff. 188r–190v. See also Kermina, *Marie de Médicis*, 70–1, and Battifol, *Marie de Médicis*, 117–18. On the marquise's disrespectful attitude towards Marie during this period, see *Les amours de Henri IV*, 1: 194, and Merki, *La marquise de Verneuil*, 93.

252 Notes to pages 48–9

92 Innocenzo del Bufalo to Cardinal Pietro Aldobrandini, Paris, 31 January 1602, originally in cipher, deciphered version transcribed as Letter #130 in Barbiche, ed., *Correspondance du nonce en France*, 247–8. The Barberini Library's collection (now at the BAV) includes a copy of Henri's 1599 letter of promise to Henriette d'Entragues; see Barb. lat. 7978, f. 12. On the context for the king's promise of marriage to Henriette d'Entragues after her earlier delivery of a stillborn son, see *Histoire des amours du Grand Alcandre*, 264. Henriette d'Entragues wrote a letter about her children to Maffeo Barberini in September 1601 prior to his arrival at the French court as extraordinary nuncio sent to honour the future Louis XIII's birth; see BAV, Barb. lat. 7978, ff. 3–4. For copies of Maffeo Barberini's letters describing his audiences with Henri and Marie, see BAV, Vat. lat. 12431, ff. 69r–70r, 71r–v.
93 Later, Henriette d'Entragues embroiled herself in a plot against Henri IV – but with the Spanish, not the Huguenots. I discuss these events further in chapter 2. L'Estoile reports that it was a Leaguer who had imported this book to France from Flanders, and that those of the League, fearing discovery, had started the rumour that this seditious book was the work of Protestants (*Journal*, 2: 60–1). Del Bufalo would no doubt have leapt at any occasion, calumnious or not, by which to discredit the Huguenots; on his frequent yet unsuccessful attempts to convince the king that they presented a threat to the dauphin, see Barbiche, "Clément VIII," 111.
94 On Marie's early recognition of her own precarious situation and that of her children, particularly the dauphin, see Rubin, "The Heroic Image," 60, 63, 67.
95 Fenlon, "Origins," 20. See also Burke, *Historical Anthropology of Early Modern Italy*, 132–49.
96 Immediately after her arrival France, as Bartoli Bacherini points out, Marie had occasion to show off her skills in social dance: in Lyon, as soon as her marriage was consummated, Marie ended a celebratory royal banquet by dancing with her husband a long "chiaranzana," a slow dance played on the lute and often accompanied by song ("Musiche," 145).
97 Burke, *History and Social Theory*, 67–71.
98 Solerti, *Gli albori*, 2: 58.
99 "Ben potete dunque a gran ragione gloriarvi, poi che le più belle che adornino i luminosi campi a gli occhi vostri in questa sera leggiadramente ballando si rappresentano, nè certo per altro che per rallegrare la nobil alma e renderle men gravi cure, le quali con sì lieta fronte sì prende, per alleggerire in parte l'alto pondo che della Monarchia di Toscana sostiene il serenissimo Ferdinando suo consorte."

100 Bertaut, *Recueil des quelques vers amoureux*, ed. Terreaux, 242–3. I am grateful to Margaret McGowan for her suggestions regarding my translation of this stanza and the one cited above.
101 For the fact of the marquise's appearance in this ballet, its effect on Henri IV's decision regarding the marriage of Leonora Galigaï and Concino Concini, and other proofs of "bienveillance" with which the queen honoured Henriette d'Entragues, see *Histoire des amours du Grand Alcandre*, 268–71. See also *Les Amours du Grand Alcandre par Mlle de Guise*, 1: 87–90, 89; *Les amours de Henri IV*, 1: 203; Dreux du Radier, *Mémoires historiques*, 6: 157; *Histoire des amours de Henry IV*, 14: 337–8; Saint-Edme, *Amours et galanteries*, 2: 64–6; Pardoe, *Life*, 1: 122–65; Freer (Robinson), *Henri IV and Marie de Medici*, 2: 277–80, 304–5; Merki, *La marquise de Verneuil*, 94–7; Kermina, *Marie de Médicis*, 102; and Thiroux d'Arconville, *Vie de Marie de Médicis*, 1: 57–8. Del Bufalo does not mention the marquise dancing in this ballet, but this nuncio's 31 January 1602 letter to Cardinal Pietro Aldobrandini, which notes a book claiming the royal marriage to be illegitimate as well as an alleged Huguenot plot to make the marquise de Verneuil's infant son heir to the throne, does explain that "una donna chiamata Leonora, che si menò di Fiorenza, maritata in Concino Concini" has great influence over the queen, and that she and her husband are in agreement with the king that the marquise should be tolerated by the queen ("che la regina sopporti la marchesa"). See del Bufalo, *Correspondance du nonce en France*, ed. Barbiche, 147–8 (Letter #130).
102 In 1599, during her first appearance at court, "Mademoiselle d'Entragues danced a couranto [sic] in a ballet with her brother the count d'Auvergne, with such grace as to attract the attention of the king ... Henry conversed for some time with this bewitching damsel; and honoured her by an invitation to dance." Freer (Robinson), *Henry IV and Marie de Medici*, 2: 59. Gabrielle d'Estrées, duchesse de Beaufort, Henri IV's late mistress, had led courtly dances at court, in 1594–5 for example (ibid., 2: 252–3), while Henriette may have danced in the 1599 *Ballet des cinq hommes et cinq filles fait par Mrs. De Rohan, de Termes, Mlle d'Entragues, M. Néon et autres*, as cited in McGowan, *L'art du ballet de cour*, 256.
103 On the social recognition associated with dancing in a royal ballet, see Kettering, "Favour and Patronage," and *Power and Reputation*, 42, as well as Battifol, *Le Louvre*, 111, who writes of the fever surrounding preparations for these ballets in which "[i]l n'est courtisan qui ne grille d'en être. Les plus grands princes tiennent à honneur d'y figurer" [there

is no courtier who does not burn [with desire] to be in one. The greatest princes hold it an honour to appear in one].
104 Regarding the 1602 *Ballet of the Sixteen Virtues*, Battifol writes that Marie "choisit les princes et princesses qui figureront dans ce ballet" (ibid., 112).
105 Pardoe, *Life*, 1: 134. On a subsequent occasion, when angered by the king and marquise, Marie seems to have refused to dance a ballet in which Henri IV asked her to include in her troupe another of his mistresses, Jacqueline de Bueil, comtesse de Moret. See *Les amours du Grand Alcandre*, 103; *Les amours de Henri IV*, 2:23; Saint-Edme, *Amours et galanteries*, 2: 91–2.
106 See especially Bourdieu, *Logic of Practice*, 98–134. Other important theorists of gift exchange include Mauss, *The Gift*, Bataille, *Visions of Excess*, 116–29, and Derrida, *Given Time. 1*. Especially relevant to the period of my study are Davis, *The Gift in Sixteenth-Century France*, Burke, *Historical Anthropology of Early Modern Italy*, and Burke, *History and Social Theory*, 67–71.
107 Mauss, *The Gift*, 39–41.
108 Bourdieu, *Logic of Practice*, 115.
109 Van Orden, *Music*. Cf. Anglo, "The Barriers."
110 After this first edition in 1605, Matthieu's *Histoire de France & des choses memorables* was reprinted in 1606, 1609, 1613, and 1615. In 1640, moreover, Malingre quotes directly from Matthieu's description of this ballet (without citing Matthieu as source); see note 55 above.
111 Bourdieu, *Logic of Practice*, 123.
112 Ibid.

2 Royal Women's Ballet and/as Royal Ceremonial

1 See the list of sources identified for a "Deuxième Ballet de la Reyne le 13 janvier" 1605 in McGowan, *L'art du ballet de cour*, 262. Among these sources McGowan includes "Malherbe. Mss, Fr. 24357, f. 177v," but this manuscript in fact references Malherbe's verses for Marie's third ballet in 1609 (the manuscript itself misidentifies this poem as having been composed for a queen's ballet for the year 1610).
2 The quoted phrase is from Andrea, "Elizabeth I and Persian Exchanges," 184.
3 This phrase is the Venetian ambassador Angelo Badoer's, written in 1605, as qtd. in Dickerman and Walker, "Monuments of His Own Magnificence," 177.
4 On royal minorities as dangers to the system of personal monarchy, see Courtright, "Garden," 59.

5 Cosandey, *La reine de France*, 27–52 (esp. 43), 296–332; Crawford, *Perilous Performances*, 13–21, 20. For a discussion of such ideas in relation to earlier regencies, see McCartney, "The King's Mother and Royal Prerogative," 117–41.
6 Buisseret, *Henry IV*, 108.
7 Lee Jr, *James I and Henry IV*, 24–5 and n21.
8 Baccio Giovannini to Ferdinando I de' Medici, Paris, 3 June 1603, qtd. and cited in Millen and Wolf, *Heroic Deeds*, 100. See also Zeller, *Henri IV et Marie de Médicis*, 180.
9 Lee Jr, *James I and Henry IV*, 24–5 and n21.
10 Dickerman, "Henri IV and the Juliens-Clèves Crisis," 631.
11 *Propago imperii* might also be translated, more simply, as "the imperial line"; see Jones, "Guillaume Dupré," 330. For a nuanced discussion of the 1603 medal's visual iconography along with the letter patent by Henri IV, see Courtright, "New Place for Queens," 276–8, and Courtright, "A Garden and a Gallery," 75 and n78. Cf. Barbiche, "Marie de Médicis, reine régnante," 42–3, who argues that this position on the council did not in fact give Marie access to any real political power. On Marie's addition to the council and the 1603 medal's commemoration of this event see also Millen and Wolf, *Heroic Deeds*, 100–4, Dubost, *Marie de Médicis*, 114, and Dubost, "L'Épouse," 104. Regarding later variants of the 1603 medal, the obverse of which formed the model for Rubens' "Consignment of the Regency," see Millen and Wolf, *Heroic Deeds*, 101–4, and Dubost, *Marie de Médicis*, 197–9.
12 On this plot, see, for example, Buisseret, *Henry IV*, 125, and Mousnier, *Assassination of Henry IV*, 125–6, 136. Earlier, in 1602, d'Auvergne had been implicated in another conspiracy against Henri IV led by the ducs de Biron and Bouillon, aided and abetted by the Spanish governor of the Milanese as well as King Philip III of Spain (Mousnier, *Assassination of Henry IV*, 126, and Buisseret, *Henry IV*, 111–15).
13 Toby Mathew as cited in Buisseret, *Henry IV*, 128.
14 Jones, "Guillaume Dupré," 320, 329–31; Mann, *Wallace Collection Catalogues*, 137 (cf. the 1603 medal, described on 138); Seelig-Teuwen, "Barthélemy Prieur," 342, 344 fig. 8. Millen and Wolf misidentify 1604 as the date for this medal's first variant (*Heroic Deeds*, 101); they cite Mazerolle, who himself gives the date as 1605 in *Les médailleurs français*, II. 129 no. 642 and III. Plate XXVI.
15 La Force, *Mémoires*, 1: 389–90 (letter dated 10 January 1605) and 1: 390–1 (letter dated 25 January 1605).
16 See Mss, Fr. 24357, f. 313v, as well as Lesure, "Le Recueil de Ballets de Michel Henry," 209–10. McGowan, *L'art du ballet de cour*, 262, cites Henry

and follows his dating. Her index of ballets also references for this same production Philidor's transcription of the dance music for a "ballet de la reine" dated "1606": two entrées (the second being multi-part) and a *grand ballet*. See Philidor, *Recueil de plusieurs anciens ballets*, ff. 40–1.

17 Giovannini to Ferdinando I de' Medici and Belisario Vinta, ASF, Mediceo del Principato, filza 4617a, f. 392; BI, ms 1794, ff. 429r–430v. For an edited transcription and translation of this letter and an initial analysis of its importance for *ballet de cour* historians and theorists, see Gough, "New Evidence and Analysis." All subsequent quotations from this document, as well as explanations of particular words and phrases, draw on this published edition, emended to follow L'École nationale des chartes guidelines (rather than Record of Early English Drama guidelines, as was the case in that earlier article).

18 Gough, "New Evidence and Analysis," 124.

19 "Je n'ai jamais vu une si grande assemblée dans le Louvre, car la Cour est fort grande" (La Force, *Mémoires*, 1: 390–1).

20 The phrase "ils marchent doucement," describing the violins' entry, can also indicate a specific dance step. For further discussion, see Gough, "New Evidence and Analysis," 127 nii.

21 Ibid., 123.

22 Ibid.

23 Ibid.

24 Ibid.

25 For a more detailed discussion of this document's provenance and a textual description, see Gough, "New Evidence and Analysis," 118–20.

26 Gravit, *Peiresc Papers*, 1–2.

27 Ibid.

28 The internal order of the sheets in these two *recueils* on ceremonial is most likely Peiresc's. The volumes were bound after his death by Peiresc's friend and correspondent Pierre Dupuy, but Peiresc himself had sorted his *registres* by subject matter and organized them into *fagots* or packets (one hundred and five of them, at the time of his death), and it is believed that Dupuy used this system when binding these packets now held at Carpentras. See ibid., 4–5.

29 BI, ms. 1794, ff. 431–2.

30 "[C]arousel, n," *OED Online*.

31 Gassendi, *Vie*, 78–9. Peiresc also wrote a letter from Aix dated 15 February 1605 to one Monsieur Clusius at Leyden; see *Lettres de Peiresc*, 7: 955–6.

32 Malherbe to Peiresc, undated letter from February 1606, in *Œuvres complètes*, ed. Lalanne, 3: 2.

33 BI, ms 1794, f. 338r.

34 Valavez to Peiresc, Paris, 18 September 1610, BI, ms. 1794, f. 453ff. Peiresc himself added a title in capitals and repeated it in the left hand corner.
35 Valavez to Peiresc, Aix, 29 November 1622, BI, ms 1794, f. 201v.
36 See Mss, Fr. 10424–10429 for Jolly's "Nouvelle collection de cérémonies et de festes, depuis Clovis jusqu'à la mort de Louis XIII." The fourth of these five manuscript volumes, Mss, Fr. 10428, is dedicated to ceremonial under Henri IV and Louis XIII, and Jolly's transcription of the document describing the queen's 1605 ballet can be found on ff. 119r–120v.
37 Jolly, *Projet d'un nouveau cérémonial françois*. Although Jolly's table for the projected work appeared in print, the work itself was never printed, meaning that some of the accounts of specific ceremonial occasions that Jolly had transcribed from earlier manuscript sources – including the account of the ballet danced by Marie de Médicis in 1605 – were never published.
38 Giesey, *The Royal Funeral Ceremony*; Giesey, *Cérémonial et puissance souveraine*; Giesey, *Rulership in France*; Sarah Hanley, *The 'Lit de Justice'*; Jackson, *Vive le roi!*; Bryant, *The King and the City* and *Ritual, Ceremony and the Changing Monarchy*. Work on royal ceremonial that draws on and extends work by these scholars includes Fogel, *Les cérémonies de l'information*, McCartney, "Queens in the Cult of the French Renaissance Monarchy," Cosandey, *La reine de France*, and, in perhaps a more critical vein, Sternberg, *Status Interaction*.
39 For statements identifying these as the four key or foundational state ceremonies, see Giesey, *Cérémonial et puissance souveraine*, Giesey, *Rulership in France*, 239–49, 240, and Bryant, *Ritual, Ceremony and the Changing Monarchy*, 2.
40 Cosandey, *La reine de France*, 124.
41 Bryant, *Ritual, Ceremony and the Changing Monarchy*, 226. By the seventeenth century, Bryant notes, the "meanings of royal ceremonies changed to be symbolic of a universal practice among all subjects to exalt divinely ordained rulers" and the historiographers and antiquarians who developed the new taxonomy of royal ceremonial which supported this view also created new "fiction[s]" of "fundamental ceremon[ies] for representing the ancient continuity of French dynastic and absolutist kingship" (5–6).
42 Watanabe-O'Kelly, "The Early Modern Festival Book," 1: 3–17, 5–6; Knecht, *The French Renaissance Court*, 94; Bryant, *Ritual, Ceremony and the Changing Monarchy*, 7.
43 Fantoni, "The City of the Prince," 39–52, 41–3.
44 "Je n'ai jamais vu une si grande assemblée dans le Louvre, car la Cour est forte grande, nous y en eumes jusqu'à une heure après minuit; il y avoit

encore deux autres grandes assemblées à la ville, où la Reine l'alla danser à l'Arsenal et à l'Evêché. Le Roi s'y voulut trouver partout, de sorte que nous n'avons fait que trotter toute la nuit, et étoit jour quand le Roi a été de retour au Louvre." La Force, *Mémoires*, 1: 390–1.

45 Buisseret mentions the king's propensity to "act the part of host" at Marie's ballets by arranging the seating and ordering the rooms, though he does not mention any specific instances (*Henry IV*, 105).

46 "[L]e temps du ballet s'approchant environ une heure apres mynuyt le roy habillé à la coustumée aiant une enseigne et une plume au chapeau une chayne de senteur en escharpe son espée au costé son manteau sur le bras gauche et un baston à la main sortit de sa chambre et vint dans la Grand salle du Louvre." Gough, "New Evidence and Analysis," 122, 125.

47 Hackenbroch, *Enseignes*, 2. According to Battifol, the king generally abjured luxurious dress, and on a day to day basis dressed simply, often in stained and worn clothing; nevertheless, for great ceremonies, "il saura tout de meme se vêtir de façon royale et se couvrir de bijoux" (*Le Louvre*, 75).

48 Gough, "New Evidence and Analysis," 122, 126.

49 Battifol claims that according to official accounts, ballet audiences at the court of Louis XIII could be as large as four thousand people (ibid., 21, 110, 229). See also Christout, "Court Ballet in France." At the court of Louis XIII, Christout asserts, "even making allowances for chroniclers' natural tendency to exaggerate, it is certain that several thousand people" viewed royal ballets (7). Productions danced by Louis XIII most often took place first in the Grande Salle du Louvre or the Petit Bourbon and then at various Paris hotels, including those at which his mother had danced her ballets.

50 See note 44 above.

51 Letter from Paris dated 6 February 1605, ASF, Mediceo del Principato, filza 4860, unpaginated.

52 "J'entens que la presse fut si grande que l'on y eût peu de plaisir." Villeroy to Beaumont, 26 January 1605, King's MSS., cxxvii, f. 143, in Sullivan, *Court Masques*, 197.

53 The original phrases are "des douzaines de copeurs de bourses," "des fripons des chapeaus et manteaus," and "des troupes de papes" [*sic*]; see Gough, "New Evidence and Analysis," 124. Christout also mentions "pickpockets" and "scoundrels" among ballet audiences ("Court Ballet in France," 5).

54 Duindam, "Palace, City, Dominions," 87.

55 "[P]our faire Ranger tout le monde les ambassadeurs danglaterre d'un costé le nonce du pape de l'autre et les princes de mesme." Gough, "New Evidence and Analysis," 122.

56 For a discussion of "monsieur le chevallier" as Henri IV himself, see Gough, "New Evidence and Analysis," 126. In that article, I translate "rompit" in this same passage as "rapped." The verb *rompre* means "to break," but in the seventeenth century it could also indicate the action of violently reducing, with one knock or stroke, a recalcitrant object or person (*Dictionnaire historique de la langue française*, 3290–1). Given the jesting tone of this letter overall, the author's use of this term seems to indicate that a person sitting next to him in the ballet's audience has been rapped or struck by the king's baton as part of Henri IV's efforts to bring the assembly to order.
57 *Le romant des chevaliers de Thrace*, 3–4.
58 The social status of spectators at royal ballets in Paris has received little scholarly attention. Christout proposes that audiences were composed of "spectateurs de conditions diverses mais nobles pour la plupart" [spectators from diverse ranks, but for the most part from the nobility] ("Les ballets-mascarades," 9; translation mine). Kettering notes further that "[t]here was no admission fee, so anyone who could get in could see the performance. Besides court nobles, the audience included ordinary Parisians with their wives and children, students, servants, and anyone well-dressed enough to slip past the guards at the door, who were selling places surreptitiously, anyway" (*Power and Reputation*, 39). See also Christout, *Ballet occidental*, 21. Regarding social privilege in connection with masque spectatorship in England during this same period, including the social and political ramifications of exclusion from royal masque audiences, see Butler, *The Stuart Court Masque*, 34–62.
59 One of the ten costumed tournament masquerades for a 1596 Stuttgart christening witnessed by Thomas Platter featured Janus on horseback in the form of conjoined twins, preceded and followed by two additional figures each having two faces; see Katritzky, *Healing*, 199. Du Choul discusses the figure of Janus as taken up by Roman emperors in architecture and medals in his *Discours de la religion*, 15–22.
60 Valladier, *Labyrinthe royal*, 145–6. On this badge or *devise* for Henri IV, see www.heraldica.org/topics/france/frarms.htm (accessed 13 July 2016). The Avignon entry further reinforced parallels between Henri IV and Janus by placing inside the Temple of Janus an effigy of the king painted in oil, at the top of which appeared an emblem of the god's head, with two faces, animated by the king's device "Duo Protegit Unus" ("the one protects the two," i.e., the two kingdoms of France and Navarre).
61 *Le polemandre*.
62 Howard, *Politics of Courtly Dancing*, 16.

63 Because Maximilien de Béthune is best known by his ducal title, for the sake of convenience I refer to him hereafter as Sully.
64 La Force, *Mémoires*, 1: 389–90 (letter dated 10 January 1605). La Force's letters about the marriage and ballet are also quoted briefly in Laugel, *Henry de Rohan*, 35, and Vray, *Catherine de Parthenay*, 114. McGowan cites Laugel and La Force as part of her index of sources for the *ballet de la reine* of 1605 (*L'art du ballet de cour*, 262).
65 Barbiche and Dainville-Barbiche, *Sully*, 169; Vray, *Catherine de Parthenay*, 112–13; Laugel, *Henry de Rohan*, 34.
66 Vray, *Catherine de Parthenay*, 110; Laugel, *Henry de Rohan*, 32.
67 Laugel outlines the state of Henri de Rohan's penury and asserts that "Le mariage avec la fille de Sully venait sans doute à propos pour tirer Rohan de ses embarras financiers" [the marriage with Sully's daughter came about, no doubt, in order to save Rohan from his financial difficulties] (ibid., 36).
68 Ibid. On Sully's own pretensions to sovereignty at this time, see Dickerman and Walker, "Monuments."
69 Laugel, *Henry de Rohan*, 34–6; Vray, *Catherine de Parthenay*, 112–14.
70 Buisseret, *Henry IV*, 137. In March the next year Henri IV would personally march against Bouillon, who capitulated without a fight (ibid., 141).
71 Barbiche and Dainville-Barbiche, *Sully*, 169–70. On Guy de Laval, see L'Estoile, *Journal*, 2: 164 and n122 bis.
72 Barbiche and Dainville-Barbiche, *Sully*, 169–70; La Force, *Mémoires*, 1: 387 (letter dated 28 December 1604); Vray, *Catherine de Parthenay*, 112.
73 Baccio Giovannini, ASF, Mediceo del Principato, filza 4860, insert dated 20 February 1605, second unpaginated folio, verso. This view would have been shared by the papacy since, as Barbiche has noted, Rome throughout the first decade of the seventeenth century sought to brand French Protestants as especial enemies to the dauphin (Barbiche, "Clément VIII et la France (1592–1605)," 111).
74 Later, when Rohan's interests clashed with Marie's, his mother the dowager duchesse de Rohan took steps to mediate between her eldest son and the regent such that in the end, courteous relations were maintained; see Vray, *Catherine de Parthenay*, 138–40, and Buissert, *Sully*, 182–3. When Rohan did actually take up arms against Louis XIII in 1620, moreover, he did so in concert with other Catholic princes (including Mayenne and Soissins) in support of Marie, during the second war of mother and son; see Tapié, *France in the Age of Louis XIII*, 116.
75 Vray, *Catherine de Parthenay*, 105.
76 La Force, *Mémoires*, 1: 389 (letter dated 10 January, 1605); Laugel, *Henry de Rohan*, 35.

77 McGowan, *L'art du ballet*, 54–61; Prunières, *Le ballet de cour en France*, 95–7; Parthenay, *Ballets allégoriques*; Paquot, "Madame de Rohan"; Paquot, "Comédies-Ballets"; Vray, *Catherine de Parthenay*, 83–4.
78 BNF, 500 Colbert, 86, f. 237r.
79 Catherine de Lorraine, duchesse de Nevers, seems to have been very retiring, avoiding appearances at court whenever possible. She was loyal to the monarchy, however, so much so that in February 1618, despite being ill, Catherine acquiesced to Anne d'Autriche's request that she attend a ballet performed at the Louvre; she died the next day. Baudson, *Charles de Gonzague*, 154–6.
80 Boyer, "Giulio Caccini."
81 Dubost, *Marie de Médicis*, 280.
82 On the inclusion of women in royal women's ballets as a form of patronage meant to facilitate more powerful kinship alliances for these women's families, particularly at the court of Louis XIII and Anne d'Autriche, see Kettering, "Favour and Patronage."
83 Giovannini, the Florentine representative in Paris, reports that according to Sully, Marie's efforts on behalf of Leonora Galigaï had this effect. *Négotiations diplomatiques*, ed. Desjardins, 5: 467.
84 For a more detailed discussion of longevity of noble bloodline in connection with early modern ideas of race, or "social racism," see chapters 3 and 4.
85 On the rank of foreign prince or *prince étranger* and its particular relation to the French king, see Oresko, "Princes Étrangers"; Parrott, "A 'Prince Souverain' and the French Crown"; Antonetti, "Les princes étrangers"; Spangler, *Society of Princes*, 19–41; Poumarède, *Pour en finir avec la croisade*, 389; Sternberg, *Status Interaction*, 19.
86 Circumstances surrounding Anne d'Autriche's 1623 *ballet de la reine* reinforce the idea that Bourbon authority required participation of women from prominent families in queens' ballets. Louis XIII had offered to make Henri de Rohan *connétable de France* (commander in chief of the king's army) if he would convert to Catholicism, thereby abdicating his de facto role as Protestant insurrectionist. Rohan refused and the king had him arrested in February 1623. Rohan was only released when his wife Marguerite de Rohan (née Béthune) made clear that she would not dance in the queen's ballet that carnival season as planned, thereby causing a major scandal. On this episode, see Vray, *Catherine de Parthenay*, 153, and Van Orden, *Music, Discipline and Arms*, 106.
87 Note that the princes of the blood, angered by the king's willingness at Marie's urging to position her sister the duchess of Mantua in a place of

honour above their own at the baptism ceremonies for the dauphin and his sisters in 1606, boycotted the celebrations. These ceremonies were an important element in the larger royal effort, begun in 1603, to bolster the queen's position. As Dubost notes, official reports such as the *Mercure françois* carefully covered over this scandal because of the political threat to the dynasty caused by such challenges to the queen's legitimacy as mother of the king's heir (*Marie de Médicis*, 145). On these events see also Thiroux d'Arconville, *Vie de Marie de Médicis*, 1: 81, and Chatenet, "Henri IV et l'évolution du cérémonial."

88 Dubost, *Marie de Médicis*, 62, 71–5. On Louis de Gonzague and Henri IV, see Wolfe, "Piety and Political Allegiance."
89 Dubost, *Marie de Médicis*, 73–4.
90 On these particular aspects of the foreign queen's vulnerability upon the death of her husband, see Crawford, *Perilous Performances*, 13.
91 Cosandey explains this concept concisely: "Mariée sous le régime de la séparation, la reine est placée hors de l'État, au titre de sa personnalité juridique privée. Mais, mariée avec le roi, elle acquiert la dignité royale qui fait d'elle une reine de France, par 'ceste communication des honneurs, dignitez et privileges qui se fait par le moyen du mariage.' Ainsi, elle apparaît dans et hors de l'État, intégrée par son mariage en même temps qu'exclue, souveraine et sujette. Cette ambiguïté de la reine, cette dualité du personnage est donc inhérente à son statut puisque marquée par le sceau du mariage, à l'origine de son existence" [Married under a contract that specifies separation of property, the queen is placed outside of the state, due to her private juridical personality. But, married to the king, she acquires the royal dignity that makes of her a queen of France, by this communication of honours, dignities, and privileges that occurs through marriage. Thus she appears both inside and outside of the state; integrated by her marriage at the same time that she is excluded; sovereign and subject. This ambiguity of the queen, this duality of personhood, is inherent to her statute since marked by the seal of marriage, at the origin of her existence" (*La reine de France*, 87, translation mine).
92 Ibid., 125.
93 "[C]omme elle feut au millieu de la salle les musiciens chantarent le louanges *du Roy*," emphasis mine.
94 Gough, "New Evidence and Analysis," 123, 130.
95 On the dating of this portrait and its relation to Pourbus' career as a whole, see Ducos, "The Portrait of doña Maria de' Medici."
96 Dillon, *Language of Space*, 77.

97 On the dais designating the place of the king in all royal ceremonies, see Descimon and Guéry, "Un État des temps modernes?" 193. But the dais could also belong to the queen in her royal entries and *sacre*, thereby setting her apart visually as a royal person sharing in the honour belonging to the king (Cosandey, *La reine de France*, 179).
98 For the term "luxurious accessory" in connection with the socially constructed symbolic meanings ascribed to dwarfs at early modern courts. I am indebted to Van Den Berg, "Dwarf Aesthetics," 25.
99 Cosandey, *La reine de France*, 74–82.
100 Garnier, *Nains et géants*, 102. According to Garnier, in 1617 Marie de Médicis' dwarf was Merlin, who held the position of usher to the queen's cabinet, and before him, the post was held by Jean Mauderon, dit Maudricart, another dwarf. Between 1599 and 1623, the kings of France (Henri IV and then Louis XIII) had several dwarfs, while Henri de Bourbon, prince de Condé, had a dwarf named Jan Verjus. Charles IX had apparently owned nine dwarfs, given to him by the king of Poland and Holy Roman Emperor; see Johnston, "Some Observations," 706. On dwarfs at the Spanish Habsburg court, see Alvarez, *Locos, enanos, y hombres de placer*.
101 I use the term "monster" historically. In early modern Europe this designation (as opposed to the eighteenth- and nineteenth-century term "freak" or the post-1989 concept of disability) was applied to animal and human beings born with marked physical nonconformities (Katritzsky, *Healing, Performance, and Ceremony*, 193 n3). On dwarfs in connection with "extraordinary bodies" or "monsters" in early modern English drama, see Burnett, *Constructing 'Monsters'*, 15, 29. On the ancient notion that dwarfism resulted from supernatural forces and that dwarfs enjoyed a special relationship to god or the gods, see Johnston, "Some Observations," 705. See also Datson and Parks, *Wonders and The Order of Nature*.
102 Andrea, "Elizabeth I and Persian Exchanges," 184. Datson and Park include dwarfs among the "human beings of unusual or unfamiliar appearance" at early modern courts who, along with other rare "things," evoked the wonders of nature control and display which became "constituitive of what it meant to be a cultural elite in Europe" (*Wonders and the Order of Nature*, 67–8).
103 Loades, *Elizabeth I*, 316, as qtd. in Andrea, "Elizabeth I and Persian Exchanges," 184.
104 Andrea, "Elizabeth I and Persian Exchanges," 184.
105 On court dwarfs as representations of courtliness in miniature, see Datson and Park, *Wonders and the Order of Nature*, 193, and Van Den Berg, "Dwarf Aesthetics," 25–6.

106 Gough, "New Evidence and Analysis," 123, 127–8.
107 Gough, "Virtuosic Female Voice."
108 "[L]a Cecchina ha cantata due arie francesì con molto gusto del Re che ne le fece replicare due volte." This letter is transcribed in the original Italian and translated into French in Boyer, "Giulio Caccini," 245–6.
109 Cf. Dubost, *Marie de Médicis*, 239, who asserts as fact that Francesca Caccini sang in Marie's 1605 ballet, with no explanation of his basis for this claim save a reference to Battifol's paraphrase. Battifol uses the phrase "une célèbre cantatrice italienne" (*Le Louvre*, 113), yet neither the document in Peiresc's *registres* nor Jolly's transcription mentions this Italian singer's "fame," nor identifies her by name. On Francesca's particular patronage by the French monarchs, see Solerti, "Un viaggio"; Prunières, *L'Opéra Italien en France*, xxxi; Masera, "La famiglia Caccini"; Silbert, "Francesca Caccini," 52–3; Carter et al., "Caccini"; Cusick, "Francesca Caccini," *New Grove Dictionary of Women Composers*, 94; Cusick, *Francesca Caccini at the Medici Court*, 20–3. Margherita Caccini, too, was greatly admired: in another letter, Giulio boasts how his wife's voice was so pleasing to all that the king and queen, marveling at her trills each time she sang, desired to retain the entire consort; see Giulio Caccini to Virginio Orsini, Paris, 1 March 1605, as qtd. and translated in Boyer, "Giulio Caccini," 247–9; see also Cusick, *Francesca Caccini at the Medici Court*, 21. Settimia Caccini, Francesca's thirteen-year-old sister, was also much sought out. Madame de Guise, for example, seems to have approached Giulio with the request that Settimia remain with her in France; see Giulio Caccini to Virginio Orsini, Paris, 1 March 1605, in Boyer, "Giulio Caccini," 248–9. In a separate letter to his friend Piero Strozzi dated 25 February 1605, Giulio states that the French king and queen wished to retain not only Francesca but also Settimia, offering the latter a dowry of 1,000 scudi; see Bartoli Bacherini, "Giulio Caccini," 63, and Cusick, "Settimia Caccini."
110 Brooks, *Courtly Song*, 200–1.
111 According to Brooks, in 1572 Doria and Beaulieu received the kind of end-of-year financial gift paid from the royal treasury usually reserved for specially favoured musicians, particularly those "attached to the [royal] chamber," as well as a "joint royal pension of 200 livres and their wages as members of the *maison de la reine*" (ibid., 100, 105). Later that decade the couple received extensive sums as pensioners of the queen and a lesser sum from the king, and during the 1580s these kinds of subventions continued, for example in the form of regular salaries from

the household of the new queen Louise de Lorraine-Vaudemont and special payments to Beaulieu and to Doria's and Beaulieu's daughter Claude (ibid., 105, 201).
112 Ibid., 201; Brooks also indicates that Doria accompanied herself on the lute and offers a helpful transcription of this duet's final stanza in musical example 4.1 (245).
113 Giulio Caccini to Belisario Vinta, Paris, 19 February 1605, qtd. in Solerti, "Un viaggio in Francia," 709.
114 As Cusick explains, at this period high voices were thought to best express high emotion and intensity; according to Giulio Caccini the female singer produced this effect the most naturally (as opposed to through the steady, high-speed forcing of air through the vocal cords required in falsetto registers produced by uncastrated male singers) – and hence the most powerfully (*Francesca Caccini at the Medici Court*, 9, 11, 12).
115 Prunières, *Le ballet de cour en France*, 105–9.
116 Ibid., 106–8; Prunières, *L'Opéra Italien en France*, xxvi.
117 Van Orden, for example, notes that "ballets were the central cultural events of each season's social calendar" (*Music, Discipline, and Arms*, 48).
118 Dubost, *Marie de Médicis*, 73.
119 Newcomb, *The Madrigal at Ferrara 1579–1597*, 1: 94, 200.
120 On these women and the Florentine *concerto di donne*, see Carter, *Jacopo Peri*, 1: 24 and n71, and Newcomb, *The Madrigal at Ferrara*, 2: 200. Eleonora Orsini was raised at the Medici court from 1576 on, and records from 1581 to 1591 show her close association with the young Marie de Médicis (Chappell, "The Artistic Education of Maria dei Medici," 13–25, 18–19). On Ferdinando I de' Medici's dismissal of the initial female consort "as part of the policy of the new grand duke ... of purging Francesco I's luxuries from the court," particularly those associated with Francesco's mistress Bianca Cappello, see Cusick, *Francesca Caccini at the Medici Court*, 3.
121 See Introduction, note 11, above. Bartoli Bacherini suggests that the princesses mentioned here must have been Marie de Médicis and Christine of Lorraine because Marie's sister Eleonora and her cousin Virginia were both married and thus had left Florence by this date; for reasons indicated above, however, Eleonora Orsini is the more likely candidate.
122 ASF, Carte Strozziane, filza XXX, c. 6, as cited and qtd. in Solerti, "Un viaggio in Francia," 708–9.

123 On Marie's sponsorship of Italian acting troupes, see Marrow, *The Art Patronage of Maria de' Medici*, 81 n63; Mamone, *Paris et Florence*, 137–8, 145–61, 247–57; Wiley, *Early Public Theatre*, 22–4; Gilder, *Enter the Actress*, 31; Schwartz, *The Commedia dell'Arte and its Influence*, 47–9; Battifol, *La vie intime*, 122; Battifol, *Marie de Médicis*, 66–8; MacNeil, *Music and Women*, 48, 163, 173; Powell, *Music and Theatre in France*, 167; Gough, "Courtly *comédiantes*"; Brown, "The Traveling Diva"; Gether and Gough, "Advent of Women Players."

124 On the Caccini consort as a symbol of Florentine cultural preeminence and their visits to Paris and Ferrara as vehicles for Medici "cultural propaganda," see Brown, "The Geography of Florentine Monody," 158, and Cusick, *Francesca Caccini at the Medici Court*, 11.

125 On seventeenth- and eighteenth-century cosmopolitanism as both an intellectual ideal and an embodied practice that involves, among other qualities, "thinking beyond the nation," see Jacob, *Strangers Nowhere in the World*.

126 Smuts and Gorse, "Introduction," 13.

127 Dillon, *Language of Space*, 3.

128 The notion of a "school" uniting what is in fact a rather diverse body of approaches taken up by American historians of early modern French royal ceremonial can by traced in part to Alain Boureau's reflections on methodology in "Les cérémonies royales françaises." For a selected list of important studies by this so-called "neo-ceremonialist school," see notes 38 and 39 above.

129 L'Estoile, *Journal*, 2: 156–7.

130 Buisseret, *Henry IV*, 125–6.

131 Ibid., 157–8. See also Chaussinand-Nogaret, *La vie quotidienne*, 47.

3 Alliances and Others

1 Examples, which are legion, include the 1598 *Ballet des Étrangers*, which featured five "barbarous" nations arriving in France in honour of Henri IV, along with another ballet for the year 1605, sponsored and danced by Henri de Bourbon, prince de Condé, which used a similar fiction. In England during the same month as Marie de Médicis' January 1605 court ballet, Anna of Denmark, queen of England, danced her *Masque of Blackness*, the dramatic fiction of which centered on the arrival of Ethiopian nymphs having come to find in James I and his realm Brittania the true source of beauty, while in 1610, a tilt (a type of court entertainment that combined jousting and other military exercises with theatrical elements)

designed for Anna's eldest son, Henry Stuart, similarly flattered James I with the fiction of visitors arriving in England in order to see for themselves its glorious king.
2 BI, ms 1794, ff. 429r–430v. For an edited transcription and translation of this letter and an initial analysis of its importance for *ballet de cour* historians and theorists, see Gough, "New Evidence and Analysis." All subsequent quotations from this letter, as well as explanations of particular words and phrases, draw on this published edition, with transcriptions emended in keeping with the "Principles of Transcription and Translation" outlined on pp. xv–xvi of this book.
3 The term "social racism" comes from Kane with Smuts, "Politics of Race," 347.
4 Franko, "Renaissance Conduct Literature and the Basse Danse," 55.
5 Ibid.
6 Ibid., 57.
7 Ibid., 58.
8 Ibid., 63.
9 Ibid.
10 Ibid.
11 The phrase is Franko's in ibid., 58.
12 The dance term "entrechat" appears in 1609 as a Francisation of the Italian *intrecciata* (past participale of *intrecciare*). See *Dictionnnaire historique de la langue française*, 1255–6. In the January 1610 *Ballet de Monseigneur de Vendôme*, eight dwarf servants to the sorceress Alcine dance this step: "Ils étoient tous petits et choisis pour les plus dispos hommes de la Cour, et faisoient (presque toujours à saults, capriolles, et entrichats) les figures biens marquées" [They were all small and chosen for [being] the most able men of the court, and were doing (almost always with jumps, caprioles, and entrechats) the figures [i.e., the figured dances of the ballet] well defined] (27).
13 Expressions of admiration at surprising kinetic feats by small bodies were not new at the court of Henri IV: on at least one occasion prior to Marie's arrival in France, during the 1598 *Ballet des Étrangers*, the king had expressed great pleasure at the agile movements of a young boy, "very skillful and the most supple and dexterous seen in our time," who danced on a rope, jumped, flew, and made other tours of "souplesse" and "gaillardise." On this performance, see L'Estoile, *Journal*, 1: 547. The *Ballet des Étrangers* was performed to celebrate the baptism of Alexandre de Vendôme, the king's second son by his mistress Gabrielle d'Estrées,

duchesse de Beaufort. Seven years later, Marie's second ballet outdid this precedent associated with the king's late mistress by featuring one of the queen's household servants in a performance designed to elicit from the king even greater appreciation of a little person's novel feats of daring agility.

14 McGowan, "Recollections of Dancing Forms," 11.
15 On the physical skill required for elite dancing, see Nevile, "Dance in Europe 1250–1750," 35.
16 Franko, "Renaissance Conduct Literature and the Basse Danse," 60.
17 On "male and female movement vocabularies" in the *basse danse*, whereby male dance included elevation, despite its associations with the grotesque and the proud, while women social dancers remained on a largely level plane, see Franko, *Dance as Text*, 67.
18 Ibid., 63–107.
19 Ibid., 67, 70–6.
20 "Ce ballet fut fort magnifique, et à la fin entra deux grands chameaux avec deux sauvages dessus, les trompettes merchant devant eux; comme les chameaux furent devant le Roi, ils se mirent tous deux à genoux, et lors celui qui étoit dessus, descendit et présenta au Roi le cartel que je vous envoie." La Force, *Mémoires authentiques*, 1: 391.
21 The manuscript letter found among Peiresc's *registres* designates "sept chameaux montés de sept Turcs" [seven camels mounted by seven Turks], but this detail is likely erroneous given that La Force mentions two camels only (*Mémoires authentiques*, 1: 391), as does *Le romant des chevaliers de Thrace*, 6. The letter in Peiresc's papers also mentions a dozen trumpets with oboes and tambours. La Force mentions "les trompettes" without designating a number (*Mémoire authentiques*, 1: 391), but *Le romant* specifies "dix esclaves Turcs sonnans du haut bois" [ten Turkish slaves playing the oboe] with eight Moors following them (6); it is likely, then, that both the "Turks" and the "Moors" played instruments, and that the large group of "Turks" mentioned by the Louvre spectator entered on foot as fictional slaves and literal musicians rather than as riders of camels. On the exotic musical effects that seem to have accompanied a number of ballet entries featuring African and Eastern foreigners see Prunières, *Le ballet de cour en France*, 218.
22 *Le romant des chevaliers de Thrace*, 6; La Force similarly mentions prostrating camels, as does the letter found among Peiresc's papers.
23 Martin and Weiss, "'Turks' on Display," 98, 101–2.
24 Sandberg, "'The Recovery of God's Heritage'," 47; Dubost, *Marie de Médicis*, 212.

25 *Le ballet de Monseigneur de Vendôme*, 7.
26 Battifol, *Le Louvre*, 114.
27 Listing a series of gossipy questions about prominent court figures fictionally posed to him in a vision, a pamphlet by Maistre Guillaume (one of Henri IV's fools), printed in 1605, asks: "Monsieur de Nevers a-il hardé ses chameaux?" (*La response de Maistre Guillaume au Soldat François*, 44). The pamphlet's full title indicates that its content was originally delivered orally to the king in September 1604. Immediately after describing the camels kneeling in the queen's ballet, La Force's letter to his wife mentions a pamphlet that responds to the *Soldat François*; Guillaume's response was one of several such pamphlets circulating in Paris at this time. Nevers was not the only sovereign prince in France to acquire exotic animals as a sign of status: the dauphin himself prior to Henri IV's death possessed a menagerie which included a camel, while his father maintained a den of lions and an aviary at the Tuileries palace (Loisel, *Histoire des ménageries*, 92–3). In the days prior to Marie de Médicis' 1605 ballet, the king had gone out of his way to show some newly collected exotic birds to La Force (*Mémoires authentiques*, 1: 384). On Louis XIV's menagerie at Versailles, which featured animals from faraway lands as part of the king's "absolutist" model for rule, see Sahlins, "Royal Menageries."
28 Katritzky, *Healing, Performance, and Ceremony*, 110.
29 *Le romant des chevaliers de Thrace*, 6.
30 The letter archived among Peiresc's *registres* suggests that it was the king himself who threw this cartel to the princes and lords of the court, having had it presented to him in a basket that the first kneeling camel had carried on stage in his mouth. It was a copy of this cartel, presumably, that La Force sent to his wife along with his letter describing the queen's ballet. According to *Le romant des chevaliers de Thrace*, this cartel was distributed in both French and Spanish during the ballet entry (8); the cartel's text also circulated more widely in print, in both languages, via *Le romant* (8–9) and in French only via the 1605 *Recueil des cartels et deffis*, 5. The dwarf in the ballet's coda, according to *Le romant*, also presented a letter addressed directly to the king and which Henri IV read before he allowed the previously mentioned cartel to be distributed to the princes (6); for the text of this letter, see *Le romant*, 7–8, *Recueil des cartels et deffis*, 4.
31 For detailed discussion of this passage, in particular the verb "conchier" (a transitive form of "chier" deriving from the Latin "concacare," meaning to soil with excrement), see Gough, "New Evidence and Analysis," 133 n3.
32 On early modern civility and music, see in particular the chapter "The Conjunction of Arms and Letters" in Brooks, *Courtly Song*, as well as

Brooks, "Les Guises et l'air de cour." Useful discussions of the "crisis of the aristocracy" in France include Jouanna, "La noblesse française et les valeurs guerrières," Jouanna, *Ordre social*, 139–79, and Schalk, *From Valour to Pedigree*, 3–35.

33 On imaginary or imaginative geographies as a concept deriving from Edward Said's theories of Orientalism yet also applicable to a proto-Orientalist early modernity, see Andrea, "Persia, Tartaria, and Pamphilia," 24.
34 Brooks, *Courtly Song*, 127.
35 Matthieu, *L'entrée de la reine à Lyon le III Décembre M.D.C.* ([Lyon]: Thibaud Ancelin, [c. 1600]), as cited and qtd. in Dubost, "Goûts et entourages," 20.
36 Qtd. in Brooks, *Courtly Song*, 132.
37 On the particular passage describing this moment, see Gough, "New Evidence and Analysis," 133 nii.
38 See, for example, Setton, *Venice, Austria and the Turks*, 5.
39 Elder, Wolch, and Emel, "Race, Place, and the Bounds of Humanity," 183.
40 Tuan, *Dominance and Affection*, 153–61.
41 On affectation in the dance as the opposite of grace and as an indicator of inferior status, see McGowan, "Recollections of Dancing Forms," 11, and McGowan, *Dance in the Renaissance*, 25. This moment looks forward to a similar incident in the *Ballet royal du grand bal de la Douairière de Billebahaut* (1625) during which the Douairière de Billebahaut performed with "pas … mal arrestés" [steps … not well stopped] and "figures inconstamment compassées" [figures inconstantly measured], followed by *demoiselles* who failed miserably in their dancing, "cherchant et ne trouvant pas la cadence des Bransles de Boccan; et leurs pas plustost de balle que de ballets tesmoignent qu'elles ont grand tort de venir studier dans la Salle du Louvre pour aller danser ailleurs" [seeking and not finding the cadence of the branles de Bocan [dancing master Jacques Cordier, called Bocan]; and their steps rather of a ball than of ballets give evidence that they are quite wrong to come to study in the Hall of the Louvre to go to dance somewhere else] (Lacroix, *Ballets et mascarades*, 3: 188).
42 On nobility of race in early modern Europe, see especially Jouanna, *L'idée de race*; Kane with Smuts, "Politics of Race," 374.
43 For a useful explanation of this dependence, see Duindam, *Myths*, 49.
44 Scholarly consensus now debunks notions of an unbridgeable gap between East and West in the early modern period and critiques an overly anachronistic application of Said's theories of Orientalism. See, for example, Jardine, *Worldly Goods*; Matar, *Islam in Britain, 1558–1685*; Matar, *Turks, Moors, and Englishmen*; Jardine and Brotton, *Global Interests*; Goffman, *The Ottoman Empire and Early Modern Europe*; Barbour,

Before Orientalism; Andrea, *Women and Islam in Early Modern English Literature*; Vitkus, *Turning Turk*; and Jaffe-Berg, *Commedia dell'Arte and the Mediterranean*. Recent historiography that considers early modern France in light of such understandings includes Isom-Verharren, *Allies with the Infidel*, as well as "France and the Early Modern Mediterranean," a special journal issue edited by Megan C. Armstrong and Gillian Weiss and published as *French History* 29.1 (2015). For particularly nuanced discussions of "Turks" in French court ballet, see Welch, "The Specter of the Turk."

45 *Chronique du Roy Françoys Premier*, 372. On the possibility that François Ier was among these performers who personated "Turks," and on the connection between this entertainment and diplomatic relationships between France and the Sublime Porte, see Heartz, "Un ballet turc," 6. An earlier, more infamous incident involving a king of France in disguise on stage as a "Turk" or "Moor" was the *Bal des Ardents* (1393). On this occasion Charles VI, dressed as an "homme sauvage" and performing an exotic dance, accidentally caught on fire and was nearly burned alive; see ibid., 1.

46 For a brief but helpful discussion of this carousel, see McCabe, *Orientalism in Early Modern France*, 234.

47 Nervèze, "Cartel des Turcs pour le combat de la Barriere, contre les Gascons," *Les essais poétiques*, 283.

48 Rouillard, *The Turk*, 624.

49 Ibid. See also Heartz, "Un ballet turc," 1; Paquot, *Les étrangers dans les divertissements de la cour de Beaujoyeulx à Molière*, 22–3.

50 Isom-Verhaaren, *Allies with the Infidel*, 24, 115–19. Regarding the petition for naval aid, Isom-Verhaaren notes that "[b]oth French and Ottoman sources present this event [of 1543–4] in these terms: the king of France requested aid, and Süleyman sent his fleet to assist him" (115).

51 As Armstrong and Weiss note, this agreement is often misunderstood in French historiography as one that involved a balance of power rather than mutual recognition, and yet, "The 'Capitulations' remain the dominant framework for examining French-Ottoman diplomatic relations" ("Introduction: France and the Early Modern Mediterranean," 1). For additional detailed discussion regarding the agreement and the way Europeans (mis)understood it, see Veinstein, "Les Capitulations franco-ottomanes de 1536."

52 Welch, "Specter of the Turk," 92–3. On Ottoman figures in court entertainments staged during the late sixteenth and early seventeenth centuries at the court of Lorraine, whose ruling family promoted its own dynastic authority in party by claiming descent from Godefroy of Bouillon,

leader of the first crusade, see Sahin-Toth, *La France et les Français*, 88–92; Choné, *Emblèmes et pensée symbolique*, 67, 185–203; Dorothée, "Le mécénat de Catherine de Bourbon," 173, Figures 11–12, plates VI and XVI.

53 Gough, "New Evidence and Analysis," 114–15.
54 Sahin-Toth, *La France et les Français*, esp. 187–225.
55 Barberini to Cardinal Pietro Aldobrandini, Paris, 7 February 1605, ASV, Segr. Stato, Francia, 50, ff. 36r–37v. Whereas in the fifteenth and sixteenth centuries the French king was indisputably less powerful than the sultan, this gap narrowed by the second decade of the seventeenth century. The Persian-Ottoman war would end with loss of Ottoman conquests in the Caucasus, while the Sublime Porte also faced challenges in the form of many uprisings as well as a very young and less effective ruler, Ahmed I, who came to power in 1603 at the death of Mehmed III. Yet the sultan's forces were very successful in Hungary against those of the Holy Roman Emperor. On Ottoman military success and failure during this period, see Setton, *Venice, Austria, and the Turks*, 20. On internal difficulties in Ottoman governance, see Pierre, "Le père Joseph," n16.
56 La Force, *Mémoires authentiques*, 1: 391.
57 Cusick, *Francesca Caccini at the Medici Court*, 351 n41. Cusick here describes a martial entertainment at the Tuscan court in 1607. In the eighteenth century Beauchamps referenced a similar performance in passing; see his *Recherches sur les théâtres de France*, 3: 48–9 (see also Mss, Fr. 24357, f. 132r). For a useful discussion of the relationship between *ballet de cour* and the genre of court entertainment known as the barriers, see Anglo, "The Barriers."
58 *Le romant des chevaliers de Thrace*, 4–5.
59 Parrott, "A 'Prince Souverain' and the French Crown," 161.
60 *Recueil des cartels et deffis*, 4. In *Le romant*, 6–7, the wording for this letter is slightly different, indicating that at least one of these printed versions offers a recollected summary, though the text for the Thracians' cartel is identical in both sources.
61 "Nous sommes Chevalliers du Royaume de Thrace nourris dans les hazars de Mars, & les delices d'amour, deitez par nous esgalement adorées … aussi riches de palmes, que de myrtes: aussi braves au combat que doux en la paix, qui apres maintes adventures [sic] achevées sommes arrivez en ceste cour pour esprouver ce que nous sçavons faire, en guerre & en amour, & partant nous vous deffions tous au combat, & ne desirons pour prix de la victoire que l'honneur d'avoir vaincu, esperant que nos Dieux nous seront si favorables qu'armez, nous ferons veoir que nous sçavons aussi bien combatre & vaincre les Chevaliers que desarmez nous

sçavons bien aymer & servir les Dames." "Aux Palladins de France," *Recueil des cartels et deffis*, 5. Cf. the version of this text printed in *Le romant des chevaliers de Thrace*, 8–9: "Nous sommes Chevaliers du Royaume de Thrace, nourris dans les hazards de Mars, & les delices de l'Amour, Deitez par nous egalement adorées, à qui le jour & la nuict nous offrons aussi volontiers du sang de nos blesseures, que les desirs de nos coeurs: guerriers infatigables, aussi riches de palmes que de myrthes, aussi braves au combat que doux en la paix, qui après maintes advantages achevées, sommes arrivez en ceste Court pour esprouver ce que nous scavons faire en guerre & en amour: & partant nous vous deffions tous au combat, ne desirans pour prix de la victoire que l'honneur d'avoir vaincu, esperans que nos Dieux nous seront si favorables, qu'armez nous ferons voir que nous scavons aussi bien combattre & vaincre les Chevaliers, que desarmez nous scavons bien aimer & servir les dames."

62 "Autre cartel par les Thraciens. La Victoire au Roy," *Recueil des cartels et deffis*, 6–7. See also *Le romant*, 15–18.
63 Ibid., 11.
64 Brooks, "Les Guises et l'Air de Cour."
65 Hoddinnott, *The Thracians*.
66 Rouillard, *The Turk*, 13–14.
67 Parrott, "A 'Prince Souverain' and the French Crown"; Parrott, "The Mantuan Succession, 1627–31," 54.
68 McCabe, *Orientalism in Early Modern France*, 140; Bilici, *Louis XIV et son project de conquête*, 153; Parrott, "A 'Prince Souverain' and the French Crown," 162.
69 This description of the order's mandate comes from the original registration for the order as cited in Le Thiec, "*Et il y aura un seul troupeau*," 332. On Nevers' involvement in founding the *milice chrétienne* starting in 1616 and in earlier designs for crusading projects to regain Ottoman-held territories and liberate Christians living there, including in the Morea (at around 1609) and in Hungary (by joining the Imperial army at the 1602 siege of Buda), see ibid., 331–7; Baudson, *Charles de Gonzague*, 49–52; Cremer, *Der Abel in der Verfassung des Ancien Régime*, 142–68; Djuvara, *Cent projets*, 185–9; Fagniez, *Le père Joseph et Richelieu (1577–1638)*, 1: 123; Humbert, "Charles de Nevers et la milice chrétienne"; Parrott, "A 'Prince Souverain' and the French Crown"; Sahin-Toth, *La France et les Français*, 168–9, 457–78; Sandberg, "Going Off to War," 373, 376; Sauzet, *Au grand siècles des âmes*, 29, 35, 42–5, 51.
70 Parrott, "A 'Prince Souverain' and the French Crown," 161.
71 Ibid.; Parrott, "The Mantuan Succession, 1627–31."

72 Hongarus and Chavigny, *Discours parénétique*, title page.
73 Chavigny, *Pléiades*, 14.
74 Haran, *Le lys et le globe*. For the related idea that the French were elected by God to vanquish the Infidel as expressed in Père Joseph's epic poem *La Turciade*, see Sahin-Toth, *La France et les Français*, 71.
75 Haran, *Le lys et le globe*; Bilici, *Louis XIV et son project de conquête d'Istanbul*, 49, 53.
76 In 1494 Charles VIII of France, hoping for an imperial crown of his own, had purchased the title *basileus* – a Greek term connoting emperor – from Ferdinand of Aragon, who himself acquired it from the last impoverished Paleologue; see ibid. The final entry for Marie's 1605 ballet initiated by Nevers does not overtly reference the French king's subsequent claim to the eastern throne, perhaps because doing so would not have served Nevers' competing pretensions to sovereign status in Thracian territories reclaimed from the Ottomans.
77 "Sire, La renommée de vos victoires, qui vous rend redouté de tous les Rois de la terre, nous a fait quitter la Thrace pour venir en vostre Cour, offrir nos services & nos vies à vostre Majesté. Mais avant qu'oser luy demander la faveur de baiser ses mains victorieuses, nous avons pensé qu'il estoit nécessaire de nous signaler en sa presence, en nous esprouvant contre vos Chevaliers. C'est pourquoy nous la supplions tres-humblement, nous permettre de les deffier au combat: afin que par nostre valeur nous acquerions assez de merite, pour nous presenter devant elle. Nous la supplions aussi nous donner le camp & le jour, & regarder les Chevaliers de vostre Cour de ces yeux dequoy vous avez accoustumé d'animer leurs courages au combat, afin que chacun coure aux armes sans excuse, ou se monstre indigne de vos genereuses inspirations, & des inimitables exemples de vostre valeur" (*Le romant des chevaliers de Thrace*, 7–8). This passage appears differently in the *Recueil des cartels et deffis*, 4: "Sire, La renommée de vos armes victorieuses dedaignant toutes autres bornes que celles du Ciel, & remplissant la terre de leurs merveilles, a incité le courage de cinq Chevaliers Thraciens à mesurer une longue espace de terre & de mer, pour venir admirer en un mortel ce qu'en leurs pays, ils adorent aux puissants Dieux des batailles: mais comme les sacrifices presentez à ce grand Dieu, d'autre main que victorieuse luy sont desagreables: Aussi ne pensons nous point debvoir paroistre devant vostre face qui est son Image vivante, avant que luy faire voir quelque preuve digne de cest honneur & de nostre courage, & pour ce qu'on ne sçauroit en tout le reste du monde trouver autant de digne subjet de leur gloire qu'en vostre cour, ils supplient tres-humblement vostre Majesté de leur permettre de deffier

au combat de la picque, & de l'espée, les plus braves de voz Chevaliers …"
See also Mss, Fr. 24353, ff. 162v–163r.
78 *Le romant des chevaliers de Thrace*, 8.
79 Ó hAnnracháin, *Catholic Europe*, 146.
80 Ibid., 150–2. On Rome's diplomatic goals and strategies at the court of Henri IV specifically, including the use of pressure tactics regarding a crusade, see also Blet, "Un Futur Pape," and Barbiche, "Clément VIII et la France (1592–1605)."
81 Barberini to Cardinal Pietro Aldobrandini, Paris, 7 February 1605, ASV, Segr. Stato, Francia, 50, ff. 36r–37v. Whereas in the fifteenth and sixteenth centuries the French king was indisputably less powerful than the sultan, this gap had narrowed by the early seventeenth century. The Persian-Ottoman war would end with loss of Ottoman conquests in the Caucasus, while the central government also faced challenges in the form of many uprisings as well as a young and less effective ruler, Ahmed I, who came to power in 1603 at the death of Mehmed III. Yet the sultan's forces were very successful in Hungary, against those of the Holy Roman Emperor. On Ottoman military success and failure during this period, see Setton, *Venice, Austria, and the Turks*, 20. On internal difficulties in Ottoman governance see Pierre, "Le père Joseph," n16.
82 Ó hAnnracháin does not discuss this particular audience with the French king, but I rely here on his discussion of the papacy's larger objectives in *Catholic Europe*, 146.
83 Maffeo Barberini to Cardinal Pietro Aldobrandini, Paris, 7 February 1605, ASV, Segr. Stato, Francia, 50, ff. 36r–37v. See also Barberini's letter reporting his follow-up meeting with Henri IV's counsellor Nicolas Brulart de Sillery: Barberini to Aldobrandini, Paris, 7 February 1605, ASV, Misc., Arm. II, 133, ff. 58v–60r. For additional discussion of papal diplomacy at Henri IV's court with respect to Clement VIII's crusading goals, see Sahin-Toth, *La France et les Français*, 120–8.
84 Ó hAnnracháin, *Catholic Europe*, 138.
85 Ibid., 139.
86 As Isom-Verhaaren has argued, the self-interest of individual European states, continually anxious about each other's power, had led many to enter into alliances with the Ottomans designed to "balance the threatening power or if possible overcome it in any ensuing struggle" (*Allies with the Infidel*, 10, 23–48).
87 Sahin-Toth, *France et les Français*, 176.
88 Desplat, "Henri IV et les Ottomans."

89 For further discussion of the regiments that Henri IV was gathering in winter 1604–5, as well as the pamphlet debate, see chapter 5.
90 On the rank of foreign prince or *prince étranger* within France, see chapter 2, n80.
91 For this phrasing, and for his encouragement regarding this oppositionalist reading of Nevers' contributions to the queen's ballet, I am indebted to Malcolm Smuts.
92 *Le romant des chevaliers de Thrace*, 5–6.
93 Oresko, "Princes Étrangers," 1020.
94 On Mayenne's poor health as the likely reason he did not take up Mercoeur's prestigious post in Hungary, see, for example, Sahin-Toth, *France et les Français*, 372.
95 Tim Carter, "Epyllia and Epithalamia: Some Narrative Frames for Early Opera," unpublished paper.
96 For the dialogue's verse texts, see Solerti, *Musica, ballo e drammatica*, 231–8; note that I have deleted Solerti's tréma for "Oriente."
97 *Rime cantate nel giardino*; see also Solerti, *Musica*, 239–59.
98 "A la reine mere du roy, sur sa bien-venue en France," in Malherbe, *Les poésies*, ed. Lalanne, 44–5.
99 "Les Sybilles, au Roy," in Durand, *Description du Ballet de Madame*, 12–14; Durand ascribes these verses to Bordier (12).
100 Garel, *Les oracles françois*, 49–50, 69–70, 125–6.
101 Le Thiec, "*Et il y aura un seul troupeau*," 333. For additional references to Marie's connection with this project, see Baudson, *Charles de Gonzague*; Humbert, "Charles de Nevers"; Cremer, *Der Adel in der Verfassung des Ancien Régime*, 151; Sauzet, *Au grand siècle des âmes*, 35, 42; Sandberg, "'Recovery of God's Heritage'," 48.
102 Sandberg, "'The Recovery of God's Heritage'," 47–9.
103 *Le romant des chevaliers de Thrace*, 15–18, 18.
104 "Mars de vos beautez espris / Surtout de la chaste Cypris, / Dont toute la France se prise ... vous append son coeur genereux" (ibid., 87); "Aux princesses et dames," *Recueil des cartels et deffis*, 34.
105 *Le romant des chevaliers de Thrace*, 85–6; *Recueil des cartels et deffis*, 32. The phrase "marcher à l'égal de" indicates a sense of proportion, such that Marie's happiness stands in proportion to Henri's courage. Another plausible translation might be "your happiness walks in step with his courage."
106 *Le romant des chevaliers de Thrace*, 86; *Recueil des cartels et deffis*, 33.
107 Verses for the Triumph of Ladies ("Le Triomphe des Dames") extend this notion of joint rule between the king and his female consort in ways

that again drive home, as part of this barriers performance, the queen's necessity to the kingdom's internal peace and international preeminence. Addressed to all of the princes and lords who performed as troupes of knights, the triumph's verses admit that these nobles have suffered an undeniable defeat since, despite their remarkable valor, all have been vanquished by "les Soleils de ces Dames" or sun-like eyes of women in the combat's audience. These knights should not be discouraged, however. Have courage, they are told, since the sky, earth, and sea, too, have lost their liberty to love, and even the Theban Hercules, who vanquished all of the world, was himself vanquished by a beauty less powerful than those present in the Salle du Bourbon on this noteworthy occasion ["le ciel la terre & l'onde / Perdirent comme vous jadis leur liberté / Et l'Hercule Thebain qui vainquit tout le monde / Fut à la fin vaincu d'une moindre beauté"]. This image of warrior princes and lords vanquished by love may figure, in gendered terms, the relative loss of independence that the kingdom's greatest nobles had begun to experience during the early consolidation of personal monarchy under Henri IV's rule. Such verses offer a vision of consolation for this tempering of martial might and the independence from royal power that it ensured: in exchange for their political submission, figured as a form of loving service, high-ranking French nobles would win a share in the worldwide renown achieved by their king and queen. Since defeat in love is inevitable, the verses tell the barriers participants, the combatants should come forward to claim their trophies from the beautiful women of the French court, joining their laurels to the women's victorious myrtles since, in future, unknown peoples from every land will again journey to the temple of France in order to worship this beautiful alliance of the victories of Mars with those of Venus ["au temple de la France, / Viendront de toutes partes les peuples inconnus, / Pour adorer, encore, cette belle alliance, / Des victoires de Mars à celle de Venus"]. *Recueil des cartels et deffis*, 53–4.

108 Sahin-Toth, *La France et les Français*, 459–65.
109 Ibid., 168, 470. Humbert, "Charles de Nevers," 86.
110 Sahin-Toth, *La France et les Français*, 472–3.
111 Ibid., 471.
112 Early in his reign, the French king's position as leader of the Saint-Esprit had allowed Henri to outwardly demonstrate his own religious sincerity when, during a procession of the host at Dijon on 2 July 1595, the king performed visually his new-found piety wearing a "black taffeta robe setting off a magnificent collar he wore around his neck identifying him

as the head of the sacred order of *Saint-Esprit*." Finley-Croswhite, *Henry IV and the Towns*, 60.
113 Chaline, "Kingdoms of France and Navarre," 75.
114 "[S]i ricomincia a parlare della creatione de' Caval[ie]ri di S[an]t[o] Spirito a capo d'anno, e si nomina tra gl'altri … i Principi di Lorena, Guisa, Buglion, Nevers …" [Talk has started again about the creation of Knights of the Holy Spirit at New Year's eve and [people] name among [likely candidates] … the Princes of Lorraine, Guise, Bouillon, Nevers]. Agostino Gioioso to Cardinal Pietro Aldobrandini, Paris, 29 November 1604, ASV, Fondo Borghese, Serie II, 14, f. 439v. A month later, Gioioso writes that the king of France "farà in quel loco [Saint Germain] le sue solite devotioni … lasciando qua malcontenti gran numero di Sig[no] ri concorsi in Parigi con speranza di dover esser honorati della croce di san spirito" [will do in that place [Saint Germain] his usual devotions … leaving here discontented a great number of gentlemen who came to Paris with the hope of being honored with the cross of the Holy Spirit]. Agostino Gioioso to Cardinal Pietro Aldobrandini, Paris, 27 December 1604, ASV, Fondo Borghese, Serie II, 14, f. 484r.
115 Baudson, *Charles de Gonzague*, 32–3.
116 Parrott, "A 'Prince Souverain' and the French Crown," 167 n52.
117 When Marie's dwarf performed earlier in this same ballet, wearing a Janus mask and a black robe or "soutane" covered in tinsel, or metallic thread, his costume may have recalled that work by members of this same *Ordre du Saint-Esprit*. This French royal order always held its induction ceremony on the first day of January, the start of the new year presided over in Roman mythology by Janus. At this ceremony, moreover, members of the order wore ceremonial costumes featuring a coat or gown of black velour decorated with a cape made from cloth of silver – much like the dwarf's black robe covered in *clinquant*. Given Nevers' involvement in ballet's final entry, the image of the queen's dwarf with his Janus mask and black robe covered in *clinquant* might have called up for those in the know the spectre of this royal chivalric order and of its sovereign grand master, Henri IV himself. Refusing to appoint a captain to his order that year, the king insisted on his resolutely personal power to control access to himself by means of ceremonial appointments of honour. If this dwarf's entry encompasses a specific topical allusion, his dancing may have represented the first Bourbon king himself, with his "absolutist" tendencies here portrayed, satirically, as a wondrous yet also threatening force. Alternatively, this dwarf's costuming, and his "over-reaching" choreographies, may have called up the image of would-be

members of the *Saint-Esprit*, such as the duc de Nevers, commenting ironically on their own debasement at being excluded from this royal order presided over by Henri IV.
118 Sandberg, "Going Off to the War in Hungary," 374.
119 Laugel, *Henry de Rohan*, 34–6; Parrott, "A 'Prince Souverain' and the French Crown," 159; Baudson, *Charles de Gonzague*, 52–3.
120 Parrott, "A 'Prince Souverain' and the French Crown," 164–5. Parrott shows that Nevers would consistently seek to capitalize on various aspects of his independent status, most obviously during the 1620s when his assertion of indisputable sovereign rights to the duchy of Mantua and Monferrato led to the Mantua succession crisis of 1628–31. On the French crown's project to marry Louis de Gonzague to Henriette de Clèves, see Boltanski, "Les Nevers," 24–94. For a more detailed account of Nevers' complex status as duke, *prince étranger*, and independent sovereign with titular claims to an Eastern imperial throne as well as to the duchies of Mantua and Montferrato, see Parrrott, "The Mantuan Succession, 1627–31."
121 Cremer, *Der Adel in der Verfassung des Ancien Régime*, 151.
122 Ibid., 154.

4 Eros and "Absolutism"

1 For a more extended discussion of this point, see chapter 3, as well as Jouanna, *L'idée de race*; Kane with Smuts, "Politics of Race," 374.
2 Kane with Smuts, "Politics of Race," 351.
3 Crawford, "Politics of Promiscuity."
4 Duindam, *Myths of Power*, 49.
5 On Hugenot and Leaguer accusations regarding Henri III's effeminacy, see, for example, Wintroub, "Words, Deeds, and a Womanly King."
6 The early modern notion of racial degenation through vice was voiced most obviously in the accepted idea that nobles who committed treason tainted their own bloodlines and extinguished their own nobility and that of their descendants (Kane with Smuts, "Politics of Race," 351). On sexual self-control as a touchstone for royal authority, particularly in connection with imagery of Henri IV's reign, see Crawford, "Politics of Promiscuity."
7 Two different printers seem to have issued octavo editions of these collected verses: the Bibliothèque Nationale de France holds a copy of the *Recueil des vers du balet de la Reyne*, printed by Toussaint Du Bray, while the Bibliothèque Mazarine's holdings include a copy of the *Recueil des vers du Balet de la Royne* printed by Jean Nigaut.

Lacroix reproduces this ballet's verses in his *Ballets et mascarades de cour*, 1: 171–9. For the ballet's three songs adapted for amateur performance with lute accompaniment, see Bataille, *Airs de différents autheurs mis en tablature de luth*, 2° livre, 6–8. The ballet's music seems to have been composed initially by Pierre Guédron and another composer named Chevalier; see Prunières, *Le ballet de cour en France*, 109.

8 On the "chaîne" (in French also called the "haie" or "haye"), see Brainard, "Hey," Franko, "Geometrical Dance," 23 and notes 38–40, Gough, "'Not as myself'," 57, Hoogleviet, "The *Balet de la Reyne* (1609)," 82–3.

9 Prunières states erroneously that during this 1609 ballet Marie incarnated Beauty (*Le ballet de cour en France*, 108); he seems to have confused the title of this *recueil* with that for a 1618 production danced by Marie's daughter-in-law Anne d'Autriche entitled *Le ballet de la reine, représentant la Beauté & ses nymphes* (Paris: Jean Sara, 1618). I here correct my own unfortunate repetition of Prunières' error in two of my previously published papers: "'Not as myself'" and "Marie de Medici's 1605 *ballet de la reine* and the virtuosic female voice."

10 On this point, see Prunières, *Le ballet de cour en France*, 108–9; McGowan, *L'art du ballet de cour*, 67.

11 The manuscript letters written to the Gonzaga court from Paris by Vittoria and Traiano Guiscardi, dated 10 and 11 February 1609 respectively, are found in the ASMa, Archivio Gonzaga, busta 667 (unpaginated). I was first alerted to these letters by Dr Cole's mention of them in an unpublished paper entitled "Maria de' Medici, the Italian Minerva of France: Music and Theatrical Spectacle between Florence and Paris during the Early Seventeenth Century," presented at the conference "Mobility, Hybridity and Reciprocal Exchange in the Theatres of Early Modern Europe" hosted by Theater without Borders at NYU-Madrid in May 2011. A revised version of this paper, which I have not yet had the opportunity to read, is forthcoming as "Transnational Exchanges and Representations of Female Power: Musical Spectacle at the Court of Maria de' Medici, the Italian Minerva of France," in M.A. Katritzky and Pavel Drábek (eds), *Transnational Connections in Early Modern Theatre* (University of Manchester Press).

12 Vittoria Guiscardi.

13 The term *strade* here indicates, in the scenic-technical sense, the entrance routes or cleared areas along which dancers would move through or around the stage mountain. The English terms "paths," "tracks," or "roads" better indicate the notional meaning of these "ways" within the illusionistic rendering of the scene. I am grateful to Richard Andrews for his advice regarding translation possibilities in this instance.

14 Traiano Guiscardi. Vittoria refers to "una gran quantità di sonatori di viole, che facevano una dolcissima armonia tutti di concerto pomposamente

vestiti" [a great number of viol players, who made a very sweet harmony all in concert, magnificently attired]. Presumably the pages in this production carried candles or torches designed to help light the playing space, as was typical of ballets from this period.
15 Traiano Guiscardi. Vittoria Guiscardi, when describing Fame's air, references only "Sua Maestà" as the recipient of praise, yet this phrasing is ambiguous: it could mean His Majesty, i.e., the king, as it clearly does in Traiano's letter, or it could mean Her Majesty, i.e., Marie de Médicis, as it does later in Vittoria's letter when she describes the queen rising first among the nymphs from her seated position in the garden.
16 Vittoria Guiscardi.
17 Traiano Guiscardi.
18 On the *chitarrone*'s equivalence to the theorbo by the early seventeenth century, see Spencer, "Chitarrone, Theorbo and Archlute."
19 Vittoria Guiscardi.
20 Vittoria Guiscardi; Traiano similarly notes that these women were "in habito di ninfe di color celeste, incarnato, et argento, con tanti diamanti addosso ch'era una meraviglia, et fu la più bella vista del mondo" [dressed as nymphs in the colours sky blue, carnation [incarnat], and silver, with so many diamonds on their habits that it was a marvel, and it was the most beautiful sight in the world].
21 Vittoria Guiscardi; Traiano's phrase is "con leggiadria incredibile."
22 Ferrière, *Trois amoureuses*, 303–4.
23 Merki, *La reine Margot*, 425.
24 Partly because Merki's citations are haphazard, later studies do not correct him. See, for example, Ratel, "La cour," 1–2, McGowan, *L'art du ballet*, 66–7, and Hoogleviet, "The *Balet de la Reyne* (1609)," 71–2, 85, 89–90. Ratel and McGowan also cite L'Estoile and La Force, but neither of these contemporary sources indicates that Marguerite was the ballet's organizer. L'Estoile, *Journal*, 2: 427 and *Mémoires authentiques de Jacques Nompar de Caumont, duc de la Force*, 2: 216.
25 See, for example, Merki, *La reine Margot*, 425, Ratel, "La cour," 2–3, 7–8, Yon, "L'Astrée et le salon de Marguerite," 303.
26 The full passage reads: "Le samedi 31e et dernier de ce mois [janvier 1609] la reine fit, à Paris, son ballet magnifique, dès longtemps pourpensé par elle et dessiné, mais différé jusques à ce jour. Et ne fut qu'en deux lieux, à l'Arsenal et chez la reine Marguerite, où Leurs Majestés trouvèrent la collation magnifique et somptueuse que ladite dame leur avait fait apprêter (qu'on disait lui revenir à quatre mille écus). Entre les singularités de laquelle y avait trois plats d'argent, accommodés exprès à cet effet, en l'un desquels y avait un grenadier, en l'autre un oranger, et en l'autre un citronnier, si dextement et artificieusement représentés et déguisés qu'il

n'y avait personne qui ne les prît pour naturels. Et était six heures du matin, quand le roi et la reine en sortirent." L'Estoile, *Journal*, 2: 427. The Guiscardi couple did not attend the event at Marguerite's, yet Traiano Guiscardi corroborates L'Estoile's report that this ballet, after having been danced at the Arsenal, moved to Marguerite's Paris residence for a repeat performance. Queen Marguerite's financial accounts indicate numerous expenses associated with preparing her residence for this ballet and banquet (McGowan, *L'art du ballet*, 67 n92).

27 See, for example, Prunières, *Le ballet de cour en France*, 108–9, Ratel, "La cour," 12–13, and Hoogvliet, "The *Balet de la Reyne* (1609)," 75–8.

28 Fame praised Henri IV similarly in the 1605 barriers in sung verses with words by François de Rosset; see the *Recueil des cartels et deffies*, 30–1, also transcribed in Mss, Fr. 24353, f. 173.

29 McGowan, *L'art du ballet*, 66–7.

30 Traiano Guiscardi registers this shift as well, describing how Fame sang some verses in praise of His Majesty and of the nymphs of the ballet ["Cantò poi la Fama alcuni versi in lodi lode di Sua Maestà *et delle ninfe del balletto*," emphasis mine].

31 Malherbe, as Hoogleviet notes in "The *Balet de la Reyne* (1609)," participated in literary circles associated with Marguerite de Valois. But he made his first splash at court, arguably, with his famous "Ode" welcoming Marie de Médicis to France in 1600. On Marie's active patronage of Malherbe after his arrival in Paris in 1605 and his subsequent loyalty to her, see Fromilhague, *La vie de Malherbe*, 227.

32 This stanza revisits a trope familiar from pastoral literature and known to Marie de Médicis (and likely Henri IV as well) from Ottavio Rinuccini's 1590 *Maschere de bergiere* in which true beauty resides in natural settings as opposed to courts and cities. In this *mascherata*, a group of shepherdesses fleeing civil war in France had sought aid from Marie's aunt the Medici grand duchess, Christine of Lorraine, on behalf of Marie's future husband, Henri de Bourbon, to restore peace in France; verses for this *mascherata* asserted not only love's superiority over war but also the superiority of nature's unaffected beauty over the artificial trappings of beauty found in courts and cities. On this *mascherata*, see Chiarelli, "Before and After," 2.3, and appendix 4.1. For the idea that God assembles in women all of the beautiful things in the natural world, see Agrippa, *Declamation*, 51.

33 La Force, *Mémoires authentiques*, 2: 216.

34 Mousnier, *Institutions of France*, 1: 122. In Marie's *Ballet of Diana and her Nymphs*, the seven women dancers who were not princesses came from families of the sword and robe; they included, for example, Rachel de

Cochefilet, second wife of Maximilien de Béthune, duc de Sully; Catherine de Peyrusse d'Escars, wife of Honorat de Montpezat, baron de Laugnac, *gentilhomme ordinaire de la chambre du roi* under Henri III; Claude de Cassillac de Cessac, wife of Charles de Choiseul, marquis de Praslin, one of the first nobles of the sword to recognize Henri IV, captain of the first company of the king's bodyguards, and member of the king's counsel; Louise Pot de Rhodes, daughter of Guillaume Pot seigneur de Rhodes, master of ceremonies of France, and wife of Claude de l'Aubespine, seigneur de Verderonne, president of the Paris *chambre des comptes*, *secrétaire du roi*, and, until 1608, court clerk and commander of the king's highly prestigious Order of the Holy Spirit; and Charlotte de Vieuxpoint, wife of Bernard Potier de Blérancourt, chevalier and marquis d'Annebaut, a lieutenant general of the light cavalry who hailed from old robe family. The Guiscardi letters name these women as follows: "La Duchessa di Sugly," "Madama di Montpesar," "Madama di Pralin," "Madama di Verderona," and "Madama de Blerancourt." They also identify as dancers "Madama la Vidame du Mans," i.e., Catherine de Vivonne, future marquise de Rambouillet, who in 1600 had married Charles d'Angennes, vidame du Mans and future marquis de Rambouillet, and "Madama la Contessa di Tillier," i.e., Catherine de Bassompierre, sister to François de Bassompierre (one of Henri IV and Marie de Médicis' favourite courtiers) and wife of Tanneguy le Veneur II, comte de Tillières, who in 1619 would serve as French ambassador to England.
35 Duindam, *Myths*, 52. For a more detailed discussion, see Jouanna, *L'idée de race*.
36 Agrippa, *Declamation*, 50; on Agrippa's use of Marsilio Ficino's philosophy as noted by his earliest French editors, see 50 n41. Ficino's notion of beauty and its salvific potential centered on men; later commentators, including Agrippa, revised Ficinian ideas by replacing male beauty with female beauty. On the complexities of this "straightening," particularly in early modern French texts, see Crawford, *Sexual Culture of the French Renaissance*, and Reeser, *Setting Plato Straight*.
37 Du Chesne, *Figures mystiques*, 31–2. Agrippa's treatise argues that women are superior to men both in their bodies and in their moral virtue; according to Rabil, this text's first French translation appeared in 1530, it was adapted to verse in 1541, and another French translation was published in Paris in 1578 (*Declamation*, 27 n48). Lucrezia Marinella's defense of women, published in 1600, 1601, and 1621, draws on Neoplatonic equations of beauty with virtue as outlined in Agrippa as well as Leone Ebreo's *Dialoghi d'amore* to argue that the first cause of women's

beauty is their participation in the ideal Form of Beauty, while the material or immediate cause of women's corporeal beauty is the superior character of their souls. Drawing on Ebreo as well as numerous poets, Marinella states: "the more beautiful the woman, the more … it is her soul that renders grace and loveliness to her body." Marinella, *Nobility and Excellence of Women*, 57. According to Panizza, the influence in France of Marinella's *Nobility and Excellence of Women* appears to be slight (*Nobility*, 31–2). However, in 1618 Marinella's dedication of her *Amore innamorato et impazzato* to Caterina Medici Gonzaga praises the Gonzaga family and Eleonora de' Medici Gonzaga (Marie's sister), in particular. In 1605 Marinella had dedicated her pastoral novella *Arcadia felice* to Eleonora, who in 1606 had traveled to the French court in 1606 for the baptisms of Marie de Médicis' two oldest children, Louis and Elisabeth.

38 On Charron's treatise, see, for example, Rice Jr, *Renaissance Idea of Wisdom*, 205–6.
39 On the reversal of gender roles and the raising of temples to female beloveds in *L'Astrée*, see Maclean, *Woman Triumphant*, 165–9. *L'Astrée*'s first installment was published in 1607 and from François de Bassompierre's memoir we know he read it aloud to Henri IV.
40 Prunières, *Le ballet de cour*, 109; Gough, "'Not as myself'," 57. Cf. Hoogleviet's (unsupported) statements that the nymphs themselves sang this set of verses while dancing ("The *Balet de la Reyne* (1609)," 76–7, 82–4).
41 Franko, "Geometrical Dance," 23 and notes 38–40; on the "chaîne" or "haye," see also n8 above.
42 Gough, "'Not as myself'," 57.
43 On such ideas in the writings of fifteenth-century Italian humanists including Bruni and Alberti and their extension in Italian dance treatises from this period as well as Thomas Elyot's *The Boke Named the Governour*, see Nevile, *The Eloquent Body*, 92–103, 119–30.
44 On similar ideas of women's silent dancing as a visible manifestation of cosmic harmony in *Tempe Restored*, an English masque danced and organized by Henri IV and Marie de Médicis' youngest daughter Henrietta Maria, see Gough, "'Not as myself'," 55.
45 Caroso, *Courtly Dance of the Renaissance*, 89.
46 Oestreich, *Neostoicism and the Early Modern State*, 37.
47 On these ideas as they are worked out in Lipsius' *Politica* and taken up in connection with absolutist concepts of sovereignty and reason of state, see Wilkin, *Women, Imagination, and the Search for Truth*, 97–139, and Sénellart, "Le stoïcisme," 109, 119, 129.
48 Keohane, *Philosophy and the State in France*, 63–71.

49 On Lipsius' use of Aristotle, see Maclean, *Woman Triumphant*, 22 n98. On the "masculinist" governing ethos of ancient stoicism, see Wilkin, *Women, Imagination, and the Search for Truth*, 101.
50 Ibid., 61–74, 101–26.
51 Keohane, *Philosophy and the State in France*, 61; Wilkin, *Women, Imagination, and the Search for Truth*, 58, 53.
52 Hoogleviet, in keeping with my reading, finds in Fame's final stanza a claim that "the self-control of the members of the court, expressed in their physical beauty, reinforces *la Renommée*'s message of Henri IV's glorious reign" ("The *Balet de la Reyne* (1609)," 90–1). She attributes this 1609 *ballet de la reine*'s "politics of *vertu*" to the interest in neostoicism shown by Marguerite de Valois, who owned texts by Epictitus and Seneca and was personally acquainted with Montaigne, and by Henri IV, who attempted to bring Lipsius to France, but dismisses the possibility that Marie de Médicis took an active role in helping to shape this ballet and its thematic interventions.
53 Keohane, *Philosophy and the State in France*, 76–7, 81.
54 Sénellart, "Le stoïcisme," 119.
55 Arbeau, for example, writes that "dancing is a kind of mute rhetoric by which the orator, without uttering a word, can make himself understood by his movements," as qtd. in McManus, *Women on the Renaissance Stage*, 38. On early modern conflations of dance with oratory and rhetoric more generally, see ibid., 38–46.
56 On this ballet's use of the notion that glory is the reward for virtue, cf. Hoogleviet, "The *Balet de la Reyne* (1609)," 90.
57 For this singer's identity see, for example, Prunières, *Le ballet de cour*, 108 n5.
58 L'Estoile, *Journal*, 2: 427.
59 "Ce jour, je payai cinq sols les trois fadaises suivantes, qu'on m'envoya: *Recueil plus mémorable des choses avenues en ces dernières années – Déclaration sur l'élection des domiciles aux décrets. Et les vers du ballet de la reine.*" Ibid., 2: 431.
60 Cf. Hoogleviet, "The *Balet de la Reyne* (1609)," 88.
61 "[E]lle estoit née avec une si belle voix, & une telle disposition à la dance, que dès l'âge de cinq ans, elle chantoit juste, & dançoit en cadence, commençant mesme de toucher la Lire: mais avec tant de grace qu'elle charmoit tous ce qui la voyoient." Scudéry, *Artamène, ou, le Grand Cyrus*, Partie VI, Livre I, 123. Translated as: "[I]n Tire they talked of the little Elisa, as a great miracle, when she was not above five or six years of age … She had such an admirable voice, and such an inclination unto Dancing,

as that at the age of five years she was most excellent in both, beginning also to play upon the Lute [sic], which she did with such a grace, that she charmed all her hearers." Scudéry, *Artamenes, or, The Grand Cyrus*, Seventh Part, Book I, 36.

62 "Il se presenta mesme une occasion, qui comme[n]ça de faire esclater hautement le merite extraordinaire de la jeune Elise: & qui fit que non seulement on parla d'elle dans Tyr, mais dans toute la Phenicie, & dans tous les Royaumes dont il y avoit alors des Ambassadeurs en nostre Cour" (Scudéry, *Artamène, ou, Le Grand Cyrus*, Partie VI, Livre I, 124). "[O]ne occasion did present it self, which did make the rare merit of this young *Elisa* to shine, and which was not talked on only in *Tire*, but also throughout all *Phenicia*, and all the Kingdoms, whose Ambassadors were then at our Court" (Scudéry, *Artamenes, or, The Grand Cyrus*, Seventh Part, Book I, 36).

63 Kermina, *Marie de Médicis*, 104; Cousin, *La société française*, 1: 308.

64 Mousnier, *Institutions of France*, 1: 123–4; Duindam, *Myths of Power*, 51.

65 Dent, *Crisis in Finance*, 44–58. See also Greengrass, *France in the Age of Henri IV*, 203–5, Mousnier, *Institutions of France*, 2: 37–8, 40, Mousnier, *La vénalité des offices,* and Cummings, "Social Impact of the Paulette: The Case of the Parlement of Paris." During the 1590s, Henri IV had sought to restrict venal office in order to save the crown money (in wages due to officeholders) and to ensure that offices (and the right to grant these offices to loyal supporters or sell them for cash) would more frequently revert to the crown when those who held them died. Such efforts backfired financially, however, since a decrease in the number of offices, coupled with efforts to sell or transfer posts by fraudulent means in order to avoid reversion to the king, meant greater challenge for the crown in financing the massive debts it had incurred during the late sixteenth-century civil wars. They also backfired politically, due to discontent among officeholders and would-be purchasers themselves, whose loyalty and support Henri IV required. As of December 1604, when the *droit annuel* was instituted, those who held royal posts could now choose to pay an annual tax in exchange for which the king granted them the rights to resign their office even at the point of death without threat of reversion and to designate their successors, including heirs by bloodline. The *paulette* also offered officeholders a lower resignation tax. The farmer of the *droit annuel* along with his associates retained all monies from this and related taxes collected by *commis* in their hire in exchange for a substantial guaranteed yearly payment to the crown. Initially this annual payment was set at 900,000 *livres*; in 1605 the amount increased to 1,006,000 *livres*.

The crown's finances benefited greatly: corruption caused by efforts to circumvent reversion decreased, while collection of revenues became easier and more reliable. Officeholders benefited also: in exchange for a reasonable annual payment, they gained a form of insurance on the initial investment laid out in purchasing their posts: they could now sell their offices without serious risk and, crucially, they also enjoyed hereditary rights to their positions. As Cummings notes, "In taking this step, the monarchy loosened its control over staffing most positions in the royal administration and invested this power in the officials themselves." In this sense "the monarchy granted officeholders a major concession." And yet "French kings still retained some important political leverage" by establishing the *paulette* initially for a set period and by making its renewal subject to the crown's sole discretion; in this way, should officeholders resist royal demands for increased revenue or political support, the crown might refuse the *paulette*'s renewal.

66 When the king died suddenly in May 1610, the bourgeois elites of Paris immediately supported the queen as a way to mitigate the threat to peace and prosperity represented by the princes of the blood and the possibility of collateral rather than direct succession; see Dubost, *Marie de Médicis*, 302–3. The temporal gap between the king's assassination and the first (and ultimately unsuccessful) rebellions led by the princes during the regency stemmed in part from Parisians' loyalty to the crown, secured through their desire for peace but also from the *paulette*'s extension of hereditary rights of office to (former) commoners. Venality of office, which brought *roturiers* (commoners) into the culture of royal service and loyalty to the crown, thus helped to ensure political stability.

67 For a definition of financiers, see the *Encyclopédie méthodique* as qtd. and discussed in Dent, *Crisis in Finance*, 14. Lougee calls financiers "the most controversial social grouping in France" (*Le Paradis des Femmes*, 134).

68 On the appearance of rapid social mobility as a major cause for the hostility directed against the financiers by magistrates, see ibid., 176. On the notion of merit as understood by the old nobility as a combination of birth right and loyal service to the king, see Smith, *The Culture of Merit*, 11–91.

69 Tallemant des Réaux, *Historiettes*, 1: 474; see also Prunières, *Le ballet de cour*, 190 n2.

70 Tallement des Réaux, *Historiettes*, 1: 474.

71 "Il [Henri IV] alloit chez elle [Angélique Paulet] le jour qu'il fut tué; c'estoit pour y mener Monsieur de Vendosme: il vouloit rendre ce prince gallant; peut-estre s'esoit-il desjà aperceû que ce jeune monsieur n'aimait

pas les femmes: M. de Vendosme a toujours depuis esté accusé de ragoust d'Italie" (ibid.). Following these comments, Tallemant launches into further jests and songs about Vendôme's alleged sodomitical tendencies.

72 Salmon, "Afterlife," 14. On Tallemant's particular prejudices regarding women actors, see Scott, *Women on the Stage*, 18–21.

73 In 1612, for example, a pamphlet reporting the court fool Maistre Guillaume's voyage to "the other world" conflates Paulet's success as a ballet performer with her purported sexual skill. Begging his beloved master the late Henri IV to come back to life and resume his former glory as ruler, Guillaume promises the king that he will be welcomed back with open arms by loyal servants: not only will prominent nobles offer the king gifts of rare animals and foodstuffs but Guillaume himself along with "Guerin," another pamphlet writer, will make a ballet for Shrovetide at Paulet's residence, in order to teach her the dances of devotion: "Guerin & moy ferons un ballet à Caresme-prenant chez la Pollette, pour luy / apprendre les bransles de devotion" (*Le voyage de Me Guillaume*, 44). Maistre Guillaume also reports a series of questions about the court that denizens of "the other world" have asked him, including one that punningly conflates Angelique Paulet's erotic entanglements with the notorious tax on venal offices named after her father (*Le voyage de Me Guillaume*, 52); on this topical reference's indication of Paulet's low reputation, see Backer, *Precious Women*, 94. For a later satirical reference to the alleged gap between Paulet's seeming "devotions" and her hidden lasciviousness, see François de Maynard's epigram in Bever, *Les poètes satyriques*, 80. This epigram most likely references more generally the "saintly" claims to piety and virtue that Paulet seems to have been made in later years in an effort to recuperate her sullied reputation (Backer, *Precious Women*, 94). Maynard authored verses for spectacles at the court of Henri IV and Marie de Médicis, however, including the 1605 combat at the barriers discussed earlier in this book. It is possible, therefore, that Maynard was directly familiar with Paulet's performances at court during Henri IV's lifetime and that his epigram comments on them, including her entry for the queen's 1609 ballet.

74 L'Estoile, *Journal*, 2: 427. For a brief reference to Paulet's impact on listeners as a model for the singer's capacity to impart sensuality and eroticism to verbal imagery, see Durosoir, *L'air de cour en France*, 331.

75 "[V]rais larrons et sangsues" (L'Estoile, *Journal*, 2: 451). Tallemant more obviously conflates Paulet's "grâces" with promiscuous behaviour but also social mobility. His *historiette* on this young woman begins by identifying her as the daughter of a Languedocian who invented

what is called today, after his name, *la Paulette*, an invention that will perhaps cause the ruin of France: "Mademoiselle Paulet estoit fille d'un Languedocien qui inventa ce qu'on appelle aujourd'huy de son nom la Paulette, invention qui ruinera peut-estre la France." Immediately following this statement Tallemant attacks Paulet's mother for a pretension to social status marked in part by promiscuity. This woman, Tallemant reports, hailed from a people greatly defamed for passing love affairs, and though she claimed that her father was a gentleman, she herself lived "une vie assez gaillarde" [a bawdy enough life]. Continuing in this same vein, Tallemant asserts that the young Angélique was in effect pimped out by her parents: the mother being a "coquette" and the father wishing (in true financier fashion) to profit from the beauty of his daughter, this couple received all the court under their roof ["receûrent toute la Cour chez eux"], including one high-ranking noble who after taking up her parents' invitation forever after saw in his mind's eye the little thing of the little Paulet ["la petite chose de la petite Paulette"] (Tallemant des Réaux, *Historiettes*, 1: 473, 1109 n6). My translation of this final phrase relies on Scott's translation in *Women on the Stage*, 20. Scott notes also that Tallemant himself hailed from a family of bankers and financiers yet "showed no interest in the world of finance," preferring instead "the worlds of fashionable, literary, and libertine Paris" (18). Although Tallemant may have indulged in characteristic exaggeration when describing Paulet's mother as "d'une race fort dissamée pour les amourettes," even Scudéry describes this woman as "capricieuse." Scudéry, *Artamène, ou, Le Grand Cyrus*, Partie VI, Livre I, 122.
76 On this privilege in association with the position of *secrétaire du roi*, see Dent, *Crisis in Finance*, 144.
77 In this way, salacious responses to Paulet's performance not only stemmed from the period's expectations about gender and sexuality but also tapped into the period's concerns about authenticity, particularly with respect to the voice as an instrument of rhetorical prowess and its possible contamination when used for private, commercial gain. On these anxieties and their impact on contemporary responses to professional women singers and in particular the women of the Este court's *concerto delle donne*, see McClary, *Desire and Pleasure*, 80–1.
78 Attendance at court was possible for those with titles and/or powerful personal connections but also those with special skills, including artists, as Duindam points out (*Myths of Power*, 86). As a skilled musician, Paulet falls into Duindam's category of "artists."
79 Lougee, *Le Paradis des Femmes*, 9–55, 113–70.

80 Regarding dates for this salon's initial formation, see DeJean, *Tender Geographies*, 228 n3. Vittoria Guiscardi lists "Madame la vidame du Mans" (Catherine de Vivonne, the future marquise de Rambouillet) among the ballet's dancers.
81 On this ballet as initiating moment for the princesse de Condé's friendship with the marquise de Rambouillet, see Tallemant des Réaux, *Historiettes*, 1: 69.
82 Vittoria and Traiano Guiscardi name the dancer who immediately followed the queen "la Principessa di Conty." On Conti's salon, see DeJean, *Tender Geographies*, 22–3.
83 For Paulet's performances as a member of Rambouillet's salon, see, for example, Livet, *Précieux et précieuses*, 24. Angélique Paulet's code name appears as "Part[h]énie" in Antoine Baudeau de Somaize's *Grand dictionnaire des précieuses*, transcribed in Duchêne, *Les précieuses*, 244, 504, 508.
84 Scudéry, *Artamène, ou, Le Grand Cyrus*, Partie VII, Livre I, 130, 136–42; Scudéry, *Artamenes, or, The Grand Cyrus*, Seventh Part, Book I, 38, 40–1.
85 For a useful explanation of this dependence, see Duindam, *Myths*, 49.
86 Ibid., 51.
87 Carew, *A relation of the state of France*, 492.
88 Dickerman, "Henry IV and the Juliers-Clèves Crisis," 635–7.
89 Buisseret, *Sully*, 48.
90 Guidi to the Grand Duke, 25 November 1608, Paris, in *Négotiations diplomatiques de la France avec la Toscane*, ed. Desjardins, 5: 588.
91 Ibid.
92 On the importance of Gaston's birth for securing "the second generation" of Bourbons, see Bonney, "Was There a Bourbon Style of Government?," 161–77, 176.
93 "Mgr le Dauphin est venu cejourd'hui en cette ville, la Reine a voulu qu'il se trouvât à son ballet." La Force, *Mémoires authentiques*, 2: 216. From the dauphin's physician Jean Héroard we also know that a new outfit had been made for his charge to wear to the Arsenal performance: "On luy met ung habillement neuf pour aller après son souper à l'Arsenal y voir danser le Balet de la Roine ... A huict heures trois quarts, mis en carosse et mené à l'Arsenal pour voir danser le balet. Rameé à une heur après minuict." Entry dated 31 January 1609, in Héroard, *Journal de Jean Héroard*, 2: 1569.
94 This phrase is Julia Pardoe's; see my discussion in chapter 1.
95 On Caron's depiction of Catherine's fertility using imagery of flowing water, a naiad, a dolphin, and the goddess Diane as a way of asserting the queen's authority relative to her rival Diane de Poitiers, the late Henri II's powerful mistress, see Sheila ffolliott, "Casting a rival," 140.

96 Ficino, *Commentary on Plato's Symposium*, sixth speech, ch. 2, p. 183, qtd. in Agrippa, *Declamation*, 50 n41.
97 Maclean, *Woman Triumphant*, 161–5.
98 Cf. Hoogleviet, "The *Balet de la Reyne* (1609)," 85, who asserts that this ballet's most important theme "is unmistakably to put an end to the importance of love in court life."
99 Franko, "Renaissance Conduct Literature and the Basse Danse," 55.
100 Ibid., 56–7.
101 Viennot, "Diane," 471–3; Bardon, *Diane de Poitiers*, 50–81, 138–42. Images of Diana had also been developed in connection with Charles IX's mistress Marie Touchet.
102 Representations of this dual capacity for erotic appeal and virtue in Diana associated with influential women of the French Renaissance begin with Claude-Catherine de Clermont, "la maréchale de Retz," praised as Diana-Venus in the poems of Étienne Jodelle. See Bardon, *Diane de Poitiers*, 132, Courtright, "Garden," 64. For Jodelle's "Sonnet IV" dedicated to the "maréchale" de Retz, see Bever, *Les amours … d'Estienne Jodelle*, 62–3.
103 Zerner, "Diane de Poitiers: maîtresse de son image?" 343.
104 Wellman, *Queens and Mistresses*, 221–3.
105 On Gabrielle as Henri's full personal and political partner and on their unusual relationship as a form of "companionate marriage," see ibid., 333–47, 355–6.
106 Ibid., 323.
107 Bardon, *Diane de Poitiers*, 142ff; Courtright, "Garden," 74 n76. This effort to transfer the power of Diana imagery from the position of mistress to that of queen consort may owe something to artists who, after Henri II's death, as Sheila ffolliott has shown, reworked associations of Diane de Poitiers with the goddess Diana in ways that asserted Catherine de Medicis' own political authority ("Casting a rival").
108 According to Courtright, "It is not likely that the gallery was begun with Gabrielle d'Estrées in mind, who died in 1599"; rather, the contract for the Gallery of Diana states that it was to be finished by the month in which Henri married Marie, i.e., in time for her arrival in France ("Garden," 74 n76).
109 Françoise Bardon, *Le portrait mythologique*, 96, 98; Bardon, *Diane de Poitiers*, 149–50; Courtright, "Garden," 78.
110 Duerloo, "Cleopatra's Pearl," 21.
111 Cf. Marie's depiction as the moon paired with Henri as the sun in a harangue for her 1600 entry at Lyons (Bardon, *Le portrait mythologique*, 100).

112 See Du Choul, *Discours*, 92. In connection with Diane de Poitiers' estate at Anet, as Courtright notes ("Garden," 66–7), Gabriel Symeoni discusses Faustina's self-fashioning as Diana of the moon: embodying the grace and magnanimity of this goddess, Faustina was alleged to have surpassed all other princesses.
113 Courtright, "Garden," 65–6.
114 Viennot, "Diane," 473–4. See also Bardon, *Le portrait mythologique*, 228; Bardon, *Diane de Poitiers*, 148.
115 Henrard, *Henri IV et la Princesse de Condé*, 17–19.
116 Malherbe to Peiresc, "De Paris, ce soir de la Chandeleur" (2 February 1609), as transcribed in *Œuvres complètes de Malherbe*, ed. Lalanne, 3: 81.
117 See, for example, *Œuvres complètes de Malherbe*, ed. Lalanne, 3: 82 n6, and Fromilhague, *La vie de Malherbe*, 226.
118 Fromilhague, *La vie de Malherbe*, 227.
119 *Œuvres complètes de Malherbe*, ed. Lalanne, 1: 149. See also Malherbe, *Œuvres*, ed. Adam, 76–7.
120 Fromilhague, *La vie de Malherbe*, 227–8; Malherbe, *Œuvres*, ed. Adam, 821.
121 Peiresc to Malherbe, from Aix, 12 May 1609, as transcribed in Peiresc, *Lettres à Malherbe: 1606–1628*, 30. Earlier, writing to Malherbe about his verses for Fame performed during the queen's *Ballet of Diana and her Nymphs*, Peiresc had expressed his appreciation for the poet's art in primarily aesthetic terms: "je vous remercie infiniment des nouvelles que vous m'avez envoyé, et encor plus des beaux vers qui ont donné l'entier lustre au beau ballet de la Reine." Peiresc to Malherbe, from Aix, 13 March 1609, in Peiresc, *Lettres à Malherbe: 1606–1628*, 29.
122 Peiresc, *Lettres à Malherbe: 1606–1628*, 31 n1, Malherbe, *Œuvres*, ed. Adam, 822, Raymond Lebègue in Peiresc, *Lettres à Malherbe: 1606–1628*, 30.
123 Crawford, "Politics of Promiscuity," 236.
124 Bassompierre, *Journal de ma vie*, 1: 213–17; see also Guizot, *History of France*, 3: 468–9.
125 Bassompierre, *Journal de ma vie*, 1: 212.
126 For these dates and other related details, see the primary documents collected and transcribed in Samaran, "Henri IV et Charlotte de Montmorency," esp. 73 n2, 86–8. Regarding the rumours circulating about Henri's humiliation of Condé, L'Estoile wrote in April 1609 that "Sa Majesté, dit la marquise, a voulu ce mariage, pour abaisser le coeur à ce prince et lui hausser la tête" (*Journal*, 2: 451).
127 Camillo Guidi to the Grand Duke, letter from Paris dated 26 May 1609, ASF, Mediceo del principato, filza 4620, transcribed in Samaran, "Henri IV et Charlotte de Montmorency," 88.

128 As early as April 1609, the king had received an anonymous letter warning him of Condé's discussions with Spanish agents and thoughts of fleeing the realm to Spain; for the text of this letter, see ibid., 80–1.
129 The seriousness of the political crisis catalyzed by Henri's passion for Charlotte may be discerned from the audience Henri gave the Spanish ambassador in early spring 1610. When asked by the ambassador why he was raising such a powerful army and whether it was designed for war against Spain, Henri complained that Philip III had consistently incited Biron and the comte d'Auvergne, Henriette d'Entragues' brother, to treasonous actions against Henri's person and was now sustaining Condé in hiding while simultaneously underwriting imperial troops for a planned attack on France. The king then stated, "J'arme mes espaules et ma teste pour empescher qu'on ne me blesse, et mettry l'espée à la main pour frapper ceux qui me fascheront" [I arm my shoulders and head so that no one can wound me, and put my sword to hand to strike those who anger me] (ibid., 63–4).
130 For the manuscript title, cited from Mss, Fr. 9543, and its derivation from Peiresc's papers, see Malherbe, Œuvres, 821, 758.
131 Carew to Salisbury (Robert Cecil), 15 February 1609 (5 February O.S.), TNA, SP 78/55, f. 33r.
132 Carew to Salisbury (Robert Cecil), 26 February 1609 (16 February O.S.), TNA, SP 78/55, f. 41v.
133 François de Bassompierre, whom Traiano Guiscardi lists among the male nobles who danced the "brando" with the queen and her female companions immediately following their *grand ballet* or final set of figured dances on 31 January 1609 at the Arsenal, gives a date of 8 March 1609, i.e., "le premier dimanche de carême" [the first Sunday of Lent], for the ballet of the queen, the most beautiful, and the last also, of all those that she danced ["le ballet de la reine, le plus beau, et le dernier aussy, de tous ceux qu'elle a dansé"]. Bassompierre, *Journal de ma vie*, 1: 223. This was the date that Marie had originally planned for her *grand ballet* that year, as noted by Carew, but no other sources indicated that this second ballet was actually performed.
134 Considered solely as persuasive rhetoric designed to shape the king's actions, Malherbe's poem stands as an example of failed epideisis. However, as a vehicle by which to impress his other royal patron, the queen, Malherbe's verses for the *Ballet de Madame* may be considered more ingenious, and likely more successful, than has previously been supposed.
135 Wine, "Henri IV Makes Peace and Love." I am grateful to Professor Wine for her willingness to share a copy of this paper with me.

136 Printed in several versions and under various titles including *Histoire des amours du roi Henri IV*, this *roman à clef* was first published anonymously in 1651 but is thought but to have been composed by a high-ranking personage at the court of Henri IV and Marie de Médicis. It is most often attributed to Louise-Marguerite de Lorraine, princesse de Conti. On the question of Conti's involvement and the diffusion of her novel manuscript in print form, see DeJean, *Tender Geographies*, 22–3, who cites Cioranescu, *Les Romans de la Princesse de Conti*, 37–8. Other contenders for authorship, according to Kathleen Wine (in personal correspondence), include the duc de Bellegarde and one Mme de Simiers. The title of *Les Amours du Grand Alcandre* was obviously inspired by Henri's "amour" for the princesse de Condé, since the fictional name "Alcandre" was first applied to the king by Malherbe in poems addressed from Henri to Charlotte. Alcandre is taken from Homer and signifies a courageous hero; Oranthe signifies "she who holds the flower of youth and beauty." On these names and their meaning, see *Œuvres complètes de Malherbe*, ed. Lalanne, 1: 152.
137 Qtd. in Wine. Wine suggests as well that *Les Amours du Grand Alcandre*, like d'Urfé's volume published in 1610, depicts in an unflattering light the king's affair with Gabrielle, her death, and his quick shift to Henriette d'Entragues: it unmasks Gabrielle's alleged religious insincerity, for example, as a way of questioning the king's own political sincerity more generally and in particular his religious conscience, which under a new absolutist understanding had become part of the *arcana imperii* of majesty and hence unquestionable in any direct fashion.
138 Ibid.

5 Dances of Diplomacy: London, Valladolid, Paris

1 For additional discussion of this point, see this book's introduction as well as Smuts and Duerloo, "Occasio's Lock of Hair," 7.
2 Welch, *Theater of Diplomacy*, 3–4.
3 I here adapt Colantuono's concept of "mute diplomacy" in his essay "The Mute Diplomat"; for more detailed introduction to this concept as it pertains to court ballet, see this book's introduction.
4 Rivère de Carles, *Early Modern Diplomacy, Theatre and Soft Power*.
5 For a more extensive discussion of this shift in France's relationship with England, Spain, and the United Provinces, see Gough, "Dynastic Marriage."
6 Hutchings and Cano-Echevarría, "Between Courts," 107 n37.
7 Chief among these was the papal nuncio Innocenzo del Bufalo. In a missive to Cardinal Pietro Aldobrandini, del Bufalo explains that he was

invited to the ballet twice, by the king and by the queen, and that it was their desire for his presence that had convinced him to attend with all the other ambassadors: "Io [sono] stato invitato dal Re e Regina con duplicato invito, vedendo il desiderio ch'havevano che c'intervenissi, insieme con tutti gli altri Ambasc[iatori] vi fui presente." Innocenzo del Bufalo to Cardinal Pietro Aldobrandini, Paris, 26 February 1602, BAV, Barb. lat. 5831, ff. 78v–79r. To his brother, the nuncio reiterates this point: "Io una volta recusai andarci, ma vedendo che il Re e la Regina lo desideravano, non me parse far il ritroso ... Vi furno anco invitati gl'altri Ambasciatori che vi furno" [I refused to go at first, but seeing that the queen and the king desired my presence there, I thought it was not appropriate to be contrarian ... The other ambassadors who were there were also invited]. Innocenzo del Bufalo to Muzio del Bufalo, postscript to a letter from Paris dated 26 February 1602, ASR, Archivio Santacroce, busta 796, unpaginated. Letters by the papal legate thus confirm how important this international audience seems to have been for both Marie and Henri IV. For a partial summary of del Bufalo's 26 February letter to Aldobrandini, see *Correspondance du nonce*, ed. Barbiche, 251 (Letter #135).
8 Lee Jr, *James I and Henry IV*, 22–7; Mousnier, *Assassination*, 127–8; Perrens, *Les mariages espagnols*, 26.
9 On 30 July 1603, James I, Henri IV, and the United Provinces signed the secret Hampton Court Treaty (Allen, *Philip III and the Pax Hispanica*, 119–20). For further details, see Gough, "Dynastic Marriage."
10 Sullivan, *Court Masques*, 8–29. The remainder of this paragraph directly summarizes the most salient points from Sullivan's discussion of the 1603–4 festival season.
11 Ibid., 8–29; Barroll, *Anna of Denmark*, 97.
12 James had already sent similar messages through his use of diplomatic ceremonial at the banquet that celebrated his signing of the Treaty of London at Hampton Court. For this signing Philip III's official representative for the peace negotiations was Juan Fernandez de Velasco, constable of Castile and duke of Feria. During the banquet that celebrated the treaty, James placed on Velasco's finger a costly diamond ring and "coded" the rapprochement between the two crowns "in marital terms" by referring to the ring as a memorial of the "marriage" between the two kingdoms. Further, James offered to share with Velasco a melon and oranges that had been grown in the royal gardens at Somerset House, under Anna's direction. When offering this gift to Philip's representative, James reportedly drew attention to the fact that these were "fruits of Spain transplanted in England"; as Gustav Ungerer notes, this action thus

"transcended the historical moment" of the peace by "prompting the [idea of a] prospective dynastic alliance between Prince Henry and the Infanta Doña Ana" ("Juan Pantoja de la Cruz," 61–2). For further discussion, see Gough, "Dynastic Marriage."

13 As Sullivan notes, "In the presence of all the Court and of all the representatives of European powers he [the Spanish ambassador] had received and returned the compliments which announced to the world the supremacy of Spain in the matter of England's friendship." Beaumont himself complained vociferously to the king's master of ceremonies, on the day of the masque, and to James I himself, two days after the performance (*Court Masques*, 27–9, 196–7, appendices 12 and 13). In a missive to the Doge and Senate, the Venetian ambassador to England, Nicolò Molin, reported: "The Question of the marriage of the Prince of Wales with the Infanta is not only kept on the tapis but is publicly discussed, though the Spanish Ambassador has not opened the subject to his Majesty yet. I am told that a few days ago a number of Privy Councillors were in the Queen's apartments, and either by accident or on purpose the subject was touched on. Almost all of them and the Queen foremost, showed themselves favorable to this match; much more so than to the French match. They say that the daughters of France can bring no dower but a little money, and that by the Salic law, which is most rigidly observed in that kingdom, they cannot inherit any territory; whereas the daughters of Spain may not only bring territory in dower but may even succeed to the throne. This has caused great suspicion in the mind of the French Ambassador." 13 (O.S. 3) January 1605, in *The Calendar of State Relating To English Affairs in the Archives of Venice*, x, 208, no. 325, as qtd. in Sullivan, *Court Masques*, 198.

14 Hutchings and Cano-Echevarría, "Between Courts," 102–4; Cross, "'Closer Together.'"

15 The duke of Lerma made explicit mention of this idea for a royal match in a discussion with Nottingham prior to the latter's departure (Cross, "'Closer Together'"). Additionally, Philip III's gift to Nottingham of a costly "ring with a diamond … which he put upon his L[eft] finger, and as he said, in token of wedding him in true love perpetually' signaled Spain's interest in such a match: as Ungerer notes, this moment returned James' gift of a ring to the duke of Feria the previous summer. Ungerer, "Juan Pantoja de la Cruz," 62. This marriage, Philip III hoped, would help to bring about better conditions for English Catholics through the proviso that Prince Henry would be raised at the Spanish court and convert to Catholicism. By suggesting that control over the Low Countries might eventually be shared with England through Aña's marriage to Henry,

Spain also hoped to lessen James I's support for the archdukes' proposal for a negotiated peace with the Dutch "rebels," since such a peace, without guaranteed free exercise of Catholicism in the United Provinces, would damage Philip's political authority as "Most Catholic King." On the July 1605 suggestion that Aña's dowry might include part of the Low Countries, see Allen, *Philip III and the Pax Hispanica*, 159. By the end of the year, the Venetian representative to England reported that the diplomatic community in London was abuzz with the rumour "that there will be a match between the Prince of Wales and the Infanta who will bring the Low Countries as her dower." Nicolò Molin to the Doge and Senate, 30 (O.S. 20) December 1605, qtd. in Sullivan, *Court Masques*, 30; see also Lee Jr, *James I and Henry IV*, 44. On the religious concerns that led Philip III to pursue such a dynastic marriage alliance with the Stuarts, see Loomie, *Toleration and Diplomacy*; Redworth, *The Prince and the Infanta*, 8; Cross, "'Closer Together'"; Allen, *Philip III and the Pax Hispanica*, 130; Gough, "Dynastic Marriage."

16 For this masque's title see Barroll, *Anna of Denmark*, 88. On this production's diplomatic context, see also Hutchings and Cano-Echevarría, "Between Courts"; Cano-Echevarría and Hutchings, "The Spanish Ambassador."
17 Hutchings and Cano-Echevarría, "Between Courts," 92.
18 Villamediana to Philip III, 20 January 1604, trans. in Cano-Echevarría and Hutchings, "The Spanish Ambassador," 246.
19 The first English masque for the Christmas season 1604–5, to which Beaumont was invited, celebrated the marriage of Philip Herbert, James' groom of the chamber, and Susan de Vere, one of Anna's ladies. Barroll, *Anna of Denmark*, 53–4.
20 *Le Mercure françois*, I: 6v–7v. The relevant passage reads: "Le 16. de Juin il se fit un Ballet en la mesme sale où la Paix avoit esté jurée, laquelle brilloit tout en or, en flambeaux, & en lampes d'argent. Aux deux costez du poesle, sous lequel estoient assis le Roy, la Royne, & l'Infante, se voyoient deux Anges tenans chacun une trompette en main, de laquelle ils commencerent à jouer si tost que l'assistance eut pris place. À peine avoient ils finy, qu'on co[mm]ença d'ouyr un harmonieux accord de Musiciens, de haut-bois, & autres instruments. Iceux firent leur entrée en la sale devancez par dix-huit porte-flambeaux, & suivis de six Vierges, lesquelles par la diversité de leurs habits & de leurs livrées representoient plusieurs des vertus. Apres eux se voyoit un char trainé par deux petits bidets, sur lequel estoit assis l'Infant d'Espagne, ayant deux Nymphes à ses costez, & vestu en habit de Dieu, avec le sceptre à la main. Quoy

fait, on vint à ouvrir la porte de la sale où parut tout à coup un ciel de verre tout brilliant de flambeaux, & duquel comme d'une descendirent certains personages qui representoient le Roy, la Royne, & le Duc de Souye [Savoy]. Entr'autres ornemens & pierreries don't estoit parée la Royne, elle portoit un diamante estimé cent mille escus, & une perle fine de la valeur de trente mille escus. Il estoit la minuict passée quand le Roy se departit d'avec l'Ambassadeur Anglois, lequel ayant pris congé de leurs Majestez le Vendrey 17. de Juin, fut honoré de plusieus riches presens, & ainsi fit voile en Angleterre, où estant arrivez quelques jours après, il fit recit à son Maistre de ce qu'il avoit fait en son Ambassade. Quel changement est-ce icy! Aux dernieres guerres de Fra[n]ce les Espagnols on despe[n]du ta[n]t de millions, & ont ma[n]dé ta[n]t d'Ambassades pour persuader aux Fra[n]çois de n'avoir aucun accord ny condition de Paix avec les Adversaires de l'Eglise Catholique Romaine; & maintenant ils ont envoyé leurs Ambassadeurs en Angleterre, pour avoir Paix avec l'Anglois: Eux qui ne voulurent assister à aucune ceremonie ny serment que da[n]s l'Eglise, & disorient ne vouloire preferer l'Estat à la Religion; jurent Paix avec l'Anglois en la sale d'un Palais: Eux qui fasoie[n]t entretenir les Fra[n]çois en divisions sous le pretextes de Religion, & do[n]t le Cardinal de Pelué en sa harangue qu'il fit à l'Assemblée de la Ligue à Paris, l'an 1593, avoit compre leur Roy à Jovinian, ne font rechercher seuleme[n]t de Paix les Princes voisins de co[n]traine Religio[n] à la leur: mais les Hollandois qui s'estoient distraicts de l'obeissance de leur Roy, pour vouloir vivre en liberté de conscience."
21 I rely here on William Roosen's application of "stroking" – a concept from sociology and psychology – to the field of early modern diplomatic ceremonial in his essay "Early Modern Diplomatic Ceremonial," 469.
22 See chapter 2. On Rohan's military prowess, see Parrott, *Richelieu's Army*, 28. Notably, in 1606 Henri de Rohan, of his own accord and without the king's knowledge or permission, left France to fight for the cause of the Protestant rebels under the command of prince Mauritz of Nassau, and although to appease the ambassadors of Spain and the archduke Henri IV exiled him from court following this action, by November 1606 Rohan was back in France performing in a *ballet à cheval* for the baptism of the dauphin, the princess Elisabeth, and the princess Christine.
23 Laugel, *Henry de Rohan*, 37.
24 According to the Florentine representative Baccio Giovannini, those in attendance included himself and the nuncio as well as representatives from Spain, Venice, Flanders, and England (ASF, Mediceo del Principato, filza 4860, unpaginated, letter from Paris dated 6 February 1605). An

eye-witness account of this ballet archived among the collected papers of Nicolas-Claude Fabri de Peiresc similarly records that representatives from England and the court of Rome attended. For a complete transcription and translation of this letter see Gough, "New Evidence and Analysis." For additional discussion, see chapters 2 and 3 of this book. At the time of this ballet, the question of whether France would again declare outright war against Spain was being vigorously debated in French popular print. The positions argued by these various pamphlet writers include a stance in favour of attacking Spain, a pro-Spanish pacifist stance, and a third approach that warns against war with Spain but for a variety of different reasons including the need for a Christian league against the Ottomans or the necessity of continued rebuilding of France itself by attending to internal affairs and staving off factionalism within the kingdom. This debate was initiated in 1603–4 with the *Soldat François*, a widely circulated anti-Jesuit, anti-papal pamphlet which mocked even Henri IV himself and urged war against Spain. This pamphlet was originally published in the small town of Orthez but quickly spread throughout France; extant copies include several 1604 editions. In response, several pamphlets arguing against this bellicose position appeared, including the *Anti-Soldat* narrated by a "Spanish soldier" who pleaded for peace between his king and Henri IV, urging that if France must have war for the purpose of giving soldiers employment it should be in battle against the "Turk." In September 1604, Maistre Guillaume, a member of Henri IV's court, delivered a response to both positions. Guillaume claimed that what France needed was not more war but to attend to its own affairs after the wars of religion. An Edict would declare in France "one faith, one law, one king"; all rabble-rousers, including "diabolical" pages and lackeys, would be chased from the realm; and all malcontents would be forced to depart – for Canada! On this pamphlet controversy, see Mathorez, "À propos d'une campagne." Connections between the central concerns of this debate and Marie de Médicis' 1605 ballet are both general and specific, for when the duc de La Force wrote to his wife in Béarn describing the ballet occasion, he sent along with his letter, dated the day after the ballet's performance, copies of not only a cartel that was distributed at the end of the ballet (discussed in chapter 3) but also a recent pamphlet responding to the original *Soldat François* (La Force, *Mémoires Authentiques*, 1: 391).

25 For an explanation of the French king's designation as eldest son of the Catholic church see, for example, Nelson, *The Jesuits and the Monarchy*, 3.
26 Henri IV had acquiesced in 1594 to bans on the Society by the Gallican parlements of Paris, Rouen, Dijon, and Rennes following an attack on his

life by a former student at one of the Jesuit colleges. For an outline of the conditions pertaining to Henri IV's absolution by Clement VIII, including the separate and independent promise made by the king to address the pope's wishes to see the Jesuits recalled, see Barbiche, "Clément VIII et la France," 112–13. On the recall of the Jesuits as a way to repay the pope, suggested by the prelates who considered the annulment, see Dubost, *Marie de Médicis*, 219.

27 As discussed in chapter 1, during the 1602 ballet Henri IV had deliberately engaged the pope's representative in intimate conversation. Through the newly appointed royal historiographer Pierre Matthieu, moreover, news of this encounter became widely disseminated in print. On this occasion, Henri IV's treatment in the audience for his wife's first French court ballet would have signalled the sincerity of his relatively recent conversion to Catholicism and the legitimacy of his new marriage, arranged through papal dispensation, and hence of his new male heir, whose birth this ballet celebrated.

28 "Les ambassadeurs d'Anglaterre d'un costé, le nonce du pape de l'autre et les princes de mesme" (anonymous letter transcribed and translated in Gough, "New Evidence and Analysis"). The regular English ambassador in France at the time, Sir Thomas Parry, wrote to England's secretary of state Robert Cecil (made earl of Salisbury in May 1605): "What happened at the Queenes Balle, because I could not be at it my self, I forbeare to write, and leave it to y[ou]r relatis of my Lshsoph: Howard at his retour, who was present, and behaved himself lyke a noble man of his place …" Parry to Cecil, Paris 29 January 1604 (i.e., 1605), TNA, SP 78/52 (State Papers Foreign, France, 1605), ff. 20–3, 21v. The "Howard" in question, as Pauline Croft has helpfully clarified in private correspondence, was the young courtier Theophilus Lord Howard de Walden, eldest son of Thomas Howard, first earl of Suffolk. Parry suggests that Howard upon his return to England would personally describe the ballet to Cecil, with whom the Suffolks were friendly at court. According to Croft, citing HMS 17: 107, both Lord Howard de Walden and Ludovic Stuart, duke of Lennox, were back at court by March when they participated in the Accession Day tournament.

29 Lennox "fut convié à se trouver au Ballet de la Reine" and "[l]e Nonce et les autres ambassadeurs y estoient en un eschaftant à part, et ledite Duc [Lennox] en un autre accompagné des seigneurs et Gentilshommes Anglois et Escossois qui sont avec luy." Villeroy to Beaumont, 26 January 1605, in King's MSS., cxxvii, f. 143, as qtd. and cited in Sullivan, *Court Masques*, 197.

30 "La Regina fece il suo balletto, et essendo state messe le seggiole per li Amba[sciato]ri, dalla banda sinistra del Re per il Duca di Lenoz, et per l'Amb[asciato]re d'Ing[hilterr]a, et dalla destra per il Nuntio, Spagna, Ven[ezi]a et Fiandra …" Giovannini, letter from Paris dated 6 February 1605, ASF, Mediceo del Principato filza 4860 (unpaginated).
31 Rivère de Carles, quoting Lawrence Lessig, in "The Poetics of Diplomatic Appeasement," 7.
32 Ibid.
33 It was this position that de Tassis occupied at the 1604 *Vision of the Twelve Goddesses*, for example; see above.
34 Derrida, "Hostipitality"; Derrida, *On Hospitality*. Useful monograph studies of hospitality in relation to early modern English literature and society include Heal, *Hospitality in Early Modern England*; Palmer, *Hospitable Performances*.
35 Lee Jr, *James I and Henri IV*, 54. The nuncio reports that Lennox's mission was principally "per esplicare, che i capitoli della Pace conchiu[s]a con Spagna non contengono cosa pregiudiciale alla Corona di Francia, il che ha dato ombra al Rè." Maffeo Barberini, Paris, 24 January 1605, ASV, Segr. Stato, Francia, vol. 50, f. 32r. Giovannini concurs when he reports that "Il Sr. Duca di Lenoz è stato udito tre volte dal Re, et s'intende che habbia portate certiss[im]e testimonianze dell'amicitia et fr[ate]llanza del suo verso di questo, et d'havergli sin detto che se nessuno voglia dire ch'egli non sia più che mai suo aff[et]to et disposto per ogni suo contento et sodisfattione, quella M[aes]tà lo prega a non lo credere in modo alcuno, facendone l'esperienza. Credesi ch'egli se ne sia per ritornare fatto carnevale et che non tratti d'altro che di puro complim[en]to." [The Duke of Lennox has received audience three times from the king, and it is understood that he brought most certain testimonials of the friendship and brotherhood of his master towards this one [the French king], and that he [Lennox] has even reported that if anyone dares to suggest that Lennox's Master is no longer well disposed towards the king's every happiness and satisfaction, that very same Majesty [James I] begs the king of France not to believe this in any way, and in fact the opposite will be proven. It is believed, that he [Lennox] will leave to go back to England when carnival is finished, his mission here having only been words of compliment.] Baccio Giovannini, letter from Paris dated 6 February 1605, ASF, Mediceo del Principato filza 4617a, unpaginated.
36 Despite expressing to Beaumont on his return to England a general satisfaction at his treatment in Paris, Lennox complained that he had been

slighted at his initial reception by the king: he had not been conveyed to this meeting by a true prince of the blood, while during the reception itself the princes of the blood remained covered (a sign that they perceived themselves socially superior to him). Beaumont to Villeroy, 3 February 1605, TNA, 31/3/40 (this is Baschet's transcription from Mss, Fr. 3510, f. 128).

37 Bély and Poumarède, *L'incident diplomatique*, 451, 457–8.
38 Sullivan, *Court Masques*, 29, 197, appendix 14.
39 According to La Force, Henri IV's captain of the guards, the king himself had made sure that all of the visiting diplomats present in Paris were escorted to his wife's 1605 ballet: "[N]ous, les Capitaines des Gardes, eûmes tous commandement de pourvoir à tout ce qu'il fallout preparer, même à cause que le Roi avoit convié tous les Ambassadeurs à s'y trouver" (*Mémoires authentiques*, 1: 390–1).
40 Lee Jr, *James I and Henry IV*, 161–2.
41 Ibid., 120. On the strategy behind this embassy as outlined in contemporary Spanish documents, see Allen, *Philip III and the Pax Hispanica*, 213, 304 n23. Philip III simultaneously insisted that he would sign a peace or truce only if such an agreement guaranteed tolerance for Catholics in the United Provinces. Behind this action was the hope of further dissolving the Anglo-French coalition through a provision that the French king, as "oldest son of the Church," would need to appear to approve of, but which James and the Dutch as Protestants could not. On Henri IV's initial insistence that he would not continue his subsidies if the Dutch would not consider freedom of worship for Catholics in the Low Countries, and on the States' response that "internal religious affairs" fell under sovereign Dutch control, see Allen, *Philip III and the Pax Hispanica*, 161.
42 Hayden, "Continuity," 9; Perrens, *Les mariages espagnols*, X: 64, 98–106, 171. Cf. Gardiner, *History of England*, 2: 28, who claims that Henri IV was "of course impervious" to the proffered alliance.
43 For a more detailed outline of these events, including Marie's audience with Don Pedro and its diplomatic impacts both short and long term, see Gough, "Dynastic Marriage."
44 "There is news that Don Pedro di [sic] Toledo is ordered to pass through France, on his way to Germany; he to raise the question of alliance between the two Crowns. This rouses great suspicion here, and the subject has been broached to the French Ambassador. He has used the opportunity to heighten the suspicion, with a view to inducing the English to accept the proposals he had already made to them about the affairs of

Holland." Zorzi Giustinian to the Doge and Senate, 25 June (O.S. 15) 1608, in *Calendar of State Papers Relating To English Affairs in the Archives of Venice, XI (1607–1610)*, 137–43, Item 269, www.british-history.ac.uk/cal-state-papers/venice/vol11/pp137-143.

45 Lee Jr, *James I and Henry IV*, 113, 115; Gardiner, *History of England*, 2: 28. Given this outcome, it seems that Don Pedro's embassy backfired even before he had his first audience with Henri IV. On James I's efforts to keep Philip III's ambassador to England in the dark concerning the potential for this Anglo-Dutch defensive league, see Allen, *Philip III and the Pax Hispanica*, 216–17.

46 On the favour shown by James I to Boderie and by Anna of Denmark to Boderie's wife, who accompanied him during his sojourn in England, see Boderie, *Ambassades*, 1: xxvj–xxxviij; Boderie to Puisieux, London, 11 October 1606, *Ambassades*, 1: 379–86; Boderie to Puisieux, London, 15 May 1607, *Ambassades*, 2: 212–28, 224–6; Boderie to Puisieux, London, 2 August 1607, *Ambassades*, 2: 343–52, 349.

47 Boderie to Puisieux, London, 29 January 1608, *Ambassades*, 3: 42–51, 43.

48 Of Anna's behaviour at the 1604 masque Henri IV writes, "Laquelle s'est tant declarée et engagée [towards Spain] en cette occasion que je dois dorénavant non seulement tenir ses voeux pour suspects, mais aussy desirer que son autorité et puissance soit contrepoisée et refrenée par la prudence de son mary et de ceux qui vraiment affectionnent sa prosperité." Henri IV to Beaumont, 2 February 1604, in King's MSS., 124, f. 738, as qtd. and referenced in Sullivan, *Court Masques*, 194, appendix 7.

49 Ubaldini, 4 March 1608, qtd. and translated in Perrens, *Les mariages espagnols*, 92; Boderie, letter from London dated 1 January 1608, in Sullivan, *Court Masques*, 202.

50 On elite women's continued contributions to diplomatic political culture throughout the early modern period despite the rise of professional "modern diplomacy" in the form of official resident ambassadors, and on the "anxious scrutiny" to which these women's diplomatic contributions were subjected, see James, "Women and Diplomacy in Renaissance Italy," 13–14, 25.

51 Sluga and James, "Long International History," 1; see also Woodacre, "Family Ties," 41.

52 Mitchell, "Marriage Plots," 87.

53 Henri IV to Boderie, Paris, 9 May 1608, *Ambassades*, 3: 255–61, 258–9.

54 Boderie to Puisieux, London, 29 January 1608, *Ambassades*, 3: 42–51, 43–4; Sullivan, *Court Masques*, 41.

55 Boderie to Villeroy, 13 December 1608, *Ambassades*, 4: 100–7, 104; Boderie to Puisieux, 27 December 1608, *Ambassades*, 4: 133–8, 136. According to

Sullivan, *Court Masques*, 49–50, Spain should have been able to count on precedence being given to extraordinary over ordinary ambassadors in matters of diplomatic protocol. On this basis, the English would have been obliged to invite Giron, as Philip III's extraordinary ambassador, instead of Boderie, whose status in London was that of resident ambassador only. As John Adamson has clarified in personal correspondence, there was no difference, per se, between the rank of extraordinary as against ordinary ambassadors: the first were appointed for a particular purpose and were usually time- or project-limited, while the latter were usually longer-term residents. In early 1631, however, another precedence dispute between the French ordinary ambassador and Spanish extraordinary ambassador to the English court, described in detail by Sir John Finet, indicates that the Spanish certainly *believed* that extraordinary ambassadors outranked ordinary ones; see Loomie, ed., *Ceremonies of Charles I*, 34–5. The French ambassador's unwillingness to concede this point, Adamson notes, demonstrates just how complicated and combustible such matters could be, particularly since rules on these and other matters of precedence were universally agreed on prior to the Vienna Convention of 1851.

56 Boderie himself apparently confessed to his friend M. d'Andilly on several occasions that he owed most of his success as a diplomat to his wife who, having accompanied him on his embassies to Flanders and England, and having a great deal of wit and knowledge of the world, discovered in the goings on of various courtiers intrigues that might well have escaped notice by even the most attentive minister (*Ambassades*, I: xxvij). On the importance of husband-wife teams to early modern diplomacy with particular attention to the role of "ambassadrice," see Oliván Santaliestra, "Lady Anne Fanshawe."

57 Carew to Salisbury, 2 February 1609 (23 January O.S.), TNA, SP 78/55, f. 23r.

58 Villeroy to Boderie, 23 January 1609, *Ambassades*, 4: 195–201.

59 Carew to Salisbury, letter dated 9 January 1609 (30 December 1608 O.S.), TNA, SP 78/54, f. 238r.

60 Salisbury's letter in response to Carew's describing Marie's ballet asserts that Anna's "mask was put off from twelvtyde for somethings incident to itself" but also explains that Giron took his leave the previous Tuesday and then on the Thursday the French ambassador was "solemnly invited and present at the Queens ball, used with all compliment and favour." 12 February 1609 (2 February O.S.), TNA, SP 78/55, f. 27r.

61 Carew to Salisbury, 2 February 1609 (23 January O.S.), TNA, SP 78/55, ff. 19–23, esp. 22.

Notes to pages 190–3   305

62 Due perhaps to the distinction between Old and New Style dating.
63 Carew to Salisbury, 2 February 1609 (23 January O.S.), TNA, SP 78/55, f. 23.
64 Sully's ill health was also touted as a convenient excuse: "Monsieur de Sully, hath beene of late much afflicted, with the cholick and stone, so as the Queenes Ballet, on that pretence, hath been put of, for three or fower times." Carew to Salisbury, 2 February 1609 (23 January O.S.), TNA, SP 78/55, f. 22.
65 Mattingly, *Renaissance Diplomacy*.
66 James, "Women and Diplomacy," 25.
67 See Toby Mathew as cited in Buisseret, *Henry IV*, 128.
68 Camillo Guidi, the Florentine representative in France, reports that "Il Nuntio non si voleva trovare con Inghilterra per conto della Religione, ne Inghilterra con Spagna, ne Fiandra con Venezia, ne Savoia con Fiandra, ne Noi con Savoia per conto di precedenza" [The nuncio did not want to be found with England, on account of religion, nor England with Spain, nor Flanders with Venice, nor Savoy with Flanders, nor us with Savoy, on account of precedence]. Guidi, letter from Paris dated February 1609. ASF, Mediceo del Principato, filza 4620, f. 419r.
69 George Carew reports these specifics as part of a detailed description of the ballet in his letter to Robert Cecil, earl of Salisbury, from Paris, 2 February 1609 (23 January O.S.), TNA, SP 78/55, ff. 19–23, esp. 23.
70 Ibid.
71 Villeroy to Boderie, 23 January 1609, *Ambassades*, 4: 196–7.
72 On the queen consort's participation in the French king's sovereignty by virtue of her legal status as his wife, from the medieval period through to the sixteenth century, see McCartney, "Ceremonies and Privileges of Office." For a detailed discussion of the queen's simultaneous status as participant in the king's sovereignty and private subject, see Cosandey, *La reine de France*, 84–7.
73 On the early modern French dowager queen, see ibid., 88–114.
74 Seating arrangements at the actual event also honoured the pope and Spain, for Marguerite de Valois and Marie de Médicis sat themselves immediately above the king's special box next to Ubaldini and the Spanish extraordinary ambassador Don Pedro de Toledo. "In casa la Regina Margherita andò il Nunzio, et il Sig[no]r Don Pietro di Toledo, il quale da pratico mandò prima a vedere come stavano i luoghi; dove ciascuno di loro haveva a sedere, et trovato haverei il suo conto non penso ad altro. Erano molte seggiole sopra un palco ben abbigliato; le prime due per le due Regine, et dopo queste un passo più a dietro una fila d'altre, la prima

per il Nunzio; l'altra per Don Pietro." [In Queen Margherite's house went the nuncio and Mr Don Pedro de Toledo, who as a pragmatic [man] first sent [someone] to see about the places where each of them had to sit, and having found that he had what he deserved [meaning that the seating arrangement was to his advantage], he did not think about anything else. There were several chairs on a well adorned stage: the first two [chairs] for the two queens and after these, a step backwards, a row of others, the first for the nuncio, the other for Don Pedro.] Camillo Guidi, letter from Paris dated February 1609. ASF, Mediceo del Principato, filza 4620, f. 419r–v.

75 Writing about a later incident in which the princes of the blood refused to attend a particular ceremony in order to avoid setting a precedence for their demotion, in a particular status interaction, Giora Sternberg writes that "Thought the avoidance tactic technically put off an unwanted outcome, fleeing the ceremonial battlefield in this way could nonetheless be perceived as an acknowledgement of defeat" (*Status Interaction*, 38). It was this risk that I believe ultimately compelled Don Pedro to attend the queen's ballet.

76 Ibid., f. 420r. Describing this incident and its consequences, Guidi notes that the Spaniard resorted to such angry name-calling and threats only after first attempting to defer the dispute until the ballet was completed. Most reports from the period emphasize, by contrast, Don Pedro's lack of self-restraint.

77 Carew to Salisbury, letter from Paris dated 15 February 1609 (5 February O.S.), TNA, SP 78/55, f. 33r. On French perceptions of Spanish arrogance, especially Don Pedro de Toledo's, see Perrens, *Les mariages espagnols*, 114–20.

78 *Oxford English Dictionary Online*, "Rodomontade," nn 1 and 2.

79 Boderie, noting that his daughter danced with James I's son Charles (then duke of York), explained that had his health been favourable enough to allow such activity, he himself would have been invited to dance (as the Spanish ambassador had been on previous occasions). See Boderie to Villeroy, 13 February 1609 (New Style) and Boderie to Puisieux, 13 February 1609 (New Style), in Sullivan, *Court Masques*, 216–19, appendices 40 and 41. Carew also reports how these details regarding Boderie's treatment at Anna's masque had reached the French through Boderie's letters; Carew to Salisbury, letter from Paris dated 16 February 1609 (26 February New Style), TNA, SP 78/55, f. 42r.

80 "Haveva il Re determinato d'invitar tutti li Ambasciadori," Guidi, February 1609, from Paris. ASF, Mediceo del Principato, filza 4620, f. 419r.

81 "[C]hez la reine Marguerite … Leurs Majestés trouvèrent la collation magnifique et somptueuse que ladite dame leur avait fait apprêter (qu'on

disait lui revenir à quatre mille écus). Entre les singularités de laquelle y avait trois plats d'argent, accommodés exprès à cet effet, en l'un desquels y avait un grenadier, en l'autre un oranger, et en l'autre un citronnier, si dextrement et artificieusement représentés et déguisés qu'il n'y avait personne qui ne les prît pour naturels." L'Estoile, *Journal*, 2: 427.

82 Carew to Salisbury, 2 February 1609 (23 January O.S.), TNA, SP 78/55, f. 23.

83 On this letter, see Dubost, "Goûts et entourages musicaux," 20, and Dubost, *Marie de Médicis*, 236. One French precedent for Marie's avowed desire to hear and retain this Spanish woman singer was Elisabeth d'Autriche's patronage, in 1572, of Maddalena Casulana, a celebrated singer, composer, and lady in waiting to Elisabeth's mother, Maria d'Autriche, wife of Emperor Maximilian II. On Casulana and Elisabeth d'Autriche, see Brooks, *Courtly Song*, 201.

84 "The Duke of Lennox, first prince at the court of England, has heard us and has showed us much honour, and he enjoyed hearing us so much that he would have wanted to bring us to the queen of England, telling us we would receive every honour and anything we might want or require for our use. And it would be very easy for him to act together with his queen, through a letter that would intercede with the queen here [in France] for a month saying that she [Anna of Denmark] would be extremely delighted by this, and by the music and language of Italy, and would receive this favor as extremely good treatment." My English translation of Giulio Caccini's letter to Belisario Vinta, Paris, 19 February 1605; the original Italian is quoted in Solerti, "Un viaggio in Francia," 710–11. On Anna of Denmark's affinity for and knowledge of Italian language and culture, see *Hymen's Triumph by Samuel Daniel*, ed. Pitcher, x, and Lawrence, "Who the Devil Taught Thee So Much Italian?", 7–8.

85 On Marie's effort to retain Francesca Caccini and the entire consort in France, see Gough, "Marie de Medici's *ballet de la reine* and the virtuosic female voice."

86 Cole, *Music, Spectacle, and Cultural Brokerage*, 1: 245. Marie would likely have been informed about specifics regarding the 1608 Florentine *intermedii*, published in Camillo Rinuccini's official *Descrizione delle feste*. Indeed, like the 1608 *intermedii* her 1609 ballet not only used a professional woman singer but also featured Fame (as found in the first Florentine *intermedio*), a garden (recall the garden of Calypso from the third *intermedio*), and the sea (the fifth *intermedio*'s setting).

87 For this singer's identity see, for example, Prunières, *Le ballet de cour en France*, 108 n5.

88 For a detailed description of this entry as depicted in reports authored by numerous contemporaries, see chapter 4.
89 Prunières, *Le ballet de cour en France*, 107.
90 Giulio Caccini, *Le nuove musiche* (Florence, 1602), sig. C2v, qtd. in Spencer, "Chitarrone, Theorbo and Archlute," 9 and n7.
91 L'Estoile, *Journal*, 2: 427.
92 For a brief biography of Vausmenil see Gioanni, *La société aristocratique française du XVIème siècle et la musique*, 2: 89–91.
93 Scudéry also claims that Henri IV found himself "transported with admiration" ["le Roy en fut si transporté d'admiration"] at Elise's song, while the queen too "gave her [Elise] a thousand commendations" ["la Reyne ... luy donna aussi mille louanges"]. Scudéry, *Artamène, ou, le Grand Cyrus*, Partie VI, Livre I, 126, 129. English translations are from Scudéry, *Artamenes, or, The Grand Cyrus*, Seventh Part, Book I, 38.
94 Scudéry identifies Guédron (under the fictional name Crysile) as Paulet's music teacher (Cousin, *Société française*, 289). On the influence of Italian singing and in particular of the Caccini troupe's visit on Guédron's compositions, see Guédron, *Les airs de cour*, ed. Durosoir, xxxvii–xl, lxxxvi–lxxxviii.
95 Gérold, *L'art du chant*, 67.
96 "Il se presenta mesme une occasion, qui comme[n]ça de faire esclater hautement le merite extraordinaire de la jeune Elise: & qui fit que non seulement on parla d'elle dans Tyr, mais dans toute la Phenicie, & dans tous les Royaumes dont il y avoit alors des Ambassadeurs en nostre Cour." Scudéry, *Artamène, ou, le Grand Cyrus*, Partie VI, Livre I, 124. Translated as: "[O]ne occasion did present it self, which did make the rare merit of this young *Elisa* to shine, and which was not talked on only in *Tire*, but also throughout all *Phenicia*, and all the Kingdoms, whose Ambassadors were then at our Court." *Artamenes, or, The Grand Cyrus*, Seventh Part, Book I, 36.
97 Nor is this woman named in the ballet's *recueil* or in the printed music.
98 See chapter 4 for a more detailed summary of Traiano Guiscardi's eye-witness account.
99 "L'ambassadeur d'Angleterre vit ce beau ballet, à l'Arsenal; et celui d'Espagne, dom Pèdre, au logis de la reine Marguerite, pour en prendre (disait-on) un plan, et l'envoyer à l'Archiduc, pour le faire imprimer, en Espagne, en tablature de taille-douce." L'Estoile, *Journal*, 2: 427.
100 Carew to Salisbury, 2 Feburary 1609 (23 January O.S.), TNA, SP 78/55, f. 23.
101 Letters dated 24 and 28 January 1609, in La Force, *Mémoires authentiques*, 2: 216.

102 The Grand Sancy was arguably early seventeenth-century Europe's largest diamond, at 55.23 metric carats. Balfour, *Famous Diamonds*, 244.
103 Ronald, *The Sancy Blood Diamond*, 130.
104 Ibid., 127, 130–2; Balfour, *Famous Diamonds*, 246–7.
105 Ronald, *Sancy Blood Diamond*, 134. In 1603, according to the Mantuan ambassador in France, Marie de Médicis had negotiated with Harlay to purchase the Grand Sancy but Henri IV secretly had Sully break off the deal; see Bapst, *Histoire des joyaux*, 200–1.
106 Ibid.; Ronald, *Sancy Blood Diamond*, 143; Walgrave, "The Seventeenth Century: The Reign of the Diamond," 121.
107 Henri IV is said to have purchased the Beau Sancy "in order to assuage the feelings of indignation aroused in the Queen when she learned that Sancy had sold his bigger diamond to the King of England" (Balfour, *Famous Diamonds*, 46, 247). This purchase complemented a larger effort by Henri IV and Marie de Médicis to enhance the French crown jewels and exhibit them publicly. As Ronald explains, Henri and his wife wanted to build a gem collection capable of rivaling that of any other kingdom, and having sought out jewel smiths for the royal wardrobe, including several exiled from Flanders, in 1608 the king "installed twenty-seven residences and five large workshops for the best artisans in diamond cutting and jewelry making on the ground floor of the Royal Palace of the Louvre" (*Sancy Blood Diamond*, 135).
108 Ibid.
109 Frans Pourbus the Younger (1569–1622), Portrait of Marie de Médicis, 1606–7, Bilbao Fine Arts Museum, reproduced as Figure 2.3 above. On the Beau Sancy in this image along with other aspects of the portrait's composition that magnified and exalted its royal subject, see Ducos, "The Portrait of doña Maria de' Medici."
110 Carew to Salisbury, 2 Feburary 1609 (23 January O.S.), TNA, SP 78/55, f. 23. Carew's report supports Ronald's claim that Henri IV, when authorizing Sully to purchase the Beau Sancy from Harlay for the queen, declared: "I will be most at ease, to recover them [the gems] more than to allow them to outside my realm in order to be sold to strangers, as if I buy them, then no one else but I will own them" (Ronald, *Sancy Blood Diamond*, 135).
111 On connections between Habsburg territorial possessions in the new world and the art of jewellery in early modern Spain, Portugal, and the Netherlands, for example, see Schmuttermeier, "The Renaissance," 67. Harlay himself pawned the Sancy diamonds to raise funds for hiring mercenary soldiers to serve Henri III (Ronald, *Sancy Blood Diamond*, 108, 127).

112 Zor[z]i Guistinian to the Doge and Senate, *CSPV* xi, no. 154, in Sullivan, *Court Masques*, 40. Ben Jonson's text for Anna's 1608 *Masque of Beauty*, too, emphasizes this wealth. The "habit and dressing" of the female masquers, Jonson writes, was "so exceeding in riches" that "the throne whereon they sat seemed to be a mine of light struck from their jewels and garments." *Ben Jonson: The Complete Masques*, ed. Orgel, 69.

113 "Sabato sera ... la Regina fece finalment due volte il suo balletto. La prima all'Arsenale in casa di Monsr. Di Soulli; et l'altra in questi Borghi di San Germano in casa della Regina Margherita. Durò sino à giorno, et quei che lo videro affermano, che fu cosa vaghissima, et superbissima; et s'io ne potrò havrebbe una relazione, che mi è stata promessa, la manderò con questa à Madama Serenissima." Camillo Guidi, letter dated "Febbraio 1609," ASF, Mediceo del Principato, filza 4620, ff. 417–22, f. 419r. Guidi admits that he personally did not attend this particular ballet, allegedly due to his anticipated discomfort at the extremely large crowd that was expected. The "relazione" he had hoped for may have been a detailed first-hand account of the event by a private individual; alternatively, Guidi may have been anticipating the appearance, in print, of verse texts for three of this ballet's songs.

114 Giovanni delli Effetti to Cardinal Maffeo Barberini, 2 February 1609, BAV, Barb. lat. 7993, f. 1v.

115 This individual was most likely Bartolomeo Malaspina, who had been present in Florence as a representative from the Este court for the festivities celebrating Marie's wedding to Henri IV. On Malaspina in Florence, see Solerti, *Musica, ballo, et drammatica*, 23. In 1600, Malaspina had written to his home court reporting preparations for these wedding festivities; he also represented a princely dynasty well known for its patronage of literature, music, and courtly spectacle. Marie must have been keen to have him return home furnished with first-hand knowledge of her magnificently bejeweled ballet to share with his ducal masters.

116 The manuscript letters written to the Mantuan court from Paris by Vittoria and Traiano Guiscardi, dated 10 and 11 February 1609 respectively, are found in the ASMa, Archivio Gonzaga, busta 667, unpaginated. For more extensive discussion of these remarkable accounts of the ballet, discovered by Janie Cole, see chapter 4.

117 This was a great deal of money: in personal correspondence, Éliane Roux has informed me that 300,000 *scudi* was the total cost of constructing and decorating, with rare marble, bronze, and gold, what was considered the most fabulous chapel in Europe at the time: the Pauline chapel of Santa Maria Maggiore in Rome, built during 1605–15.

Conclusion

1 Louis XIII seems to have danced at least one ballet during Marie's regency – the 1611 *Ballet du roi Louis XIII* with verses referenced in McGowan, *L'art du ballet de cour*, 272. He was also entertained that same summer, together with Marie de Médicis, Marguerite de Valois, and a number of princes, princesses, and lords of the court, by "la comédie de Madame [Elisabeth]," a play based on Robert Garnier's *Bradamante*, performed at Saint-Germain by his younger siblings Elisabeth and Christine; on this production and Marie's role in encouraging its rehearsals and issuing invitations to audience members, see Gough, "Courtly *Comédiantes*." In November 1613, Elisabeth danced the lead role of Iris in a production at Fontainebleau, verses for which were gathered and published in a printed *livret* entitled the *Ballet de Madame ... par quatorze nymphes de Junon* (1613).
2 McGowan, *L'art du ballet de cour en France*, 85–9; Mamone, *Paris et Florence*; Barker with Gurney, "House Left, House Right"; Franko, "Fragment of the Sovereign as Hermaphrodite." Praise for Marie's achievement in securing dynastic marriages with Spain appears prior to the 1615 *Ballet de Madame* in the poem that ventriloquizes Elisabeth in the voice of Iris for the 1613 *Ballet de Madame*; in this ballet's printed *livret*, Iris' verses identify Marie as Juno and laud her success in achieving peace and tranquility in France and throughout the world by arranging Elisabeth's engagement to the future Philip IV of Spain (*Ballet de Madame ... par quatorze nymphes de Junon*, 5–6).
3 Gough, "A Newly Discovered Performance by Henrietta Maria."
4 See, for example, Mamone, *Paris et Florence*, 193–272, Crawford, *Perilous Performances*, 59–97. Neither of these studies discusses Marie's ballets prior to Henri IV's assassination.
5 See most notably Dubost, *Marie de Médicis*.
6 Franko, *Dance as Text*, 66, 86. McGowan, *L'art du ballet de cour en France*, 49–67, especially 61, 67, notes that during the period 1581–1610, ballet practitioners at court sought to broaden the genre's aesthetic scope and political framework in part by introducing burlesque elements; for an extension of this argument, see Lecomte, *Entre cour et jardins d'illusion*, 112–19. Neither scholar touches on burlesque elements in ballets danced by royal women, however.
7 Sternberg, *Status Interaction*, 6.
8 Ibid.
9 For a more extended discussion challenging an "arts of power" approach to early modern court entertainments, see Smuts and Duerloo, "Occasio's Lock," 9–11.

10 Sánchez, *The Empress, The Queen, and the Nun*.
11 Duindam, *Vienna and Versailles*; Duindam, "Palace, City, Dominions."
12 Duindam, "Palace, City, Dominions," 63.
13 On "personal" monarchy and "absolutism" under Henri IV, see especially Nelson, *The Jesuits and the Monarchy*.

Bibliography

Reference Works

Dictionnaire historique de la langue française, edited by Alain Rey et al. Paris: Dictionnaires Le Robert, 2006.
Grammont, Maurice. *Petit traité de versification française*. Paris: Colin, 1965.
Oxford English Dictionary Online.

Manuscript Sources

Archivio di Stato di Firenze (ASF), Mediceo del Principato

Filza 4256, f. 461. *Avviso* to the Tuscan court dated 18 October 1608, from Brussels. Describing Marie de Médicis' preparations for a ballet at Fontainebleau in honour of Vincenzo I Gonzaga.
Filza 4615a, ff. 188r–190v. Baccio Giovannini, Florentine resident in France, to Ferdinando I de' Medici's secretary, two letters partly in cipher, dated 17 February 1602. Describing at length Henriette d'Entragues' designs and actions, including her verbal insults towards the dauphin as another of the king's bastards.
Filza 4615a, ff. 192r–193r. Baccio Giovannini, Florentine resident in France, letter dated 2 March 1602 from Paris. Describing the ballet danced by Marie de Médicis on 19 February 1602.
Filza 4617a, f. 392. Baccio Giovannini, Florentine resident in France, to Ferdinando I de' Medici and Belisario Vinta, letter dated 23 January 1605. Notes that the queen's ballet is expected to be danced that evening.
Filza 4620, ff. 417–22. Camillo Guidi, Florentine resident in France, letter dated February 1609 from Paris. Describing the two performances of Marie de Médicis' ballet danced on 31 January 1609.

Filza 4860, unpaginated. Baccio Giovannini, Florentine resident in France, letter dated 6 February 1605 from Paris. Describing the ballet danced by Marie de Médicis on 23 January 1605.

Archivio di Stato di Mantova (ASMa), Archivio Gonzaga

Busta 667, unpaginated. Traiano Guiscardi and Vittoria Dalla Valle Guiscardi, letters from Paris to Vincenzo I Gonzaga and Eleonora de' Medici, respectively, dated 10 and 11 February 1609. Describing the ballet danced by Marie de Médicis on 31 January 1609.

Archivio di Stato di Roma (ASR), Archivio Santacroce

Busta 796, unpaginated.
Innocenzo del Bufalo, papal nuncio in France, to his brother Muzio del Bufalo, postscript to a letter dated 26 February from Paris.
Innocenzo del Bufalo, postscript to a letter dated 26 February 1602 from Paris. Describing the ballet danced by Marie de Médicis on 19 February 1602.

Archivio Segreto Vaticano (ASV)

FONDO BORGHESE

Serie II, 14, f. 439v. Agostino Gioioso to Cardinal Pietro Aldobrandini, letter dated 29 November 1604, from Paris. Regarding the naming of knights to the Order of the Holy Spirit.

Serie II, 14, f. 484r. Agostino Gioioso to Cardinal Pietro Aldobrandini, letter dated 27 December 1604, from Paris. Regarding Henri IV's departure for Saint-Germain without having yet appointed numerous persons to the Order of the Holy Spirit.

SEGRETERIA DI STATO (SEGR. STATO), FRANCIA

Vol. 50, f. 32r. Maffeo Barberini, papal nuncio to France, letter dated 24 January 1605, from Paris. Reporting on the duke of Lennox's arrival in Paris as extraordinary ambassador of James I.

Vol. 50, ff. 36r–37v. Maffeo Barberini, papal nuncio to France, to Cardinal Pietro Aldobrandini, letter dated 7 February 1605, from Paris. Reporting on Barberini's audience with Henri IV, shortly following the queen's ballet, pressing the French king to join a Christian league against the Ottomans.

MISCELLANEOUS ARMADIO (MISC, ARM. II)

Vol. 133, ff. 58v–60r. Maffeo Barberini, papal nuncio to France, to Cardinal Pietro Aldobrandini, letter dated 7 February 1605, from Paris. Reporting on

Barberini's meeting, following his audience with Henri IV, with the king's counsellor Nicolas Brulart de Sillery.

Biblioteca Apostolica Vaticana (BAV)

VATICANI LATINI COLLECTION (VAT. LAT.)
Vat. lat. 12431, ff. 69r–70r, 71r–v. Maffeo Barberini, extraordinary papal nuncio to France. Congratulating Henri IV and Marie de Médicis on the September 1601 birth of a dauphin.

BARBERINIANI LATINI COLLECTION (BARB. LAT.)
Barb. lat. 5831, ff. 78v–79r. Innocenzo del Bufalo, papal nuncio to France, to Cardinal Pietro Aldobrandini, letter from Paris, dated 26 February 1602. Describing the ballet danced on 19 February 1602 by Marie de Médicis.
Barb. lat. 7978, ff. 3–4, f. 12. Copy of Henri IV's 1599 letter promising marriage to Henriette d'Entragues should she birth him a son.
Barb. lat. 7993, f. 1v. Giovanni delli Effetti, secretary to Guidi, Florentine representative in France, to Cardinal Maffeo Barberini, letter from Paris, dated 2 February 1609. Describing Marie de Médicis' 31 January 1609 ballet.

Bibliothèque Inguimbertine, Carpentras (BI), Registres de Peiresc

Ms. 1794, f. 201v. Palamède de Valavez to Nicolas-Claude Fabri de Peiresc, letter dated 29 November 1622. Discussing a lengthy description of a royal entry at Aix that Valavez is sending to his brother.
Ms. 1794, f. 338r. Undated letter from Nicolas-Claude Fabri de Peiresc to an unnamed addressee. Requesting a description of a Te Deum.
Ms. 1794, ff. 429r–430v. Unsigned document entitled "Le Balet de la Reine dansé à Paris le 23 janvier 1605."
Ms. 1794, ff. 431–2. Describing a royal "carouzère" (carousel) performed in Paris in February 1606.
Ms. 1794, f. 453ff. Palamède de Valavez to Nicolas-Claude Fabri de Peiresc, letter dated 18 September 1610, from Paris. Describing "Cérémonies du renouvellement de l'Alliance d'Angleterre."

Bibliothèque Nationale de France (BNF)

CINQ CENTS DE COLBERT (500 COLBERT)
Tome 86, f. 237r. January 1605 letter from Marie de Médicis to an unnamed addressee [Henriette de Savoie-Villars, marquise de Villars and duchesse de Mayenne]. Requesting the presence of her daughter among the princesses whom the queen was gathering in Paris to dance her ballet.

MANUSCRITS FRANÇAIS (MSS, FR.)

10424–10429. François-Antoine Jolly, "Nouvelle collection de ceremonies et de festes, depuis Clovis jusqu'à la mort de Louis XIII." 18th-century manuscript.

24352–24357. Recueil de ballets, d'opéras, de pastorales, et de tragédies. 19th-century manuscript.

COLLECTION PHILIDOR

Rés. F-496. André Philidor, *Recueil de plusieurs anciens ballets dansez soul les regnes de Henri 3. Henri 4. Et Louis 13. depuis l'an. 1575. jusqu'à 1641. Recherchez et mis en ordre par Philidor l'aisné ordinaire de la musique du roy, en 1690.*

The National Archives of the United Kingdom (TNA)

CALENDAR OF STATE PAPERS (CSP) FOREIGN, FRANCE

SP 78/52, 1605. Sir Thomas Parry to Robert Cecil, first earl of Salisbury and secretary of state.

SP 78/54 and 55, 1609. Correspondence between George Carew, English ambassador to France, and Robert Cecil, first earl of Salisbury and secretary of state.

CALENDAR OF STATE PAPERS (CSP) FOREIGN, BASCHET TRANSCRIPTS

31/3/40 (Baschet's transcription from BNF, Mss, Fr. 3510)

Early Modern Printed Sources

Agrippa, Henricus. *Declamation on the Nobility and Preeminance of the Female Sex*. Edited and translated by Albert Rabil Jr. Chicago: University of Chicago Press, 1996.

Ballet de Madame s[o]evr du Roi. Devant le Roi et la Reine. Où sont représentés les météores par quatorze nymphes de Junon. Paris: F. Bourriquant, 1613.

Ballet de Monseigneur le duc de Vandosme dancé ... 1610. Paris: Chez Jacques de Heuqueville, 1610.

Bassompierre, François de. *Journal de ma vie. Mémoires du Maréchal de Bassompierre*. 4 vols. Edited by M. de Chantérac. Paris: Société de l'Histoire de France, 1870–7.

Bataille, Gabriel. *Airs de différents autheurs mis en tablature de luth*. Paris: Pierre Ballard, 1608.

– *Airs de différents autheurs mis en tablature de luth*. 2° livre. Paris: Pierre Ballard, 1609. Geneva: Minkhoff Reprints, 1980.

Beauchamps, Pierre François Godard de. *Recherches sur les théâtres de France*. 3 vols. Paris: 1735.

Ben Jonson: The Complete Masques. Edited by Stephen Orgel. New Haven: Yale University Press, 1969.

Bertaut, Jean. *Recueil de quelques vers amoureux*. Edited by Louis Terreaux. Paris: Librairie Marcel Didier, 1970.

Boderie, Antoine Le Fèvre de la. *Ambassades de Monsieur de La Boderie en Angleterre 1606–1611*. 4 vols. [Paris]: [Paul-Denis Burtin], 1750.

Caccini, Giulio. *Le nuove musiche*. Florence: Appresso i Marescotti, 1602.

Calendar of State Papers Relating To English Affairs in the Archives of Venice, Volume 11 (1607–1610). Edited by Horatio F. Brown. London: Her Majesty's Stationery Office, 1904. www.british-history.ac.uk/cal-state-papers/venice/vol11.

Carew, George. *A relation of the state of France, with the character of Henry IV. and the principal persons of the court, drawn up by George Carew, upon his return from his embassy there in 1609, and addressed to James I*. In Thomas Birch, *An Historical View of the Negotiations Between the Courts of England, France, and Brussels*. London: A. Millar, 1749.

Caroso, Fabritio [Fabrizio]. *Courtly Dance of the Renaissance: A New Translation and Edition of the Nobiltà di dame 1600*. Translated and edited by Julia Sutton; music transcribed and edited by F. Marian Walker. New York: Dover Publications, 1995.

Charron, Pierre. *De la sagesse*, 1601. Geneva: Slatkine Reprints, 1968.

Chavigny, Jean-Aimé de. *Les Pléiades du S. de Chavigny, … où en l'explication des antiques prophéties conservées avec les oracles du célèbre Nostradamus, est traicté du renouvellement des siècles, changement des empires et avancement du nom chrestien, avec les prouesses … et couronnes promises à … Henry IIII, roy de France et de Navarre …* Lyon: P. Rigaud, 1603.

Chiabrera, Gabriello. "Canzone in lode della reina." *Rime cantate nel giardino del Signor Riccardo Riccardi. Con l'occasione d'una festa fatta quivi per la Reina*. Firenze: Domenico Manzani, 1600. In Angelo Solerti, *Musica, ballo e drammatica alla corte Medicea dal 1600 al 1637: Notizie tratte da un diario, con appendice di testi inediti e rari*, 1905. New York: B. Blom, 1968.

Chronique du Roy Françoys Premier de ce Nom. Edited by Georges Guiffrey. Paris: Veuve Jules Renouard, 1860.

Correspondance du nonce en France Innocenzo del Bufalo Évêque de Camerino (1601–1604). Edited by Bernard Barbiche. Rome: Presses de l'Université Grégorienne; Paris: Éditions Boccard, 1964.

Dante Alighieri. *The Divine Comedy*. Translated with commentary by Charles S. Singleton. Princeton: Princeton University Press, 1975.

Discours de ce qui s'est passé au voyage de monseigneur le duc de Nevers & principalement au siege de Bude en Hongrie, au mois d'octobre 1602. Lyon: J. Pillehotte, 1603.

Dreux du Radier, Jean François. *Mémoires historiques, critiques, et anecdotes sur les reines et régentes de France*. 6 vols. Paris: Impr. de Mame frères, 1808.

Du Chesne, André. *Figures mystiques du riche et précieux cabinet des dames*. Paris: Chez Toussaint Du Bray, 1605.

Du Choul, Guillaume. *Discours de la religion des anciens romains illustré*, 1556. New York: Garland, 1976.

Durand, Étienne. *Description du Ballet de Madame soeur aisnée du Roy*. Lyon: F. Yvrad, 1615.

E[s]tienne, Henri. *Ane Mervellous discourse upon the liyfe, deides and behaviours of Katherine de Medicis*. 1576.

[Estienne, Henri]. *Discours merveilleux de la vie, actions et deportemens de Catherine de Medicis roine mere. Declarant les moyens qu'elle a tenus pour usurper le gouvernement du royaume de France, & ruiner l'estat d'iceluy. Seconde edition* ... 1576.

Ficino, Marsilio. *The Book of the Sun (De Sole)*. Translated by Geoffrey Cornelius et al. *Sphinx 6: A Journal for Archetypal Psychology and the Arts* (1994). www.users.globalnet.co.uk/~alfar2/ficino.htm.

– *Commentary on Plato's Symposium on Love*. Translated by Sears Jayne. Dallas: Spring Publications, 1985.

Garel, Elie. *Les oracles françois, ou explication allégorique du Balet de Madame, soeur aisnée du Roy* ... Paris: Chez Pierre Chevalier, 1615.

Gassendi, Pierre. *Vie de l'illustre Nicolas-Claude Fabri de Peiresc conseiller au parlement d'Aix par Pierre Gassendi*. Translated by Roger Lasalle with Agnès Bresson. Paris: Belin, 1992.

Godefroy, Théodore. *Le cérémonial françois, ... recueilly par Théodore Godefroy, ... et mis en lumière par Denys Godefroy* ... 1619; Paris: Sébastien Cramoisy, 1649.

Guédron, Pierre. *Airs de cour, à 4 et 5 parties*. 5 vols. Paris: Pierre Ballard, 1608.

– *Les airs de cour*. Edited by Georgie Durosoir, with lute tablature transcription by Éric Bellocq. Versailles: Éditions du Centre de Musique Baroque de Versailles, 2009.

Héroard, Jean. *Journal de Jean Héroard*. Edited by Madeleine Foisil. 2 vols. Paris: Fayard, 1989.

Histoire des amours de Henry IV. In *Archives curieuses de l'histoire de France*. Edited by M.L. Cimber and F. Danjou. Series I, vol. 14. Paris: Beauvais, 1837.

Histoire des amours du Grand Alcandre. In *Recueil de diverses pièces servant à l'histoire de Henry III, roy de France et de Pologne* ... Cologne: Chez Pierre du Marteau, 1663.

Hongarus, Georgius, and Jean-Aimé de Chavigny. *Discours parénétique sur les choses turques ... où est proposé s'il est expédient et utile à la République chrestienne de prendre les armes par communes forces ... contre ce ... pernicieux ennemi du nom chrestien* ... Lyon: P. Rigaud, 1606.

Hymen's Triumph by Samuel Daniel. Edited by John Pitcher. Oxford: Malone Society Reprints, 1994.

Jolly, François Antoine. *Projet d'un nouveau cérémonial françois, augmenté d'un grand nombre de pièces qui n'ont pas été publiées par M. Godefroy.* Paris: De l'Imprimerie de Prault père, 1746.

La Force, Jacques Nompar de Caumont, duc de. *Mémoires authentiques de Jacques Nompar de Caumont duc de La Force maréchal de France.* Edited by Le Marquis de la Grange. 4 vols. Paris: Charpentier, 1843.

La response de Maistre Guillaume au Soldat François. Faicte en la presence du Roy, à Fontainebleau, le huictiesme Septembre 1604 [1605].

La Roque, Siméon-Guillaume sieur de. *Hymne sur l'embarquement de la royne, et de son arrivée en France.* Paris: Pour Clayde de Montroeil, 1600.

Lacroix, Paul (P.L. Jacob). *Ballet et mascarades de cour de Henri III à Louis XIV, 1581–1652.* 6 vols. 1868–70. Geneva: Slatkine Reprints, 1968.

Le Mercure françois: Ou, la suite de l'histoire de la paix ... Paris: Je[a]n Richer, 1619.

Le polemandre, ou discours d'estat de la necessite de faire la guerre en Espagne. 1604.

Le romant des chevaliers de Thrace. Paris: Chez Jean Gesselin, 1605.

Le voyage de Me Guillaume en l'autre monde vers Henry le Grand. Paris: 1612.

L'Estoile, Pierre de. *Journal de l'Estoile pour le règne de Henri IV.* 3 vols. Edited by Louis Raymond Lefèvre and André Martin. Paris: Gallimard, 1948–60.

Les amours de Henri IV, roi de France, avec ses lettres galantes à la duchesse de Beaufort, et à la marquise de Verneuil ... 2 vols. London [i.e., Paris]: 1790.

Les amours du Grand Alcandre par Mlle de Guise, suivis de pièces intéressantes pour servir à l'histoire de Henri IV. 2 vols. Paris: l'Imprimerie de Didot l'Aîné, 1786.

Les entrées royales et solennelles du règne d'Henri IV dans les villes françaises. Edited by Marie-France Wagner. Paris: Classiques Garnier, 2010.

Les œuvres morales et meslées de Sénecque, traduites ... par Simon Goularrt [sic]. Paris: J. Houzé, 1595.

Les œuvres poétiques de M. Bertaut, évesque de Sées, abbé d'Aunay, premier aumosnier de la Royne, publ. d'après l'éd. de 1620, avec introd., notes et lexique par Adolphe Chenevière, 1891. Millwood NY: Kraus Reprints, 1982.

Lettres de Peiresc. Edited by Philippe Tamizey de Larroque. 7 vols. Paris: Imprimerie Nationale, 1888–98.

Malherbe, François de. *Œuvres.* Edited by Antoine Adam. Paris: Gallimard, 1971.

– *Œuvres de Malherbe.* Ed. M.L. Lalanne. 5 vols. Paris: Hachette, 1862–9.

– *Les poésies de messire François de Malherbe ...* Edited by Ludovic Lalanne. Paris: Hachette, 1862.

Malingre, Claude. *Annales générales de la ville de Paris.* Paris: Pierre Rocolet et al., 1640.

Marinella, Lucrezia. *The Nobility and Excellence of Women and the Defects and Vices of Men*. Edited and translated by Anne Dunhill. Introduction by Letizia Panizza. Chicago: University of Chicago Press, 1999.

Matthieu, Pierre. *Histoire de France & des choses memorables, advenues aux provinces estrangeres durant sept années de paix, du regne du roy Henri IIII. Roy de France & de Navarre, divisée en sept livres*. Paris: Chez P. Metayer, Imprimeur du Roy, & M. Guillemot, 1605.

Négotiations diplomatiques de la France avec la Toscane. Edited by Abel Desjardins. 6 vols. Paris: Imprimerie Impériale, 1859.

Nervèze, Antoine de. *Les essais poétiques*. Paris: Société des Textes Français Modernes, 1999.

Ovid. *Metamorphoses*. Translated by Frank Justus Miller, revised by G.P. Goold. Loeb Classical Library 42. Cambridge, MA: Harvard University Press, 1916.

Panegyric du voyage et retour de Monsieur de Nevers de la guerre contre les Turcs. Paris: 1603.

Parthenay, Catherine de, dame de Rohan. *Ballets allégoriques en vers, 1592–1593*. Edited by Raymond Ritter. Paris: Champion, 1927.

Peiresc, Nicolas-Claude Fabri de. *Lettres à Malherbe: 1606–1628*. Edited by Raymond Lebègue. Paris: Centre National de la Recherche Scientifique, 1976.

– *Lettres de Peiresc, ...* Edited by Philippe Tamizey de Larroque. 7 vols. Paris: Imprimerie Nationale, 1888–98.

Recueil des cartels et deffis tant en prose qv'en vers povr le combat de la barriere faict le xxv. de Fevrier en presence du roy, de la roine, des princes, des princesses, seigneurs & dames de la cour en la grand'salle de Bourbon. Paris: Chez Abraham Saugrain, 1605.

Recueil des vers du balet de la Reyne. Paris: Toussaincts [sic] Du Bray, 1609.

Recueil des vers du Balet de la Royne. Paris: Jean Nigaut, 1609.

Rime cantate nel giardino del signor Riccardo Riccardi con l'occasione d'una festa fatta quivi per la reina. Florence: Domenico Manzani, 1600.

Rinuccini, Camillo. *Descrizione delle feste fatte nelle reali nozze de' serenissimi principi di Toscana d. Cosimo de' Medici, e Maria Maddalena arciduchessa d'Austria*. Firenze, 1608.

Scudéry, Madeleine de. *Artamène, ou, le Grand Cyrus*. 10 vols. Paris: A. Courbé, 1650–4.

– *Artamenes, or, The Grand Cyrus an excellent new romance / written by that famous wit of France, Monsieur de Scudery ...; and now Englished by F.G., Gent*. London: 1653–5.

Sully, Maximilien de Béthune, duc de. *Mémoires de Maximilien de Bethune, duc de Sully*. 8 vols. London: 1767.

Tallement des Réaux, Gédéon. *Historiettes*. Edited by Antoine Adam. 2 vols. Paris: Librairie Gallimard, 1960.

Thou, Jacques-Auguste de. *Histoire universelle de Jacques-Auguste de Thou depuis 1543 jusqu'en 1607, traduite ... sur l'édition latine de Londres*. 16 vols. Londres [Paris]: 1734.
Valladier, André. *Labyrinthe royal de l'Hercule gaulois triomphant*. Avignon: Chez Jaques Bramereau, 1601.

Secondary Sources

Adam, Antoine. *Théophile de Viau et la libre pensée française en 1620*. Geneva: Droz, 1935. Geneva: Slatkine Reprints, 1966.
Adamson, John. "The Making of the Ancien-Régime Court." In *The Princely Courts of Europe 1500–1750: Ritual, Politics and Culture Under the Ancien Régime 1500–1750*, edited by John Adamson, 7–41. London: Weidenfeld & Nicolson, 1999.
Allen, Paul C. *Philip III and the Pax Hispanica 1598–1621: The Failure of Grand Strategy*. New Haven: Yale University Press, 2000.
Alvarez, Fernando J. Bouza. *Locos, enanos, y hombres de placer en la corte de los austrias oficio de burlas*. Madrid: Ediciones Tenas de Hoy, S.A., 1991.
Andrea, Bernadette. "Elizabeth I and Persian Exchanges." In *The Foreign Relations of Elizabeth I*, edited by Charles Beem, 169–99. New York: Palgrave Macmillan, 2011.
– "Persia, Tartaria, and Pamphilia: Ideas of Asia in Mary Wroth's *The Countess of Montgomery's Urania*, Part II." In *The English Renaissance, Orientalism, and the Idea of Asia*, edited by Debra Johanyak and Walter S.H. Lim, 23–50. New York: Palgrave Macmillan, 2010.
– "The Tartar Girl, The Persian Princess, and Early Modern Women's Authorship from Elizabeth I to Mary Wroth." In *Women Writing Back/ Writing Women Back: Transnational Perspectives from the Late Middle Ages to the Dawn of the Modern Era*, edited by Anke Gilleir, Alicia C. Montoya, and Susan van Djik, 257–81. Leiden: Brill, 2010.
– *Women and Islam in Early Modern English Literature*. Cambridge: Cambridge University Press, 2008.
Anglo, Sydney. "The Barriers: From Combat to Dance (Almost)." *Dance Research* 25.2 (Winter 2007): 91–106.
– *Martial Arts of Renaissance Europe*. New Haven: Yale University Press, 2000.
Antonetti, G. "Les princes étrangers." In *État et société en France aux XVIIe et XVIIIe siècles. Mélanges offerts à Yves Durand*, edited by Jean-Pierre Bardet et al., 33–62. Paris: Presses de l'Université Paris-Sorbonne, 2000.
Armstrong, Megan C., and Gillian Weiss. "Introduction: France and the Early Modern Mediterranean." *French History* 29.1 (2015): 1–5.

Babelon, Jean-Pierre. "Avant-propos" and "Forward." In Pierre Guédron, *Les airs de cour*, edited by Georgie Durosoir, with lute tablature transcription by Eric Bellocq, v–viii. Versailles: Éditions du Centre de Musique Baroque de Versailles, 2009.

Backer, Dorothy Anne Liot. *Precious Women*. New York: Basic Books, 1974.

Balfour, Ian. *Famous Diamonds*, fifth ed. Woodbridge: Antique Collectors' Club, 2009.

Bapst, Germain. *Histoire des joyaux de la couronne de France*. Paris: Hachette, 1889.

Barbiche, Bernard. "Clément VIII et la France (1592–1605). Principes et réalités dans les instructions générales et les correspondances diplomatiques du Saint-Siège." In *Die Papsttum, die Christenheit und die Staaten Europas 1592–1605: Forschungen zu den Hauptinstruktionen Clemens' VIII*, edited by Georg Lutz, 99–118. Tübingen: Niemeyer, 1994.

– "Conseils pour l'édition des textes de l'époque modern (XVI–XVIIIe siècle)." http://theleme.enc.sorbonne.fr/cours/edition_epoque_moderne/edition_des_textes.

– "Marie de Médicis, reine régnante, et le Saint-Siège: Agent ou otage de la réforme Catholique?" In *Le "siècle" de Marie de Médicis*, edited by Françoise Graziani and Francesco Solinas, 41–56. Alessandria: Edizioni dell'Orso, 2003.

Barbiche, Bernard, and Monique Chatenet. *L'Édition des textes anciens, XVIe–XVIIIe siècle*. 1990; Paris: Inventaire général, 1993.

Barbiche, Bernard, and Ségolène de Dainville-Barbiche. *Sully: L'homme et ses fidèles*. Paris: Fayard, 1997.

Barbour, Richmond. *Before Orientalism: London's Theatre of the East, 1576–1626*. Cambridge: Cambridge University Press, 2003.

Bardon, Françoise. *Diane de Poitiers et le mythe de Diane*. Paris: Presses Universitaires de France, 1974.

– *Le portrait mythologique à la cour de France sous Henri IV et Louis XIII: Mythologie et politique*. Paris: Picard, 1974.

Barker, Sheila, with Tessa Gurney. "House Left, House Right: A Florentine Account of Marie de Medici's 1615 *Ballet de Madame*." *The Court Historian* 20.2 (2015): 137–65.

Barroll, Leeds. *Anna of Denmark, Queen of England*. Philadelphia: University of Pennsylvania Press, 2001.

Bartoli Bacherini, Maria Adelaide. "Giulio Caccini. Nuove fonti biografiche e lettere inedite." *Studi musicali* 9.1 (1980): 59–71.

– "Musiche e danze per una regina." In *Maria de' Medici (1573–1642) una principessa fiorentina sul trono di Francia*, edited by Caterina Caneva and Francesco Solinas, 141–4. Florence: Sillabe, 2005.

Baschet, Armand. *Les comédiens italiens à la cour de France sous Charles IX, Henri III, Henri IV et Louis XIII* ... Paris: E. Plon, 1882.
Bassani Pacht, Paola et al., eds. *Marie de Médicis: Un gouvernement par les arts*. Paris: Somogy; Blois: Château de Blois, 2003.
Bataille, George. *Visions of Excess: Selected Writings, 1927–1939*. Edited by Allan Stoekl. Minneapolis: University of Minnesota Press, 1985.
Battifol, Louis. *Le Louvre sous Henri IV et Louis XIII: La vie de la cour de France au XVIIe siècle*. Paris: Calmann-Lévy, 1930.
– *Marie de Médicis and the French Court in the XVIIth Century*. Translated by Mary King, edited by H.W. Carless Davis. London: Chatto and Windus, 1908.
– *La vie intime d'une reine de France au XVIIe siècle*. Paris: Calmann-Lévy, 1906.
Baudson, Émile. *Charles de Gonzague duc de Nevers de Rethel et de Mantoue 1580–1637*. Paris: Perrin, 1947.
Baumgartner, Frederic J. *Radical Reactionaries: The Political Thought of the French Catholic League*. Geneva: Librairie Droz, 1975.
Beam, Sara. *Laughing Matters: Farce and the Making of Absolutism in France*. Ithaca: Cornell University Press, 2007.
Bély, Lucien, and Géraud Poumarède. *L'incident diplomatique (XVIe–XVIIIe siècle)*. Paris: Pedone, 2010.
Bever, Adolphe van. *Les amours et autres poésies d'Estienne Jodelle* ... Paris: E. Sansot, 1907.
– *Les poètes satyriques des XVIe et XVIIe siècles* ... Paris: Bibliothèque Internationale d'Édition, 1903.
Bilici, Faruk. *Louis XIV et son project de conquête d'Istanbul*. Ankara: Imprimerie de la Société d'Histoire Turque, 2004.
Blet, Pierre. "Un futur pape, nonce en France auprès d'Henri IV." *Études* 300 (1959): 203–20.
Boltanski, Ariane. "Les Nevers: Une maison noble, et ses clientèles dans la trame de l'État royal (vers 1550 – vers 1620)." PhD diss., Université de Paris I, 2001.
Bonney, Richard. "Was There a Bourbon Style of Government?" In *From Valois to Bourbon: Dynasty, State and Society in Early Modern France*, edited by Keith Cameron, 161–77. Exeter: University of Exeter Press, 1989.
Boureau, Alain. "Les cérémonies royales françaises entre performance juridique et compétence liturgique." *Annales. Économies, Sociétés, Civilisations* 46 (1991): 1253–64.
Bourdieu, Pierre. *The Logic of Practice*. Translated by Richard Nice. Stanford: Stanford University Press, 1990.
Boyer, Ferdinand. "Giulio Caccini à la cour d'Henri IV (1604–05) d'après des lettres inédites." *Revue Musicale* (1926): 241–50.

Brainard, Ingrid. "Hey." In *The International Encyclopedia of Dance*, edited by Selma Jean Cohen. 1998. Oxford Reference, 2012.

Britland, Karen. "An Under-Stated Mother in Law: Marie de Médicis and the Last Caroline Court Masque." In *Women and Culture at the Courts of the Stuart Queens*, edited by Clare McManus, 204–23. New York: Palgrave Macmillan, 2003.

– *Drama at the Courts of Queen Henrietta Maria*. 2006. Cambridge: Cambridge University Press, 2009.

Brooks, Jeanice. *Courtly Song in Late Sixteenth-Century France*. Chicago: University of Chicago Press, 2000.

– "Les Guises et l'Air de Cour: Images Musicales du Prince Guerrier." In *Le mécénat et l'influence des Guises: acts du colloque organisé par Centre de recherche sur la littérature de la Renaissance de l'Université de Reims*, edited by Yvonne Bellenger, 187–210. Paris: H. Champion, 1997.

Brown, Howard Mayer. "The Geography of Florentine Monody: Caccini at Home and Abroad." *Early Music* 9.2 (1981): 147–68.

Brown, Pamela Allen. "The Traveling Diva and Generic Innovation." *Renaissance Drama* 44.2 (Fall 2016): 249–67.

Brown, Pamela Allen, and Peter Parolin, eds. *Women Players in England, 1500–1660: Beyond the All-Male Stage*. 2005. Aldershot: Ashgate, 2008.

Bryant, Lawrence M. *The King and the City in the Parisian Royal Entry Ceremony: Politics, Ritual, and Art in the Renaissance*. Geneva: Librairie Droz, 1986.

– *Ritual, Ceremony and the Changing Monarchy in France, 1350–1789*. Farnham and Burlington: Ashgate Variorum, 2010.

Buisseret, David. *Henry IV*. London and Boston: G. Allen & Unwin, 1984.

– *Sully and the Growth of Centralized Government in France, 1598–1610*. London: Eyre and Spottiswoode, 1968.

Burke, Peter. *The Historical Anthropology of Early Modern Italy: Essays on Perception and Communication*. Cambridge: Cambridge University Press, 1987.

– *History and Social Theory*. Cambridge: Polity Press, 1992.

Burnett, Mark Thornton. *Constructing 'Monsters' in Shakespearean Drama and Early Modern Culture*. New York: Palgrave Macmillan, 2002.

Butler, Martin. *The Stuart Court Masque and Political Culture*. Cambridge: Cambridge University Press, 2008.

Campbell, Julie. *Literary Circles and Gender in Early Modern Europe*. Aldershot: Ashgate, 2006.

Caneva, Caterina, and Francesco Solinas, eds. *Maria de' Medici (1573–1642) una principessa fiorentina sul trono di Francia*. Florence: Sillabe, 2005.

Cano-Echevarría, Berta, and Mark Hutchings. "The Spanish Ambassador and *The Vision of the Twelve Goddesses*: A New Document [with Text]." *ELR* 42.2 (2012): 223–57.

Canova-Green, Marie-Claude. "Dance and Ritual: The *Ballet des nations* at the Court of Louis XIII." *Renaissance Studies* 9.4 (1995): 395–403.
– *La politique-spectacle au grand siècle: Les rapports franco-anglais*. Paris, Seattle, and Tübingen: Biblio 17, 1993.
Canova-Green, Marie-Claude, Jean Andrews, and Marie-France Wagner, eds. *Writing Royal Entries in Early Modern Europe*. Turnhout: Brepols, 2013.
Carter, Tim. "Epyllia and Epithalamia: Some Narrative Frames for Early Opera." Unpublished paper.
– *Jacopo Peri 1561–1633: His Life and Works*. 2 vols. New York: Garland Publishing, 1989.
Carter, Tim, and Richard Goldthwaite. *Orpheus in the Marketplace: Jacopo Peri and the Economy of Late Renaissance Florence*. Cambridge: Harvard University Press, 2013.
Carter, T., H. Hitchcock, S. Cusick, and S. Parisi. Caccini family. *Grove Music Online*. 2001. http://www.oxfordmusiconline.com/grovemusic/view/10.1093/gmo/9781561592630.001.0001/omo-9781561592630-e-0000040146.
Chaline, Olivier. "Kingdoms of France and Navarre: The Valois and Bourbon Courts c. 1515–1750." In *The Princely Courts of Europe: Ritual, Politics and Culture Under the Ancien Régime 1500–1750*, edited by John Adamson, 67–93. London: Weidenfeld and Nicolson, 1999.
Chappell, Miles. "The Artistic Education of Maria dei Medici." In *Le 'siècle' de Marie de Médicis. Actes du Séminaire de la Chaire rhétorique et société en Europe (XVIe–XVIIe siècles)*, edited by Françoise Graziani and Francesco Solinas, 13–25. Alessandria: Edizioni dell'Orso, 2003.
Chatenet, Monique. "Henri IV et l'évolution du cérémonial des Valois aux Bourbons." In *Henri IV: Art et pouvoir*, edited by Colette Nativel, 187–95. Tours et Rennes: Presses Universitaires François Rabelais, Presses Universitaires de Rennes, 2016.
Chaussinand-Nogaret, Guy. *La vie quotidienne des femmes du roi: d'Agnès Sorel à Marie-Antoinette*. Paris: Hachette, 1990.
Chiarelli, Francesca. "Before and After: Ottavio Rinuccini's *Mascherate* and Their Relationship to the Operatic Libretto." *Journal of Seventeenth-Century Music* 9.1 (2003). https://sscm-jscm.org/v9/no1/chiarelli.html.
Choné, Paulette. *Emblèmes et pensée symbolique en Lorraine: 1525–1633: "Comme un jardin au coeur de la chrétienté."* Paris: Klincksieck, 1991.
Christout, Marie-Françoise. "Les ballets-mascarades des *Fées de la Forêt Saint-Germain* et de la *Douairière de Billebahaut* et l'oeuvre de Daniel Rabel." *Revue d'histoire du théâtre* XIII (1961): 7–24.
– *Ballet occidental: Naissance et metamorphoses XVIe–XXe siècles*. Paris: Desjonquères, 1995.

- "The Court Ballet in France: 1615–1641." In *Dance Perspectives* 20: 5–37. New York: Dekker, 1964.
Cioranescu, Alexandre. *Les romans de la princesse de Conti*. Paris: Ecole roumaine en France, 1935–6.
Ciseri, Ilaria. "Ballets et carrousels: immagini simboliche nello spettacolo di corte." In *Le "siècle" de Marie de Médicis. Actes du Séminaire de la Chaire rhetorique et société en Europe (XVIe–XVIIe siècles)*, edited by Françoise Graziani and Francesco Solinas, 137–44. Alessandria: Edizioni dell'Orso, 2003.
Cohen, Sarah R. *Art, Dance, and the Body in the French Culture of the Ancien Régime*. Cambridge: Cambridge University Press, 2000.
- "Rubens's France: Gender and Personification in the Marie de Médicis Cycle." *The Art Bulletin* 85.3 (2003): 490–522. http://www.jstor.org/stable/3177384.
Colantuono, Anthony. *Guido Reni's Abduction of Helen: The Politics and Rhetoric of Painting in Seventeenth-Century Europe*. New York: Cambridge University Press, 1997.
- "High Quality Copies and the Art of the Thirty Years War." In *The Age of Rubens. Diplomacy, Dynastic Politics and the Visual Arts in Early Seventeenth-Century Europe*, edited by Luc Duerloo and R. Malcolm Smuts, 111–26. Turnhout: Brepols, 2016.
- "The Mute Diplomat: Theorizing the Role of Images in Seventeenth-Century Political Negotiations." In *The Diplomacy of Art, Acts of the International Colloquium, Villa Spelman, The Johns Hopkins University Center for Italian Studies, Florence, Italy, July 1998*, edited by Elizabeth Cropper, 51–76. Florence: Leo S. Olschki; Baltimore: The Johns Hopkins University Press, 2000.
Cole, Janie. "Maria de' Medici, the Italian Minerva of France: Music Spectacle between Florence and Paris during the Early Seventeenth Century." Unpublished conference paper.
- *Music, Spectacle, and Cultural Brokerage in Early Modern Italy: Michelangelo Buonarroti Il Giovane*. 2 vols. Firenze: Leo S. Olschki, 2011.
- "Transnational Exchanges and Representations of Female Power: Musical Spectacle at the Court of Maria de' Medici, the Italian Minerva of France." *Transnational Connections in Early Modern Theatre*, edited by M.A. Katritzky and Pavel Drábek, forthcoming from the University of Manchester Press.
Conroy, Derval, *Ruling Women*. 2 vols. New York: Palgrave MacMillan, 2016.
Cosandey, Fanny. *La reine de France. Symbole et pouvoir XVe–XVIIIe siècle*. Paris: Gallimard, 2000.
- "Représenter une reine de France. Marie de Médicis et le cycle de Rubens au palais du Luxembourg." *Clio. Femmes, Genre, Histoire* 19 (2004). http://journals.openedition.org/clio/645.

Cosandey, Fanny, and Robert Descimon. *L'absolutisme en France*. Paris: Seuil 2002.
Courtright, Nicola. "A Garden and a Gallery at Fontainebleau: Imagery of Rule for Queens." *The Court Historian* 10.1 (2005): 55–84.
- "The King's Sculptures in the Queen's Garden at Fontainebleau." In *Medieval, Renaissance and Baroque: A Cat's Cradle for Marilyn Aronberg Lavin*, edited by David A. Levine and Jack W. Freiberg, 129–48. New York: Italica Press, 2010.
- "A New Place for Queens in the Art and Political Imagination of 17th-Century France." Unpublished paper.
- "A New Place for Queens in Early Modern France." In *The Politics of Space: European Courts ca. 1500–1750*, edited by Marcello Fantoni, Malcolm Smuts, and George Gorse, 267–92. Rome: Bulzoni, 2009.
Cousin, Victor. *La société française au XVIIe siècle d'après Le Grand Cyrus de Mlle de Scudéry*. 2 vols. Paris: Didier, 1858.
Crawford, Katherine. *Perilous Performances: Gender and Regency in Early Modern France*. Cambridge: Harvard University Press, 2004.
- "The Politics of Promiscuity: Masculinity and Heroic Representation at the Court of Henry IV." *French Historical Studies* 26.2 (Spring 2003): 225–52.
- *The Sexual Culture of the French Renaissance*. Cambridge: Cambridge University Press, 2010.
Cremer, Albert. *Der Adel in der Verfassung des Ancien Régime: Die Châtellenie d'Epernay und die Souveraineté de Charleville im 17. Jahrhundert*. Bonn: Ludwig Röhrscheid Verlag, 1981.
Crépin-Leblond, Thierry. "Le développement des arts décoratifs: un modèle médicéen?" In *Marie de Médicis: Un gouvernement part les arts*, edited by Paola Bassini Pacht, T. Crépin-Leblond, N. Sainte Fare Garnot, and F. Solinas, 226–31. Paris: Somogy; Blois: Château de Blois, 2003.
Cross, Robert. "'Closer Together and Further Apart' – Religious Politics and Political Culture in the British-Spanish Match, 1596–1625." In *Stuart Marriage Diplomacy: Dynastic Politics in Their European Context, 1604–1630*, edited by Valentina Caldari and Sara J. Wolfson. Woodbridge: Boydell and Brewer, 2018.
- "To Counterbalance the World. England, Spain, and Peace in the Early Seventeenth Century." 2 vols. PhD diss., Princeton University, 2012.
Crouzet, Denis. *Les guerriers de Dieu: La violence au temps des troubles de religion (vers 1525 – vers 1610)*. Paris: Champs Vallon, 1990.
- *Le haut coeur de Catherine de Médicis*. Paris: Albin Michel, 2005.
- "King of Reason." *From Valois to Bourbon: Dynasty, State and Society in Early Modern France*, edited by Keith Cameron, 73–106. Exeter: Exeter University Press, 1989.

Cummings, Mark. "The Social Impact of the Paulette: The Case of the Parlement of Paris." *Canadian Journal of History/Annales canadiennes d'histoire* 15.3 (1980): 329–54.

Cusick, Suzanne G. "Francesca Caccini." In *New Grove Dictionary of Women Composers*, edited by Julie Anne Sadie and Rhien Samuel, 94–8. London: Macmillan, 1994.

– *Francesca Caccini at the Medici Court: Music and the Circulation of Power.* Chicago: University of Chicago Press, 2009.

– "Settimia Caccini." In *New Grove Dictionary of Women Composers*, edited by Julie Anne Saide and Rhian Samuel, 98–9. London: Macmillan, 1994.

Dartois-Lapeyre, Françoise. "Turcs et turqueries dans les 'représentations en musique' (XVIIe–XVIIe siècles)." In *Turcs et turqueries: XVIe–XVIIe siècles*, preface by Lucien Bély, 161–215. Paris: Presses de l'Université Paris-Sorbonne, 2009.

Datson, Lorraine, and Katharine Parks. *Wonders and The Order of Nature, 1150–1750*. New York: Zone Books, 1998.

Davis, Natalie Zemon. *Fiction in the Archives: Pardon Tales and their Tellers in Sixteenth-Century France.* Stanford: Stanford University Press, 1987.

– *The Gift in Sixteenth-Century France.* Madison: University of Wisconsin Press, 2000.

DeJean, Joan. *Tender Geographies: Women and the Origins of the Novel in France.* New York: Columbia University Press, 1991.

Dent, Julian. *Crisis in Finance: Crown, Financiers, and Society in Seventeenth-Century France.* Newton Abbot: David and Charles, 1973.

Derrida, Jacques. *Given Time. 1. Counterfeit Money.* Translated by Peggy Kamuf. Chicago: University of Chicago Press, 1992.

– "Hostipitality," translated by Barry Stocker with Forbes Morlock. *Angelaki* 5.3 (December 2000): 3–18.

– *On Hospitality: Anne Dufourmantelle Invites Jacques Derrida to Respond.* Stanford: Stanford University Press, 2000. Originally published as *De l'hospitalité: Anne Dufourmantelle invite Jacques Derrida à répondre.* Paris: Calmann-Lévy, 1997.

Descimon, Robert, and Alain Guéry. "Un état des temps modernes?" In *L'État et les pouvoirs*, edited by Jacques Le Goff, 181–356. Paris: Seuil, 1989.

Desplat, Christian. "Henri IV et les Ottomans." In *Henri IV, le roi et la reconstruction du royaume: Volume des actes du colloque Pau-Nérac, 14–17 septembre 1989*, 395–422. Pau: Association Henri IV; J&D Editions, 1990.

Dickerman, Edmund H. "Henri IV and the Juliens-Clèves Crisis: The Psychohistorical Aspects." *French Historical Studies* 8.4 (1974): 626–53.

Dickerman, Edmund H., and Anita N. Walker. "Monuments of His Own Magnificence: Henrichemont and the Archaeology of Sully's Mind." *French History* 6 (1992): 159–84.
Dictionnnaire historique de la langue française. 1998. 3 vols., edited by Alain Rey. Paris: Le Robert, 2006.
Diefendorf, Barbara. "Henri IV, the Dévots and the Making of a French Catholic Reformation." In *Politics and Religion in Early Bourbon France*, edited by Alison Forrestal and Eric Nelson, 157–79. New York and London: Palgrave Macmillan, 2009.
Dillon, Janette. *The Language of Space in Court Performance, 1400–1625*. Cambridge: Cambridge University Press, 2010.
Djuvara, T.G. *Cent projets de partage de la Turquie (1281–1913)*. Paris: Librairie Félix Alcan, 1914.
Dobbins, Frank. "Les airs pour luth de Charles Tessier." In *Luths et luthistes en Occident. Actes du colloque organisé par la cité de la musique, 13–15 mai 1998*, 169–84. Paris: Cité de la Musique, 1999.
– "Caroubel, Pierre Francisque." *Grove Music Online*. http://www.oxfordmusiconline.com/grovemusic/view/10.1093/gmo/9781561592630.001.0001/omo-9781561592630-e-0000004988.
– "The Lute Airs of Charles Tessier." *Lute Society Journal* 20 (1978): 23–42.
Dorothée, Vincent. "Le mécénat de Catherine de Bourbon et les arts du spectacle à la cour de Lorraine (1589–1604)." In *Henri IV: Art et pouvoir*, edited by Colette Nativel, 163–78. Tours et Rennes: Presses Universitaires François Rabelais, Presses Universitaires de Rennes, 2016.
Dubost, Jean-François. "L'Épouse." In *Marie de Médicis et le Palais du Luxembourg*, edited by Marie-Noëlle Baudouin-Matuszek, 101–10. Paris: Délégation à l'action artistique de la ville de Paris [Hachette], 1991.
– "Goûts et entourages musicaux auprès de Marie de Médicis (v. 1600–1620)." In *Poésie, musique et société: L'air de cour en France au XVIIe siècle*, edited by Georgie Durosoir, 19–27. Sprimont: Mardaga, 2006.
– *Marie de Médicis: La reine dévoilée*. Paris: Éditions Payot & Rivages, 2009.
Duchêne, Roger. *Les précieuses, ou comment l'esprit vint aux femmes*. Paris: Librairie Arthème Fayard, 2001.
Ducos, Blaise. "The Portrait of doña Maria de' Medici by Frans Pourbus the Younger or, the Habsburg temptation at the French court." *B'09: Buletina = Boletín = Bulletin* (Bilbao Fine Arts Museum) 5 (2010): 109–37.
Duerloo, Luc. "Cleopatra's Pearl: Jewellery and the European Courts." In *Brilliant Europe: Jewels from European Courts*, edited by Diana Scarisbrick, Christophe Vachaudez, and Jan Walgrave, 14–27. Brussels: Mercatorfonds; Brussels: ING, 2008.

- "Marriage, Power and Politics: The Infanta and Archduke Albert." In *Isabel Clara Eugenia: Female Sovereignty in the Courts of Madrid and Brussels*, edited by Cordula van Wyhe, 154–79. Madrid: Centro de Estudios Europa Hispanica; London: Paul Holberton Publishing, 2011.
Duerloo, Luc, and R. Malcolm Smuts, eds. *The Age of Rubens. Diplomacy, Dynastic Politics and the Visual Arts in Early Seventeenth-Century Europe*. Turnhout: Brepols, 2016.
Duindam, Jeroen. *Myths of Power Norbert Elias and the Early Modern European Court*. Amsterdam: Amsterdam University Press, 1995.
- "Palace, City, Dominions: The Spatial Dimension of Habsburg Rule." In *The Politics of Space: European Courts ca. 1500–1750*, edited by Marcello Fantoni, Malcolm Smuts, and George Gorse, 59–90. Rome: Bulzoni, 2009.
- *Vienna and Versailles: The Courts of Europe's Dynastic Rivals, 1550–1780*. Cambridge: Cambridge University Press, 2003.
Durosoir, Georgie. *L'air de cour en France 1571–1655*. Liège: Mardaga, 1991.
- "L'allégorie de la renommée royale dans les airs de ballet au temps de Louis XIII." In *Le chant, acteur de l'histoire*, edited by Jean Quéniart, 77–88. Rennes: Presses Universitaires de Rennes, 1999.
- *Les ballets de la cour de France au XVIIe siècle*. Geneva: Papillon, 2004.
Elder, Glen, Jennifer Wolch, and Jody Emel. "Race, Place, and the Bounds of Humanity." *Society and Animals* 6 (1998): 183–202.
Fagniez, Gustave. *Le père Joseph et Richelieu (1577–1638)*. 2 vols. Paris: Librairie Hachette, 1894.
Fantoni, Marcello. "The City of the Prince: Space and Power." In *The Politics of Space: European Courts ca. 1500–1750*, edited by Marcello Fantoni, Malcolm Smuts, and George Gorse, 39–57. Rome: Bulzoni, 2009.
Fantoni, Marcello, Malcolm Smuts, and George Gorse, eds. *The Politics of Space: European Courts ca. 1500–1750*. Rome: Bulzoni, 2009.
Fenlon, Iain. "The Origins of the Seventeenth-Century Staged Ballo." In *Con Che Soavità: Studies in Italian Opera, Song, and Dance, 1580–1740*, edited by Iain Fenlon and Tim Carter, 13–40. Oxford: Clarendon Press, 1995.
Feret, M. L'Abbé P. *Henri IV et l'église*. Paris: Librairie Victor Palmé, 1875.
Ferrière, Hector de la. *Trois amoureuses au XVIe siècle*. Paris: Calmann Lévy, 1885.
ffolliott, Sheila. "Casting a Rival into the Shade: Catherine de' Medici and Diane de Poitiers." *Art Journal* 48.2 (Summer 1989): 138–43.
- "Catherine de' Medici as Artemisia: Figuring the Powerful Widow in Early Modern Europe." In *Rewriting the Renaissance: The Discourses of Sexual Difference in Early Modern Europe*, edited by Margaret W. Ferguson, Maureen Quilligan, and Nancy Vickers, 227–41. Chicago: University of Chicago Press, 1986.

Finley-Croswhite, S. Annette. *Henry IV and the Towns: The Pursuit of Legitimacy in French Urban Society, 1589–1610*. Cambridge: Cambridge University Press, 1999.
Fogel, Michele. *Les cérémonies de l'information dans la France du XVIe au XVIIIe siècle*. Paris: Fayard, 1989.
Forrestal, Alison, and Eric Nelson, eds. *Politics and Religion in Early Bourbon France*. New York and London: Palgrave Macmillan, 2009.
Franko, Mark. *Dance as Text: Ideologies of the Baroque Body*. Cambridge: Cambridge University Press, 1993.
– "Fragment of the Sovereign as Hermaphrodite: Time, History, and the Exception in *Le Ballet de Madame*." *Dance Research* 25.2 (Winter 2007): 119–33.
– "Geometrical Dance in French Court Ballet." In *Proceedings of the Ninth Annual Conference of Dance History Scholars*, 13–30. N.p.: University of California Riverside, 1986.
– "Renaissance Conduct Literature and the Basse Danse: The Kinesis of Bonne Grace." In *Persons in Groups: Social Behavior as Identity Formation in Medieval and Renaissance Europe*, edited by Richard C. Trexler, 55–66. Binghamton, NY: Medieval and Renaissance Texts and Studies, 1985.
Frappier, Louise. "Construction de la figure monarchique et perfection divine dans les récits d'entrée royale à Avignon (1600 et 1622)." *EMF: Studies in Early Modern France* 12 (2008): 26–43.
Freer (Robinson), Martha. *Henry IV and Marie de Medici*. 2 vols. London: Hurst and Blackett, 1861.
Fromilhague, René. *La vie de Malherbe, apprentissages et luttes, 1555–1610*. Paris: A. Colin, 1954.
Galletti, Sara. *Marie de Médicis et le Palais du Luxembourg, 1611–1642*. Paris: Éditions Picard, 2012.
Gardiner, Samuel R. *History of England from the Accession of James I to the Outbreak of the Civil War 1603–1642*. 10 vols. London: Longmans, Green, and Co., 1883.
Garnier, Edouard. *Nains et géants*. Paris: Hachette, 1884.
Gérold, Théodore. *L'art du chant en France au XVIIe siècle*. Strasbourg: Commission des Publications de la Faculté des Lettres, 1921.
Giesey, Ralph. *Cérémonial et puissance souveraine. France, XVe–XVIIe siècles*. Paris: A. Colin, 1987.
– "The Juristic Basis of Dynastic Right to the French Throne." *Transactions of the American Philosophical Society* 51.5 (1961): 3–47.
– *Le rôle méconnu de la loi salique. La succession royal, XIVe–XVIe siècles*. Translated by Frank Regnot. Paris: Les Belles Lettres, 2007.
– *The Royal Funeral Ceremony in France*. Geneva: Librairie Droz, 1960.

- *Rulership in France, 15th–17th Centuries*. Aldershot: Ashgate, 2004.
Gilder, Rosamond. *Enter the Actress: The First Women in the Theatre*. Boston: Houghton Mifflin, 1931.
Gioanni, Florence. *La société aristocratique française du XVIème siècle et la musique: Le cas de Marguerite de Valois (1553–1615)*. 2 vols. Villeneuve d'Ascq: Presses Universitaires du Septentrion, 1996.
Goffman, Daniel. *The Ottoman Empire and Early Modern Europe*. Cambridge: Cambridge University Press, 2002.
Gough, Melinda J. "Courtly *Comédiantes*: Henrietta Maria and Women's Amateur Stage Plays in France and England." In *Women Players in Early Modern England, 1500–1650: Beyond the "All-Male Stage,"* edited by Pamela Allen Brown and Peter Parolin, 193–215. Aldershot: Ashgate Press, 2005.
- "Dynastic Marriage, Diplomatic Ceremonial, and the Treaties of London (1604–05) and Antwerp (1609)." *Stuart Marriage Diplomacy: Dynastic Politics in Their European Context, 1604–1630*, edited by Valentina Caldari and Sara J. Wolfson, 287–301. Woodbridge: Boydell and Brewer, 2018.
- "Marie de Medici's 1605 *ballet de la reine*: New Evidence and Analysis." *Early Theatre* 15.1 (June 2012): 109–44.
- "Marie de Medici's 1605 *ballet de la reine* and the Virtuosic Female Voice." *Early Modern Women: An Interdisciplinary Journal* 7 (2012): 127–56.
- "A Newly Discovered Performance by Henrietta Maria." *Huntington Library Quarterly* 65.3–4 (2002): 435–47.
- "'Not as myself': The Queen's Voice in *Tempe Restored*." *Modern Philology* 101.1 (August 2003): 48–67.
Gough, Melinda J., and Perry Gethner. "The Advent of Women Players and Playwrights in Early Modern France." *Renaissance Drama* 44.2 (Fall 2016): 217–32.
Gough, Melinda J., and Clare McManus, eds. "Transnational Mobility and Female Performance in Early Modern Europe." *Renaissance Drama* 44.2 (2016): 187–275.
Gravit, Francis W. *The Peiresc Papers*. Ann Arbor: University of Michigan Press, 1950.
Graziani, Françoise, and Francesco Solinas, eds. *Le 'siècle' de Marie de Médicis. Actes du Séminaire de la Chaire rhétorique et société en Europe (XVIe–XVIIe siècles)*. Alessandria: Edizioni dell'Orso, 2003.
Greene, Thomas M. "The King's One Body in the *Ballet Comique de la Royne*." *Yale French Studies* 86 (1994): 75–93.
Greengrass, Mark."Epilogue. Regime Change: Restoration, Reconstruction, and Reformation." In *Politics and Religion in Early Bourbon France*, edited by

Alison Forrestal and Eric Nelson, 246–60. New York and London: Palgrave Macmillan, 2009.
- *France in the Age of Henri IV: The Struggle for Stability*. London: Longman, 1995.
Guichard, Léon. "L'entrée de la reine Marie de Médicis à Avignon en 1600." In *Poesia e musica nell'estetica del XVI e XVII secolo: [Atti] convegni internationali di musicologia del centro studi Rinascimento musicale, villa medica "La Ferdinanda" Artimino (Firenze): 3–10 maggio 1976*, 23–34. Firenze: Centro Studi Rinascimento Musicale, ca. 1979.
Guillo, Laurent. *Pierre I Ballard et Robert III Ballard, imprimeurs du roy pour la musique (1599–1673)*. 2 vols. Sprimont: Mardaga, 2003.
Guizot, M. [François]. *The History of France From The Earliest Times to 1848*. Translated by Robert Black. 8 vols. New York: John B. Alden, 1885.
Hackenbroch, Yvonne. *Enseignes*. Firenze: Studio per Edizioni Scelte, 1996.
Hamilton, Alaistair, and Francis Richard. *André du Ryer and Oriental Studies in Seventeenth-Century France*. London: Oxford University Press, 2004.
Hanley, Sarah. "Configuring the Political Authority of Queens in France, 1600s–1840s." *Historical Reflections/Réflexions Historiques* 32.2 (2006): 453–64.
- ed. *Les droits des femmes et la loi salique*. Paris: Indigo & Côté-femmes, 1994.
- "Engendering the State: Family Formation and State Building in Early Modern France." *French Historical Studies* 16.1 (1989): 4–27.
- *The "Lit de Justice" of the Kings of France: Constitutional Ideology in Legend, Ritual, and Discourse*. Princeton: Princeton University Press, 1983.
- "The Monarchic State in Early Modern France: Marital Regime, Government and Male Right." In *Politics, Ideology and the Law in Early Modern Europe*, edited by Adrianna E. Bakos, 107–26. Rochester: University of Rochester Press, 1994.
Hanning, Barbara R. "Glorious Apollo: Poetic and Political Themes in the First Opera." *Renaissance Quarterly* 32.4 (Winter 1979): 485–513.
Haran, Alexandre Y. *Le lys et le globe. Messianisme dynastique et rêve impérial en France à l'aube des temps modernes*. Seyssel: Champ Vallon, 2000.
Hayden, Michael J. "Continuity in the France of Henry IV and Louis XIII: French Foreign Policy, 1598–1615." *Journal of Modern History* 45.1 (1973): 1–23.
Heal, Felicity. *Hospitality in Early Modern England*. Oxford: Oxford University Press, 1990.
Heartz, Daniel. "Un ballet turc à la cour d'Henri II: Les branles de Malte." *Baroque* 5 (1972): 1–8.
Henrard, Paul. *Henri IV et la princesse de Condé, 1609–1610*. Brussels: Merzbach and Falk, 1885.

Hoddinnott, R.F. *The Thracians*. London: Thames and Hudson, 1981.
Hoogleviet, Margriet. "The *Balet de la* Reyne (1609) and the Politics of Vertu: Media and Political Communication." In *Selling and Rejecting Politics in Early Modern Europe*, edited by Martin Gosman and Joop W. Koopmans, 71–91. Leuven: Peeters, 2007.
Howard, Skiles. *The Politics of Courtly Dancing in Early Modern England*. Amherst: University of Massachussetts Press, 1998.
Humbert, Jacques. "Charles de Nevers et la milice chrétienne 1598–1625." *Revue Internationale d'Histoire Militaire* LXVIII (1988): 85–114.
Hutchings, Mark, and Berta Cano-Echevarría. "Between Courts: Female Masquers and Anglo-Spanish Diplomacy, 1603–5." *Early Theatre* 15.1 (2012): 91–108.
Isom-Verhaaren, Christine. *Allies with the Infidel: The Ottoman and French Alliance in the Sixteenth Century*. London: I.B. Tauris, 2011.
Jackson, Richard A. *Vive le roi!: A History of the French Coronation from Charles V to Charles X*. Chapel Hill: University of North Carolina Press, 1984.
Jacob, Margaret C. *Strangers Nowhere in the World: The Rise of Cosmopolitanism in Early Modern Europe*. Philadelphia: University of Pennsylvania Press, 2006.
Jaffe-Berg, Erith. *Commedia dell'Arte and the Mediterranean: Charting Journeys and Mapping "Others."* Farham: Ashgate Publishing Limited, 2015.
James, Carolyn. "Women and Diplomacy in Renaissance Italy." In *Women, Diplomacy and International Politics since 1500*, edited by Glenda Sluga and Carolyn James, 13–29. New York and London: Routledge, 2016.
Jardine, Lisa. *Worldly Goods: A New History of the Renaissance*. New York: W.W. Norton, 1996.
Jardine, Lisa, and Jerry Brotton. *Global Interests: Renaissance Art Between West and East*. Ithaca: Cornell University Press, 2000.
Johnston, Francis E. "Some Observations on the Roles of Achondroplastic Dwarfs through History." *Clinical Pediatrics* 2.12 (1963): 703–9.
Jones, Ann Rosalind. *The Currency of Eros: Women's Love Lyric in Europe, 1540–1620*. Bloomington: Indiana University Press, 1990.
Jones, Mark. "Guillaume Dupré (c. 159–1640)." In *The Currency of Fame: Portrait Medals of the Renaissance*, edited by Stephen K. Scher, 319–37. New York: The Frick/Harry N. Adams, 1994.
Jouanna, Arlette. *L'idée de race en France au XVIe siècle et au début du XVIIe*, revised ed. 2 vols. Montpellier: Presses Imprimerie de Recherche-Université Paul Valéry, Montpellier III, 1981.
– "La noblesse française et les valeurs guerrières au XVIe siècle." In *L'homme de guerre au XVIe siècle*, edited by Gabriel-André Perouse, André Thierry, and André Tournon, 205–17. Saint-Etienne: Université de Saint-Etienne, 1993.

– *Ordre social: Mythes et hiérarchies dans la France du XVIe siècle*. Paris: Hachette, 1977.
Kane, Brendan, with R. Malcolm Smuts. "The Politics of Race in England, Scotland, and Ireland." In *The Oxford Handbook of the Age of Shakespeare*, edited by R. Malcolm Smuts, 346–63. Oxford: Oxford University Press, 2016.
Katritzky, M.A. *Healing, Performance, and Ceremony in the Writings of Three Early Modern Physicians: Hippolytus Guarinonius and the Brothers Felix and Thomas Platter*. Burlington: Ashgate, 2012.
Kelly, Donald E. "Murd'rous Machiavel in France: A Post Mortem." *Political Science Quarterly* 85.4 (1970): 545–59.
Keohane, Nannerl O. *Philosophy and the State in France: The Renaissance and the Enlightenment*. Princeton: Princeton University Press, 1980.
Kermina, Françoise. *Marie de Médicis: Reine, régente et rebelle*. Paris: Librairie Académique Perrin, 2010.
Kettering, Sharon. "Favour and Patronage: Dancers and Patronage in the Court Ballets of Early Seventeenth-Century France." *Canadian Journal of History/Annales canadiennes d'histoire* 43 (Winter/Hiver 2008): 391–415.
– *Power and Reputation at the Court of Louis XIII: The Career of Charles D'Albert, duc de Luynes (1578–1621)*. Manchester: Manchester University Press, 2008.
Kingdon, Robert M. "Calvinism and Resistance Theory, 1550–1580." In *The Cambridge History of Political Thought 1450–1700*, edited by J.H. Burns, 193–218. Cambridge: Cambridge University Press, 1991.
Knecht, R.J. *The French Renaissance Court, 1483–1589*. New Haven: Yale University Press, 2008.
Kociszewka, Ewa. "War and Seduction in Cybele's Garden: Contextualizing the *Ballet des Polonais*." *Renaissance Quarterly* 65.3 (Fall 2012): 809–63.
Kristeller, Paul O. "The European Significance of Florentine Platonism." In *Medieval and Renaissance Studies: Proceedings of the Southeastern Institute of Medieval and Renaissance Studies, Summer 1967*, edited by John M. Headley, 206–29. Chapel Hill: University of North Carolina Press, 1968.
Lacombe, Étienne Charles Mercier de. *Henri IV et sa politique*, second ed. Paris: Librairie Académique/Didier, 1863.
Lancaster, Henry. "Errors in Beauchamps's *Recherches sur les théâtres de France*." *MLN* 37 (1922): 466–9. Reprinted in Henry Lancaster, *Adventures of a Literary Historian*, 349–52. 1942. Freeport, NY: Books for Libraries Press, 1968.
Landini, Roberta Orsi. "Lo stile fiorentino alla corte di Francia: Il guardaroba di Maria." In *Maria de' Medici (1573–1642), una principessa fiorentina sul trono di Francia*, edited by Caterina Caneva and Francesco Solinas, 146–50. Florence: Sillabe, 2005.

Larson, Katherine R. *Early Modern Women in Conversation*. New York: Palgrave Macmillan, 2011.
Laugel, Auguste. *Henry de Rohan, son rôle politique et militaire sous Louis XIII (1579–1638)*. Paris: Firmin-Didot, 1889.
Lawrence, Jason. *"Who the Devil Taught Thee So Much Italian?" Italian Language Learning and Literary Imitation in Early Modern England*. Manchester: Manchester University Press, 2005.
Le Roux, Nicolas. *La faveur du roi. Mignons et courtisans au temps des derniers Valois (vers 1547 – vers 1589)*. 2000. Seysell: Éditions Champ Vallon, 2013.
– "The Politics of Festivals at the Court of the Last Valois." In *Court Festivals of the European Renaissance: Art, Politics and Performance*, edited by J.R. Mulryne and Elizabeth Goldring, 101–17. Aldershot: Ashgate, 2002.
Lecomte, Nathalie. *Entre cours et jardins d'illusion. Le ballet en Europe (1515–1715)*. [Pantin]: Centre National de la Danse, 2014.
Lecoq, Anne-Marie. *François Ier imaginaire: Symbolique et politique à l'aube de la Renaissance française*. Paris: Macula, 1987.
Lee Jr, Maurice. *James I and Henry IV: An Essay in Foreign Policy, 1603–1610*. Urbana: University of Illinois Press, 1970.
Les arts au temps d'Henri IV. Pau: Association Henri IV 1989; J&D Editions, 1992.
Lesure, François. "Le Recueil de Ballets de Michel Henry." In *Les fêtes de la Renaissance*, edited by Jean Jacquot, 205–19. Paris: Éditions du Centre National de la Recherche Scientifique, 1956.
Lesure, François, and G. Thibault. *Bibliographie des éditions d'Adrian Le Roy et Robert Ballard (1551–1598)*. Paris: Société Française de Musicologie, 1955.
Livet, Charles Louis. *Précieux et précieuses*. Leipzig, Paris: Welter, 1895.
Loades, David. *Elizabeth I*. London: Hambledon Continuum, 2003.
Loisel, Gustave. *Histoire des ménageries de l'antiquité à nos jours*. Paris: Doin et Fils, 1912.
Loomie, Albert J. *Toleration and Diplomacy: The Religious Issue in Anglo-Spanish Relations, 1603–1605*. N.p.: The American Philosophical Society, n.s., vol. 53, part 6, 1963.
– ed. *Ceremonies of Charles I*. New York: Fordham University Press, 1987.
Lougee, Carolyn. *Le Paradis des Femmes: Women, Salons, and Social Stratification in Seventeenth-Century France*. Princeton: Princeton University Press, 1976.
Maclean, Ian. *Woman Triumphant: Feminism in French Literature 1610–1652*. Oxford: Clarendon Press, 1977.
MacNeil, Anne. *Music and Women of the Commedia dell'Arte in the Late Sixteenth Century*. New York: Oxford University Press, 2003.
Maître, Myriam. *Les précieuses: Naissance des femmes de lettres en France au XVIIe siècle*. Paris: Champion, 2008.

Mamone, Sara. *Dei, semidei, uomini: Lo spettacolo a Firenze tra neoplatonismo e realta borghese (XV–XVII secolo)*. Rome: Bulzoni, 2003.
– "Feste e spettacoli a Firenze e in Francia per le nozze di Maria de' Medici con Enrico IV." *Quaderni di teatro* 2 (1980): 206–28.
– *Paris et Florence. Deux capitales du spectacle pour une reine: Marie de Médicis*. Translated by Sophie Bajard and Françoise Decroisette. Paris: Seuil, 1990. Originally published as *Firenze e Parigi: Due capitali dello spettacolo per una regina, Maria de' Medici*. Milan: Silvana Editoriale, 1988.
– "Slittamenti progressivi della festa da Firenze a Lione per le nozze di Maria de' Medici con Enrico IV di Francia." *Medioevo e Rinascimento* 1 (1987): 309–22.
Mann, J.G. *Wallace Collection Catalogues. Sculpture, Marbles, Terra-cottas and Bronzes, Carvings in Ivory and Wood, Plaquettes, Medals, Coins, and Wax-reliefs*. London: H.M. Stationery Office, 1931.
Marchante-Aragón, Lucas. "Temples of Dynastic Memory in the Seventeenth Century: Valladolid and London." *Viator* 36 (2005): 603–24.
Marrow, Deborah. *The Art Patronage of Maria de' Medici*. Studies in Baroque Art History. N.p.: University of Pennsylvania, 1978.
Martin, Meredith, and Gillian Weiss. "'Turks' on Display during the Reign of Louis XIV." *L'Esprit Créateur* 53.4 (Winter 2013): 98–112.
Martin-Ulrich, Claudie. *La persona de la princesse au XVIe siècle: Personnage littéraire et personnage politique*. Paris: Champion, 2004.
Masera, Maria Giovanna. "La familia Caccini alla corte di Maria de' Medici." *Rassegna musicale* 13 (1940): 481–4.
Matar, Nabil. *Islam in Britain, 1558–1685*. Cambridge: Cambridge University Press, 1998.
– *Turks, Moors, and Englishmen in the Age of Discovery*. New York: Columbia University Press, 1999.
Mathorez, J. "À propos d'une campagne de presse contre l'Espagne." *Bulletin du bibliophile et du bibliothécaire* (1913): 313–29.
Mattingly, Garrett. *Renaissance Diplomacy*. 1955. New York: Cosimo Classics, 2008.
Mauss, Marcel. *The Gift: The Form and Reason For Exchange in Archaic Societies*. 1925. Translated by W.D. Halls. New York: W.W. Norton, 1990.
Mazerolle, Fernand. *Les médailleurs français du XVe siècle au milieu du XVIIe*. Paris: Imprimerie Nationale, 1902–4.
McCabe, Ina Baghdiantz. *Orientalism in Early Modern France*. Oxford and New York: Berg, 2008.
McCartney, Elizabeth. "Ceremonies and Privileges of Office: Queenship in Late Medieval France." In *Power of the Weak: Studies on Medieval Women*, edited by Jennifer Carpenter and Sally-Beth McLean, 178–219. Urbana: University of Illinois Press, 1995.

- "The King's Mother and Royal Prerogative in Early-Sixteenth-Century France." In *Medieval Queenship*, edited by John Parsons, 117–41. New York: St Martin's Press, 1993.
- "Queens in the Cult of the French Renaissance Monarchy: Selected Studies in Royal Ceremonial, Public Law, and Political Discourse, 1484–1610." PhD diss., University of Iowa, 1998.

McClary, Susan. *Desire and Pleasure in Seventeenth-Century Music*. Berkeley and Los Angeles: University of California Press, 2012.

McClure, Ellen. *Sun Spots and the Sun King: Sovereignty and Mediation in Seventeenth-Century France*. Champaign: University of Illinois Press, 2006.

McGowan, Margaret. *L'art du ballet de cour en France 1581–1643*. Paris: Éditions du Centre National de la Recherche Scientifique, 1963.

- ed. and intro. *Le ballet comique par Balthazar de Beaujoyeulx* (1581). Binghamton, NY: Medieval and Renaissance Texts and Studies, 1982.
- *Dance in the Renaissance: European Fashion, French Obsession*. New Haven: Yale University Press, 2008.
- ed. *Dynastic Marriages 1612/15: A Celebration of the Habsburg Bourbon Unions*. Farnham: Ashgate, 2013.
- "Les Jésuites à Avignon. Les fêtes au service de la propaganda politique et religieuse." In *Les fêtes de la Renaissance III*, edited by Jean Jacquot and Elie Konigson, 153–71. Paris: Éditions du Centre National de la Recherche Scientifique, 1975.
- "Recollections of Dancing Forms from Sixteenth-Century France." *Dance Research* 21.1 (2003): 10–26.

McIlvenna, Una. *Scandal and Reputation at the Court of Catherine de Medici*. London and New York: Routledge, 2016.

- "'A Stable of Whores'? The Flying Squadron of Catherine de Medici." In *The Politics of Female Households: Ladies-in-Waiting across Early Modern Europe*, edited by Nadine Akkerman and Birgit Houben, 181–208. Leiden: Brill, 2014.

McManus, Clare. *Women on the Renaissance Stage: Anna of Denmark and Female Masquing in the Stuart Court 1590–1619*. Manchester: Manchester University Press, 2002.

Merki, Charles. *La marquise de Verneuil (Henriette de Balzac d'Entragues) et la mort d'Henri IV*. Paris: Plon-Nourrit, 1912.

- *La reine Margot et la fin des Valois (1553–1615) d'après les mémoires et les documents*. Paris: Plon-Nourrit, 1905.

Millen, Ronald Forsyth, and Robert Erich Wolf. *Heroic Deeds and Mystic Figures: A New Reading of Rubens' Life of Marie de' Medici*. Princeton: Princeton University Press, 1989.

Mitchell, Silvia Z. "Marriage Plots: Royal Women, Marriage Diplomacy and International Politics at the Spanish, French and Imperial Courts, 1665–1659." In *Women, Diplomacy and International Politics since 1500*, edited by Glenda Sluga and Carolyn James, 86–106. New York and London: Routledge, 2016.

Morselli, Raffaella. "Rubens and the Spell of the Gonzaga Collections." In *The Age of Rubens. Diplomacy, Dynastic Politics and the Visual Arts in Early Seventeenth-Century Europe*, edited by Luc Duerloo and R. Malcolm Smuts, 21–37. Turnhout: Brepols, 2016.

Morton, Adam. "Introduction: Politics, Culture and Queens Consort." In *Queens Consort, Cultural Transfer and European Politics, c. 1500–1800*, edited by Helen Watanabe-O'Kelly and Adam Morton, 1–14. London and New York: Routledge, 2017.

Mousnier, Roland. *The Assassination of Henry IV*. Translated by Joan Spencer. London: Faber and Faber, 1973.

– *The Institutions of France under the Absolute Monarchy 1598–1789*. 2 vols. Chicago: University of Chicago Press, 1979.

– *La vénalité des offices sous Henri IV et Louis XIII*. Paris: Presses Universitaires de France, 1971.

Mousset, Albert. "Les droits de l'infante Isabelle-Claire-Eugénie à la couronne de France." *Bulletin Hispanique* 16.1 (1914): 46–79. https://doi:10.3406/hispa.1914.1849.

Nativel, Colette, ed. *Henri IV: Art et pouvoir*. Tours et Rennes: Presses Universitaires François Rabelais, Presses Universitaires de Rennes, 2016.

Nelson, Eric. *The Jesuits and the Monarchy: Catholic Reform and Political Authority in France (1590–1615)*. Aldershot and Burlington: Ashgate; Rome: Institutum Historicum Societatis Iesu, 2005.

– "*Religion Royale* in the Sacred Landscape of Paris: the Jesuit Church of Saint Louis and the Resacralization of Kingship in Early Bourbon France (1590–1650)." In *Layered Landscapes: Early Modern Religious Space across Faiths and Cultures*, edited by Eric Nelson and Jonathan Wright, 277–302. London: Routledge, 2017.

– "Royal Authority and the Pursuit of a Lasting Religious Settlement: Henri IV and the Emergence of the Bourbon Monarchy." In *Politics and Religion in Early Bourbon France*, edited by Alison Forrestal and Eric Nelson, 107–31. New York: Palgrave Macmillan, 2009.

Nevile, Jennifer. "Dance in Europe 1250–1750." In *Dance, Spectacle, and the Body Politick, 1250–1750*, edited by Jennifer Nevile, 7–64. Bloomington: Indiana University Press, 2008.

– *The Eloquent Body: Dance and Humanist Culture in Fifteenth-Century Italy.* Bloomington: Indiana University Press, 2004.
Newcomb, Anthony. *The Madrigal at Ferrara 1579–1597.* 2 vols. Princeton: Princeton University Press, 1980.
Nordera, Marina. "Ballet de cour." Translated by Jonathan Steinberg. *The Cambridge Companion to Ballet,* edited by Marion Kant, 19–31. Cambridge: Cambridge University Press, 2007.
Ó hAnnracháin, Tadhg. *Catholic Europe, 1592–1648: Centre and Peripheries.* Oxford: Oxford University Press, 2015.
Oestreich, Gerhard. *Neostoicism and the Early Modern State.* Edited by Brigitta Oestreich and H.G. Koenigsberger, translated by David McLintock. Cambridge: Cambridge University Press, 1982.
Oliván Santaliestra, Laura. "Lady Anne Fanshawe, Ambassadress of England at the Court of Madrid (1664–1666)." In *Women, Diplomacy and International Politics since 1500,* edited by Glenda Sluga and Carolyn James, 68–85. New York and London: Routledge, 2016.
Oresko, Robert. "Princes Étrangers." In *Dictionnaire de l'ancien régime,* edited by Philippe Guignet et al., 1018–20. Paris: Presses Universitaires de France, 1996.
Palmer, Daryl W. *Hospitable Performances: Dramatic Genre and Cultural Practices in Early Modern England.* West Lafayette: Purdue University Press, 1992.
Paquot, Marcel. "Comédies-ballets représentés en l'honneur de Madame, soeur du roi Henri IV." *Revue Belge de philologie et d'histoire* 10 (1931): 965–95.
– *Les étrangers dans les divertissements de la cour de Beaujoyeulx à Molière, 1581–1673.* N.p.: La Renaissance du Livre, n.d.
– "Madame de Rohan, auteur de comédies-ballets." *Revue Belge de philologie et d'histoire* 8 (1929): 801–29.
Pardoe, Julia. *The Life of Marie de Medicis, Queen of France, Consort of Henry IV, and Regent of the Kingdom Under Louis XIII.* 3 vols. London: Colburn and Co., 1852.
Parolin, Peter, ed. "Access and Contestation: Women's Performance in Early Modern England, Italy, France, and Spain." Special Volume. *Early Theatre* 15.1 (2012).
Parrott, David. "The Mantuan Succession, 1627–31: A Sovereignty Dispute in Early Modern Europe." *English Historical Review* 112 (1997): 20–65.
– "A 'Prince Souverain' and the French Crown: Charles de Nevers, 1580–1637." In *Royal and Republican Sovereignty in Early Modern Europe,* edited by Robert Oresko, G.C. Gibbs, and H.M. Scott, 149–87. Cambridge: Cambridge University Press, 1997.

- *Richelieu's Army: War, Government and Society in France, 1624–1642.* Cambridge: Cambridge University Press, 2001.

Paster, Gail Kern. "Eschewing Politeness: Norbert Elias and the Historiography of Early Modern Affect." *PMLA* 130.5 (October 2015): 1443–9.

Perrens, F.T. *Les mariages espagnols sous le règne de Marie de Médicis (1602–1615).* Paris: Didier, 1869.

Pierre, Benoist. "Le père Joseph, l'empire Ottoman et la Méditerranée au début du XVIIe siècle." *Cahiers de la Méditerranée* 71 (2005): 185–202. http://journals.openedition.org/cdlm/968.

Poumarède, Géraud. *Pour en finir avec la croisade: Mythes et réalités de la lutte contres les Turcs aux XVIe et XVIIe siècles.* Paris: Presses Universitaires de France, 2004.

Powell, John S. *Music and Theatre in France 1600–1800.* Oxford and New York: Oxford University Press, 2000.

Prest, Julia. "Performing Violence to End Violence: Theatrical Entertainment for the Marriage of Marguerite de Valois and Henri de Navarre." In *Gender, Agency and Violence: European Perspectives From Early Modern Times to the Present Day*, edited by Ulrike Zitzlsperger, 38–55. Newcastle upon Tyne: Cambridge Scholars Publishing, 2013.

- *Theatre under Louis XIV: Cross-Casting and the Performance of Gender in Drama, Ballet and Opera.* New York: Palgrave Macmillan, 2006.

Prieto, Elisa García. "*Isabel Clara Eugenia* of Austria: Marriage Negotiations and Dynastic Plans for a Spanish Infanta." In *Isabel Clara Eugenia: Female Sovereignty in the Courts of Madrid and Brussels*, edited by Cordula van Wyhe, 130–53. Madrid: Centro de Estudios Europa Hispanica; London: Paul Holberton Publishing, 2011.

Pruiksma, Rose. "Dansé par le Roi: Constructions of French Identity in the Court Ballets of Louis XIV." PhD diss., University of Michigan, 1999.

Prunières, Henri. *Le ballet de cour en France avant Benserade et Lully.* 1914. New York and London: Johnson Reprint Corporation, 1970.

- *L'opéra italien en France avant Lully.* Paris: E. Champion, 1913.

Ramsey, Ann W. "The Ritual Meaning of Henry IV's 1594 Parisian Entry." In *French Ceremonial Entries in the Sixteenth Century: Event, Image, Text*, edited by Nicolas Russell and Hélène Visentin, 189–205. Toronto: CRRS, 2007.

Ratel, Simonne. "La cour de la Reine Marguerite: Partie I." *Revue du seizième siècle* 11 (1924): 1–29.

Redworth, Glyn. *The Prince and the Infanta: The Cultural Politics of the Spanish Match.* New Haven: Yale University Press, 2000.

Reeser, Todd. W. *Setting Plato Straight: Translating Ancient Sexuality in the Renaissance.* Chicago: University of Chicago Press, 2016.

Rice Jr, Eugene F. *The Renaissance Idea of Wisdom*. Cambridge: Harvard University Press, 1958.

Rivère de Carles, Nathalie, ed. *Early Modern Diplomacy, Theatre and Soft Power: The Making of Peace*. London: Palgrave Macmillan, 2016.

- "The Poetics of Diplomatic Appeasement in the Early Modern Era." In *Early Modern Diplomacy, Theatre and Soft Power: The Making of Peace*, edited by Nathalie Rivère de Carles, 1–23. London: Palgrave Macmillan, 2016.

Rodier, Yann. "Marie de Médicis et le culte marial: langage et langue de l'immaculatisme politique et tridentin d'une reine de France (1605–1617)." *Annali di Storia moderna e contemporanea* 16 (2010): 185–202.

Ronald, Susan. *The Sancy Blood Diamond: Power, Greed, and the Cursed History of One of the World's Most Coveted Gems*. Hoboken: John Wiley and Sons, 2005.

Roosen, William. "Early Modern Diplomatic Ceremonial: A Systems Approach." *Journal of Modern History* 52.3 (1980): 452–76.

Rouillard, Clarence Dana. *The Turk in French History, Thought, and Literature (1520–1660)*. Paris: Boivin, 1940.

Royster, Don Lee. "Pierre Guédron and the Air de Cour, 1600–1620." PhD diss., Yale University, 1973.

Rubin, Elaine. "The Heroic Image: Women and Power in Early Seventeenth-Century France, 1610–1661." PhD diss., George Washington University, 1977.

Sahin-Toth, Péter. "La France et les Français face à la 'longue guerre' de Hongrie (1591–1606)." 2 vols. PhD diss., Université François Rabelais (Tours), Centre d'Études Supérieures de la Renaissance, 1997.

Sahlins, Peter. "The Royal Menageries of Louis XIV and the Civilizing Process Revisited." *French Historical Studies* 35.2 (2012): 237–67. doi: 10.1215/00161071-1498463.

Sauzet, Robert. *Au grand siècle des âmes: Guerre sainte et paix chrétienne en France au XVIIe siècle*. N.p.: Perrin, 2007.

Saint-Edme (Edme-Théodore Bourg). *Amours et galanteries des rois de France*. 2 vols. Paris: Amable Costes, 1830.

Salmon, J.M.H. "The Afterlife of Henry of Navarre." *History Today* 47.10 (October 1997): 12–18.

- "Catholic Resistance Theory, Ultramontanism, and the Royalist Response, 1580–1620." In *The Cambridge History of Political Thought 1450–1700*, edited by J.H. Burns, 219–53. Cambridge: Cambridge University Press, 1991.

Samaran, C. "Henri IV et Charlotte de Montmorency princesse de Condé (Décembre 1608–Décembre 1609) d'après des documents en partie nouveaux." *Annuaire-bulletin de la Société de l'Histoire de France* (1950–1): 53–119.

Sánchez, Magdalena S. *The Empress, The Queen, and the Nun. Women and Power at the Court of Philip III of Spain*. Baltimore and London: Johns Hopkins University Press, 1998.

Sandberg, Brian. "Going Off to the War in Hungary: French Nobles and Crusading Culture in the Sixteenth Century." *Hungarian Historical Review* 4. 2 (2015): 346–83.

– "'The Recovery of God's Heritage': Maria de' Medici and French Religious Politics in the Eastern Mediterranean." In *The Grand Ducal Medici and the Levant. Material Culture, Diplomacy, and Imagery in the Early Modern Mediterranean*, edited by Maurizio Arfaioli and Marta Caroscio, 45–52. London/Turnhout: Harvey Miller Publishers/Brepols, 2016.

Saslow, James M. *The Medici Wedding of 1589*. New Haven: Yale University Press, 1996.

Schalk, Ellery. *From Valor to Pedigree: Ideas of Nobility in France in the Sixteenth and Seventeenth Centuries*. Princeton: Princeton University Press, 1986.

Schmuttermeier, Elisabeth. "The Renaissance: Between Uniformity and Internationalism." In *Brilliant Europe: Jewels from European Courts*, edited by Diana Scarisbrick, Christophe Vachaudez, and Jan Walgrave, 62–119. Brussels: ING Belgium and Mercatorfonds, 2008.

Schwartz, I.A. *The Commedia dell'Arte and its Influence on French Comedy in the Seventeenth Century*. Paris: H. Samuel, 1933.

Scott, Virginia. *Women on the Stage in Early Modern France, 1540–1750*. Cambridge: Cambridge University Press, 2010.

Scott, Virginia, and Sara Sturm-Maddox. *Performance, Poetry and Politics on the Queen's Day: Catherine de Médicis and Pierre de Ronsard at Fontainbleau* [sic]. Aldershot: Ashgate, 2007.

Seelig-Teuwen, Regina. "Barthélemy Prieur, portraitiste d'Henri IV et de Marie de Médicis." In *Les arts au temps d'Henri IV: Volumes des actes du colloque, Fontainebleau, 1992*, 331–54. Pau: Association Henri IV 1989, 1992.

Sénellart, Michel. "Le stoïcisme dans la constitution de la pensée politique: les *Politiques* de Juste Lipse (1589)." In *Le stoïcisme au XVI et XVIIe siècles. Actes du colloque CERPHI (4–5 juin, 1993), organisé par Pierre-François Moreau*, edited by J. Lagrée, 109–30. *Cahiers de philosophie politique et juridique* 25. Caen: Presses Universitaires de Caen, 1994.

Setton, Kenneth M. *Venice, Austria and the Turks in the Seventeenth Century*. Philadelphia: American Philosophical Society, 1991.

Sframeli, Maria. "Perle e diamanti per la Regina." In *Maria de' Medici (1573–1642), una principessa fiorentina sul trono di Francia*, edited by Caterina Caneva and Francesco Solinas, 146–50. Florence: Sillabe, 2005.

Silbert, Doris. "Francesca Caccini, Called La Cecchina." *Musical Quarterly* 32.1 (1946): 50–62.
Skinner, Quentin. *The Origins of Modern Political Thought*. Cambridge: Cambridge University Press, 1978.
Sluga, Glenda, and Carolyn James, eds. *Women, Diplomacy and International Politics since 1500*. New York and London: Routledge, 2016.
Smith, Jay M. *The Culture of Merit: Nobility, Royal Service, and the Making of Absolute Monarchy in France, 1600–1789*. Ann Arbor: University of Michigan Press, 1996.
Smuts, Malcolm, and George Gorse. "Introduction." In *The Politics of Space: European Courts ca. 1500–1750*, edited by Marcello Fantoni, Malcolm Smuts, and George Gorse, 13–38. Rome: Bulzoni, 2009.
Smuts, Malcolm, and Luc Duerloo. "Occasio's Lock of Hair: The Artist and the Ruler in Pursuit of Opportunity." In *The Age of Rubens. Diplomacy, Dynastic Politics and the Visual Arts in Early Seventeenth-Century Europe*, edited by Luc Duerloo and R. Malcolm Smuts, 5–19. Turnhout: Brepols, 2016.
Solerti, Angelo. *Gli albori del melodramma*. 3 vols. Milan: Libraio della Real Casa, 1904; Hildesheim: G. Olms, 1969.
– *Musica, ballo e drammatica alla corte Medicea dal 1600 al 1637: Notizie tratte da un diario, con appendice di testi inediti e rari*. 1905. New York: B. Blom, 1968.
– "Un viaggio in Francia di Giulio Caccini, 1604–05." *Rivista musicale italiana* 10 (1903): 707–11.
– Review of Franceso Raccamadoro-Ramelli, *Ottavio Rinuccini: Studio Biografico e Critico*, Tipografia gentile, 1900. *Giornale storico della letteratura italiana* 39 (1902): 403–4.
Spangler, Jonathan. *The Society of Princes: The Lorraine-Guise and the Conservation of Power and Wealth in Seventeenth-Century France*. Farnham and Burlington, VT: Ashgate, 2009.
Spencer, Robert. "Chitarrone, Theorbo and Archlute." *Early Music* 4.4 (October 1976): 408–22.
Sternberg, Giora. *Status Interaction During the Reign of Louis XIV*. Oxford: Oxford University Press, 2014.
Strong, Roy. *Art and Power: Renaissance Festivals 1450–1650*. 1973. Berkeley and Los Angeles: University of California Press, 1984.
– *The Cult of Elizabeth: Elizabethan Portraiture and Pageantry*. London: Thames and Hudson, 1977.
Strunck, Christina. *Christiane von Lothringen am Hof der Medici. Geschlechterdiskurs und Kulturtransfer zwischen Florenz, Frankreich und Lothringen (1589–1636)*. Petersberg: Michael Imhof Verlag, 2017.

Sullivan, Mary. *Court Masques of James I: Their Influence on Shakespeare and the Public Theatres*. New York and London: G.P. Putnam's Sons, 1913.
Tapié, Victor-L. *France in the Age of Louis XIII and Richelieu*. Translated by D. McN. Lockie. New York: Prager Publishers, 1975.
Thiroux d'Arconville, Marie Geneviève Charlotte. *Vie de Marie de Médicis, princesse de Toscane, reine de France et de Navarre*. 3 vols. Paris: Chez Ruault, 1774.
Tomlinson, Sophie. *Women on Stage in Stuart Drama*. 2005. Cambridge: Cambridge University Press, 2009.
Tuan, Yi-Fu. *Dominance and Affection: The Making of Pets*. New Haven: Yale University Press, 1984.
Tucker, Holly. *Pregnant Fictions: Childbirth and the Fairy Tale in Early Modern France*. Detroit: Wayne State University Press, 2003.
Ungerer, Gustav. "Juan Pantoja de la Cruz and the Circulation of Gifts between the English and Spanish Courts, 1604/5." *SEDERI* 9 (1998): 59–78.
Van Den Berg, Sara. "Dwarf Aesthetics in Spenser's *Faerie Queene* and the Early Modern Court." In *Recovering Disability in Early Modern England*, edited by Allison P. Hobgood and David Houston Wood, 23–42. Columbus: The Ohio State University Press, 2013.
Van Orden, Kate. *Music, Discipline, and Arms in Early Modern France*. Chicago: University of Chicago Press, 2005.
Van Whye, Cordula, ed. *Isabel Clara Eugenia: Female Sovereignty in the Courts of Madrid*. Madrid: Centro de Estudios Europa Hispanica; London: Paul Holberton Publishing, 2011.
Veinstein, G. "Les Capitulations franco-ottomanes de 1536: Sont-elles encore controversables." In *Living in the Ottoman Ecumenical Community: Essays in Honour of Suraiya Faroqhi*, edited by V. Costantini and M. Koller, 71–88. Leiden: Brill, 2008.
Viennot, Eliane. "Diane parmi les figures du pouvoir feminin." In *Actes du colloque Le mythe de Diane en France au XVIe siècle*, edited by Jean-Raymond Fanlo and Marie-Dominique Legrand, 463–78. *Albineana* 14 (2002).
Vitkus, Daniel J. *Turning Turk: English Theater and the Multicultural Mediterranean, 1570–1630*. Houndmills: Palgrave, 2003.
Vivanti, Corrado. "Henri IV, the Gallic Hercules." *Journal of the Warburg and Courtauld Institutes* 30 (1967): 176–97.
Vray, Nicole. *Catherine de Parthenay, duchesse de Rohan: Protestante insoumise 1554–1631*. Paris: Librairie Académique Perrin, 1998.
Wagner, Marie-France, Louise Frappier, and Claire Latraverse, eds. *Les jeux de l'échange: Entrées solennelles et divertissements du XVe au XVIIe siècle*. Paris: Champion, 2007.

Walgrave, Jan. "The Seventeenth Century: The Reign of the Diamond." In *Brilliant Europe: Jewels from European Courts*, edited by Diana Scarisbrick, Christophe Vachaudez, and Jan Walgrave, 120–54. Brussels: ING Belgium and Mercatorfonds, 2008.

Watanabe-O'Kelly, Helen. "The Early Modern Festival Book: Function and Form." In *Europa Triumphans. Court and Civic Festivals in Early Modern Europe*. 2 vols. Edited by J.R. Mulryne et al., 1: 3–17. Aldershot and Burlington, VT: Ashgate, 2004.

Watanabe-O'Kelly, Helen, and Adam Morton, eds. *Queens Consort, Cultural Transfer and European Politics, c. 1500–1800*. London and New York: Routledge, 2017.

Watkins, John. "Toward A New Diplomatic History of Medieval and Early Modern Europe." *Journal of Medieval and Early Modern Studies* 38.1 (Winter 2008): 1–14.

– ed. *Toward New Medieval and Early Modern Diplomatic History*. Special volume. *Journal of Medieval and Early Modern Studies* 38.1 (Winter 2008).

Welch, Ellen R. "Dancing the Nation: Performing France in Seventeenth-Century Ballets des Nations." *Journal for Early Modern Cultural Studies* 13.2 (Spring 2013): 3–23.

– "National Characters: Playing Against Type in the *Ballet des Muses* (1666–67)." *Seventeenth-Century French Studies* 32.2 (2010): 191–205. doi: 10.1179/026510610X12857561930912.

– "Rethinking the Politics of Court Spectacle: Performance and Diplomacy Under the Valois." In *French Renaissance and Baroque Drama: Text, Performance, Theory*, edited by Michael Meere, 101–16. Newark: University of Delaware Press, 2015.

– "The Specter of the Turk in Early Modern French Court Entertainments." *L'Esprit Créateur* 53.4 (Winter 2013): 84–97.

– *A Theater of Diplomacy: International Relations and the Performing Arts in Early Modern France*. Philadelphia: University of Pennsylvania Press, 2017.

Wellman, Kathleen. *Queens and Mistresses of Renaissance France*. New Haven: Yale University Press, 2012.

Wiley, W.L. (David). *The Early Public Theatre in France*. Cambridge: Harvard University Press, 1960.

Wilkin, Rebecca M. *Women, Imagination, and the Search for Truth in Early Modern France*. Aldershot: Ashgate, 2008.

Wine, Kathleen. "Henri IV Makes Peace and Love." Unpublished conference paper.

Wintroub, Michael. "Words, Deeds, and a Womanly King." *French Historical Studies* 28.3 (2005): 387–413.

Wolfe, Michael. "Piety and Political Allegiance: The Duc de Nevers and the Protestant Henri IV, 1589–1593." *French History* 2 (1988): 1–21.
Woodacre, Elena. "Family Ties, Political Ambition and Epistolary Diplomacy in Renaissance Europe." *Women, Diplomacy and International Politics since 1500*, edited by Glenda Sluga and Carolyn James, 30–45. New York and London: Routledge, 2016.
Yates, Frances A. *Astraea: The Imperial Theme in the Sixteenth Century*. 1975. London: Pimlico, 1993.
– *The French Academies of the Sixteenth Century*. 1947. Nendeln, Liechtenstein: Kraus Reprints, 1973.
Yon, Bernard. "L'Astrée et le salon de Marguerite." In *Marguerite de France, reine de Navarre et son temps. Actes du Colloque d'Agen (12–13 octobre 1991)*, edited by Cl.-G. Dubois and de M. Lazard, 297–308. Agen: Centre Matteo Bandello, 1994.
Zanger, Abby. *Scenes from the Marriage of Louis XIV. Nuptial Fictions and the Making of Absolute Power*. Stanford: Stanford University Press, 1997.
Zeller, Berthold. *Henri IV et Marie de Médicis, d'après des documents nouveaux tirés des archives de Florence et de Paris*. Paris: Didier, 1877.
Zerner, Henri. "Diane de Poitiers: maîtresse de son image?" In *Actes du colloque: Le mythe de Diane en France au XVIe siècle*, edited by Jean-Raymond Fanlo and Marie-Dominique Legrand, 335–43. *Albineana* 14 (2002).

Index

Abbas I the Great, shah of Persia (embassy to Henri IV), 114
absolutism, 3, 12–14, 98, 125, 142–3, 160, 166, 169–70, 208, 210, 240n28, 243n7, 257n41, 269n27, 278–9n117, 284n47, 294n137, 312n13
Acevedo, Pedro Enríquez de, count of Fuentes and (Spanish) governor of Milan, 255n12
Achilles, in association with Catholic warrior-prince ideal, 109–10
Adam, Antoine, 163
Adamson, John, 304n55
Agrippa, Henricus, 39–40, 134, 283n36, 283–4n37; *Declamation on the nobility and preeminence of the female sex*, 39, 134, 282n32, 283n36, 283–4n37, 291n96
Ahmed I, sultan of the Ottoman empire, 107, 113, 272n55, 275n81
"Air: pour le balet de la Reyne, La Renommée au Roy" (Malherbe), 127–8, 131–2, 135, 144–5, 151–2, 159, 167, 199, 281n15
airs de cour. See *ballets de cour*; music
Albert VII. See Austria, archduke of
Alberti, Leon Battista, 284n43
Alcandre. See *under* Henri IV: association with
Alcine, in the *Ballet de Monseigneur de Vendôme* (1610), 96, 267n12
Aldobrandini, Pietro, Cardinal, 38, 47, 246n36, 248n53, 250n75, 252n92, 253n101, 272n55, 275nn81, 83, 278n114, 294–5n7
ambassadors: of England, 45, 56, 66, 106, 153, 159, 167, 175, 177–83, 186, 188, 191–3, 204, 207, 298–9n24, 300n28 (*see also* Carew, George; Parry, Thomas; Lennox, duke of [Ludovic Stuart]; Winwood, Ralph); of Ferrara, 246n29, 310n115 (*see also* Malaspina, Bartolomeo); of France, 66, 74, 176–7, 180, 183, 185–91, 194–5, 203–4, 283n34, 296n13, 302–3n44, 303–4n55, 304nn56, 60 (*see also* de Béthune, Philippe; Le Fèvre de la Boderie, Antoine; Beaumont, comte de [Christophe de Harlay]; Tillières, comte de [Tanneguy Veneur II]); of the Holy See (*see* Barberini, Maffeo; del Buffalo, Innocenzo; nuncios, papal); of

350 Index

Mantua, 128 (see also Guiscardi, Traiano); of Spain, 106, 174–6, 179, 183–4, 186, 188, 190–5, 293n129, 295n12, 296n13, 298–9n24, 303n45, 303–4n55, 305–6n74, 306n79 (see also de Giron, don Fernando de; de Toledo, don Pedro; Villamediana, first count of [Juan de Tassis y Peralta]; de Velasco, Juan Fernandez); as spectators at ballets and masques, 4, 52, 66, 171–2, 174–83, 188–96, 204–5, 209, 241n34, 242n36, 259n58, 298–9n24, 300n27, 303n48, 303–4n55, 305n68, 305–6n74; of Tuscany, 38, 58, 154, 165, 180, 182, 205, 261n83, 298–9n24, 305n68 (see also Giovannini, Bacio; Guidi, Camillo); of Venice, 106, 180, 182, 192, 194, 204, 254n3, 296n13, 296–7n15, 298–9n24, 305n68 (see also Badoer, Angelo; Giustinian, Giorgio [Zorzi]; Molin, Nicolò)
"American neo-ceremonialist school," 11, 64–5, 89, 266n128
Aminta (Tasso), performed in 1590 by Marie de Médicis, 8, 87
Les Amours du Grand Alcandre (Louise Marguerite de Guise-Lorraine), 169, 250n78, 253n101, 294nn136–7
Andrea, Bernadette, 84, 254n2, 263n103, 270n33
Andreini, Isabella, 88
d'Angennes, Charles. See Rambouillet, marquis de
Anglo-Spanish match, 175–6, 178, 296n13, 296–7n15
animals, exotic: in ballets de cour, 12, 93, 99–103, 105, 107–9, 112, 268nn20–2, 269nn27, 30; in masquerades, 259n59; in royal menageries, 269n27, 288n73
Anjou et d'Alençon, duc d' (François de France), 4
Anna of Denmark, queen of Scotland, England, and Ireland, 173–8, 181–4, 186–90, 194–5, 204–6, 241n34, 242n40, 266–7n1, 295–6n12, 297nn16, 19, 303nn46, 48, 304n60, 306n79, 307n84, 310n112
Anne de Bretagne, queen of France, 41, 105–6
Annebaut, marquis d' (Bernard Potier de Blérancourt), 283n34
Apollo, 19–24, 27–8, 33, 44, 67, 159, 244nn11–12
Arbeau, Thoinot, 285n55
Arcadia felice (Marinella), 284n37
Archilei, Vittoria, 197
aristocracy, crisis of, 101, 269–70n32
Aristotle, 36, 142, 285n49; Nichomachean Ethics, 36
Armand de Bourbon, prince de Conti, 73, 77, 164
Armstrong, Megan, 271nn44, 51
Arsenal, 59, 75, 101, 131, 189, 191–3, 195–6, 205, 257–8n44, 281–2n26, 290n93, 293n133, 308n99, 310n13
Artamène, ou Le Grand Cyrus (de Scudéry), 145, 150, 285–6n61, 286n62, 289n75, 290n84, 308nn93, 96
arts, revival of, following the French civil wars, 9, 10, 17, 23–7, 35–7, 67–8, 196–205. See also magnificence
Astraea, goddess of Justice, 9, 18, 20, 24–5, 27, 40–1, 214–15, 239, 249n61
L'Astrée (D'Urfé), 41, 138, 157, 169, 284n39

Atlas, daughters of, 30, 48
de l'Aubespine, Claude. *See* Verderonne, seigneur de
audiences for court ballets. *See ballets de cour*: audiences
Augustus, Roman Emperor, 18, 41, 68
Aurora, beauty of compared to that of Marie de Médicis, 117
Austria, archduchess of (Isabel Clara Eugenia), 5–6, 56, 142, 197
Austria, archduke of (Albert VII), 165, 175, 200
Auvergne, comte d' (Charles Valois), illegitimate son of Charles IX and Marie Touchet, half-brother of Henriette d'Entragues, marquise de Verneuil, 57, 90, 253n102, 255n12, 293n129
d'Auvergne, Henri de La Tour. *See* Bouillon, duc de
Avignon, royal entry (1600) at, 23, 68, 70, 244n12, 259n60

Badoer, Angelo, Venetian ambassador to France, 192, 194, 254n3
bal des Ardents, Le (1393), 271n45
Balkans. *See* Thrace
Ballard, Pierre, 145, 234–5, 244n15
ballet à cheval, 298n22
Le ballet comique de la royne (1581), 8, 35–7, 52, 85, 208, 239n18
Le ballet de Diane et ses nymphes [Ballet of Diana and her Nymphs] (1609), also referred to as *Le Ballet de la reine* (1609), 9, 13, 16, 125–70, 185, 218–29, 234–5, 250n73, 282n34, 291n101, 292n121. *See also under* Henri IV; Marie de Médicis

Le ballet des Étrangers (1598), 243–4n8, 266n1, 267n13. *See also* Henri IV; Beaufort, duchesse de (d'Estrées, Gabrielle)
ballet *La félicité de l'âge d'or* (1610), 237n1
Le ballet de Madame (1609), 13, 16, 125–7, 160–70, 145–6, 160–70, 230–3, 235, 292n121, 293nn133–4. *See also under* Elisabeth of France; Henri IV; Marie de Médicis
Le ballet de Madame ... par quatorze nymphes de Junon (1613), 311nn1, 2. *See also under* Elisabeth de France; Marie de Médicis
Le ballet de Monseigneur de Vendôme (1610), also known as *Ballet de Monseigneur de Vandosme*, 96, 100, 267n12, 269n25. *See also* Vendôme, duc de (César de Bourbon)
Le ballet de la Nuit (1653), 69
Le ballet de la reine (1605), 3, 10, 11, 13, 54–93, 96, 98, 100–4, 106, 108, 110–11, 113–15, 117, 119, 122–3, 167–8, 174, 178–83, 196, 237n1, 254n1, 256n16, 257nn36–7, 260n64, 264n109, 266n1, 269n27, 274n76, 299n24, 302n39. *See also under* Marie de Médicis
Le ballet royal du grand bal de la Douairière de Billebahaut (1625), 270n41
Le ballet des Seize Vertus [Ballet of the Sixteen Virtues] (1602), 3, 9, 16–53, 65, 67, 76–7, 92, 98, 154, 173, 179, 212–17, 234, 243n5, 243–4n8, 244–5n15, 245nn16–17, 247n38, 250n75, 254n104, 300n27. *See also* Louis XIII; Marie de Médicis;

352 Index

Verneuil, marquise de (Henriette d'Entragues)
Le ballet du Triomphe de Minerve (1615), also known as *Ballet de Madame*, 118, 207, 241n31, 311n2. See also Elisabeth of France; Marie de Médicis
ballets de cour (see also magnificence; Marie de Médicis: ballets produced and/or danced by; music; *titles for individual ballets*):
- audiences, 3–4, 28, 33, 37, 49, 59, 62, 70–1, 85, 92, 100, 102–3, 106–7, 129, 135, 138, 140–1, 143, 145, 148, 151–2, 155–9, 161, 167, 194, 199, 205, 207, 240n27, 248n50, 258n53, 311n1; casting of, 65–6, 68, 71, 79, 179, 183, 205, 242n36, 259n56; foreign, 14, 122, 172–4, 200, 295n7 (see also under ambassadors); precedence in, 15, 66–7, 89–90, 175–7, 179–83, 186–7, 191–5, 205; size of, 11, 44, 59, 65–6, 258n49; social standing of, 11, 101, 141, 259n58
- avant-garde developments in: imagery, 41–2; dance, 10–12, 14–15, 85, 97, 173, 210; music, 3–4, 14–15, 88, 97–8, 173, 210, 239n20
- burlesque aspects, 12–13, 68, 92–3, 97–8, 101–4, 106–7, 147–8, 208, 240n27, 311n6; cross-dressing, 12–13, 59, 93, 97–8, 103, 278; representations of "barbarous" nations (see Ottomans in court entertainments). See also animals, exotic; dwarfs
- choreographies, 10, 12–13, 55, 71, 80–1, 89, 92, 95–8, 103, 140, 208, 278–9n117. See also under dance, courtly; kinesis
- contemporary accounts: in manuscripts, 10–11, 18, 38, 44, 54, 58–60, *61*, 62–6, 89, 93–5, 99, 106–9, 116, 128, 140, 168, 172, 196, 203, 205, 248n52, 257nn36–7, 268n21, 282n26, 298–9n24, 305n69, 308n98, 310nn113, 116; printed, 10–11, 18–20, 23–4, 28–30, 38, 40, 45, 50, 53, 63–4, 70, 99, 118, 129, 133, 243n5, 249n55, 257n37 (see also cultural capital, primitive accumulation of)
- costumes: gendered cross-dressing, 12, 59, 93, 97–8; opulence, 17–19, 23, 27–38, 45, 51–3, 84, 89, 105, 128, 171–3, 183, 195–6, 204–5, 248n46; precious materials, 11, 14, 18, 29, 33–5, 37–8, 55, 59–60, 89, 104, 128–9, 172, 200, 204–5, 216–17, 248n42, 250n75, 258n47, 278–9n117, 281n20. See also gems; masks, worn in ballets
- dancers: animals, 12, 93, 99–103, 105, 107–9, 112, 268nn20–2, 269nn27, 30; dwarfs, 55, 59, 68, 70–1, 81, 83–4, 93, 96–100, 102–3, 108, 112, 263nn98, 100–2, 105, 267n12, 269n30, 278–9n117; women, 30, 33, 35, 38, 49–50, 55, 71, 75, 76, 79–81, 92, 95, 97, 129, 133–4, 144, 151–2, 154, 167, 205, 268n17, 282–3n34; from royal and princely families, 4, 8, 35, 38, 71, 75–81, 85, 90, 92, 97, 116, 123–4, 133–4, 150, 152, 154, 158, 179, 261nn79, 82, 86, 271n45, 290n82. See also de Bourbon, Catherine; Louis XIII; Louis XIV; Louise de Lorraine-Vaudemont; Marie de Médicis; Vendôme, duc de

Index 353

(César de Bourbon); Verneuil,
marquise de (Henriette d'Entragues)
– imagery and iconography:
Christian, 9, 18, 118–19, 239n15;
classical, 9, 18, 25, 28–30, 44, 68,
71, 161, 239n15, 291n107; celestial,
18, 27–8, 30, 33, 39, 46, 48–50,
140–1, 246n35, 284n44 (*see also*
heavens, references to in *ballets
de cour*); imperial, 41–2, 54, 120,
204; Marian, 9, 41–2, 47, 50. *See
also under* Marie de Médicis;
Neoplatonism
– scenic effects, 14, 18, 27–8, 35,
37–8, 128, 129, 140, 155, 159, 167,
196–8, 204, 268n21, 280n13, 281n15
– verse texts, 10, 17–27, 30–3, 35,
38–41, 49–50, 52, 85–6, 120, 125–9,
131, 139, 143, 145, 153, 155, 158,
161–3, 166, 168–9, 198–9, 212–35,
243nn4–5, 243–4n8, 244–5n15,
245nn16, 17, 19, 247n38, 254n1,
293n134, 310n113, 311n2; *livrets*
(printed editions), 10, 16–17, 21,
24, 35, 42, 52–3, 96, 118, 127–8,
131–2, 145, 198–9, 234, 243–4n8,
244–5n15, 245n17, 279n7, 311nn1, 2;
as cultural capital, 17, 24, 52–3.
See also *cartels*; *individual names
of poets*
balli. *See under* dance, courtly
banquets, 32, 105–6, 117, 252n96,
282n26, 295n12
Bar, duc de (Henri de Lorraine),
73, 78
Barberini, family, 15, 252n92
Barberini, Maffeo, Cardinal, 113, 181,
205, 252n92, 272n55, 275nn81, 83,
301n35, 310n114
barriers. *See* combat at the barrier

Barroll, Leeds, 241n34
Bartoli Bacherini, Maria Adelaide,
30, 238n11, 252n96, 265n121
basse danse. *See under* dance, courtly
de Bassompierre, Catherine, 282–3n34
de Bassompierre, François, 163–4,
284n39, 293n133
Bastille, 90
Bataille, Gabriel, 21, 131, 145, 234–5
Battifol, Louis, 100, 248n49, 254n104,
258nn47, 49, 284n109
de Bavière, Jean II. *See* Deux-Ponts,
duc de
Bayonne summit (1565), festivities
for, 106
Beaufort, duchesse de (Gabrielle
d'Estrées, mistress of Henri
IV), 47, 73, 83, 97, 108, 159, 169,
253n102, 267–8n13, 291n108
de Beaulieu, Claude, 264–5n111
de Beaulieu, Girard, 85, 264–5n111
Beaumont, comte de (Christophe
de Harlay), French ambassador
to England, 66, 176–7, 180, 182–6,
190, 258n52, 296n13, 297n19,
300n29, 301–2n36, 303n48
Beaumont-lez-Tours, convent of, 90
beauty: as residing in natural
settings, 9, 12, 98, 132, 221n10,
282n32; as virtue, 18, 27–8, 30,
33–4, 39–40, 117, 127, 132–5, *136*,
138, 140, 143–4, 151, 153, 156, 159,
277, 283n36, 283–4n37, 285n52;
women's, 27–9, 32, 33, 39–40, 50,
134–5, 150, 157, 283n36, 283–4n37
Bedford, countess of (Lucy Russell),
174–5
Beik, William, 240n28
Bellegarde, duc de (Roger de Saint-
Lary de Termes), 294n136

Bély, Lucien, 182
Berenice. *See* Atlas, daughters of
Bertaut, Jean, 20, 24–7, 33, 35, 38, 40–1, 49–50, 214–15, 234, 244–5n15, 245nn16, 17, 19, 247n38. *See also* "Voyant la douce Paix et la divine Astrée"
de Béthune, clan, 74–5, 178–9; interest in ballet, 178
de Béthune, Marguerite. *See* Rohan, second duchesse de
de Béthune, Maximilien. *See* Sully, marquis de Rosny, duc de
de Béthune, Philippe, 74
de Billebahaut, Douairière. *See ballets de cour*
Blérancourt, Bernard Potier. *See* Annebaut, marquis d'
bloodline, royal. *See* dynasty, royal
Bodin, Jean, 142; *Six livres de la république*, 142; *De la démonomanie des sorciers*, 142
Book of the Courtier (Castiglione), 157
Bosphorus. *See* Thrace
Bouillon, duc de (Henri de La Tour d'Auvergne), 73, 121, 164, 183, 255n12, 260n70, 278n114
de Bouillon, Godefroy, 271n52
de Boulanger, Guillaume. *See* Vaumesnil, sieur de
Bourbon dynasty, 3–5, 8–9, 11–14, 17–18, 23–4, 27–8, 33, 36–8, 41, 44, 46–7, 49, 52–8, 73, 75, 77, 80–1, 83–4, 90–1, 93, 103, 111, 113, 115, 118, 121, 123, 125–6, 133–4, 165, 167, 169, 172, 178–9, 183–5, 190–1, 193, 195–6, 198, 200, 204, 206–8, 210, 240n28, 278n117, 290n92. *See also individual names of Bourbon members*

de Bourbon, Alexandre, chevalier de Vendôme, second illegitimate son of Henri IV by Gabrielle d'Estrées, 267n13
de Bourbon, Armand, 73
de Bourbon, Catherine, sister of Henri IV, 8, 72–3, 75, 160, 239n14
de Bourbon, César. *See* Vendôme, duc de
de Bourbon, Charles. *See* Soissons, comte de
de Bourbon, Gaston Henri, illegitimate son of Henri IV by Henriette d'Entragues. *See* Verneuil, duc de
de Bourbon, Henri. *See* Henri IV
de Bourbon, Henri II. *See* Henri II de Bourbon
Bourbon, Petit, 258n49
Bourdieu, Pierre, 52–3
Boureau, Alain, 266n128
Bradamante (Robert Garnier), 311n1
de Brèves, Savary (French ambassador at the Sublime Porte), 100, 121
Brittania, 266n1. *See also* masques, English; *Masque of Blackness*
Brooks, Jeanice, 109, 244–5n15, 264–5n111, 265n12
Bruni, Leonardo, 284n43
Brussels, 237n1
Bryant, Lawrence, 10, 63–4, 240n23, 257n41. *See also* "American neo-ceremonialist school"
Buda, 107, 121, 273n69. *See also* Nevers, second duc de (Charles Gonzaga)
de Bueil, Jacqueline. *See* Moret, comtesse de
del Bufalo, Innocenzo (papal nuncio in France), 38, 47, 248nn53–4,

250n75, 252nn92–3, 253n101, 294–5n7
del Bufalo, Muzio, 38, 250n75, 294–5n7
Buisseret, David, 250n77, 258n45
Bulgaria. *See* Thrace
Burke, Peter, 48
Byzantines, Byzantine kings, 110–12, 115. *See also* emperors, Eastern Roman; Paleologues, dynasty

Caccini, Francesca ("La Cecchina"), 84–8, 197, 264n109
Caccini, Giulio, 76, 84–8, 197–9, 264n109, 265nn113–14, 307n84
Caccini, Lucia, 87
Caccini, Margherita, 84–6, 88, 197, 264n109
Caccini, Pompeo, 84
Caccini, Settimia, 84–6, 88, 197, 264n109
Caccini consort, 76, 84–8, 196–9, 266n124
Callisto. *See* Atlas, daughters of
Calypso, garden of, in the 1608 *intermedii*, 307n86
de Camere, Isabel, 197
Candlemas, as date for court performances, 190
Canova-Green, Marie-Claude, 240n23
"Canzone in lode della Reina" (Chiabrera), 31–3, 246n36
Cappello, Bianca, 265n120
Carew, George, 153–4, 159, 167–8, 186–96, 200, 203–4, 293nn131–3, 304nn57, 59–61, 305nn63–4, 69, 306nn77, 79, 307n82, 308n100, 309n110. *See also* ambassadors: of England

Carew, Thomasine, 189, 192–3
carnival festivities, ballets as, 17–20, 38, 44–5, 54, 67, 70, 72, 85, 87, 98, 100, 102, 123, 167, 178, 185, 196, 238n11, 250n75, 261n86, 301n35
Caroso, Fabritio, 27, 141; *Nobiltà di dame*, 141
carousel (or *carouzère*), 62, 104, 271
cartels, in court ballets, 100, 105, 108–9, 119, 268n20, 269n30, 271n47, 272n60, 272–3n61, 273n62, 274n77, 299n24
Carter, Tim, 8
Castiglione, Baldassare, 157. See also *Book of the Courtier*
Casulana, Maddalena, 307
Catherine de Médicis, 7, 8, 12, 14, 33, 35, 42, 130, 238n8, 239n18, 241n31, 247n41, 291n107. See also *Le ballet comique de la royne* (1581)
de Caumont, Jacques Nompar. *See* La Force, duc de
Cecil, Robert. *See* Salisbury, earl of
Cérémonial françois (Godefroy), 63, 257n37
ceremonial: coronations (*sacres*), 8, 11, 63, 76, 79, 81, *201–2*, 203, 240n23; descriptions of, 11, 60, 62–5, 256n28, 257nn36–8, 41; elements of in ballets, 4, 10–11, 14–15, 37, 54, 58, 63–5, 71, 79–80, 89–90, 92, 171, 181; diplomatic ceremonial, 121–2, 172, 182, 194, 197, 209, 295n12, 306n75; *lits de justice*, 11, 63; processions, 63; royal births and baptisms, 5, 18, 60, 63, 261–2n87, 267–8n13, 283–4n37, 298n22; royal marriages and funerals, 11, 63, 104, 240n23. *See also* "American

356 Index

neo-ceremonialist school";
entries, royal; Te Deums
chaîne (hay). *See under* dance, courtly
Charles I, king of England, Scotland, Ireland, and Wales, 19, 207
Charles III. *See* Lorraine, duc de
Charles V, Holy Roman emperor, 104–5
Charles VI, king of France, in the *Bal des ardents* (1393), 271n45
Charles VIII, king of France, 274n76
Charles IX, king of France (Valois dynasty), 5, 8, 17, 23, 35, 41–2, 73, 85, 239n18, 263n100, 291n101
Charlotte-Marguerite de Montmorency, princesse de Condé, 125, 150, 161–7, 169, 290n81, 293n129, 294n136
Charron, Pierre, 95, 135, 137, 138–9, 284n38
de Chavigny, Jean Aimé, 111
Du Chesne, André, 39, 134–5, 138; *Figures mystiques du riche et précieux cabinet des dames*, 39, 134, 136. *See also* Neoplatonism
Chevalier (composer), 279–80n7
Chiabrera, Gabriello, 31–3, 246n36. *See also* "Canzone in lode della Reina"
de Choiseul, Charles. *See* Praslin, marquis de
Christ child, 18, 39, 41–2
Christendom, 105, 111, 113, 115. *See also* crusades
Christian Militia. *See* *milice chrétienne*
Christine of France, second daughter of Henri IV and Marie de Médicis and duchess of Savoy, 184, 207, 210, 298n22, 311n1
cinq pas. *See under* dance, courtly

Circe, in *Le Ballet comique de la royne*, 35
Ciseri, Ilaria, 30
civility, early modern, 13, 93–6, 101, 103, 108–9, 112, 114, 126, 157–8, 241n30, 269–70n32. *See also* aristocracy, crisis of; combat at the barrier; tilts, English
Claude de France, queen of France, 41, 105, 243n2
Clement VIII, pope, 4, 70, 112–13, 179, 246n36, 275n83, 299–300n26, 305n74
de Clermont, Claude-Catherine. *See* Retz, "la maréchale" de
Clèves, duchy of, 123, 165
Clèves, duke of. *See* Jülich and Clèves, duke of
de Clèves, Henriette, 279n120
de Cochefilet, Rachel. *See* Sully, duchesse de
Colantuono, Anthony, 15, 293n3
Cole, Janie, 128, 280n11
de Coligny, François. *See* de Laval, Guy XX
combat at the barrier (entertainment), 67, 100, 104, 106, 107–8, 112, 115, 119–21, 272n57, 276–7n107, 282n28, 288n73. *See also* carousel; Knights of Thrace; *Le romant des chevaliers de Thrace*; Thrace; tilts, English
commedia dell'arte, 87, 194
Commentary on Plato's Symposium (Ficino), 27
concerto di donne, 87, 265n120. *See also* Marie de Médicis: patronage, artistic
Concini, Concino, 51, 253n101
Condé, prince de. *See* Henri II de Bourbon

Condé, princesse de. *See* Charlotte-Marguerite de Montmorency
conspiracy, Biron, 121, 255n12, 293n129
consumption, conspicuous, 7, 11, 14–15, 19, 36, 38, 48, 51–2, 89, 148–9, 159, 172–3, 196, 204, 310n112. *See also* gems; magnificence
Conti, prince de. *See* Armand de Bourbon
Conti, princesse de. *See* Louise Marguerite de Guise-Lorraine
Cordier, Jacques, called Bocan, 270n41
Cosandey, Fanny, 11, 42, 45, 63–4, 79–80, 83, 239n15, 240n23, 249n67, 262n91
Cosimo il Vecchio. *See* Tuscany, grand duke of (Cosimo I de' Medici, il Vecchio)
cosmopolitanism, 88, 266n125
Courtright, Nicola, 9, 57, 160, 240n26, 291n108, 292n112
Crawford, Katherine, 126, 164
Cremer, Albert, 123
Crépin-Leblond, Thierry, 53
Croft, Pauline, 300n28
cross-dressing. See under *ballets de cour*
Crouzet, Denis, 26, 245n21
crusades, 93, 105–8, 110–19, 122–3, 271–2n52, 273n69, 274n74, 275nn80, 83. *See also under* Henri IV; Nevers, second duc de (Charles Gonzaga)
cultural capital, primitive accumulation of, 17, 47–53, 83, 200. *See also* Bourdieu, Pierre
Cummings, Mark, 286–7n65
Cupid, 29, 98, 134–5, 138–40, 152, 155–6, 160–3, 166–7, 169–70,

223n14. *See also* Love personified, in court entertainments
Cusick, Suzanne, 85, 265n114, 272n57
Cyprigna (Cypria). *See* Venus
Cypris. *See* Venus

dance, courtly: *bal* (ball), 24, 38, 101, 270n41, 271n45, 304n60; *ballo*, 8, 30, 36, 38, 49, 85, 246n29, 247n38; *basse danse*, 71, 94, 96, 103, 152, 158, 246n36, 268n17; capers, 59, 96–7; *chaîne*, 127, 140–1, 226n22, 280n8, 284n41; *cinq pas*, 93, 97, 103; *entrechats*, 96, 267n12; *galliard*, 97, 250n70; *intrecciata*, 267n12; jumps, 96–7, 267; leaps, 59, 68, 93, 96–8, 199; marching, 22, 29, 59–60, 95, 99, 256n20; reverence, 59, 93–7, 100; walking, 93–8; silent noble dance as rhetoric, 144, 150–2, 158, 284n44, 285n55; as vehicle for exhibiting or teaching virtue, 27–9, 33–5, 101, 141–4, 151–2, 156–8, 170. See also *ballets de cour*; masques; revels; *saraos*
Daniel, prophet, vision of four empires as taken up in France, 111
Dardenelles. *See* Thrace
dauphin, future Louis XIII. *See* Louis XIII, king of France
Day of the Dupes (Marie de Médicis' exile from France in 1631), 42, 150, 207
Declamation on the nobility and preeminence of the female sex (Agrippa), 39–40, 134, 282n32, 283n36, 283–4n37
Delia, 33
Derrida, Jacques, 181–2

Desportes, Philippe, 24
Deux-Ponts, duc de (Jean II de Bavière), 72, 74, 75
Deux-Ponts, duchesse de (Catherine de Rohan), 72, 74, 75
Dialoghi d'amore (Leone Ebreo), 283–4n37
Dialogo di Giunone e Minerva (1600), 117
Dialogues (Tahureau), 97
Diana, 9, 31, 117, 128, 132–3, 138–41, 152, 155–6, 158–61, 166–7, 220–4, 230–1, 290n95, 291nn101, 107–8, 292n112. See also *Le ballet de Diane et ses nymphes*; Marie de Médicis: allegorical association with
dignity, royal, 45, 47, 55, 79–81, 177, 183, 189, 192–3, 262n91
Dillon, Janette, 11, 81, 89
diplomacy, "mute," 15, 172. See also Colantuono, Anthony
"diplomatic ambiguation," 15, 180. See also Rivère de Carles, Nathalie
"diplomatic incident," 182–3. See also Bely, Lucien
Discours parénétique sur les choses turques (de Chavigny), 111
dolphins, 127–8, 146–7, 154–5, 198, 222–3, 290n95
Doria, Violante, 85, 264–5n111, 265n12
Du Bray, Toussaint, 136, 234, 279n7
Du Choul, Guillaume, 259n59
Dubost, Jean-François, 77, 86–7, 262n87
Duerloo, Luc, 160
Duindam, Jeroen, 66, 134, 209–10, 289n78
Dupré, Guillaume, 57–8
Dupuy, Pierre, 256
Durosoir, Georgie, 45, 243n5

dwarfs, 55, 59, 68, 70–1, 81, 83–4, 93, 96–100, 102–3, 108, 112, 263nn98, 100–2, 105, 267n12, 269n30, 278–9n117. See also *ballets de cour*: dancers; *individual names*
dynastic marriage, 7, 83, 144, 173–4, 178, 187, 206, 210, 296n12, 297n15, 311n2. See also queen of France: foreignness
"dynastic wooing," 175, 178, 195, 204

East. See Orient
East, Near. See Mediterranean, Eastern
Ebreo, Leone, 283n36. See also *Dialoghi d'amore*
Eden, 41
Edict of Nantes (1598), 4, 17, 37, 119
delli Effetti, Giovanni, 205, 310n14
Elias, Norbert, 13
Élisabeth d'Autriche, queen of France, 85, 307n83
Elisabeth of France, eldest daughter of Henri IV and Marie de Médicis and queen of Spain and Portugal, 184, 210, 284n37, 298n22, 311nn1, 2; ballets danced by, 125, 127, 162, 166–7, 207, 311nn1, 2
Elise, Angélique Paulet as, 145, 150, 200, 286n62, 308nn93, 96
Elizabeth I, queen of England, 172, 174, 176, 184, 203
emperors, Eastern Roman, 110, 259n59. See also Paleologues, dynasty
emperors, Holy Roman, 41, 84, 104–5, 107, 111, 263n100, 275n81
Empire, Holy Roman, 110
England: diplomatic relations with Spain, 70, 114, 172, 174–8, 182,

185–6, 295–6n12, 296n13, 296–7n15, 303n45; relations with France, 114, 172, 176–95, 205–7, 210, 294n5, 301n35, 301–2n36. *See also* ambassadors: of England; masques, English; *individual names of rulers*

d'Entragues, Charles Balzac, father of Henriette d'Entragues, marquise de Verneuil, 57, 90

d'Entragues, Henriette Balzac. *See* Verneuil, marquise de

entries, royal, 11, 23, 26, 36, 60, 62–3, 68, 79, 81, 104, 159, 240n23, 244n12, 248n48, 249n64, 259n60, 263n97, 291n111

Epictitus, 285n52

eroticism, in court entertainments, 9, 12, 29, 49, 145–57, 127, 134, 145, 147–8, 159–60, 167, 208, 240n27, 288nn73–4, 289n77. See also *Le ballet de Diane et ses nymphes*; Paulet, Angélique

d'Escars, Catherine de Peyrusse, 282–3n34

de L'Estoile, Pierre, 44, 47, 130–1, 145, 148, 152, 196, 198, 200, 252n93, 281n24, 282n27, 292n126

d'Estrées, Gabrielle. *See* Beaufort, duchesse de

Euridice (opera), 8

Fame, goddess of (la Renommée), 120, 127–8, 131–5, 141, 144–5, 151–2, 158–9, 161, 167, 170, 199, 218–23, 281n15, 282nn28, 30, 285n52, 292n121, 307n86

Fantoni, Marcello, 64–5

Far East, 114, 204. *See also* Orient

Faustina, empress of Rome, 160, 292n112

female monody. *See* monody, female

feminism, proto-, 134, 145–52

Fenlon, Iain, 36, 48

Ferdinand II, Holy Roman emperor, 107, 272n55

Ferrara: court of (Este), 87, 246n29, 266n124, 289n78, 310n115

de la Ferrière, Hector, 130–1

fertility, of queens consorts and royal mistresses, 5, 23, 155, 174, 290n95

festival studies, 3, 64, 295n10

Le Fèvre de la Boderie, Antoine (French ambassador to England), 186

Ficino, Marsilio, 27–8, 156, 245n24, 283n36. See also *Commentary on Plato's Symposium*; *De Sole*

Figures mystiques du riche et precieux cabinet des dames (Du Chesne), 39, 134, *136*

Finet, Sir John, 304n55

Flanders. *See* Netherlands

Florence, 8, 36–7, 48, 76, 83, 87, 117, 120, 197, 237n1, 246n29, 247n38, 248n52, 265n121, 280n11, 310n115

Florise. *See* Charlotte-Marguerite de Montmorency

Fogel, Michele, 10, 257n38

Fontainebleau, 46, 159, 237n1, 311n1

La Force, duc de (Jacques Nompar de Caumont), 58–9, 65–6, 72, 99, 107, 133, 200, 268nn21–2, 269nn27, 30, 281n24, 299n24, 302n39

France, political positioning of under Henri IV and Marie de Médicis: alliance with Ottomans (*see* Franco-Ottoman alliance); new Bourbon dynasty of (*see* Bourbon dynasty); relations with England, 114, 172, 174, 176–95, 205–7, 210, 294n5, 301n35, 301–2n36 (*see also* ambassadors: of England); relations with Spain, 11, 173–4, 177–9, 181, 183–6, 196, 206–7, 209–10, 294n5, 298–9n24, 311n2 (*see also* ambassadors: of Spain); supporting the United Provinces, 114, 172–4, 178, 181, 183–4, 186, 194, 206, 294n5, 295n9, 298n22; unity of, 55, 70, 91. *See also* ambassadors: of France; *individual names of rulers*

Francisque, Pierre, 249n69

Franco-Ottoman alliance, 13, 100, 104–6, 114–15, 119, 121, 208, 271nn45, 50–1. *See also* François Ier; Henri IV: foreign policy under; Süleyman the Magnificent

François Ier, king of France, 41, 104, 114, 243n2, 249n64, 271n45

François II, king of France, 5, 17, 42

François de France. *See* Anjou et d'Alençon, duc d'

Franko, Mark, 94–5, 97–8, 158, 208, 240n27

Franks, as legendary rulers of Thrace. *See* Thrace

Friedrich I. *See* Württemberg, duke of

Fromilhague, René, 162

Galigaï, Leonora, 51, 77, 253n101, 261n83

Gallery of Diana. *See* Fontainebleau

galliard. *See under* dance, courtly

Garnier, Robert, 311n1

Gaston de France. *See* Orléans, duc d'

Gaultier, Léonard, 42

I Gelosi (*commedia dell'arte* troupe), 88. *See also* Andreini, Isabella

gems: symbolic dimensions of, 14, 38, 65, 159–60, 204, 309nn107, 111; worn by dancers at court, 14, 18–20, 27–9, 32–8, 60, 129, 159–60, 171–3, 177, 200–5, 281n20, 298n20, 310nn112, 115. *See also* Sancy diamonds

Giesey, Ralph, 63, 240n23

gift exchange, 19, 51–2, 254n106. *See also* Bataille, Gabriel; Bourdieu, Pierre; Mauss, Marcel

Gioioso, Agostino, 122, 278n114

Giovannini, Baccio, Florentine representative to France, 58, 66, 74–5, 180, 182, 248n52, 251n91, 255n8, 256n17, 260n73, 261n83, 298n24, 301nn30, 35

de Giron, Don Fernando, extraordinary Spanish ambassador to England, 188–9, 303–4n55, 304n60

Girone, Ferdinando, 189

Giudiccioni, Laura, 87, 238n11, 265n121

Il giudizio di Paride, 197

Giustinian, Giorgio (Zorzi), Venetian ambassador, 106, 310n112

Glaucus, duet with Tethys, in *Le ballet comique de la royne*, 85

Godard de Beauchamps, Pierre François, 237n1

Godefroy, Théodore, 63. *See also Cérémonial françois*

Golden Age, 18, 20–1, 24–5. *See also* Pax Romana

De Gondi, Henri. *See* Paris, bishop of

Gonzaga, Caterina de' Medici. *See* de' Medici Gonzaga, Caterina

Gonzaga, Charles (also known as Charles de Gonzague). *See* Nevers, second duc de

Gonzaga, Eleonora de' Medici, sister of Marie de Médicis. *See* Mantua and Monferrat, duchess of
Gonzaga, Federico, 110
Gonzaga, Ludovico (also known as Louis de Gonzague). *See* Nevers, first duc de
Gonzaga, Marie Henriette de, sister of Charles Gonzaga, duc de Nevers, and wife of Henri de Lorraine, eldest son of Charles de Lorraine, duc de Mayenne, 78
Gonzaga, Vincenzo I. *See* Mantua and Montferrat, duke of
Gorse, George, 88
Goulart, Simon, 25. See also *On Clemency*
grace, in dance, 12, 31, 93–8, 123, 128–9, 141, 152, 156, 246n36, 253n102, 270n41, 283–4n37, 285–6n61, 292n112
La Grande Salle du Louvre (Great Hall of the Louvre Palace). *See under* Louvre palace
Guédron, Pierre, 21, 24, 199, 234, 243nn4–5, 243–4n8, 279–80n7, 308n94
Guidi, Camillo, Florentine representative in France, 205, 290n90, 292n127, 305n68, 305–6n74, 306n76, 80, 310n113
Guidiccioni, Caterina, 238n11
Guidiccioni, Laura, composer, 87, 238n11
Guillaume, Maistre, 269n27, 288n73, 298–9n24
Guillo, Laurent, 244n15
Guiscardi, Traiano, secretary to the Mantuan ambassador in France, 128–9, 131, 133, 135, 140, 145, 150, 155–6, 161, 200, 280n11, 280–1n14, 281nn15, 17, 21, 281–2n26, 282n30, 282–3n34, 290n82, 293n133, 308n98, 310n116
Guiscardi, Vittoria Dalla Valle, 128–9, 131, 133, 135, 140, 145, 150, 155–6, 159, 161, 205, 280nn11–12, 281nn15–16, 19–21, 281–2n26, 282–3n34, 290nn80, 82, 310n116
Guise, house of, 73, 77, 78, 109, 116, 122, 154
Guise, Mademoiselle de. *See* Louise Marguerite de Guise-Lorraine

Habsburg dynasty (Spanish and Austrian branches), 4–6, 18, 56–7, 70, 83, 107, 111, 114–15, 118, 166, 172–3, 175, 177–9, 181, 185, 189, 194–5, 204, 206–7, 263n100, 309n111
Hanley, Sarah, 63, 240n23
de Harlay, Christophe. *See* Beaumont, comte de
de Harlay, Nicolas. *See* Sancy, seigneur de
hat badge (*enseigne*): symbolism of, 65; worn by Henri IV, 65, 259n60; worn by James I (Mirror of Great Britain), 201, 203
heavens, references to in *ballets de cour*, 21, 23–4, 26, 30, 32, 35, 41, 48, 50, 101, 132, 153, 216, 218–19, 220–1
Helen of Troy, 39
Helicon, Mount, and Heliconian spring, 23
Henrard, Paul, 161
Henri de Navarre, later Henri IV, king of France. *See under* Henri IV
Henri I, king of France, 41–2, 71
Henri II, king of France, 41–2, 104, 158, 243n2, 249n64, 290n95

362 Index

Henri II de Bourbon, prince de Condé, 77–8, 123, 161–7, 263n100, 266n1, 292n126, 293nn128–9

Henri II de Rohan. *See* Rohan, duc de

Henri III, king of France, 4, 5, 8, 17, 33, 35–6, 41–2, 85, 121, 126, 239n18, 249n69, 279n5, 282–3n34, 309n111

Henri IV, king of France:
- association with: Alcandre, 162, 169, 294nn136–7; Apollo, 19–24, 27–8, 33, 44, 67, 159, 244nn11–12; Augustus, 41, 68; Janus, 70–1, 259n60, 278n117; the Gallic Hercules, 41, 68; Mars, 57, 108–9, 112, 119–20, 159, 163, 232, 276–7n107; royal virtue, 18, 22–7, 35, 37, 125–6, 141–5, 165, 167, 243nn6–7 (*see also* "Maintenant les vertus sacrées"; virility)
- challenges to rule of: assassination, 3, 147, 166, 185, 207, 287n66, 311n4; claim to French throne (contested), 4–6, 56, 142, 178, 210 (*see also* law, Salic); conspiracies against, 5, 48, 57–8, 90, 121, 191, 252n93, 253n101, 255n12
- foreign policy under: 4–5, 13, 14–15, 18, 69–70, 93, 113–14, 119, 121, 123–4, 165–6, 171, 172–206, 293n129, 298–9n24, 299–300n26 (*see also* Franco-Ottoman alliance)
- governance: arrangement of ballet audiences, 65–8, 70–1, 79, 173, 179–81, 183, 205, 242n36, 258n45, 306n74; arrangement of noble marriages, 71–5, 90, 163–6, 173–4, 178–9, 184; clemency of, 18, 21, 25, 37, 67, 169, 243n7; pacification of the kingdom, 17, 18, 21–3, 26, 41, 67–71, 131, 159, 169, 172

- as Henri de Bourbon, roi de Navarre, 4–5, 46, 87, 282n32
- marital and sexual relations of: divorce from Marguerite de Valois, 5, 47, 68, 179, 193; marriage with Marie de Médicis, 5, 9, 12, 31, 37, 45, 47, 49, 56–7, 70, 83–4, 113, 179, 191, 252n96; mistresses of (*see* mistresses, royal); philandering of, 4–5, 9, 47, 125–6, 147, 156, 169, 208, 279n6; progeny, 6, 19, 39, 46–8, 57–9, 73–5, 83, 90, 97–8, 147, 153–4, 187, 251n90, 253n101, 267n13 (*see also* Charlotte-Marguerite de Montmorency; Beaufort, duchesse de; Marie de Médicis; Verneuil, marquise de [Henriette d'Entragues])
- religious status: absolution of, 4, 70, 179, 299–300n26; apostacy of, 4, 18, 21, 47, 113, 126, 179, 300n27; commitment to Catholicism, 5, 18, 21, 74, 113, 179, 191, 300n27 (*see also under* Protestantism)

Henrietta Maria of France, youngest daughter of Henri IV and Marie de Médicis, queen of England, 207, 210, 242n40, 284n44; English masques danced and organized by, 210, 284n44

Henry, Michel, 44–5, 58, 237n1, 249n69

Henry Stuart, prince of Wales, son of James I and Anna of Denmark, 174–5, 266–7n1

Herbert, Philip, 297n19

Hercules, 41, 68, 276–7n107

hereditary rule, 4, 17, 37, 42, 45–6, 125–6, 146, 160, 238n4

Héroard, Jean, 290n93

heroide, untitled (Rinuccini), 32–3, 247n38
Heroides (Ovid), 32
Histoire des amours du Grand Alcandre, 45, 169, 250n78, 252n92, 253n101
historiographers, court, 10, 19, 52, 257n41, 300n27. *See also* Malingre, Claude; Matthieu, Pierre
history, new diplomatic, 187
Holy See. *See* Clement VIII; nuncios, papal; Paul V
Holy Spirit, Order of the. See *Ordre du Saint-Esprit*
Homer, 109, 294n136. See also *Iliad*
de L'Hôpital, Michel, 141
"hostipitality," 178–83, 301n34. *See also* Derrida, Jacques
Howard, Skiles, 71
Howard, Thomas. *See* Suffolk, earl of
Howard de Walden, Theophilus Lord, 300n28
Huguenots, 4–5, 17–18, 46, 48, 73–5, 79, 122, 173, 178–80, 191, 237n2, 252n93, 253n101
Hungary, 107, 110, 113, 114, 121, 122, 272n55, 273n69, 275n81, 276n94. *See also* Buda
"Hymne sur l'embarquement de la royne, et de son arrivée en France" (de La Roque), 23

Iliad (Homer), 109
imagery in *ballets de cour*. See under *ballets de cour*
instruments, musical, in *ballets de cour*: 20, 23, 60, 101; *chitarrone*, 198, 281n18; *chitarrone* in connection with female monody, 198; drums, 99, 101–2, 116; lutes, 21, 23–4, 41, 59–60, 80, 85, 99, 101, 109, 127, 129, 145–6, 149, 198, 217, 250n97, 263n112, 278n7, 284n61; oboes, 99, 101, 116, 268n22; theorbo, 129, 150, 198, 281n18; trumpets, 99, 102, 116, 268n21; violas, 128; violins, 59, 60, 80, 101–2, 256n20; viols, 128
intermedii, 7, 8, 30, 36, 150, 197, 307n86. *See also* Andreini, Isabella; Archilei, Vittoria; Marie de Médicis: patronage, artistic
intrecciata. *See under* dance
Iris, 311nn1, 2
Isabel Clara Eugenia, Infanta of Spain. *See* Austria, archduchess of
Islam, Islamicate world, 5, 12, 94–104, 108, 111, 113, 117, 119, 124, 270–1n44, 274n74, 282n32

Jackson, Richard, 63
James I, king of Scotland, England, Ireland, and Wales, 70, 114, 172–7, 180, 184–90, 194–5, 197, *201*, 203–5, 242n36, 266–7n1, 295n9, 295–6n12, 296n13, 296–7n15, 297n19, 301n35, 302n41, 303nn45–6, 306n79
James, Carolyn, 190
Janus, 59, 68, *69*, 70–1, 96, 259nn59–60, 278n117. *See also* Henri IV: association with; *Le ballet de la reine* (1605)
Jeanne d'Albret (Jeanne III), queen of Navarre and mother of Henri de Navarre (later Henri IV, king of France), 104
Jerome, Saint, 40
Jerusalem, 117
Jesuits, 68, 169, 179, 243n7, 298–9n24, 299–300n26
jetons (tokens), 57, 58, 70
Jodelle, Étienne, 291n102

Jolly, François-Antoine, 63, 100, 252nn36–7, 264n109
Jonson, Ben: *Masque of Beauty* (verse texts), 112. See also *Masque of Beauty*; *Masque of Blackness*
Joseph, Père (François Leclerc du Tremblay), 110, 118, 123, 274n74; *La Turciade*, 274n74
Jove, 30, 48
Julia, empress of Rome, 160
Jülich and Clèves, duke of (William I), 104, 123, 165
Jupiter, 39, 132, 220–1
Justice, 9, 18, 32, 40–1. See also Astraea

Kettering, Sharon, 51, 259n58
kinesis, 94–5, 141. See also ceremonial
kings of France, as ballet performers. *See under individual names*
Knights of Thrace, 93, 107–12, 115. See also Thrace

Lacroix, Paul (P.L. Jacob), 235, 279–80n7
Laugel, Auguste, 72, 260nn64, 67
Laugnac, baron de (Honorat de Montpezat), 282–3n34
Laurus (Lorenzo de' Medici il Magnifico), 246n36
de Laval, Guy XX (François de Coligny), 72, 74, 260n71
law, Salic, 5, 238n4, 296n13; in connection with Henri IV's kingship, 5–6, 56, 142, 178, 210. See also Hanley, Sarah
Lebègue, Raymond, 163, 292n122
Leda, 39
Lennox, duke of (Ludovic Stuart), extraordinary ambassador in Paris, 176, 180–3, 197, 300nn28–9, 301n35, 301–2n36, 307n84
Lent, 44, 168, 93n133
Lessig, Lawrence, 15, 301n31
the Levant. See Mediterranean, Eastern
Lille, 105
Lipsius, Justus, 141–2, 144, 284n47, 285nn49, 52. See also *Politica*
"living breathing luxury items," 12, 55, 83
Livre de meslanges (de Ronsard), 102
Loades, David, 83
London, 121, 173–5, 183, 185, 187–8, 190, 193–4, 197, 295n12, 296–7n15, 303nn46, 47, 49, 54, 303–4n55
Lorraine, ducal court of, ballets at, 8
de Lorraine, Charles. See Mayenne, duc de
Lorraine, Christine of, wife of Ferdinando I de' Medici and aunt of Marie de Médicis. See Tuscany, grand duchess of
Lorraine, duc de (Charles III), 73
de Lorraine, Françoise. See Mercoeur, duchesse de
de Lorraine, Henri. See Bar, duc de
de Lorraine, Louise Marguerite, mademoiselle de Guise, princesse de Conti. See Louise Marguerite de Guise-Lorraine
de Lorraine, Philippe Emmanuel. See Mercoeur, duc de
de Lorraine-Mayenne, Catherine. See Nevers, duchesse de
de Lorraine-Mayenne, Renée, 76, 116, 164
Lougee, Carolyn, 149
Louis XIII, king of France: ballets at the court of, 98, 208, 239n18,

258n49, 261nn82, 86; ballets danced by, 207, 258n49, 311n1; birth of, 19, 44–5, 47, 243n2, 252n92; as dauphin, 5, 42, 98, 118–20, 147, 154, 184, 207; reign of, 118, 150, 257n36, 260n74

Louis XIV, king of France, 68, 69, 99, 209–10, 235, 239n18, 241–2n35

Louise de Lorraine-Vaudemont, wife of Henri III and queen of France, 8, 35, 85, 264–5n111

Louise Marguerite de Guise-Lorraine, princesse de Conti, 45, 73, 150, 154, 169, 290n82, 294n136

Louise de Savoie, queen of France, 41

Louvre palace, 3, 9, 24, 32, 44, 46–7, 65, 195, 203, 258, 309n107; ballets danced at the, 10, 37, 44, 54, 58–60, 65–6, 85, 94, 96, 101–2, 107, 116, 161, 173, 179, 191, 249n55, 250n73, 256n19, 257–8n44, 259n56, 261n79, 309n107; Grande Salle du, 54, 58, 65, 68, 71, 79, 96, 179, 248n50, 258n49, 270n41

Love personified, in court entertainments, 27, 29, 32, 34, 49, 108–9, 119, 134, 138–40, 152, 158, 162–3, 166–7, 216, 217, 220–34

Low Countries. *See* Netherlands

Lully, Jean-Baptiste, 69. See also *Le ballet de la Nuit*

Lycurgus, 19–20

Lyon, royal entry at, 23, 102, 243n6, 253n96

Macedonia, republic of. *See* Thrace
madrigals, 87, 238n11

Maestro, Giovanni del, 87

magnificence, 17–19, 27–38, 45, 51–3, 84, 105, 128, 171–3, 183, 195–6, 204–5, 248n46. *See also* Aristotle; consumption, conspicuous; "living breathing luxury items"

"Maintenant les vertus sacrées" (Guédron), *air de cour* for Marie's 1602 *Ballet of the Sixteen Virtues*, 20–7, 52, 212–15, 217, 234, 243nn4–5. See also *airs de cour*

Malaspina, Bartolomeo, 205, 310n115

de Malherbe, François, 62, 117, 134, 161–2, 254n1, 256n32, 282n31, 292nn116, 121, 293n134, 294n136; "De petites Nymphes qui mènent l'Amour prisonnier. Au roi" (verses for the 1609 *Ballet de Madame*), 162–3, 166, 168, 230–3, 235, 293n134; "Air: pour le balet de la Reyne, La Renommée" (verses for the 1609 *Ballet of Diana and her Nymphs*), 128, 131, 159–61, 218–23. *See also* Henri IV: association with

Malingre, Claude, 212nn4–5, 234, 249n55, 254n110

Mamone, Sara, 243n6

Mantua, 83, 115, 128, 130, 205, 279n120, 310n116. *See also* ambassadors: of Mantua; *individual names of rulers*

Mantua, duchess of (Margherita Paleologus), 110

Mantua and Montferrat, duchess of (Eleonora de' Medici), sister of Marie de Médicis, wife of Vincenzo I de Gonzaga, 78, 128, 130, 205, 261–2n87, 265n121, 283–4n37

Mantua and Montferrat, duke of (Vincenzo I Gonzaga), 78, 128, 130, 200, 203, 205, 237n1

Marchesani [Gian Battista], at the court of France in 1602, 248n52

Margarita de Austria, queen of Spain, 175, 178, 200, 204

Marguerite de Valois, queen of Navarre and of France, 5, 10, 45, 47, 68, 74, 126, 130–1, 190–6, 210, 281n24, 281–2n26, 282n31, 285n52, 305–6n74, 306–7n81, 308n99, 311n1

Maria of Austria (Maria d'Autriche), Infanta of Spain and Holy Roman empress, spouse of Maximilian II, mother of Elisabeth of Austria (wife of Charles IX of France), 307n83

Maria Maddalena of Austria. *See* Tuscany, grand duchess of

Marie de Médicis, queen of France (see also *ballets de cour*; Henri IV; queen of France):
- allegorical association with: Diana, 9, 31, 152, 155–6, 159–60 (*see also Le ballet de Diane et ses nymphes*; Diana); a heavenly star, 30–4; Love, 29–34, 49, 109, 119, 134, 138–40, 158; Minerva (Pallas), 57, 117; Penthesilea, 33; the Virgin Mary, 9, 18, 38–42, 43, 44–6, 50, 249n67; the Virtues, 8–9, 18, 19–22, 24, 26, 28–38, 40, 49–53 (see also *Le Ballet des Seize Vertus*)
- ballets produced and/or danced by, 3, 7–11, 15, 17, 19, 30, 33, 38, 44, 49–50, 55, 65, 71, 81, 92, 96, 107, 116, 118, 130, 132, 143, 150, 160, 171, 187, 200, 207–8, 210, 237n1, 241n31, 246nn29, 36 (see also *Le Ballet de Diane et ses nymphes*; ballet *La félicité de l'âge d'or*; *Le Ballet de Madame*; *Le ballet de Madame ... par quatorze nymphes de Junon*; *Le Ballet de la reine*; *Le Ballet des Seize Vertus*; *Le ballet du Triomphe de Minerve*)
- building social networks with powerful princely families, 4, 10, 13, 51, 54, 71, 74–8, 80–1, 90–4, 103–4, 107–9, 115–19, 121, 123–4, 253–4n103, 275nn91, 101, 278n117
- involvement in Medici grand ducal court spectacle: 7–8, 30–3, 48–9, 87–8, 208, 246nn29, 36, 247n38
- navigation of international relations, 4, 11, 13, 14–15, 36–8, 73–5, 115–20, 171–206, 207–10, 237n1, 242n1, 246nn29, 36, 294–5n7, 298–9n24, 301n30, 305–6n74, 310n115, 311nn1, 2 (*see also* ambassadors; *ballets de cour*: audiences; consumption, conspicuous; magnificence)
- patronage, artistic: of female musicians, 8, 11–13, 55, 59–60, 81, 84–8, 101–2, 145–57, 196–200, 238n11, 264n109, 265n120, 307n83; of Italian acting troupes, 88, 266n123; of the visual arts, 9–10, 36, 37, 42, 239n15, 249n67, 255n11 (see also *ballets de cour*: avant-garde developments in)
- portraits of, 37; by Peter Paul Rubens (heroic cycle), 9, 42, 23n15, 249n67, 255n11; by Pourbus the younger, 81, *82*, 202, 203, 262n95, 309n109
- political status and activities: as devout Catholic, 5, 37–40, 47, 113, 116–19, 179 (see also *milice chrétienne*); as foreign (Medici) princess, 6–8, 11–12, 23, 27–38,

45–9, 70, 76–8, 81–8, 120, 179, 196–200, 246n36, 247n38, 282n32; as juridical subject of the king, 10–11, 55–6, 65, 71, 78–81, 143–4, 192, 210, 262n91, 305n72; as legitimate royal consort and mother of the true dauphin, 4–5, 6, 8, 9, 11–12, 18–19, 42, 44–8, 52, 55–8, 76–8, 81, 83, 90–3, 98, 103–4, 116, 120, 126–7, 173–4, 190–2, 208, 243n2, 250n77, 250–1n78, 251nn81, 91, 252nn92–4, 253n101, 261–2n87, 300n27; as member of the royal council, 56–7, 255n11; as royal guardian and regent, 6, 14, 42, 55–6, 75, 78, 92, 117–19, 123, 145, 154, 164, 185, 207–8, 241n31, 255n11, 260n74, 287n66, 311nn1, 2

Marinella, Lucrezia, 283–4n37. See also *Arcadia felice*; *Nobility and Excellence of Women*

Mars, 57, 105, 108, 112, 119–20, 159, 163, 232–3, 272–3n61, 276n104, 277n107

Marseille, 75, 119

Mary, Virgin, mother of God. See Virgin Mary

La Mascherata di stelle (Rinuccini), 8, 30–2, 48, 246nn29, 35

mascherate (or *maschere*). See masquerades

Maschere di bergiere (Rinuccini), 87, 282n32

masks, worn in ballets, 7, 17, 38, 68, 70, 96, 100, 250n75, 278n117

Masque of Beauty (1608), 186, 188–9, 204, 310n112. See also Jonson, Ben

Masque of Blackness (1605), 174–5, 178, 181–2, 184, 186, 266n1, 296n13. See also Jonson, Ben

Masque of the Knights of India and China (The Orient Knights, 1604), 176

Masque of Queens (1609), 173, 186, 188–90, 194–6, 205

masque *Tempe Restored* (1632), danced by Henrietta Maria of France, queen of England, 284n44

Masque of the Twelve Goddesses (1604), 174–8, 186, 190, 303n48, 306n79

masquerades, 8, 100, 250n75, 304n59

masques, English, 176–7, 186, 188–90, 241n34, 242n36, 259n58, 284n44, 297n19. See also individual titles of masques

Matthieu, Pierre, 19–24, 28–30, 33, 35, 38, 44, 46, 52, 102, 234, 243n5, 249n55, 254n110, 300n27

Mattingly, Garrett, 190

Mauderon, Jean, dit Maudricart, dwarf and usher of the queen's cabinet, 83–4, 263n100

Maurice of Nassau, prince of Orange, 298n22

Mauss, Marcel, 51–2, 254n106

Maximilian II, Holy Roman emperor, 307n83

Mayenne-Lorraine-Gonzaga, Catherine de. See Nevers, duchesse de

Mayenne, duc de (Charles de Lorraine), 76, 78, 116–17, 164, 260n74, 276n94

Mayenne, duchesse de (Henriette de Savoie-Villars), 76, 78

de Mayenne, Renée. See de Lorraine-Mayenne, Renée

de Maynard, François, 288n73

McGowan, Margaret, 9, 97, 131, 239n18, 248n51, 250n70, 253n100, 254n2, 260n64, 281n24, 311n6

368 Index

Medici: dynasty, 36, 47, 49, 77, 83, 88, 151, 196, 238n8, 266n124; grand ducal court (Tuscany), 7, 18, 23, 30–1, 36, 83–4, 86–8, 117, 180, 244n11, 247n38, 248n46, 265n120, 266n124, 272n57
de' Medici, Cosimo I (Cosimo il Vecchio). *See* Tuscany, grand duke of
de' Medici, Cosimo II. *See* Tuscany, grand duke of
de' Medici, Don Giovanni, 119
de' Medici, Eleonora, sister of Marie de Médicis, wife of Vincenzo I Gonzaga. *See* Mantua and Montferrat, duchess of
de' Medici, Francesco I. *See* Tuscany, grand duke of
de' Medici, Ferdinando I. *See* Tuscany, grand duke of
de' Medici, Lorenzo de', il Magnifico. *See* Tuscany, grand duke of
de' Medici Gonzaga, Caterina, dedication to, 283–4n37
de Médicis, Catherine, wife of Henri II and queen of France, 7, 33, 42, 238n8, 247n41, 291n107; ballets and related entertainments at the Valois court organized by, 8, 12, 14, 35, 130, 239n18, 241n31
Mediterranean, Eastern, 13, 93, 112, 118, 119
Mehmed III, sultan of the Ottoman empire, 272n55, 275n81
Mercedarians, 119
Mercoeur, duc de (Philippe Emmanuel de Lorraine), 117, 276n94
Mercoeur, duchesse de (Françoise de Lorraine), 73

Le Mercure françois, 177–8, 262n87, 297n20
Merki, Charles, 130, 281n24
Merlin, dwarf, in household of Marie de Médicis, 263n100
Metamorphoses (Ovid), 29
"methodologies of authority," Bourbon, 131–44
de Mézeray, François Eudes, 169
milice chrétienne, 110, 118, 123, 273n69
Minerva, 57, 117
Mirror of Great Britain, 203
mistresses, royal: 4–5, 8–9, 17, 19, 47, 49, 53, 73, 76–7, 83, 97, 126, 150–1, 153–6, 158–60, 164, 166, 169, 240n27, 253n102, 254n105, 267–8n13, 290n95, 291nn101, 107. *See also* Charlotte-Marguerite de Montmorency; Beaufort, duchesse de; Verneuil, marquise de (Henriette d'Entragues)
Mitchell, Silvia Z., 187
Molin, Nicolò, 296–7
monody, female, 85, 129, 196–8, 200. See also *ballets de cour*; Caccini, Francesca; Caccini, Giulio; Caccini, Settimia; music
monsters: "beast-like" figures, 12, 23; human, 12, 83, 263n101. *See also* Python
de Montaigne, Michel, 285n52
de Montmorency, Charlotte-Marguerite. *See* Charlotte-Marguerite de Montmorency
Montpezat, Honorat de. *See* Laugnac, baron of
"Moors," 13, 93, 99, 103, 106–7, 111–12, 268n1. *See also* Ottomans in court entertainments

the Morea, proposed military order to liberate from Ottoman "tyranny," 110, 273n69
Moret, comtesse de (Jacqueline de Bueil), 254n10
the muses, in court entertainments, 19–27, 28, 33, 44, 67, 212–15
music: *airs de cour,* 20–1, 85 (*see also* "Air: pour le balet de la Reyne; La Renommée au Roy"); composers, 21, 24, 84–5, 87, 145, 198–9, 238n11, 243nn4, 5, 243–4n8, 278–9n7, 307n83, 308n94 (*see also* Caccini, Giulio; Chevalier; Guédron, Pierre); harmonic modulation, 22; ornamentation, 22, 85; sung *récits,* 84–6 (*see also* "Récit de la naiade portée sur un dauphin"); violons du roi, 249n69. See also *ballets de cour*: avant-garde developments in; instruments, musical, in *ballets de cour*; Marie de Médicis: patronage, artistic; monody, female; musicians; singers; songs
musicians, 27–8, 59–60, 68, 84, 88, 92, 96, 100, 129, 264n111, 268n21; women, 84–5, 87–8, 149, 198. *See also* musical instruments; *individual names of singers*
Muslims. *See* Islam, Islamicate world

naiads, 127–9, 131, 135, 138–40, 145, 148–9, 152, 155–6, 158, 200, 222–7, 290n95. *See also* Paulet, Angélique; "Récit de la naiade portée sur un dauphin"
Near East. *See* Mediterranean, Eastern
Neoplatonism, 9, 18, 27–38, 54, 34, 138, 156–7, 245n24, 247n38, 283–4n37. *See also ballets de cour*: imagery and iconography
neostoicism, 138, 141–5, 285n52. *See also* Lipsius, Justus
de Nervèze, Antoine, 104
Netherlands, 141; Spanish, 6, 114, 172, 181, 183, 309n111; United Provinces, 114, 172–4, 178, 181, 183–6, 194, 206, 294n5, 295n9, 296–7n15, 302n41, 303n45
de Neufville, Nicolas. *See* Villeroy, marquis de
Nevers, duchesse de (Catherine de Lorraine, wife of Charles de Gonzague), 76, 261n79
Nevers, first duc de (Ludovico Gonzaga, also known as Louis de Gonzague), 78, 109, 262n88
Nevers, second duc de (Charles Gonzaga, also known as Charles de Gonzague), 76, 78, 92, 99–100, 107–9, 121–4, 269n27, 273n69, 274n76, 276nn91, 101, 278n114, 278–9n117, 279n120. See also *milice chrétienne*
newsletters, 10. See also *Le Mercure françois*
Nichomachean Ethics (Aristotle), 36
Nigaut, Jean, 234, 279n7
nobility, new definition of, 101, 269–70n32. *See also* race: discourses on nobility of; racism, "social"
Nobility and Excellence of Women (Marinella), 284n37
Nobiltà di dame (Caroso), 141
Nordera, Marina, 7
Nottingham, earl of (Charles Howard), 175, 177, 296n15, 300n28
nuncios, papal, 28–33, 38, 44, 48, 52, 66, 113, 122, 179–81, 190–3, 195,

205, 252n92, 253n101, 294–5n7, 298n24, 300n27, 301n35, 305n68, 305–6n74. *See also* Barberini, Maffeo; del Bufalo, Innocenzo

Ó hAnnracháin, Tadhg, 113, 275n82
"Ode to the Queen" (Malherbe), 117
"Odelette," 23
On Clemency (Seneca; translated into French by Simon Goulart), 25–6
opera, 8, 23, 36, 86–7. *See also* Marie de Médicis: patronage, artistic; music
"opinion management," 144
Ordre du Saint-Esprit, 121, 278n117
Orient, 117, 218–19. *See also* Far East
Orientalism, proto-Orientalism, 13, 104, 270n44
Orléans, duc d' (Gaston of France), 187, 290n92
Orpheus, 109–10
Orsini, Eleonora, 87, 265nn120–1
Orsini, Virginio, 264n109
Ottoman: court, 84; empire, 13, 18, 93, 100–1, 104–7, 110–11, 113–19, 121, 123, 272n55, 273n69, 274n76, 275nn81, 86, 298–9n24; French anti-Ottoman sentiment, 93, 104–7, 110–11, 114–19, 298–9n24. *See also* Ahmed I; Franco-Ottoman alliance; Mediterranean, Eastern; Mehmed III; Süleyman the Magnificent
Ottomans in court entertainments, 271–2n52; "Moors," 13, 93, 99, 103, 106–7, 111–12, 268n21, 271n45; "savages," 12, 99, 102; "Turks," 13, 93, 99–100, 104–7, 111–12, 268n21, 270–1n44, 271n45; "Tartars," 13, 93, 99, 112
Ovid, 29, 32. *See also Heroides*; *Metamorphoses*

palaces, 3, 236n11, 263n121. *See also* Louvre palace; Palazzo Vecchio; Paris, bishop of: palace of; Pitti palace; Riccardi palace; Saint-Germain-en-Laye, palace of; Tuileries palace
Palazzo Vecchio (Florence), 117
Paleologues, dynasty, 110–15, 274n76
Paleologus, Margherita. *See* Mantua, duchess of
Pallas, 57
Pardoe, Julia, 45, 51, 290n94
Paris: dauphin's first public appearances in, 46, 154; Henri II's 1549 entry in, 249n64; Marie de Médicis' entry in, 8, 17, 44; Parlement of, 37, 58, 90, 153, 166, 286n65, 299n26
Paris, bishop of (Gondi, Henri de), 37, 44, 59; palace of, 37, 44, 59
Parisians, ordinary, in audiences for royal ballets, 259n58
Parlement of Paris. *See under* Paris
Parrott, David, 110, 122, 279n120
Parry, Sir Thomas, 56, 300n28
de Parthénay, Catherine. *See* Rohan, first duchesse de
patronage: artistic. *See* arts, revival of; Marie de Médicis: patronage, artistic
Paul V, pope, 184, 193
Paulet, Angélique, 13, 145–57, 198–200, 287–8n71, 288n73, 288–9n75, 289nn77–8, 290n83. See also *Artamène, ou Le Grand Cyrus*; Elise, Angélique Paulet as
Paulet, Charles, sieur de Coubéron, 148
paulette tax, 13, 126, 146, 198, 286–9n65, 289n66, 288–9n75. *See also* Paulet, Angélique; Paulet, Charles

Pax Romana, 18, 25, 41
peace, civic, 5, 9, 14, 17–18, 23–6, 68, 71, 173–4, 247n41, 276–7n107, 287n66; restoration of, 17–18, 20–2, 26–7, 41, 67–8, 70, 120, 159, 172, 282n32, 311n2. *See also* Pax Romana
Peace of Vervins, 70
Pedro, Don. *See* de Toledo, Don Pedro
Peiresc, Nicolas-Claude Fabri de, 58, 60, 62–6, 84, 88–9, 95–7, 99–100, 103, 107, 116, 163, 256nn28, 31–2, 257nn34–5, 264n109, 269nn21–2, 30, 292nn116, 121–2, 293n130, 299n24
La Pellegrina (play), 117
Penthesilea, 33
de Péréfixe de Beaumont, Hardouin, 169
Persians, 107, 111, 113–14, 272n55, 275n81. *See also* Abbas I the Great
De petites Nymphes qui mènent l'Amour prisonnier. Au roi (Malherbe), 162, 166, 230–3, 235
Phenicie, king of, Henri IV as (*Artamène, ou Le Grand Cyrus*), 286n62, 308n96
Philidor, 256
Philip II, king of Spain, 6, 70
Philip III, king of Spain, 57, 113, 165, 174–5, 179, 184, 191, 193–4, 200, 255n12, 293n129, 295–6n12, 296–7n15, 297n18, 302n41, 303n45, 303–4n55
Philip of Austria, king of Castile, 105
Piraeus, 20
Pitti Palace, 8
Plato, 27, 33–4, 216–17. *See also* Neoplatonism

plays, 7, 36, 87, 311n1; pastoral, 139, 157, 238n11, 263n121, 266n123. *See also Aminta* (Tasso); *commedia dell'arte*; *La Pellegrina*
Pléiade, 226n22
Pleiades (Elettra, Alcinoe, Celeno, Maya, Asterope, Taigete, Merope), in the *Mascherata di stelle* (1596), 30, 246n31
Pluto, 29
poets, courtly, 18, 24, 30–1, 86, 161–2. *See also ballets de cour*: verse texts; Bertaut, Jean; Chiabrera, Gabriello; Desportes, Philippe; Jonson, Ben; de Malherbe, François; de Nervèze, Antoine; Pléiade; Rinuccini, Ottavio; de La Roque, Siméon-Guillaume
Poitiers, Diane de, mistress of Henri II, king of France. *See* Valentinois, duchesse de
Politica, 141, 142, 284n47
Portrait of Marie de Médicis (Pourbus the Younger). *See* Marie de Médicis: portraits of
Pot, Guillaume. *See* Rhodes, seigneur de
Pourbus the Younger, Frans, 81, *82, 202, 203,* 262n95, 309n109
Praslin, marquis de (Charles de Choiseul), 282–3n34
précieuses, 149–50
le Prévost, Jeanne, 186
princes, of the blood and foreign (*princes étrangers*) in ballets and stylized combats at the French court, 4, 10, 51, 73–5, 92–4, 100–1, 107–17, 119, 122–4, 129, 141, 253–4n103, 254n104, 269n30, 276–7n107. *See also individual names of princes*

princesses, of the blood and foreign (*princesses étrangères*) in ballets at the French court, 4, 10–11, 19–20, 24, 35, 38, 44, 51, 59, 71, 75–81, 84, 92, 95–7, 99, 103–4, 116, 124, 127, 132–41, 150–8, 161, 169, 189, 250n75, 254n104, 282–3n34. *See also individual names of princesses*
Prosperi, Bartolomeo, 246n29
Protestantism: Henri IV's abjuration of, 4, 47–8, 179; of Henri IV's foreign allies, 4–5, 18, 73–4, 114, 123, 173, 178–9, 181, 206, 298n22, 302n41. *See also* Henri IV
protocols in ballets (kinetic, spatial, and temporal), 4, 11, 89. *See also* ceremonial
Prunières, Henri, 86, 239n20, 280n9
Puisieux, vicomte de (Nicolas Brulart de Sillery), chancelier de France, 303nn46–7, 303n54, 303–4n55, 306n79
Python, defeated by Henri IV (as Apollo), 23

queen of France (*see also* Cosandey, Fanny; law, Salic; Marguerite de Valois; Marie de Médicis; regency, female, in France):
– femaleness, political deficit implied by, 5–7, 12, 79–80, 142–3, 191–3, 210
– foreignness of, 6–7, 11, 83–4
– participation in royal ceremonial, 11, 23, 63–4, 68–70, 76, 79–81, 202, 203, 240n23, 243n6, 244n12, 263n97
– as political subject of the French king, 11, 55, 65, 78–81, 89, 143–4, 191–3, 262n91, 305n72

– sovereign dignity of, 9, 11–13, 45, 55, 57, 65, 78–81, 89, 91, 160, 191–3, 262n91, 305n72

race: discourses on nobility of, 93–5, 102–4, 110, 125–7, 151, 251n85, 270n42, 279n6; "ideas of," 10, 95, 134, 239n22, 261n84
racism, "social," 94, 239n22, 261n84, 267n3. *See also* Smuts, Malcolm
Rambouillet, marquis de (Charles d'Angennes), 283n34
Rambouillet, marquise de (Catherine de Vivonne), 150, 283n34, 290nn80–1
Il rapimento di Cefalo (opera), 23
des Réaux, Tallemant, 147–8, 287–8n71, 288n72, 288–9n75; *Les Historiettes*, 147–8, 288–9n75
récit, sung. *See* music
"Récit de la naiade portée sur un dauphin" (for the 1609 *Ballet of Diana and her Nymphs*), 127–9, 131, 135, 138–40, 145, 152, 156, 158, 222–6. *See also* naiads; Paulet, Angélique
Recueil des vers du balet de la Reyne (Du Bray), 145, 234, 279n7
Recueil des vers du Balet de la Royne (Nigaut), 145, 234, 279n7
Recupito, Ippolita, 197
regency, female, in France, 6–8, 55–6, 89–91, 238nn4–8. *See also under* Marie de Médicis; queen of France
religion royale, 36
la Renommée. *See* Fame, goddess of
Republica christiana, 113, 115
Retz, "la maréchale" de (Claude-Catherine de Clermont, duchesse de Retz), 37, 44, 250n73, 291n102

revels, 92, 141, 174–5, 195
reverence. *See under* dance, courtly
rhetoric: of divine right, 13, 17; epideictic, 127, 168, 198
de Rhodes, Louise Pot, 283
Rhodes, seigneur de (Guillaume Pot), 283
Riccardi palace, 117
Richelieu, Armand Jean du Plessis de, Cardinal, 123, 150
Richeome, Louis, 42, 43. See also *Tableaux sacrés des figures mystiques du très-auguste sacrifice et sacrement de l'Eucharistie*
Rinuccini, Ottavio, 8, 30, 32–3, 48–9, 86–7, 246nn31, 35, 247n38. See also *heroide*, untitled; *Maschere di bergiere*; *La Mascherata di stelle*
rituals. *See* ceremonial
rivalry, between elite women, 5, 8, 19, 47–53, 197–8, 267–8n13. *See also* Verneuil, marquise de (Henriette d'Entragues)
Rivère de Carles, Nathalie, 15, 172
Rodier, Yann, 42
Rohan, Benjamin de. *See* Soubise, duc de
Rohan, duc de (Henri II), 71–2, 74–5, 122, 178, 179, 260nn67, 74, 261n86
Rohan, first duchesse de (Catherine de Parthénay), 72, 74–5, 260n74
Rohan, second duchesse de (Marguerite de Béthune), 71–2, 74–5, 253n102, 260n67, 261n86
Rohan clan, 72–5, 178–9
roman à clef, 45, 169, 294n136
Le romant des chevaliers de Thrace, 67, 99–100, 107, 109, 115, 268n21, 269n30, 272–3n61, 274–5n77

de Ronsard, Pierre, 102. See also *Livre de meslanges*
Roosen, William, 298n21
de La Roque, Siméon-Guillaume, 23–4. *See also* "Hymne sur l'embarquement de la royne, et de son arrivée en France"
Rosny, marquis de. *See* Sully, marquis de Rosny, duc de (Maximilien de Béthune)
Roux, Éliane, 9–10, 62–3, 310n117
le Roux, Nicolas, 36
Royster, Don Lee, 22, 234, 243n4
Rubens, Peter Paul, 9, 42, 239n15, 249n67, 255n12
Russell, Lucy. *See* Bedford, countess of

Safavid dynasty, Persian empire, 107, 113
Sahin-Toth, Péter, 107, 121
Said, Edward, 270n33, 270–1n44
Saint-Esprit, Ordre du (Order of the Holy Spirit), 121–2, 277–8n112, 278n114, 278–9n117, 283n34
Saint-Germain-en-Laye, palace of, 46, 122, 154, 162, 167, 278n114, 311n1
Saint-Germain-en-Laye, Treaty of, 73
Saint-Lary de Termes, Roger de. *See* Bellegarde, duc de
Salic law. *See* law, Salic
Salisbury, earl of (Robert Cecil), 186, 188, 293nn131–2, 300n28, 304nn57–61, 305nn63, 65, 69, 306nn77, 79, 307n82, 308n100, 309n110
salons, women-led, 149–50, 157, 250n73, 290nn80, 82–3
Sánchez, Magdalena, 209

Sancy, seigneur de (Nicolas de Harlay), 203, 205, 309nn105, 110–11
Sancy diamonds: the Beau Sancy (or Petit Sancy), 159–60, 200, 203–5, 309nn107, 109–11; the Grand Sancy (also known as the Great Sancy), *201*, 203–5, 309nn102–5, 111. See also Carew, George; gems; Henri IV; James I; Mantua and Montferrat, duke of (Vincenzo I Gonzaga); Sancy, seigneur de (Nicolas de Harlay)
saraos, in Spain, 173, 175, 177–8, 195, 204
"Sarasins" (Muslims). See Islam, Islamicate world
Saturn, 23
"savages." See Ottomans in court entertainments
de Savoie-Villars, Henriette. See Mayenne, duchesse de
de Scudéry, Madeleine, 145, 150, 199–200, 285–6n61, 286n62, 288–9n75, 290n84, 308n93–4, 96. See also *Artamène, ou Le Grand Cyrus*
Seneca, 25–6, 285n52
Sénellart, Michel, 144
Sibyls, 118
de Sillery, Nicolas Brulart. See Puisieux, vicomte de
de Simiers, Madame, 294n136
singers: in *ballets de cour*, 11, 28, 44, 55, 80–1, 84–7, 148, 152, 196–7, 199, 307n86; chorus of (Music), 59–60, 80, 84; in early opera, 86–7; women, 11–12, 55, 59–60, 81, 84–7, 148, 152, 196–7, 200, 264n109, 265n114, 288n74, 289n77, 307nn83, 86. See also de Beaulieu, Gerard;

Caccini consort; de Camere, Isabel; Doria, Violante; Paulet, Angélique; Vaumesnil, sieur de (Guillaume de Boulanger)
slaves, 99–100, 102, 111–12, 119, 268n21. See also *ballets de cour*: burlesque aspects
Smith, Jay, 147
Smuts, Malcolm, 10–11, 88, 276n91
Soissons, comte de (Charles de Bourbon), 77, 160, 164
De Sole (Ficino), 28
Solerti, Angelo, 238n11, 246n29, 247nn38–9
Somerset House, royal gardens at, 295
songs, 20–1, 23–4, 28, 31, 44, 60, 67, 84–7, 102, 120, 127–8, 131–5, 138–41, 145–52, 155–8, 196–200, 221n11, 243n8, 246n35, 252n96, 279–80n7, 282n28, 287–8n71, 308n93, 310n113; solo female, 85, 128–9, 196, 198. See also *airs de cour*; music; singers; *individual names of singers*
La Sophonisbe (Mairet), 150
Soubise, duc de (Benjamin de Rohan), 179
sovereignty, female. See under Marie de Médicis; queen of France
space, playing, 28–9, 33, 66, 71, 80, 98–9, 107, 109, 112, 119, 128, 140, 175, 280–1n14; and social priority, 10–11, 50, 71, 81, 97. See also stage
Spain: dynastic marriages planned by, 70, 185, 296–7n15; kings of, 6, 57, 70, 113, 165, 174–5, 179, 184, 191, 193–4, 200, 210, 255n12, 293n129, 295–6n12, 296–7n15, 297n18, 302n41, 303n45, 303–4n55, 311n2; participation in plots against Henri IV, 4–5, 57, 90,

165, 293n129; peace treaty with England, 70, 114, 172, 174, 176, 295–6n12, 296n13. *See also* ambassadors: of Spain; *saraos*; *individual names of rulers*

spectators at ballets. See *ballets de cour*: audiences

sprezzatura, 95

stage: court 18, 20–2, 24, 26–8, 35, 37, 40, 50, 54, 71, 77–8, 80, 83–4, 89, 95, 96, 98–102, 107, 109–10, 116–17, 127–31, 143–4, 152–7, 161, 166, 175, 199, 269n30, 271n45; machinery, 14, 196, 198, 204, 280n13; objects on, 7, 60, 81, 89, 305–6n74 (*see also* dwarfs; "living breathing luxury items")

Sternberg, Giora, 209, 306n75

stoicism, 142, 285n49. *See also* neostoicism

stones (precious). *See* gems; Sancy diamonds

Stuart: court, of England, 186, 203, 242n36, 259n58; dynasty, 173–4, 177–8, 193, 195, 203, 296–7n15

Stuart, Henry, son of James I and Anna of Denmark, and prince of Wales. *See* Henry Stuart

Stuart, Ludovic. *See* Lennox, duke of

Stuttgart, tournament with camels in, 1596, 100; account of by Thomas Platter, 259n59

Sublime Porte. *See* Ottoman

Suffolk, earl of (Thomas Howard), 300n28

Süleyman the Magnificent, sultan of the Ottoman empire, 104, 271n50

Sullivan, Mary, 242n36, 295n10, 303–4n55

Sully, duchesse de (Rachel de Cochefilet), 282–3n34

Sully, marquis de Rosny, duc de (Maximilien de Béthune), 37, 59, 72–7, 174, 178, 189, 191, 248n51, 260nn63, 67–8, 261n83, 282–3n34, 305n64, 309nn105, 110

symbolism: celestial, 18, 27–8, 30, 33, 39, 46, 48–50, 140–1, 246n35, 284n44 (*see also* heavens, references to in *ballets de cour*); Marian (*see under* Marie de Médicis)

Tableaux sacrez des figures mystiques du très-auguste sacrifice et sacrement de l'Eucharistie (Richeome), 42, 43

Tahureau, Jacques, 97

Tallemant des Réaux, Gédéon, 147–8, 288nn71–2, 288–9n75

"Tartars." *See* Ottomans in court entertainments

de Tassis y Peralta, Juan. *See* Villamediana, first count of

Tasso, Torquato, 8, 87. See also *Aminta*

Tasso the younger (Tassino), 238n11

Te Deums, 46, 60, 62, 64, 251n86

Tempe Restored (1632). *See* masque *Tempe Restored* (1632)

Thessaly. *See* Thrace

Thomas, Saint, 36

de Thou, Jacques-Auguste, 44

Thrace, 6, 93, 99–100, 104–13, 115, 122, 272–3n61, 274n76, 274–5n77. See also *Le romant des chevaliers de Thrace*

Tillières, comte de (Tanneguy Veneur II), French ambassador to England, 282–3n34

tilts, English, 266–7n1
de Toledo, Don Pedro, Spanish extraordinary ambassador to France, 184, 200, 302–3n44, 305–6n74, 306n77
Touchet, Marie, mistress of Charles IX, 291n101
tournaments, 62, 259n59, 300n28. *See also* carousel
travesti, 12, 59, 93, 97–8. See also *ballets de cour*: costumes; Vendôme, duc de (César de Bourbon)
Treaty of London (1604–5), 173–4, 184–5, 187, 295n12
Troy, 39, 110
Truce of Antwerp (1609), 183, 185, 206
Tuan, Yi-Fu, 102
Tuileries palace, 267n27
"Turks," in *ballets de cour* and other court entertainments. *See under* Ottomans in court entertainments
Tuscany, grand duchess of (Christine of Lorraine, wife of Ferdinando I de' Medici and aunt of Marie de Médicis), 30, 49, 84, 88, 246n29, 282n32
Tuscany, grand duchess of (Maria Maddalena of Austria), 197
Tuscany, grand duke of (Cosimo I de' Medici, il Vecchio), 36, 197
Tuscany, grand duke of (Cosimo II de' Medici), 197
Tuscany, grand duke of (Ferdinando I de' Medici), 7, 30, 49, 70, 78, 84, 87–8, 168, 252n99, 255n8, 256n17, 265n120
Tuscany, grand duke of (Francesco I de' Medici), 87, 265n121
Tuscany, grand duke of (Lorenzo de' Medici, il Magnifico); author of courtly dances, 246n36

Ubaldini, Roberto, 191, 193–4, 303n49, 305n74
Ungerer, Gustav, 296–7n12
United Provinces. *See* Netherlands
D'Urfé, Honoré, 41, 138, 157, 169, 249n61, 294n137. See also *L'Astrée*

Du Vair, Guillaume, 142
de Valavez, Palamède, 62–3, 257nn34–5
Valentinois, duchesse de (Diane de Poitiers), 8, 158–9, 290n95, 291nn101, 107, 292n112
Valladier, André, 23, 68, 70
Valladolid, 173–5, 177–8, 183, 197, 204
de Valois, Charles. *See* Auvergne, comte d'
Valois dynasty, 5, 17–18, 33–7, 42, 45–6, 85, 104, 111, 113, 126, 130, 142, 155, 177, 196, 198, 208, 249n64. *See also* Anjou et d'Alençon, duc d' (François de France); Catherine de Médicis; Charles IX; François Ier; Henri II; Henri III; Marguerite de Valois
Van Orden, Kate, 23, 52, 265n117
Vaumesnil, sieur de (Guillaume de Boulanger), 198
de Velasco, Juan Fernandez, constable of Castile and duke of Feria, 295–6n12
Vendôme, duc de (César de Bourbon), first illegitimate son of Henri IV by Gabrielle d'Estrées,

29, 59, 73, 93, 96–8, 100, 103, 147, 287–8n71. See also *Ballet de Monseigneur de Vendôme*
Veneur II, Tanneguy. *See* Tillières, comte de
Venice, 194, 305n68. *See also* ambassadors: of Venice
Venus, 29, 31, 98, 120, 246n36, 277n107, 291n102
Venus (Lorenzo de' Medici, il Magnifico), 246n36
Verderonne, seigneur de (Claude de l'Aubespine), 282–3n34
Verjus, Jan, dwarf, 263n100
Vernaccini, Madeleine dite "Médicis," 99–100
Verneuil, duc de (Gaston Henri de Bourbon), 57, 154
Verneuil, marquise de (Henriette d'Entragues), 5, 9, 19, 47–53, 57–8, 74–8, 83, 90, 116, 151, 153–5, 166, 251nn81, 90–1, 252nn92–3, 253nn101–2, 293n129, 294n137
"Vers Masculins Pour La Chaisne du Mesme Balet," verses for the 1609 *Ballet of Diana and her Nymphs*, 127, 139, 226–9
Victory, personified, 108, 119–20
Viennot, Éliane, 160
de Vieuxpoint, Charlotte, 282–3n34
Villamediana, first count of (Juan de Tassis y Peralta), 174–7, 190, 297n18. *See also* ambassadors: of Spain
Villeroy, marquis de (Nicolas IV de Neufville), 56, 66, 121, 168, 180, 182, 188–92, 258n52, 300n29, 301–2n36, 303–4n55, 304n58, 305n71, 306n79
violence, symbolic, 51–3

Virgil, 18, 23, 41; *Fourth Eclogue*, 18, 41
Virgin Mary, 18, 38–42, 43, 44–6, 50, 249n67
virility, 125–6, 165. *See also* Henri IV: marital and sexual relations of
the Virtues, as personified in court ballets, 18, 20–7, 29, 33–4, 39–40, 50, 85, 141, 159, 167. See also *Ballet of the Sixteen Virtues*; "Maintenant les vertus sacrées"; neostoicism
virtuosity, 15, 85–8, 102–3, 172, 199–200
de Vivonne, Catherine, vidame du Mans. *See* Rambouillet, marquise de
de Vivonne, Julie (daughter of the marquise de Rambouillet), 150
Voeux de Faisan banquet, 105
"Voyant la douce Paix et la divine Astrée" (Bertaut), 20, 24–7, 40–1, 214–17

Wagner, Marie-France, 240n23
Wales, prince of, son of James I and Anna of Denmark. *See* Henry Stuart
Warburg Institute, 209
wars, French civil, 5, 8, 17–19, 35, 37, 41, 46, 72–3, 87, 142, 155, 177, 286–7n65
Weiss, Gillian, 270–1n44, 271n51
Welch, Ellen, 106, 172, 239n18, 241n33
Wellman, Kathleen, 159
Wilkin, Rebecca M., 142
William I. *See* Jülich and Clèves, duke of
Wine, Kathleen, 169, 293n135, 294nn136–7

Winwood, Ralph, 45, 250n77
Württemberg, duke of (Friedrich I), 100

Xanthus, river, 33

Yates, Frances, 41, 239n18
York, duke of. *See* Charles I

Zerner, Henri, 158

www.ingramcontent.com/pod-product-compliance
Lightning Source LLC
Chambersburg PA
CBHW030300080526
44584CB00012B/380